The View from Within

The View from Within

Writers and Critics on Contemporary Arabic Literature

A selection from
Alif: Journal of Comparative Poetics

Edited by
Ferial J. Ghazoul and Barbara Harlow

The American University in Cairo Press

All of the articles in this volume were first published in *Alif: Journal of Comparative Poetics,* and are reprinted here by permission of Radwa Ashour, Saadi Youssef, Gamal al-Ghitany, Adonis, Anni Kanafani, Mona Takieddine Amyuni, Mahmoud El Lozy, Hamdi Sakkut, Ahmad Shams al-Din al-Haggagi, Ceza Kassem Draz, Marilyn Booth, Samia Mehrez, Shukry Ayyad, Jabra Ibrahim Jabra, S. Samar Damluji, Mohamed Choukri, Edwar al-Kharrat, Latifa al-Zayyat, Edward Said, and Denys Johnson-Davies. Two lines of verse by Mahmoud Darwish are reproduced by permission.

Copyright © 1981, 1982, 1983, 1984, 1985, 1986, 1987, 1990, 1991, 1993 by the Department of English and Comparative Literature, the American University in Cairo

Copyright © 1994 by
The American University in Cairo Press
113 Sharia Kasr el Aini
Cairo, Egypt

All rights reserved. No part of this publication may be reproduced, stored in a retrieval system or transmitted in any form or by any means, electronic, mechanical, photocopying, recording or otherwise, without the prior written permission of the copyright owner.

Dar el Kutub No. 7830/93
ISBN 977 424 327 7

Printed in Egypt at the Printshop of the American University in Cairo

Contents

Introduction   1
Ferial J. Ghazoul and Barbara Harlow

Testimonies

My Experience With Writing   7
Radwa Ashour
On Reading the Earth   12
Saadi Youssef
Intertextual Dialectics   17
Gamal al-Ghitany
Language, Culture, and Reality   27
Adonis
Thoughts on Change and the 'Blind Language'   34
Ghassan Kanafani

Essays

The Image of the City: Wounded Beirut   53
Mona Takieddine Amyuni
Brecht and the Egyptian Political Theater   77
Mahmoud El Lozy
Naguib Mahfouz and the Sufi Way   90
Hamdi Sakkut
The Mythmaker: Tayeb Salih   99
Ahmad Shams al-Din al-Haggagi
Opaque and Transparent Discourse in Sonallah Ibrahim's Works   134
Ceza Kassem Draz
Force and Transitivity: Bayram al-Tunisi and a Poetics of
Anticolonialism   149
Marilyn Booth
Poetic Experimentation and the Institution: The Case of
Ida'a 77 and *Aswat*   177
Samia Mehrez

Interviews

Shukry Ayyad	197
On Criticism and Creativity	
Jabra Ibrahim Jabra	207
On Interpoetics	
Hassan Fathy	213
On the Poetics of Space	
Mohamed Choukri	220
Being and Place	
Edwar al-Kharrat	228
The Relative and the Absolute in Avant-Garde Narration	
Latifa al-Zayyat	246
On Political Commitment and Feminist Writing	
Edward Said	261
People's Rights and Literature	
Denys Johnson-Davies	272
On Translating Arabic Literature	
Sources	283
Notes on Contributors	285
Index	292

The View from Within

> And seeds from a withered ear
> With wheat shall fill the valley
> —*Mahmoud Darwish*

Introduction

❖

Ferial J. Ghazoul
Barbara Harlow

When the first issue of *Alif: Journal of Comparative Poetics* appeared in Cairo in the spring of 1981, it was celebrated by the many—contributors, editors, readers—who had participated in its inception, production, and reception as marking the result of long efforts to translate disciplinary and aesthetic divisions into a collective practice of cultural exchange. The issue represented the first step in a project of intercultural dialogue—both within the Arab world and between the Arab world and its global interlocutors. Indeed, *Alif*'s beginnings and continued history in Cairo are not inconsequential. The capital of Egypt, historically a center of Arab intellectual and artistic activity, geographically located at the intersection of the Arab, African, and Mediterranean worlds, and of critical impact on transformations in the Arab social order, Cairo and its cultural dynamics are integral to the complex of analyses, debates, and essays that have animated the first thirteen issues, and the first thirteen years, of *Alif*'s publication.

The importance of place, of Cairo in particular, but an insistence too on place more generally as historically significant, shapes the interviews, testimonies, and literary articles, selected from those first thirteen years, to comprise this anthology of Alif studies in contemporary Arabic literature. By 'place' is intended both the setting of the text and the problematized topos written into the text—places such as the Arab cities of Cairo, Beirut, Jerusalem, Tangier, the public and institutional spaces of academia, establishments, and their oppositional fronts, as well as their conceptual alternatives. Site specificity grounds this collection of writings, then, on and from contemporary Arabic literature by critics and creative artists whose committed relationship to Cairo itself, the premises on and for which it stands, informs their analyses of the current cultural situation. Thus Cairo stands here not simply as a geographical site, but as a symbolic focus of the Arab world, the Third World, and the South in their struggles against forces of marginalization and obliteration. Cairo's very specificity, however, engages no less urgently an interactive cultural discourse within the crucial, if contested, parameters of the historically globalized debates on issues of postcoloniality, liberationist national independences, and persistent cultural and economic dependencies. It references too the recent history of the Arab world, its moments of crisis, rise and decline—of radical change in which the very urgency of events enjoins the necessity of intellectual responsibility and critical accountability.

Alif emerged as a project in a particularly turbulent period where accepted ideas and unchallenged values were crumbling. The need to make sense in such a historical conjuncture and to start from the very beginning led to choosing *Alif* as a title for the journal. 'Alif' is the first letter in the Arabic alphabet; thus it stands for a linguistic beginning and underlines the crucial importance of language as an indispensable medium for meaningful dialogue and genuine development. The Arabic form of the first letter was selected to point to the direction of the journal and its concerns while highlighting the often marginalized media of the peripheries.

Against the panoramic historical trajectory articulated at its extremes by the Camp David Accords and the Gulf War, and within which the Palestinian intifada marked an insurgent space, *Alif* proposed a literary critical discursive arena for assessing current events certainly, but, more significant perhaps, for relocating and reenvisioning these within a longer, more expanded narrative of Arab cultural practices. If the first decade of the publication of *Alif* coincided with a protracted moment of socioartistic crisis in the Arab Middle East, itself the culmination of decades of accumulated regional and international crises, such a critical period was neither unique to the Arab world, nor even to *Alif*. But whereas other such instances have elsewhere produced alternative responses, such as 'withdrawal' into an aesthetics of 'art for art's sake', for example, or 'alienation' and cults of the 'absurd', *Alif*'s project demonstrates rather an engagement with what might be termed, from within the Arabic lexicon and its grammar, *ta'sil*, an effort to grasp the roots and radicals themselves of the contemporary critical conjuncture.

The Arabic root *'sl*, from which *ta'sil* (rooting) is derived, signifies a number of things—root, origin, source, cause, reason, foundation, principle—and connotes what is primary, authentic, noble, genuine, and sound. *Alif*'s project for rooting runs counter to dispersion and counterfeiting—so common in the irresponsible world of mass media—and to entrenched stereotypes. Our time is characterized by the word 'crisis', as the Egyptian critic Shukry Ayyad has emphasized, and is best described by the Iraqi poet Saadi Youssef as a situation of "siege." In this critical impasse *Alif* aspired to contribute a practical solution, and to surmount simultaneously the confusing outbreak of new methodologies of literary studies as well as reevaluating the relevance of the

Introduction

literary legacy and its approaches. The project of *Alif*, then, searches for the primary building blocks and the necessary conditions for establishing an authentic exchange. It does not seek a nostalgic and self-indulgent search for roots, nor does its project stem from a dazzled admiration for the achievements of the Other. It seeks to demystify and demarginalize simultaneously, to pave the channels of intercourse between cultures, and to reestablish a 'circulation'—to borrow the words of the Palestinian writer Ghassan Kanafani—in order to achieve a healthy global culture. Thus, in addition to *ta'sil* (rooting), *Alif* has been concerned about *tawsil* (communicating). *Alif* chose to create a two-way forum (Arabic and English, and occasionally French) for communication, while keeping in mind that intercultural dialogues can become most fruitful among people joined by a certain common concern or discipline.

The project of *Alif* was a response to the lack of meaningful interactions between different cultural traditions, and an effort to heal such a state. The journal chose to dedicate each issue to a theme or a problematic. The focuses of *Alif* have been varied, while trying to fill the gaps in the current critical discourse by complementing, revising, and questioning; or by illuminating different facets of the same phenomenon—even trying to locate its parallel or precursor in the Self and the Other, in the past and the present.

Thus, for example, the first issue of *Alif* was devoted to "Philosophy and Stylistics" (1981). It reexamined not only classical and Arabic poetics but their reintegration in modern literature as well. The consequences of the breach in the dialogue between East and West are thus seen not only to be codified in the philosophical concepts of the respective cultures and their canonical traditions but to be carried as well in the styles of their languages and constituting ideologies. The process of adaptation and transformation at work in the rhetorics of Aristotle and Avicenna, as analyzed in *Alif* 1, have implications for the theories of modern linguistics and the development of modern style.

The most recent issue of *Alif*, published in 1993, focused on "Human Rights and Peoples' Rights in Literature and the Humanities." It explored the embryonic and implied presence of the concept of elemental rights of individuals and peoples in literary texts, proverbs, and philosophical reflections. It viewed the denunciation of repressive violence, social oppression, dehumanizing practices, and the representations of inhumanities in literature and the humanities as attesting to a consciousness informed by ideas and notions of human rights. Thus, the formalization of the concept of human rights and peoples' rights—which is a relatively recent phenomenon—should not dismiss its earlier informal presence and manifestations in the literary discourses and the human sciences.

Some issues dealt with innovative trends such as "Criticism and the Avant-Garde" (*Alif* 2, 1982) and "Poetic Experimentation in Egypt Since the Seventies" (*Alif* 11, 1991). Others addressed specifically rhetorical strategies such as "Intertextuality" (*Alif* 4, 1984) and "Metaphor and Allegory in the Middle Ages" (*Alif* 12, 1992). On one hand the journal covered textual concerns as in "The Mystical Dimension in Literature" (*Alif* 5, 1985) and "Interpretation and Hermeneutics" (*Alif* 8, 1988), and on the other it handled themes with social implications such as "The Self and the Other" (*Alif* 3, 1983), "The Third World: Literature and Consciousness" (*Alif* 7, 1987), and "Marxism and the Critical Discourse" (*Alif* 10, 1990). An issue on "Poetics of Place" (*Alif* 6, 1986) was followed by an issue on "Questions of Time" (*Alif* 9, 1989).

Literary studies, when isolated within a single cultural or linguistic tradition, forfeit, often for the sake of authority and hegemony, much of their critical potential. Western criticism and scholarship, for example, the results of an established tradition of theory and practice, come finally to serve the perpetuation of that very tradition itself—its canon and criteria. Arabic literature and thought, for their part, have long been judged by the same criteria. What does not conform to Western norms is either ignored as lacking sophistication or dismissed as deviation. *Alif*, as a journal of comparative poetics, proposed to account for this discrepancy and to redress the imbalance that now exists. It sought, in other words, to inaugurate a new locus of critical discourse, one in which the very differences between the respective literary traditions and styles contribute to a reformulation of methodological perspectives and cultural horizons.

In this anthology contributions of writers from the Arab world provide a window onto Arabic literature and thought. The anthology presents the pressing debates, polemics, and preoccupations of Arab writers and literary Arabists who have shared in the Arab cultural experience and lived in the Arab world in the eighties and nineties. The view, therefore, is from within without being exclusive of non-Arabs. Being an insider, or for that matter an outsider, is not a matter of ethnicity or nationality, but a matter of experience and commitment.

The anthology consists of (1) literary testimonies and theoretical proclamations by creative writers, (2) essays and articles by critics and comparatists, and (3) interviews and dialogues with distinguished writers. The organization corresponds respectively to the first person, third person, and second person; or what has been sometimes called the lyrical, the narrative, and the dramatic modes. Originally these pieces belonged to *Alif* issues which focused on given themes. They stood juxtaposed to contributions on the same themes by critics specialized in other literatures and exploring similar concerns. The diverse orientations and varied examples of approach provided the framework for comparative speculation. Many of the articles of *Alif* were comparative in perspective and attempted to analyze a literary issue through calling upon works from different traditions or periods. This present anthology, however, brings together the pieces that revolved specifically around contemporary Arabic literature. Given the location of the journal in Cairo and the cultural weight of Egypt within the Arab world, it is not surprising that many of the contributors, interviewers, and translators are from Egypt. If other anthologies would come out of *Alif* with different focuses, such as cultural studies, medieval poetics, or comparative literature, then a different configuration of participants would surface. The testimony and interview in *Alif* tended to probe into the views of the writer and explore in depth the writer's position on the particular theme of that issue. In some ways this limited the focus of the interview and confined it to the concern of the particular issue, but also allowed deeper investigations of the ideas of the interviewed writer. The interviews with one interviewer (Jabra Jabra by Najman Yasin, Hassan Fathy by S. Samar Damluji, Edwar al-Kharrat by Sabry Hafez, Edward Said by Jonathan Rée) were orally conducted, taped, and transcribed. The rest of the interviews were carried out in writing by several interviewers well read in the works of those interviewed. The testimonies were either written specifically for *Alif*, as in the case of Gamal al-Ghitany, or selected for translation from speeches, proclamations, and manifestos issued by the writers.

In all thirteen issues, which present concerns of over a decade, an effort was made to introduce varied cultural and critical perspectives. From these issues, articles that were selected for this anthology were not only deemed the best but also those that together constituted a representative sample of the current intellectual and literary debates of the Arab world. Writers from Iraq to Morocco, from Sudan to Syria, are represented as well as the three literary genres: poetry, drama, and narrative. Genders are equally represented and the voices of the younger generation of writers and critics appear next to those of established figures. In order to achieve this comprehensive anthology, six pieces that appeared originally in Arabic in *Alif* were translated specifically for this collection. The testimony of Gamal al-Ghitany and the two articles on Naguib Mahfouz and Tayeb Salih, as well as the three interviews with Mohamed Choukri, Edwar al-Kharrat, and Latifa al-Zayyat, were translated into English specifically for this anthology to complement the rest of the pieces which had appeared in English in *Alif*. As is customary with *Alif*, the translators selected are skilled in the two languages and are specialists in the material of their translation.

What transpires from the present configuration is a certain insistence from within—not only on the relevance of literature, but also on its necessity in various human struggles. The most intrinsic and aesthetic perspectives, based on stylistic and rhetorical analysis, seem to uncover issues pertaining to liberation, while the most socially inclined approaches are conscious of the poetic dimension in combats. Clearly, the human propensity to overcome is still alive in this corner of the world. Perhaps the most persisting concern that can be detected in this anthology is how to preserve Arab cultural specificity and simultaneously belong to a global culture, how to be one's self and at the same time be a part of a larger human order that happens to be inequitable and, more often than not, hostile.

Alif as a project could not have worked without the enthusiasm and support of hundreds of people whose sense of *Alif*'s mission had led them to contribute articles and advice. Contributions of prominent intellectuals as well as emerging scholars appeared in the pages of *Alif* thanks to the dedication of an editorial group drawn from the American University in Cairo, the Egyptian national universities, and universities elsewhere in the world: Nasr Hamid Abu-Zeid, Stephen Alter, Galal Amin, Gaber Asfour, Ceza Kassem Draz, Sabry Hafez, Malak Hashem, Ahmad Taher Hassanein, Pauline Kaldas, Thomas Lamont, Samia Mehrez, Doris Enright-Clark Shoukri, Daniel Vitkus, and Hoda Wasfi. Needless to say, such a project could not have worked without the institutional support of the American University in Cairo and the cultural ambience of Egypt, and above all, the enthusiastic support of the students of the Department of English and Comparative Literature who have regularly assisted in *Alif*: Maggie Awadalla, Hala Halim, Hoda Hassanein, Faten Morsi, Noha Nassar, and Mounira Soliman.

As this anthology is addressed to contemporary English-speaking readers of all continents, we have chosen to simplify typographical decisions by opting for the minimum of diacritical marks in transliteration and confined (most) Arabic citations to English translations with reference to their locations in the original sources, or to published translations where possible.

For the production of this anthology thanks are due to Maggie Awadalla, Neil Hewison, and especially to Simon O'Rourke.

My Experience With Writing

❖

Radwa Ashour

I write because I love writing. I mean I love it in a way that makes the question, Why do I write? seem strange and incomprehensible to me.

Having said that, I also write because I have a fear of lurking death. What I mean is not just the sense of death at the end of it all, but death in its many different guises, in every nook and cranny, in the street, in the house, at school. I am talking about the live burial and assassination of potential.

I am an Arab woman and a citizen of the Third World, and my heritage in both cases is stifled. I know this truth right down to the marrow of my bones, and I fear it to the extent that I write in self-defense and in defense of countless others with whom I identify or who are like me. I want to write because reality fills me with a sense of alienation. Silence only increases my alienation, while confession opens me up so that I may head out toward the others or they may come to me themselves.

Am I a writer? The question has long perplexed me and come between me and my sleep (and still does).

I renounced writing. I said that I was no good, and my resolution hit home as sharply and decisively as a guillotine. Several years passed and then all of a sudden, I found that writing reappeared with an insistent, importuning presence.

On the convalescence couch after a protracted illness, I found myself returning to writing for the first time since the breach. I took hold of the pen and wrote:

> When I left childhood and untied the handkerchief that my mother and my aunt had left for me, I found in it its defeat. I cried, but both crying and reflection done with, I flung away the handkerchief and moved on. I was angry.

I think that in my case the act of writing began by assimilating then rejecting and attempting to answer the question: What would I leave in *my* knotted handkerchief?

To me writing is about a relationship with three things: a relationship with the surrounding reality, that is, the reality that I see, endowed principally with its social and historical conditioning; a relationship with the language and behind it the cultural and literary legacies shaped within and through the language; and a relationship with the craft of writing and the experiences acquired in the daily 'workshop'.

The first relationship begins with the self and the vocabulary that is peculiar to it and gives it its distinguishing features. For me, they are a river and a palm tree, the tomb of an old king harboring a dream of the everlasting, the lives of thousands of slaves forced to build it, a university mosque, alleyways branching off around it and leading to tombs lived in by people, a dead bird, a cane, a man that I love, a child formed from the very beginning in my womb, the voice of a woman singing, and a rose. I am talking about the vocabulary of my life, about Cairo where I was born, and Egypt from where I come. I am talking about myself, and it is strange to think that in doing so I am also talking about history and geography. I am saying that this is the vocabulary of my life, then I say that the vocabulary of my life is just a door opening onto a time and place.

My second relationship is that with the Arabic language in which I see a homeland whose limits range from Qur'anic Arabic to the call of the peddler, from the national anthem issuing from the mouths of children at school in the morning to the speech of a hypocritical politician. In Arabic I see a vast homeland, clear-cut yet ambiguous, familiar yet surprising. I know it and still I cannot pin it down. I live in it, and I know that it too dwells in me, that in everything I say or do I carry its stamp, its mark. Arabic is my tool it is true, but I am equally one of its tools. Arabic is my book whose pages are filled with my heritage, my story with time, and my ambition is to add a new line to those already there within it.

While the relationship with language, and with it the national culture and literature, is a relationship both inherited and acquired, the relationship with the craft of writing (assuming the presence of talent) requires pressing diligence and effort, exploration and pursuit, observation, discovery and acquisition—all of which are acquired, pure and simple.

In the writing 'workshop', I see myself as a young pupil who is consumed and exhausted by problem-solving. Then, filled with uncontrollable joy on reaching the solution, the little schoolgirl hides behind another woman who is filled with vain confidence. But the moment does not last. The pupil goes back to anxiously biting her nails, faced with the question: Have I succeeded?

I now realize that in my effort to define clearly what I thought were the requirements for writing, I presented the relationships with reality, with language, and with the craft of writing as if they were three separate entities. But this is not the case. They interconnect and interweave because the process of producing reality in writing comes about through language, and language is both the vessel for what is produced and its tool. Neither is the craft just a skill, suspended alone in midair. It consists of tools whose uses are discovered in the workshop when actually handling the specific material whose building blocks are both reality and language. It is also the precision tool which regulates the needle to the correct wavelength and allows for the transmission of the message without interference.

This leaves the actual writing, which is a special case each time. It is to a certain extent, an independent project, with its own motivating forces, associations, and goals.

In 1980 I returned to writing when the question struck me, What if death were to descend on me? At that moment I decided that I would write in order to leave something of my own, however small, behind me 'in my knotted handkerchief'. I also realized, and I was thirty-four, that it is far wiser to accept the relative than to cling to the absolute, that the time had come to be free from the feeling that I had to 'bring forth that which those before me had not produced', or turn my back, in weakness and fear . . . and with pride too.

In 1980 I embarked upon an autobiographical project. I wrote pages on my life's experiences in the years between 1946 (the year when I was born) and 1956. I discovered that the threads which made up the consciousness of a ten-year-old girl, and those which wove the history of that period, were tighter and more closely interwoven than that which I was capable of writing on. I found myself stumbling when writing about the relationship between the personal and the general which were interlocked to a degree that made it difficult to distinguish one from the other. I was afraid of slipping into rhetoric or lyricism. The material that I was dealing with was not just personal experience, but also the history of the nation, and I stopped, feeling ill-equipped and fearful. I decided that I needed a workshop where I could train and learn. The writing of *al-Rihla: ayyam taliba misriya fi amrika* (The journey: an Egyptian student's days in America) was the workshop to which consciously I gave my attention, thinking of it as a workshop of preparation.

The material used in *al-Rihla* was part of my personal biography, and no difficulties would arise in grasping and understanding it. Writing began to seem possible. I wanted to present a testimony of my American journey that would be different from and yet form a part of the sequence of texts written by Egyptian men of letters who had gone to the West as students, the vast majority of whom had recorded how they had been dazzled by the imperial lights. My experience was an extension of theirs, but it differed in that I set out full of doubt and fear, perhaps even bitterness toward the imperial other. I belonged to a different generation with a different ideological stance, and, then, I was a woman. The eye that sees and the perception that classifies and organizes the vocabulary of experience, both impose their different constraints which are in turn reflected in the purport of the experience and the writing of it.

Al-Rihla was the first long text that I completed. I would write daily with a regular quota of between two and five pages. The work absorbed me from nine in the morning until two in the afternoon. In this daily workshop, I learned how to accomplish an extended project. I gained stamina, if I may put it that way. I learned how to move from a total preoccupation with the presentation of the object in its every detail to the overall frame which sets up the objects and links them with one another. I also learned about the transposition of time, which allows for an incident lasting minutes to consume pages while a situation enduring for years can be written about in two lines. I went over what I had written many times, sometimes even ten times, to find a reasonable middle road between economy, density, and depth on one hand and simplicity and clarity of communication on the other. Then, as I was writing *al-Rihla*, I realized for the first time that I was aware of the great value of analogy as a tool of rhetoric, and it is probably the most useful of all.

I believe that writing *al-Rihla* gave me faith in myself and eased the burden of that petulant question which dogged me insistently for twenty years: Am I right for writing? In short, I attained something of a reconciliation with myself as a possible writer. That was at the end of 1981.

About three months later, I began on the text of a full-length novel which was subsequently to be published under the title *Hajar dafi'* (Warm stone). It was not my conscious intention to write something based on characters but more to write about an epoch and a place—the project was Egypt in the 1970s—to capture a collection of images of the place at a specific moment in time. (I realize now that history, in the sense of the recording of a historical reality, was always something that engrossed me.) Because of the nature of the project, the style was descriptive, for the most part restrained, overtly neutral, and as far removed as possible from lyrical expression.

Hajar dafi' is my first attempt at a novel. (*Al-Rihla* was a full-length text, but it was the result of an experience that I had lived through and people that I knew. Of course I influenced the arrangement of the material and the conclusions drawn therein, both implicitly and explicitly. But I did not invent any of the situations or characters that are portrayed in it.) As for *Hajar dafi'*, it was the first time ever that I created a world with all its own features, both in terms of time and place, putting into it characters who bore these features and who moved within its confines. It was not easy; indeed, it was riddled with dangers and stumbling blocks which in most cases, I think, I was unable to overcome.

In 1976 I had begun a novel and then unfortunately, or perhaps luckily, I read a great novel by a Latin American author and there was nothing left to do but tear up my own novel. The strange thing was that in May of 1985, when I had just finished writing the last chapter of *Hajar dafi'*, I found before me, complete in every detail, the first scene of the novel that I had torn up: the same characters, even their names and the exact dialogues, were all there. I was astonished, and I confess too that I was delighted and I told myself repeatedly: 'Perhaps I am a writer after all . . . nothing could press me with such urgency were it not genuine'. This is the book that I am about to finish now. I started to write it two and a half years ago and found myself obliged to stop on account of my work which uses up a large amount of my intellectual and physical energy. In order to write a full-length work, I need extended periods of free time which hold in them the assurance that there will be no chance interruption. I cannot write a long work by gleaning half a day here and half a day there; at least I have been unable to until now. As for the short story, that is a different matter. The idea springs to mind suddenly, or I see a scene in life which makes the story, and then there is nothing more to it but to write, and that rarely demands much time, a matter of a day or so.

I have said that writing is dear to me because I love it and because death is at hand and I am afraid of it. I have said that I feel alienation and have indicated that I write because I am committed and I want to win over the others. (I am aware of the ideological element in what I write—it is always present in writing by any author, but I am conscious of its presence.) But were you to ask me now do you write in order to win the others over to your vision, I would answer without hesitation that this is only a part of what motivates me. I write because I love writing and I love writing because life arrests me, astonishes and preoccupies me, embraces, confuses, and frightens me, and because I am impassioned by it, impassioned until driven to write.

On Reading the Earth

❖

Saadi Youssef

In this humid evening, a leaden Paris evening, on the fifth of January 1992, I think of forty years back when I published my first poetic text. I was in the days of need then and I borrowed ten dinars from an uncle of mine to print a long poem in a booklet. I returned the sum to my uncle, not in one banknote or two as I received it, but in a sack of coins of varied marks and sounds. From the poem I gained a great deal: a leather belt and a seat in the movie theater.

Today I delight in the same sentiments: I gird myself, I take matters in my hand, and I reach for art.[1]

How was I destined—I, the child of an impoverished village and villagers— to reach out for art and to persist in doing so until this evening, until this moment?

How was I destined to cross deserts and oceans, and to exchange one country for other countries, the grandfather's home for semi-furnished apartments and cheap hotels, and my first library for stacks of books, folded and unfolded like luggage?

How was I destined to cross the bridge between the mosque of Hamdan village[2] and the public road, that umbilical cord, which is birth and death?

How was I destined to bear the strain and the hardship, to endure them and to dialogue with them even when "the bones within me are feeble and my head is all aflame with hoariness"?[3]

The days rotate, the years turn into decades and there are neither landmarks on the trail nor a beacon on the mountaintop.

Peace upon you . . . therefore.

Peace upon you, O hidden eternity in the wrap.

I write about people: I am fond of them and I defend them, but there is no beacon on the mountaintop.

I remember, once, my detention: I was taken from home to the police station. After passing nights there, a policeman led me handcuffed to the train station—the train was going up from Basra to Baghdad where I would be tried.

We—the policeman and I—were on foot. The road between the police station and the train station passes by all the places I know and where I am known: the souk, the cafés, and the bookstore. People were stirring in their daily bustle and I was walking handcuffed among them. No one said to me "Peace upon you." No eyes batted for me. The people were preoccupied with their own affairs, which had nothing to do with me. O for the dreary endeavor! But at the last turn towards the train station I saw a lad whose eyes whispered to me that he would tell the town my story.

Of this lad I wrote.

The artist discovers his beacon and raises his mountain where the flame blazes.

In Beirut in 1982, during the first days, starting with the fourth of June, I began to write personal poems. The first raid came upon the Sports Center while I was writing a poem tracing the Virgin Mary in the poetry of Rilke. The transformations of Mary started taking place reaching her last transfiguration in the poem entitled "Mary Comes," which I wrote on the twenty-fifth of July.

How did I pick up the material of the poem?

I used to be constantly on the move—before the air raids reached their barbaric intensity—visiting nearby positions, talking to fighters, going to risky spots, spending the night at times with young fighters in dark shelters, turning on broadcasting sets, straining my ears for news from here and there. I used to feel that my life was gushing forth in such a way that if death arrived it would be a crowning. The artist reveals his reality, purifies it, and picks it out. He raises his very reality into a beacon on the mountaintop.

Often the term 'surprising' is associated with poetry and what poetry evokes. The expression has arrested my attention for a long time and made me recall a verse of al-Muraqqish the Younger:

They were adorned with sapphires, set gems and gilt
With onyx of Zufar and twinned pearls[4]

The women of al-Muraqqish the Younger, those adorned beauties, how did they stand out for us in their glorious halo of art? The women of Saint-John Perse and Rilke, how did they reach us?

Al-Murraqish the Younger said nothing more than naming things. They were things we know, but the poet placed them in front of us in such a way as to see them for the first time. He granted us color and form. He provided us with delightful touches and wide-open eyes, and he invited us through touching and seeing to enter into an imaginative and visionary universe which we would have never been able to enter without him, without that surprise pouring in front of us like colored rain.

The senses, therefore, are the target of the poet's spell. They are addressed because they receive, and because imaginative and visionary elements go first through the senses and then continue their trajectory towards the subsequent artistic operation; that is the second half of the operation which is related to the reader—the reader who will pick up the elements and rearrange them after his own inclination and level.

Where, then, is the surprise in this?

I think the surprise is in the elements of reality and the things selected by the poet—the raw material (the elements and the thing) addresses the senses by alluding and not through declarations; that is, the relationship between the person and the world is returned to its beginning, to its starting point, to its sudden truth. This provokes reactions not answers: it moves. I have read a study that investigated the corporal responses to certain poetic texts, such as the twitching of facial muscles, the fluttering of eyelids, the hair's standing on end, and the manner of breathing. The affinity between early poetry and dance is but one example in this context.

But the issue is not as deceptively simple as it is in theoretical interpretation. In the creative process you will find yourself confronted with crucial practical decisions to make, pushing you with an amazing centrifugal force outside the current and the predominant. For example, inasmuch as things are your material, and language is made up of signs for things—and not the things themselves—then what will you do with language? For example, if the 'verb' *(al-fi'l)* and the 'defective noun' *(al-ism al-jamid)* are the closest to describing the raw material, then what will you do with the 'verbal noun' *(al-masdar)* and the 'derivative noun' *(al-mushtaqq)*?[5] And, for instance, if you were to see the ethics of the artistic process as inseparable from its raw material—its primary material which is available in the primordial language—then what will you do with memory? Can you present the goblet freely, like this, in your hands, while memory is crowded with goblets: Socrates', al-Khayyam's, and Umm Kulthum's? And for instance, if poetry is a re-view and a critique of the world, and given the fact that imagery is its instrument, what place is left for the idea? That is, does the idea precede the artistic process or does it follow it?

Is it the poet who arrives at the idea, or is it the reader?

For questions like these you will not find answers except in practice, that is in writing through extended time and cumulative effort. And it will remain so, as long as the road to art is longer than life.

On the table in front of me there is a paper, a matchbox, an ashtray, and a cigarette. There are four things in front of me, and it is up to me to play. These four things have their familiar conventional order. You forget the paper, you light the cigarette with a matchstick, you smoke, then you put the cigarette in the ashtray. This is what we do daily, but it is up to me to play, to change the familiar conventional order, to make my poem diverge, differ, and at the same time I must conserve the keys for me and the reader—my keys are the things. Thus I shall take out a cigarette from its pack and light it with a matchstick, but I shall not put it, lit, in the ashtray. I shall bring in the paper in the scene and put the lit cigarette on the paper, leaving things to interact outside the familiar context. I leave them to interact in the alchemy of poetry.

The seventh of January 1992. Another Paris morning: rain and leaden sky. It is 8:30 and darkness is still total. Only the windows light the jet-black morning in this working class suburb where I live. The roar of the cars and the buses penetrates the double glass. People are going to their factories and businesses while my papers, awaiting, remain blank.

Why am I in Paris? Why am I here and there, there and here, in migrations that started thirty-five years ago? Moscow–Damascus–Kuwait–Beirut–Algiers–Damascus–Beirut–Cyprus–Beirut–Damascus–Aden–Cyprus–Belgrade–Tunis, and at last: Paris.

What am I doing in Paris?

What am I doing in non-Arab land?

Exile includes the idea of abrogation—abrogating the relationship of the individual with heaven, earth, and society. There is a vertical line connecting heaven—where the worshipped is—with earth—where the ancestors lie in the long repose of death. And there is a horizontal line ordering the village or the town where homes, memories, and childhood playgrounds are. At the point of intersection between those two lines stands the individual.

The horror of exile is in the uprooting of the individual from this point of intersection and transplanting him in another spot which is not a point of intersection, where neither heaven is the primordial one nor the ancestors are ancestors, where there are no homes, no memories, and no childhood playgrounds.

What is left therefore?

Hardship only: toil and pain in order to preserve the primordial composition, the stock that is threatened by extinction, the root that is drying up.

But the rules of the artistic process make such preservation an extremely laborious task. The more someone makes an advance in art's way, the more his need for deeper roots increases—deeper roots at the point of intersection, not in the soil of exile.

I think of the Arab land with its beautiful people and its even more beautiful language. I think of its civilization and wealth, and simultaneously I think of where we have ended, encircled by bleak times, and I say to myself: We are not the only ones among nations afflicted and besieged. Many nations, other than ourselves, have been through and are going through bleak times. They have come out of them and they are coming out of them, because they preserved the firebrand smoldering or kindling. This firebrand is nothing but the core: it is the counterculture, alone capable of supplying every new generation with reasons justifying the branding of it as "new."

I wonder what would we have done without Taha Hussein?

His banner precedes us in blind times![6]

Translator's notes

1 This speech was delivered by Saadi Youssef when he was awarded the Sultan al-'Uways Poetry Prize for 1992. It appeared in the cultural page of the newspaper *al-Ittihad* (Abu Dhabi) on February 28, 1992.
2 Hamdan is a village near Basra in southern Iraq.
3 The quotation is from Surat Maryam in the Qur'an (XIX:4), rendered in A. J. Arberry's translation.
4 Al-Muraqqish the Younger, the nephew of al-Muraqqish the Elder and the uncle of Tarafa ibn al-'Abd, was of the Bani Rabi'a. He is a pre-Islamic poet known as a lover and a fighter. The line is from the conventional erotic prelude of a poem; see for further details *al-Mufaddaliyat*, edited by Ahmad M. Shakir and 'Abd al-Salam M. Harun (Cairo: Dar al-Ma'arif, n.d.), p. 245.
5 By using grammatical Arabic terms, the poet is contrasting the basics of the language as expressed in its core of radical verbs and primary nouns versus its elaborate armature of varied derivatives.
6 The ironic reference here is to the physically blind yet progressive and lucid Egyptian intellectual Taha Hussein (1889–1973).

Intertextual Dialectics

❖

Gamal al-Ghitany

I can easily remember the first book I read. I recall on one of my childhood days, I was crossing al-Husayn square during the feast when I stopped at a newspaper stand. It was there that I first saw the Beirut edition of the translation of Victor Hugo's *Les Misérables* in Arabic which I bought for seven piastres. When one of my relatives saw it, he exclaimed: "This is too difficult for you." But I read the book and I still recall entire lines from it. Later on, I discovered reading through two main sources: the library at Gammaliya Primary school, where I studied; I remember reading the entire collection of *al-Sindibad* (The Sinbad) magazine which was published in Arabic by Muhammad Sa'id al-'Irian. I also read from the collection *Awladuna* (Our children) where I was introduced to *Pinocchio* and *Juha fi Ganbulad*. The second source of readings came from the used book stands along al-Azhar sidewalk. There I found old paperback editions and *Arsène Lupin, Rocambole*, Samuel Johnson, Ben Jonson, and the Tarzan stories. I also read the paperback editions of Raphael Sabatini, Dostoevsky, Eugène Sue's *The Wandering Jew*, Emile Zola, and others. Those were all very spontaneous readings for I received no guidance at all. I used to read whatever I could get my hands on. Sometimes I even read novels whose title page had been ripped off, or whose first pages were missing. I remember reading voluminous novels, translated at the beginning of this century such as *Ghara'ib al-ittifaq* (Fantastic coincidence) by an author whose name I cannot recall, and a novel entitled *Warda* (Rose) by a German historian on pharaonic history. I also read *Sunuhe: The Egyptian* by Mika Waltari and was greatly influenced by it. In addition, I read Jurji Zaydan's works on Islamic history. The novels I read about the French Revolution lead me to several historical texts of which I remember a book entitled *Ashhar qadaya al-tarikh al-kubra* (The most renown historical issues). Among the books I recall is *al-Mughamir al-misri: Hafiz Najib* (Hafiz Najib: the Egyptian adventurer), a detective story. At al-Azhar bookstands, I also discovered the Arabic literary heritage—books like *al-Amali* (Dictations) by Abu 'Ali al-Qali, *Kitab al-ma'arif* (Book of knowledge) by Ibn Qutayba, and *al-Kamil* (The perfect) by al-Mubarrad. To this day, I still have in my library a copy of *Nafh al-tib* (Breath of perfume) by al-Maqqari which I had purchased for a few piastres. To put it briefly, then, my readings proceeded in two directions: that of world literature and that of the Arabic literary heritage, all quite spontaneously and intuitively. However, all these readings planted seeds which would bloom later.

My readings took a new turn when I discovered Bab al-Khalq where Dar al-Kutub (the National Library) is located and where I borrowed the books I could not afford to buy. I read whole translations which were published by Dar al-Yaqza al-'Arabiya in Damascus, especially those by the impressive Russian writers: Tolstoy's War and Peace (four volumes); Maxim Gorky's autobiography; Mother; Foma Gordeyev; The Lower Depths; The Outcasts, as well as stories by Chekhov and Ivan Turgenev. I also read The Storm and The Fall of Paris by Ilya Ehrenburg and The Bold Guard by Alexander Vadeyev. I recall that at the time a collection entitled "Eastern Publications" appeared in which I read Alexander Kuprin's The Garnet Bracelet, an excellent translation of Dostoevsky with an introduction by Dr. Muhammad al-Qassas, a collection of short stories by Saltykov-Shchedrin, and some novels by Turgenev.

My trips to Dar al-Kutub represented a more developed reading phase during which I bade farewell to a stage where I had been identifying with Lupin, the honorable thief, and dreaming of following his example in stealing from the rich to give to the poor. This period perhaps represents my earliest socialist leanings.

Simultaneously, I was becoming more familiar with the Arabic literary heritage, especially the historical sources on Egypt during the Islamic period. I benefited tremendously during that stage from having been introduced, at an early age, to the late Amin al-Khuly and his weekly, roundtable discussions—"al-'Umana'"—which took place on Sundays. His guidance changed the course of my readings in the Arabic literary heritage. Many years have passed since that period, which extended to the beginning of the sixties. I published my first short story in 1963 in the Lebanese literary journal, *al-Adib*, and during the same month I wrote a review article of *The Psychological Novel* by Leon Edel, a book which introduced me to James Joyce, Henry James, and Martin du Gard, whose novel *The World of the Thibaults* I read many years later. Today I can trace in this intuitive beginning some of the characteristics of my writing. I proceeded reading along these two parallel lines: translations of world literature and the Arabic literary heritage. They remain parallel to this day with further development and depth.

However, I did not read contempoary Arabic literature as much. I used to read those great writers and dream of writing like them. Yes, I developed in their footsteps and was influenced by them. Some of the novels I read a quarter of a century ago continue to influence me now: I still recall George Orwell's

1984. I did not read Muhammad 'Abd al-Halim 'Abdallah, nor Yusuf al-Siba'i. Even Yusuf Idris I read after I was twenty, in bits and pieces, out of curiosity.

The only contemporary Arab writer at whose work I stopped at length and read extensively and carefully was Naguib Mahfouz. My interest in his work started when I was fifteen years old, at approximately the same time that I was introduced to him in person. The strong relationship which I established with him and his work influenced me on a personal level because the titles of his novels were placenames from the area where I lived in Cairo: Khan al-Khalili, Bayn al-Qasrayn, al-Sukkariya, Qasr al-Shawq. I paused at his works for long, perhaps because I found that they were no less impressive than other world literature that I had read and through which I had been shaped.

I read Tawfiq al-Hakim's *Yawmiyat na'ib fi-l-aryaf (Maze of Justice: Diary of a Country Prosecutor)* at a later age and liked it tremendously. As for *'Awdat al-ruh (Return of the Spirit)*, I feel it has more historical than literary value. The work which most influenced me by al-Hakim, written in diary form, is *Zahrat al-'umr* (The flower of life). As for his plays, I remain ignorant of them. Now turning to Yahya Haqqi, I must say that I consider his collection *Dima' wa tin* (Blood and soil) one of the pioneering works in modern Arabic literature.

I have also read in psychology. Perhaps one of the books which I read at an early age and which influenced me to a great extent was Freud's *The Interpretation of Dreams*. I had borrowed it from Dar al-Kutub in a translation by Mustafa Safouan. I very much wanted to own this book, but I couldn't afford it (it cost LE1.50), so I started to recopy it by hand. That is why I have almost memorized entire pages of it. I also read several other works by Freud. At sixteen I discovered philosophy. It all started with materialist philosophy when I read *Fundamental Principles of Philosophy* by Georges Poulitzer, a book which circulated underground. From then on I read extensively in philosophy and political theory. Generally speaking, my readings until age sixteen followed one from the other by association so that when I read a novel on pharaonic history I would seek historical texts that dealt with that period, and so forth in all other areas.

In our literary heritage, I was particularly attached to history as a result of a powerful feeling of the passage of time. I read historiographical texts and historical annals closely, starting with Ibn al-Hakam, up to al-Jabarti, where the record of everyday life remains very vivid, especially in the texts of al-Maqrizi and Ibn Iyas. I read in pharaonic history, especially the encyclopedia of Salim Hasan, as well as in foreign sources. I found the pharaonic history very distant, but Islamic history, and more specifically perhaps the Mamluk period, is still alive. I lived in an area in Cairo that was always mentioned in the early Islamic sources: whole areas and streets still bear the same names. One of my hobbies is to trace the transformations that befell a place: what had been built here, who had lived there, what were the conditions of the time. After the 1967 defeat I rediscovered Ibn Iyas, who had lived a similar historical moment when the Ottomans crushed the Egyptian army in the battle of Marj Dabiq. This historian depicted the defeat with national fervor and genuine grief comparable to my own feelings during that bleak period of 1967.

Persian literature was one of the areas in which I took interest because of its specificity, especially the *Shah-Nama* (Book of the kings) by al-Firdawsi, Hafez's poetry, and Iranian mythology. Of late, I also read in Islamic Sufism and mysticism, besides the spiritual teachings in different religions: Hinduism, Sabian practices, Buddhism, as well as primitive beliefs.

From the start I felt the urge to write something, the like of which I had not read before. I went through different stages. After I had read Leon Edel's *The Psychological Novel*, I discovered many possible techniques: the subversion of linear time and the interior monologue. This further developed into a desire to innovate in narrative style itself, with one eye on world literature and the other on the Arabic literary heritage. But I remained incapable of finding the right form until 1967. During the period between 1963 and 1968 I published numerous stories and two short novels: *Hikayat muwadhdhaf kabir* (Stories of a distinguished civil servant) in the Lebanese paper *al-Muharrir,* and *Hikayat muwadhdhaf saghir* (Stories of an insignificant civil servant) in the Lebanese journal *al-Jumhur al-jadid*. But when my first collection *Awraq shabb 'asha mundhu alf 'am* (Journal of a young man who lived a thousand years ago) appeared in 1969, I only included five stories, all written after 1967. I had started to be inspired by our literary heritage in creating new forms of expression. Despite that, I had a strong internal urge to transcend the narrative forms which I had read. This required a relentless effort on my part; one could say that starting with my novel *Khitat al-Ghitani* (The itineraries of al-Ghitany) and more specifically in the novel I am now writing, *Kitab al-tajliyat* (The book of epiphanies), I finally succeeded in transcending conventional forms. In other words, I could rid myself of the inner feeling that I was dominated by the standards of the classical novel; I was equally freed from the waves of innovation that characterized the literary work of Europe and the United States. Only now can I say that I am beginning to move more freely toward new modes of expression, inspired mainly by the Arabic literary heritage.

This is not to say that I am inventing a new literary form; rather I am trying to innovate within the framework of narrative art. The western or conventional novel, starting with *Don Quixote* and proceeding to the Nouveau Roman, in Europe and the United States, represented the model which Arab writers had to follow. What I am trying to do really is an attempt to establish a narrative form that derives its very foundations from our heritage at large, beginning with the oral, popular tradition which I have internalized to a great extent because of my upbringing in Upper Egypt and in Gammaliya, all the way to the written heritage. Until recently, I believed that what was being written in world literature represented the measuring stick for any novel. However, I now feel that I have completely rid myself of these standards which were imposed by literary criticism or by writers' acceptance of the stipulations for a good novel. Here I must note that my continuous preoccupation with a new narrative form was not just a search for form, rather it was an attempt to locate a new narrative form that would insure more space for freedom of expression, and in keeping with my own experience. I am in constant struggle with the *how* of what I want to express, in order to have more freedom. I think I have freed myself, to a great extent, from the hegemony of existing narrative forms in my most recent work, *Kitab al-tajliyat*.

This does not mean that I do not have specific standards that I have developed from within world literature, but I have always tried to transcend conventional forms. Now I have my own standards which are derived from our heritage. I do not work in a vacuum. I work with models drawn from Arabic narration latent in poetry, the Sufi tradition, historical texts, or folk life. But this is a vast subject which is difficult to address in detail. What I do is name the literary conventions I wish to transcend in world literature. I try to benefit from them, not in order to imitate or apply ready-made models, but rather in order to transcend them through my own individual heritage. For example, there are many narrative techniques and strategies for character development, but Muhi al-Din ibn 'Arabi has a unique way of narrating the incident, or depicting a particular character—a unique method which I never encountered in any novel. This mode is closer to my own psyche and I am capable of appreciating it. Why should I not inhabit it and try to make of it a starting point, just as I had attempted earlier with written history, specifically Ibn Iyas? Another example: the internal rhythm in Sheikh 'Abd al-Karim al-Jili's work is by far different from any other style I have come across because the spiritual experience is itself different and could only exist within the reality which I inhabit and know. It is in this respect that I do not work in a vacuum, or invent forms from nothingness. I am tryng to create a form that has assimilated both universal and spiritual traditions. I am trying to create something original; this is every artist's dream. Because of my upbringing, my disposition, and my interests, the Arabic literary heritage is my stool: I stand on tiptoe and try to reach higher to create my special form that relies on all the rest.

It is true that I am a product of my own experiences. But these same readings have been consulted by others who did not try [to do likewise]. Our literary heritage has always been available. The only Arab writer who has tried to use it is the Palestinian Emile Habiby in his novel *al-Waqa'i' al-ghariba fi ikhtifa' Sa'id Abu al-Nahs al-mutasha'il* (*The Secret Life of Saeed, the Ill-fated Pessoptimist*). Incidentally, for me Habiby is the most important Arab writer because we have chosen parallel routes despite differences in our ultimate goals. In recent years, Naguib Mahfouz has discovered the potentials of Arabic literary narrative art. This is evident in his *Layali alf layla (Arabian Nights and Days)* preceded by *al-Harafish (The Harafish)* and more recently *Rihlat Ibn Fattuma (The Journey of Ibn Fattouma)*. Many intellectuals looked down on our heritage: they either used the most frequently cited texts or they were simply ignorant of it all. The Arabic literary heritage is rich and diverse and requires much effort to familiarize oneself with it. Knowing it is not enough to benefit from it. The important thing is how. Of late, this endeavor has become doubly difficult, what with the increasing surrender to easy solutions in every field and the existence of an inferiority complex vis-à-vis Western culture and its modes of creative production. The late Amal Dunqul, one of the poets of my generation, was aware of the importance of our heritage and learned from it. But I must confess that there has been an increasing consciousness of the like during recent years, not just in Egypt, but in the Arab world at large. Some had said that my experimentation would lead me to a dead end, because traditional forms are limited, hence my experience itself. But such statements reveal ignorance as to the scope of our heritage and what it has to offer. I personally feel I need five centuries in order to exhaust the possibilites inherent in the Arabic heritage.

Experiments take place in many different frameworks: in the West, for example, whether we speak of the English, French, Spanish, or Italian novel we will find that experimentation takes place within the framework of each one of these civilizations. In my case, there is a different experience, a different heritage not known there, laden with visions that reflect a specific way of being, in harmony with my own. True, every period and every place has its own specificity and conventions. Hence I believe that understanding the potentials of my own heritage is very important in allowing me to transcend earlier creative forms and to advance toward something new, different, something I have never read before. Such is my ambition.

For me, it is the content that dictates the form. In my own experience with *al-Zayni Barakat (Zayni Barakat)*, I was recreating an entire period. The subject matter in itself is a familiar one throughout history, i.e. issues of oppression and the politics of surveillance. Here I wish to explain that the spy apparatus I depicted in *al-Zayni Barakat* did not exist during the sixteenth century, the timeframe of the novel. It belongs to our time. And because I was reconstructing a whole period I had to recreate some of its minutest details: language, style, kinds of food, costumes, street-names in Cairo, and neighborhoods. All this in order to evoke an entire period. I deal with this perennial subject matter—that of oppression and surveillance—in *Khitat al-Ghitani* through a contemporary setting but a historical format. *Waqa'i' Harat al-Za'farani (Incidents in Zaafarani Alley)* is different: the whole narrative is a series of files and reports, and hence I adopted a detached documentary style. As for *Kitab al-tajliyat*, the experience has to do with death, time, oblivion, and the afterlife; hence my recourse to the Sufi heritage.

There is certainly a great difference between the style of my creative writing and that of my articles. Because I am a journalist, I am obsessed with keeping them separate. For example, I never use the pen with which I write my articles to write my literary works; my evenings are completely dedicated to literature—I would never write an article during that time; when I don't write, I read. When I was a military correspondent I wrote my articles in the car, but those were exceptional circumstances.

In *Waqa'i' Harat al-Za'farani* I employ the language of detached reporting since, as I mentioned before, language emerges from the work itself. Here I would like to speak about something personal. Three years ago I decided I wanted to study French. At the same time I was beginning to discover the Sufi idiom and style and I realized that the stylistic experiment which later appeared in *Kitab al-tajliyat* would require my undivided attention. Actually Arabic itself is a plural language: poetic, epistolatory, and Sufi. Evoking any of them requires tremendous effort. For example, when I started to study Sufi style I did not content myself with reading *al-Futuhat al-makkiya* (Meccan revelations) by Ibn 'Arabi, or *al-Insan al-kamil* (The perfect man) by 'Abd al-Karim al-Jili, or *al-Isharat al-ilahiya* (Divine signs) by al-Tawhidi, rather I used to recopy, by hand, slowly and diligently, whole pages of these texts for no reason other than to immerse myself in the secret of their style, so that it would penetrate me. It is crucial that one be sensitive to the characteristics of style. So, this is how I gave up French to study this style. When I started writing *Kitab al-tajliyat,* I put all that I learned aside in order to forge my own language. I think that recently I have become more concerned with the details of language. In the beginning, I focused primarily on form and mood in general, but of late I have become more interested in detail. This I suppose is part of maturation. In *Waqa'i' Harat al-Za'farani* I benefited from Ibn Iyas's linguistic experience despite the fact that my subject matter was not historical. Ibn Iyas used to record the most horrific incidents with the same composure he recorded the most mundane ones. He maintained an objective distance between himself and the event. In *Waqa'i' Harat al-Za'farani*, therefore, I record events with neutrality because I am writing a report. I could not have adopted a poetic language within a report. Generally speaking, I am now more interested in and concerned with the minute details of language.

I think that language is an active and influential component of the literary work. For me, language is also a state of mind and not just a style that one can perfect and use as a tool. States of mind change of course; that is why my language changes from one work to the other. I think I have two major experiments in language: one via the historical sensibility and the other via the Sufi sensibility. When I wrote my short stories "Hidayat ahl al-wara li-ba'd ma jara fi-l-Maqshara" (Guiding mankind to some of the happenings in the prison-house of Maqshara), "Ithaf al-zaman bi-hikayat Jalabi al-sultan" (The most beautiful stories of the sultan's Jalabi), "Ibn Sallam" (The son of Sallam), "Taybugha" (Wailing Taybugha), then *al-Zayni Barakat,* I used to transmigrate into the spirit of the historical language of the sixteenth century. In order to penetrate the spirit and essence of this style, I read extensively in medieval texts, not just *Bada'i' al-zuhur fi waqa'i' al-duhur* by Ibn Iyas. This great writer represented the base for me. Many other texts rotated in his orbit and served to heighten my sensibility for the period, especially in the wake of the 1967 defeat, the mirror image of the defeat in Marj Dabiq in 1517. I used to read aloud whole pages of *Bada'i' al-zuhur* and recopy others in an attempt to achieve the inner rhythm of Ibn Iyas' language. In fact, sometimes I used to imagine Ibn Iyas himself during those distant evenings when he recorded the incidents that had taken place or which he had witnessed: the way he sat, his composure, pen in hand gliding over the paper. It is a very private state interwoven with public circumstances (the 1967 defeat and the 1517 defeat at Marj Dabiq), an acute sense of time and many other emotions, all of which led to the creation of this language. After I finished *al-Zayni Barakat*, I felt I was bidding farewell to the state of mind that had created this language and I found such a moment enormously difficult. It was as if you had spent tremendous energy in order to master a language and then decided deliberately to forget it or not speak it! I was actually bidding farewell to the Mamluk period, but not to my desire to create new forms relying on the Arabic heritage. Several years later, I relived an experience similar to the one I had with *Bada'i' al-Zuhur fi waqa'i' al-duhur* by Ibn Iyas, for I had read him before the defeat but then rediscovered him after June 1967. During the late seventies, I became immersed in *al-Futuhat al-makkiya* by Sheikh Ibn 'Arabi. I would constantly look at it and wonder about what that huge book might contain. In effect, I started reading it while consulting some contemporary studies, or orientalist works, in order to unravel its secrets. Then came the sudden death of my father in 1980 while I was traveling. For me, this was the heaviest blow ever. I went through a period of profound grief during which I once more sought refuge in *al-Futuhat al-makkiya*. Once again, I began to rediscover it and I tried to penetrate the essence of its Sufi idiom so akin to a profound spiritual experience concerning the human being and the universe. It became intermingled with my grief. This state led to my current novel *Kitab al-tajliyat* of which the first volume, *al-Sifr al-awwal* (The first book) has appeared. I have completed the second volume, *al-Sifr al-thani* (The second book) and am now beginning *al-Sifr al-thalith* (The third book). Once again *al-Futuhat al-makkiya* became the sun around which other planets orbited. With it I relived the Islamic Sufi tradition, beginning with al-Junayd, al-Hallaj, al-Qushayri, Imam al-Sha'rani, and continuing with Ibn Sab'iyn, al-Suhrawardi, and Abd al-Karim al-Jili. I also read and continue to cohabit with the Islamic Sufi heritage from Iran. Thus the language of *Kitab al-tajliyat* was a product of such a state of mind. This situation made of the language of the text a major protagonist. Before writing the novel such an idea was not very clear in my mind. It gradually took substance when I heard some of the criticism which circulated after the publication of *al-Sifr al-awwal*. Purpose and deliberation were not the main thrust in my creation of new literary forms. I remember that a friend of mine had read my short story "Hidayat ahl al-wara li-ba'd ma jara fi-l-Maqshara," and told me that it represented a new stage in short story writing. I listened in silence and disbelief wondering if I could possibly be creating a new form. I thought he was flattering me. But then, after the appearance of my first collection *Awraq shabb 'asha mundhu alf 'am*, the critics wrote confirming my friend's statement, who had only read the story in manuscript form.

The question of time is one that has long preoccupied me. It was one of the important reasons for my interest in the different stages of history. For me, history is time, colossal, overpowering, reviving, deadly in its awesome process. It is that which diverts us endlessly to the past, that which brings forth memory and forgetfulness. For long I have contemplated and reflected on time, starting with the simple mechanical movement of seconds, minutes, and hours, and proceeding to the movement of the galaxies, the succession of night and day, the passage of years, life and death. For me, history is over and done with: there is no difference between a moment that terminated seconds ago and another, which occurred thousands or millions of years ago. Neither can be recaptured. That is why I do not agree with those who say that "you are writing a historical novel." Everything proceeds to the past, a past that is impossible to repossess. For long I have contemplated time and I still do. I have also read about time in ancient thought, in mythology, religion, philosophy, except that I have not found an answer to my ever-pressing question. For me, there is one certain truth: the only thing in the world that cannot be vanquished, resisted, or challenged is time. Despite our conscious understanding of this truth, since we all know that life has a determined end through death, the glory of humanity is that it refuses to surrender. It resists to the end. True, death is forthcoming and fate is inevitable, but the human glory lies in this challenge which is at times visible but more often invisible. If we were to reflect on the history of art, especially of ancient times, we will find that its essence lay in the attempt to vanquish annihilation, an attempt to vanquish this invisible time: materially, through the great pyramid for example, or through a memorable life, or by imagining the existence of another world with another life. When human civilization reached a peak, the expression of human desire for immortality also attained its peak. Art, for me, is the most refined human endeavor against annihilation. However, my preoccupations have taken a different turn in the aftermath of several general and personal experiences. Among the personal ones was my father's death; among the public ones was the 1967 defeat, followed by the late President Sadat's visit to Jerusalem and the peace treaty with Israel, which most violently affected me. After my father's death, I became profoundly immersed in the Islamic Sufi heritage. Some of the Muslim Sufi thinkers believed that the human being (*insan*) was named after forgetfulness (*nisyan*); in fact, they deal extensively with forgetfulness. One of the things that left a heavy resentment within me was having to live during an age where basic principles were being reversed, where many things with which we grew up were being squandered. Yes ... perhaps in the distant future there will be a change, for nothing remains at a standstill. But there is a great difference between reading about such things and actually living the moments of transition, or experiencing oblivion and being consumed by these fires. One often reads about death, but when death approaches us through a dear one, it all becomes very different. I returned to Ibn 'Arabi after my father's death, in the same way I had rediscovered Ibn Iyas after the 1967 defeat. I am in constant contemplation of the relationship between man and the universe. I always reflect on the invincible: time or fate (*dahr*) as I prefer to call it, because I am convinced that the universe does not exist absurdly. There is a power that organizes and directs it. Through my own contemplation I have become convinced that fate is God. I was surprised to find my idea was echoed in my readings of Ibn 'Arabi and others, and that the word *dahr* (fate) was, in fact, one of the ninety-nine Islamic names of God; that it is indeed His ninety-ninth name, the very last name. There is a *hadith* of the Prophet Muhammad that says: "Do not curse fate for fate is God."

I am not a Sufi in my conduct, but I consider myself close to the Muslim Sufis' vision of time and of fate. Much of my inner suffering and toil found expression through our heritage. In this respect, the suffering was fundamental in my orientation toward the heritage. It was not simply a matter of search for technique. Certainly there was the attraction to the delicate purity of the language itself, which I consider sweeter than poetry. I invite you to read *al-Isharat al-ilahiya* by Abu Hayyan al-Tawhidi or *al-Insan al-kamil* by 'Abd al-Karim al-Jili. Of course there is also *al-Mawaqif* by al-Niffari and *al-Tawasin* by al-Hallaj. Fate is my main preoccupation, fate in all its guises starting with the coming moment, all the way to past and future time, the period, the epoch. All of these are names for one invincible thing, with no beginning or end, with an unknown face, even though we see its signs and marks every passing instant. Human yearnings will proceed to nothingness without art. Human life will lose its features without art. Art, in its various forms, is the sole sincere attempt, on the part of humanity, to confront this unconquerable power—to resist nothingness and annihilation.

Language, Culture, and Reality

❖

Adonis

The dominant cultural trend in Arab society is a devotion to the culture of the past. It is presumed that if traditions are preserved, so is the existence of society itself. This devotion is not simply a dogma; it is manifested in life itself: in educational programs, in cultural institutions, and in intellectual currents. It reflects a specific idea of culture, namely, that it is knowledge of the texts of the past, or knowledge of that which does not contradict such texts. The representatives of this dominant trend—the educated, the intellectuals, and the writers— speak of this knowledge in a tone bordering on religious reverence. Thus, they believe that the strength of Arab society is dependent on the power, impact, and persistence of traditional culture. This is why Arab culture continues to be based on memorization and transmission. In other words, the relation between the Arabs and their traditional culture remains analogous to the relation of the fallible with the infallible, the pupil with the teacher. Questioning, rejecting, and transcending are viewed not only as transgressions of culture, but also as attacks on society itself, to the point that anything which is out of the ordinary is not considered original, but, seen as something arising from some type of madness, it is looked at with curiosity and astonishment. Our daily life is nothing but a reflection of our culture: an alienating world of orders and commands.

Language is not only a means of expression, but it is also a way of thinking. Every social situation, therefore, has its own language: our prevailing language is the language of our prevailing circumstances. These circumstances are backward on all levels; that is why our language is backward on all levels. It is the language of rhetoric, artifice, and ornament, and in this case, society consumes words as an individualistic pleasure, as if they were consumer goods. Thus, our language has lost the vitality of innovation and the intensity of life. It has become something like a scrap-heap which opposes action. It glorifies the moment of speech, not the moment of action; the moment of consumption, not the moment of production.

It is impossible to generate consciousness by reading the cultural legacy (*al-turath*) or by studying it, for such reading transmits a culture external to actual life and from above, that is, it transmits a culture which is both didactic and abstract. In addition, the Arab masses live in closed circles; they do not interact with and integrate into a unified, effective, and dynamic social network. Since the culture of the Arab masses is a part of their forefathers' (*salaf*) culture, their life is a continuation of their forefathers' life. Their concern, therefore, is not to innovate but to imitate. There is no future, however, except for those who innovate. As for those who are satisfied with transmission and imitation, it is as if they reject the future and live in an extending past. The Arab masses continue to live in a cultural era which has died. They continue, therefore, to face history with what has become extraneous to history.

The Arabs' becoming revolutionary is, therefore, dependent on acquiring complete freedom in theoretical and actual revolutionary practice, and in a continual radical revision of the inherited concepts and values, as well as achievements. By this alone, the old world crumbles and, from its debris, a new world arises—a world overflowing with forms, configurations, and ideas.

From here, the meaning of the relation between the revolutionary intelligentsia and that which is inherited changes. It is not a relation of revival or glorification. It is, rather, a relation of criticism, analysis, and transcendence. In this way, we realize that the role of innovation does not lie in the preservation, but rather, in the explosion and development of the inherited cultural system. Every intellectual who does not do this remains below the revolutionary standard: he does not create, but rearranges what has become unfastened from the chains of words preserved in books and memory. Revolution is the science of changing reality; revolutionary writing is the visionary dimension of this science that produces change.

We cannot create a revolutionary Arab culture without a revolutionary language. (Revolutionizing the language is part of revolutionizing society as a whole. This discussion on revolutionizing language does not mean, therefore, to isolate it from this whole.) How can we therefore make out of Arabic a revolutionary language? This, to me, seems to be one of the most complicated problems that faces the Arab revolutionary movement. But what do we mean by the 'revolution of language'? We mean that the word—and hence, writing—becomes a force for creativity and change, placing the Arab in an atmosphere of investigation, questioning, and inquiry.

The word, as we have inherited it, does not express an emotional or visionary density, but it simply expresses an external relation. It is quasi-neutral because it is filled with earlier significance brought from the outside. When Abu Tammam, for example, tried to rebel against such language, it was said that he "corrupted poetry," meaning that he changed the traditional paradigm of speech. For this reason, the readers and critics who inherited and preserved this system did not understand him.

The linguistic revolution lies in destroying the function of the old language, that is to say, by emptying it of the prevailing traditional meanings. In this way, the word becomes an act that has no 'past'; it becomes a mass radiating with unfamiliar associations.

The revolution that we are striving for in the Arabic language, therefore, is not formal or aesthetic, limiting its concern to literal meanings, to external sound and to the harmony of tone and articulation. Rather, it is an explosion of the language from within. When the revolution of language is limited to form, sound, and its tonal rhythms, it turns into a sickly regurgitation.

Nor is this revolution a return to the roots or the origin. A return like this makes a sacred entity out of language, a language beyond language. That is, it is detached from history, time, and man, and is transformed into a rite moving man in the direction of eternity. In this way, language becomes a foreshadowing of paradisiac residency; it therefore refuses to be polluted by the earth's dust or to be integrated into daily reality, because this reality is constant change, that is to say, perpetual annihilation.

Language, according to that view, does not favor the transient but rather the permanent. Language thus overlooks the present because it is only a fleeting crossing toward eternity. Yet devotion to eternity leads to complete passivity. It becomes a complete alienation from the movement of history—and this causes language to exist outside of time and society. It follows, therefore, that reality is destroyed in order to construct speech. But the time of speech is itself false because it aspires to melting and fusing with the origin and root in eternity.

Unity in a language such as this one is not a unity harmonizing various elements, but it is like the unity of the Arabesque: the unity of a recurring element, a dispersed unity. It is the unity of the word which is shaped like the pearl, the unity of a single verse of poetry.

The fundamental difference between the 'old' language and the 'modern' one is that in the former, meaning already exists and the writer shapes it in a new form. But meaning in 'modern' (revolutionary) language is established in the writing and afterwards. Meaning in 'modern' language succeeds rather than precedes the writing.

The problem of the bond between the masses and the revolutionary writer arises from this point. (This problem does not exist for the nonrevolutionary writer.) The revolutionary writer who lives among masses such as ours is isolated by virtue of his creativity (that is to say, his revolutionism) on the one hand, and by virtue of the inherited backwardness that clouds these masses, on the other hand. The masses embrace, nay, cling to, everything they preserve of the world they are familiar with. The writer, however, is not revolutionary except in so far as he shakes his familiar, inherited world in order to create a new and pure one.

Revolution in language cannot be separated from revolution in life. We, in Arab society, face together this dual problem: to revolutionize life and to revolutionize language. And if we are still suffering under the yoke of decline caused by the backwardness unjustly imposed on us by Ottoman rule, we are now also facing the burden of decline of another type, which I call the decline caused by the progress imposed on us by modern civilization—the civilization of the Image (cinema, television, photo magazines, and so forth) wherein culture is transformed into a passive process, which we receive and in which we do not participate. If it is in the nature of the word to address the mind, and in the nature of the image to address the senses, we are facing the danger of moving, with perfect ease, from the sphere of repression which was imposed on us by foreign political imperialism, to the sphere of surrender of thought, entirely of our own will and desire, and this is what modern civilization, with its simple but tempting passive consumerism, imposes on us.

The contemporary Arab writer faces a problematic of creativity that could be summed up as follows: he politicizes his writing theoretically without having, in the practical sense, political influence. In this way, the writer often relinquishes his role as creator of the world of the word without being able to undertake the role of creator in the world of politics.

I do not intend to differentiate between politics and writing. Every great piece of writing is, in my opinion, political writing in one form or another. What I mean is that the creative writer—in order to remain faithful to himself and to his writing—cannot but turn the life of words into his primary obsession. Like politics, writing has its special problems—they are many, complex and always changing. A writer is a writer inasmuch as he bears them in mind and lives with them. When he is detached from them or occupied with other matters, he becomes—in relation to the act of writing—like someone who wants to swim while out of water.

The Arab liberation movements that have emerged until now are nonrevolutionary, whether in their manner of thinking or in their means of struggle. They inherit the past and perpetuate it. The Arab, man or woman, cannot be an effective factor in the struggle without being personally liberated. And he cannot function as long as he is subservient to the culture of the past, as long as he is subservient to the inherited system of social relations, as long as he is subservient to a heritage that has ceased responding to any of the problems which he is confronting. Faced with this situation, the revolutionary Arab poet finds that, on the one hand, he cannot but support these movements in fighting colonialism and imperialism, and that, on the other hand, he cannot but oppose them because of their lack of a revolutionary foundation.

Topics exploding before the Arab writer threaten not only his daily tranquillity but also his entire existence. Moreover, when some writers come to express them, these topics generate nothing other than styles which past themes called for in past eras. To other writers, however, these topics call for expressive modes which traditional styles fail to provide. Nothing expresses life that explodes forth in a sudden, unprecedented deluge except a style that explodes forth, likewise, in a sudden, unprecedented deluge. I shall formulate this more precisely: when writing on a topic deviating from the familiar paradigm of life, the writer must deviate from the familiar paradigm of writing. Deviation from the familiar system of writing, by necessity, means deviation from the system of language and the system of thought. That is, the writer would contradict—by necessity— everything that convention persists in calling 'natural writing'. For his writing would indeed be 'unnatural' or would contradict the nature of 'language and style' or 'deviate from tradition and its spirit' as some others like to say in a tone of racist ignorance. Similarly, 'nonsense', 'orderlessness', and 'chaos' are, in the true revolutionary product, means of expressing what has changed life and filled it with chaos, orderlessness, and nonsense. Just as the revolution rises from the failure of static life, so revolutionary writing will rise from the failure of earlier writing. Revolutionary writing, from this perspective, is an attempt to struggle with and overcome impotence. It is, therefore, writing that failed, if viewed from standpoints of the past, except that its success, strictly speaking, lies in this very failure—I mean, in this distance from writing of the past.

Revolutionary writing is not fuel but fire, a fire that burns only in the depths of humans filled with the sun. More simply, the word as creation cannot gain for the revolution a person for whom the creativity of life, as well as its transformation, does not form an essential part of his existence and thought. It may gain him as a 'material mass', as an 'inherited accumulation', but, in this case, he would be no more than fuel. And that which is fundamental, for him, for the revolution and for the future, is that we make out of him a pit of fire, not a dry piece of firewood. The true role of the revolutionary writer is represented in what I call deconstruction of traditional time. The prevailing means of expression, whether in poetry or prose, music or painting, acting or singing, are still ornamental motifs sticking to the planes and walls of this time. They have lost, like this era, the ability of creation. Thus, one must have the courage to reject this era and these means, and one must penetrate deeply into what is behind them: to explosions capable of recreating the Arab and inciting all of his thought and his being in the direction of revolution. There must be courage to acknowledge that this era has died, that its way and meaning have died, and that it is impossible for us to revolt with either of them. Without this, we will be like one fighting childhood with decrepitude, or the sun of the future with the darkness of the past.

Sartre, in a study on Mallarmé, defines the "word" as a way of possessing something. It is a possession that transfers the thing to the other, that is to say, man writes in order to convey to the other what he writes. Mallarmé, however, does not use language to bring the world closer to him, but rather to keep it at a distance. But can language communicate the reality of the world? Many researchers in linguistics doubt the possibility of this communication. Language, according to them, cannot go beyond the surface of experience. As for the rest, it remains outside of language, absent, enveloped by silence. The word becomes more and more incapable of realizing the world of cosmic energy, the world of spatial continuity, relative time, and the atomic structure of beings. It is, therefore, as if reality now begins outside of language.

But some of them do not see the crisis of language in language itself as much as they see it in the absence or non-existence of new prophets or sorcerers who can shake the dust off and resurrect a language glowing like the morning sun.

From ancient times, the Arabs treated the potential of language to embrace the world and its things and what is beyond them. The scholars of Basra considered language a mirror reflecting concepts, phenomena, and things with exactitude. They, therefore, saw that language must include the rules and laws which thought follows in life and nature. Thus, they concerned themselves with its rules and principles, and with furnishing the links between words and meanings. In this way, they brought linguistics into the models of the mind, as it is in the case of logic, sociology, or science. As for the scholars of Kufa, their opinions were completely the opposite. They dismissed principles and rules of logic and, instead, deduced by analogy. In this way, linguistics for them came to be a collection of specific statutes applicable to each case in and of itself. This science was directed by an apprehensiveness of general rule and by a tendency toward diversity greatly valuing the specific and the unique, and the exceptional, or what we call deviant. From this point, formulas and linguistic patterns increased, and they considered everything that appeared on the Arabs' tongue as a basic foundation even if it opposed logic and reason. Thus, they believed that the exception to the rule, from the Basra scholars' point of view, was in fact a foundation from which analogy could proceed. The foundation is not to be found in the general logical rule, but in life.

Jabir ibn Hayyan, in his book *Mizan al-huruf* (The scale of letters), pointed out that language is not a product of convention nor is there a system to explain it, but rather, it springs from the soul. This implies an essential and intimate link between the nature of language and the nature of the body, resembling the essential and intimate link between the melody and the string. Therefore, the nature of the foundation of the word corresponds to the nature of that which is signified. This is Plato's theory of language itself.

Modern development, however, has confused the relationship of our language with the world, by increasing their separation. For example, the words that we use frequently are lost; they are the past that our thought has transcended, but, at the same time, they are the past that still continues in our institutions. They, therefore, express neither our reality and present nor our future, but the delusion of our continuing existence. This difference between language and reality has begun to increase day by day. And when words no longer have meaning, any word becomes appropriate for anything or for any meaning. Hence, we talk in order to kill words or to not say anything, or we speak a language that only says what contradicts it: the despot discusses freedom; the hypocrite, candor; and the liar, truth.

In the light of this, we discover that the failure of expression, of comprehending the world and its secrets, usually attributed to language, does not lie in language itself, but in the absence of he who knows how to unburden language of its ancient night and to retrieve it into its primal innocence. This is where the secret of poetic creativity is hidden. It is on this level alone that one may say that poetry is, first of all, language.

But if we wanted to study this relationship between language and subject—on a sociopolitical level—in the Arab world, which is moving towards revolution, what do we notice? We notice that there is a gap between, on the one hand, revolution as language and thought, as a reality thinking and expressing, versus, on the other hand, revolution as work and change, as a reality changing its precepts and values in its infrastructure and superstructure.

This gap is revealed, clearly and directly, in that the revolutionary Arab still deals, on the one hand, with abstractions, and is fused, on the other hand, in universal revolutionary thought. In other words, he combines rather than contrasts. This syncretism develops into a dependency approaching annihilation, because, until now, he does not move toward distinction or difference. This distinction, however, cannot be achieved except under two conditions: 1) breaking forth from the Arab reality which we inherit and which we are now living; 2) rediscovery of revolutionary thought and theories in the light of this reality, that is to say, in the light of analyzing, understanding, and comprehending it.

The basis, therefore, of the establishment of Arab revolutionary thought is the analysis of Arab reality. So why doesn't the Arab intellectual analyze this reality? I do not believe that the reason for this is attributable to the lack of those who can analyze or of analytical tools, as some think. Rather, it is due to the absence of freedom of analysis, that is, to the absence of courage on the part of those who would analyze. Every analysis, in order to be both revolutionary and realistic, must deal with Arab reality as a whole, beginning with the human being, and passing by the social, political, and economic institutions, and ending with ideology. Here is the dilemma: no Arab revolutionary thought will be established without beginning from this analysis, and this analysis is almost impossible as long as there is neither freedom nor courage. Thus, the Arab 'revolutionary' thinker takes refuge in 'speech' detached from the reality in which he lives, discussing the other reality in which the other revolutionary thought lives, and covering all of this in Arab wrapping.

Thoughts on Change and the 'Blind Language'

❖

Ghassan Kanafani

Introduction

Thoughts on Change and the 'Blind Language' *(Afkar 'an al-taghyir wa-l-lugha al-'amya')* was originally presented by Ghassan Kanafani on March 11, 1968 as part of a public lecture series in Beirut that invited major Arab writers and intellectuals to consider the impact of the June 1967 defeat on Arab society and thought. As such, Kanafani's text can be located within the context of the enormous corpus of theoretical, historical, ideological, emotional, literary, and lyrical reassessments of the limited successes and multiple defeats and setbacks of recent Arab history that emerged in the immediate aftermath of the war and that continue even today, some two decades later, to characterize much of contemporary Arab cultural production. As Faysal Darraj has pointed out,

> The June 1967 defeat was the most serious event in modern Arab history. Its significance and results surpassed those brought about by the establishment of Israel in 1948. Israel's establishment was an expression of the defeat of the Palestinian people and the impotence of the Arab regimes in a certain historical period when they were dependent on the colonial forces. But the June defeat was an expression of the defeat of the Arab revolution as a whole.[1]

"Thoughts on Change and the 'Blind Language'," however, distinguishes itself, in 1968 when it was written and again twenty years later, within this particular literary history by its materially grounded critical analysis of the tendency to an unreconstructed and tyrannical fetishization of 'self-criticism'.

Ghassan Kanafani is best-known, if not exclusively so, in English translation for his literary writings, the short stories and novels such as *Men in the Sun*,

Return to Haifa, and *All That's Left to You*.[2] Consistent with the international division of labor as applied to global economic development, the metropolis, in the cultural arena, has in recent years 'discovered' the literary work of its former colonies. The importation of the 'raw material' of poetry, fiction, and even drama has in turn provided the resources for the theory factories of the West where these materials are processed and transformed into consumable commodities for an elite audience—and only later reexported to their places of origin. What is conscientiously neglected in this redistribution of goods is the critical and theoretical contribution from the 'periphery' that would challenge a dominant paradigm of economic and cultural dependency. And while Kanafani's literary narratives themselves elaborate a rigorous critique, on the basis of class and ethnicity, of distorted social and political relationships of power, he was furthermore a major critic, historian, journalist, and theorist of the Palestinian resistance until his assassination by the Israeli Mossad in a car-bomb explosion in Beirut in July 1972. Indeed, the last text written by Kanafani before his death and published posthumously, on the case of Abu Hamidu and cultural cooperation with the enemy,[3] suggested the outlines of a radical analysis of, first, the role of gender within the revolutionary movement, and, second, the material conditions limiting the strategic relations between select representatives of the Israeli and Palestinian parties to the 'Middle East conflict'.

"Thoughts on Change and the 'Blind Language'" itself proposes a similarly critical reading of the Arab sociopolitical arena, and the essay's combined lexicon of political scientific terminology, such as 'patriarchy' *(qa'idat al-'ubuwa)* and 'party activism' *(hizbiya)* and the more metaphorical terms of organicity such as 'blind language' *(al-lugha al-'amya')* and the 'circulation of blood' *(al-dawra al-damawiya)* makes manifest the necessary and critical intersection in Kanafani's work of what has often been dichotomized into the cultural and the political. Contained in each of these apparently disparate but theoretically interconnected key terms is Kanafani's focus in the essay on the 'younger generations' in the Arab world and the possibilities for social and political renewal that they represent. That same commitment to a younger generation informs as well his fictional works where it is often the child who introduces the historicizing potential inherent in the dynamics of contradiction. In the beginning pages of *Men in the Sun* (1962), for example, Abu Qais's son reminds his father of the difference between an educated critical analysis and the defeatism of religious resignation, just as in *Return to Haifa* (1969) the Palestinian child, Khaled/Dov, abandoned by his parents in their flight from Haifa in 1948 and now a recruit in the Israeli army, instructs his parents, when they find him again in 1967 on "returning" home following the "defeat" and the opening of the borders between Israel and the now-Occupied Territories, in the lessons of secularism and the danger of too sectarian a definition of nationalism. So too, the young boy in the early short story, "The Slope" (1961), provides the liberatory example, to both his father and his teacher, of refusing the finalities of historical and narrative closure. Like Edward Said's polemical concept of "affiliation" perhaps,[4] Kanafani's argument for the restoration of the 'circulation of blood' in the Arab and Palestinian social and political corpus demands a radical restructuring of the patriarchal and authoritarian ties of genealogical and hereditary filiation into the more collective, 'democratic' bonds of affiliation.

The projective historical narrative of defeat and still immanent renewal traced in Kanafani's analysis—in "Thoughts on Change and the 'Blind Language'"—of the material and intellectual conditions of the Arab world in its immediate post-1967 phase can be further located within the larger political debates of the period, the apogee perhaps of the struggles for national liberation throughout Africa, Asia, and Latin America, as well as the Middle East, that marked the end of territorial imperialism. The need stressed by Kanafani for an adequate assessment of the real material and political strengths of the 'enemy', as well as of one's own concrete possibilities within historically determined circumstances, is likewise critical to the resistance agendas of 'Third World' theorists such as Amilcar Cabral of Guinea Bissau and Frantz Fanon, as was the debate between vanguardism and popular struggle in resistance organizations from Nicaragua and El Salvador to the Philippines and China. Kanafani's examination of the multiple contradictions, of greater and lesser magnitude, confronting the Arab world in the aftermath of the defeat responds critically to Mao Zedong's 1957 statement "On the Correct Handling of Contradictions among the People." And the essay's insistence on the vital importance of the party, of party formation, and party activism in creating cadres as well as a popular democratic revolution, together with the critique of an overweening fetishization of the 'leader', is not without its analogue in the work of Antonio Gramsci on revolution, the state, the intellectual, and the people, in particular *The Modern Prince*. The theoretical premises and specific historical analyses elaborated by Kanafani in Thoughts on Change and the 'Blind Language'" thus firmly ground the essay not only in the political controversies in the Arab world in particular but in the international arena of the time as well.

Read now, twenty years later, in the period of post- (or neo-) colonialism, those same theoretical premises resonate once again, albeit within a new historical configuration, that of economic imperialism, 'technological underdevelopment', and multinational capital. The promise seen by Kanafani as offered by Lebanon has been forfeited in the wake of civil war and the Israeli invasion to sectarianism and the power struggles of ever-more-fragmented militias and their respective sponsors. On a more extended theoretical level, according to Faysal Darraj, "the essential character of the prevailing Arab culture is not manifested in political allegiance or a partisan position, but in a series of ideological stereotypes which fight the defeat from defeated positions."[5] A new concatenation of dates has succeeded to 1967 in the Arab historiographical narrative: 1973, 1975–76, 1982. Since December 1987, however, the calendric trajectory is no longer punctuated by decisive years, but projected through the continuation of the Palestinian intifada in the Occupied Territories: "in the first, second, third . . . twentieth month of the intifada . . . ." The urgent theoretical issues raised by Kanafani in "Thoughts on Change and the 'Blind Language'"—issues of patriarchy, party, blind language, the circulation of blood, democracy—are currently being resubmitted from within occupied Palestine to the challenge of new historical developments. In an article entitled "The Intifada: Political Creativity and Popular Memory," Faysal Darraj has, in response to these challenges of theory, practice, and the demands of history, claimed that "the intifada does not deliver a theoretical speech, but is making out of its multiple practices the highest form of theoretical discourse." Darraj goes on, however, to ask: "if its practice of creative theory without articulating it, its practice of revolutionary theory, leaves to 'others' the task of translating practice into the realm of written theory, when will the practice write its theory?"[6]

The urgency with which Ghassan Kanafani's work continues to speak to the social and political issues of the Arab world certainly, but of the global context as well, raises still another question: if Ghassan Kanafani were alive today, are there not still those who would feel it necessary to assassinate him?

—*Barbara Harlow*

❖ ❖ ❖

This platform has seen now many qualified professors examining different sides to the reasons for the defeat *(al-hazima)*, its underlying circumstances, the challenge it raises, and the immediate obligations with which that defeat confronts one side or another of our society. Everything that has been said until now proves one point at least, a point on which there is complete agreement: given what has happened, what is happening, and what will happen, the issue must be considered from different sides, for there is no single perspective, no single mistake. The defeat cannot be summarized in a slogan nor vindicated by accusation.

This very platform then is a condensation of sorts of what is happening in practice throughout the Arab world in the aftermath of a profound crisis: discussion breaks out from all sides, reproducing the situation. The different sides cannot be expressed on a single front nor by a single individual. The effort to comprehend all that has been said will alone give the discussion its meaning, its usefulness, and its future.

But before beginning my own intervention into this discussion I want to make clear that the position from which I speak can be a meaningful part of the subject—if it is to have any meaning at all—only in the context of the many defined dimensions provided already by colleagues on this platform. There are points that I am omitting, reasons greater perhaps than the ones I will indicate, more important clarifications than what I see to be the order of priorities. The following pages do not negate this, however, but rather form an interconnected link in the chain of actual meaning. The role of outside forces in the story must be explored in depth, as must the role and extent of counterforces from within. Then there are the results of the interactions of social and economic forces and the Arab style of political work over the last ten years. There are other reasons and concerns even the enemy is unable to categorize or deny; and, since they are not categorizable, they are not pertinent.

Taken in isolation, the presentation proposed here is perhaps partial, but, located within the larger story of this platform and sixteen other voices, it finds, if you will, a kind of completion.

Periods of defeat in a people's history are witness to a rapid growth in critical spirit that can often develop into resentment and anger. Yet this critical spirit, even in the form of resentment and anger, remains an indispensable constructive capacity. The human power to rise from a fall is the power to judge and find guilty, the capacity to correct a mistake is indeed the capacity to discover that mistake in the first place. Thus a people's periods of defeat take on a rigorous and stern examining character, an internal sort of self-punishment, its basic aim being to increase its capability of self-defense. This critical spirit in times of defeat seems all at once to awaken human feelings in times of danger, feelings that double the capacity for both self-awareness and confrontation. All this is, no doubt, a constructive phenomenon—both necessary and indispensable—as long as it is basically motivated by an exit from defeat.

Periods of defeat, however, witness not only the awakening of a spirit of criticism and reexamination, but another very closely related phenomenon as well, namely that of the spirit of criticism gone beyond its own limits into a kind of withdrawal through an exaggerated form of self-punishment. Such a phenomenon represents a still more dangerous side to periods of defeat. In describing the awakening of a critical spirit, we are using the analogy of a human being who, confronting danger, doubles the capabilities for feelings of self-awareness and confrontation. The description of the critical spirit surpassing its own limits may trigger in another human being who, surrounded by danger, would lose the courage of the awakening of this feeling, thereby adding the specter of illusions to the dangers he confronts. He, thus, loses not only the ability to evaluate his capacities, but that of directing them as well.

In any case, we are presently confronting a combination of the two situations: in the face of the tendency to courageous reexamination that we observe here and there, there is another tendency to lamentation that leads only to a withdrawal behind a veil of criticism. In the name of criticism and reexamination in periods of defeat, this latter tendency, less capable of steadfastness (*sumud*), plays a game of suicide. It thus enters into the confusion

Thoughts on Change and the 'Blind Language' 39

of assessing things, factors, and situations and makes enormous mistakes in understanding their real weight and place within the shaky picture that it has sketched. Such a game finds fertile ground amid the ruptures generalized now by the defeat. From here it acquires its dangerous capacity for destruction.

In these critical periods, the task of the researcher takes on a deeper role than it has had at any other time in the past, requiring a twofold courage: on the one hand a critical power; and on the other, a devotion to what must not be destroyed. The distinction between these two sides of the task is an extremely precise one. If the researcher takes just one extra step in the direction of criticism, he falls into the confusion of assessment. One step too many in the direction of devotion to traditional givens and he falls into a state of resignation in the face of what is now unacceptable. The danger of a period of defeat—that it carries within it both the seeds of construction and the seeds of destruction—requires a true grasp of what must be rejected and what must be defended. Only absolute rejection is easier than absolute devotion.

Our generation used to see in its schoolbooks an unforgettable photograph. This photograph, taken in the second decade of this century, shows a man mounted gloriously on a charger. A shining sword glistens in his hands with which he boldly confronts a Turkish airplane about to destroy him. This was a true picture—not a film, nor mere sensationalism—but a unique and terrifyingly realistic representation of how the Arabs looked on the twentieth century from within the great Arab revolution.

Exactly half a century separates this picture-symbol from ourselves. And if we step back from the maelstrom engulfing us and troubling our own time, we will see that what has happened over the last half century seems to be a miraculous development. Nonetheless, it has not been quite half a century, since in reality the Arabs confronted the age not much more than twenty five years ago when 'local men' *(al-rijal al-mahalliyun)* took over the leadership of an immense territory that had only just, in the last quarter century or so, emerged from out of the Middle Ages.

The Arabs in this short period have accomplished for themselves something enormous, when taken in the balance of history, in escaping from under the dark cloak thrown over them by a backward Ottoman rule. For centuries such has been the essential value in the history of modern humankind, a history that has seen numerous examples of rapid awakening, as in Japan and Germany. These awakenings, however, do not spring from a void but rather from a given technological, political, and military stratum *(tabaqa),* even when that stratum had been shattered by war. The Arabs, by contrast, began their entry into the age from a complete void.

Our generation, for example, has seen an amazing development, but our closeness to it has made us incapable of estimating its true value. The basic difference separating us from our fathers is unprecedented. Only rarely has history seen such a distance between two successive generations, but it is perceptible in the face of our brothers and sisters. The wheel turns more quickly than we can grasp. This fact, however, is important only insofar as it refutes the theory of Arab unworthiness and the Arab incapacity to enter into the spirit of the age, a theory that is used not only to justify the invasion of the Arabs but that also provides the theoretical criterion for some of our authors, passing under the veil of criticism.

The difference between our generations can no longer be measured in years. The incalculable speed of development gives rise to one of the most significant contemporary problems, in fundamental contradiction with the social foundation of our life and yet inseparable from it, what we are designating principally with the term 'patriarchy' *(qa'idat al-'ubuwa)*. Older men, both in terms of age and by custom, demand always of the younger the right of respect and submission. If this custom formed the basis of social organization in times of stagnation, then it forms now, in the midst of a dynamism that intensifies daily, a difficult fetter with dangerous consequences. And while this does not mean abandoning the familial institution, it does necessarily mean adding to it a further vital and fundamental article: that the older men likewise respect the younger.

What we are calling 'patriarchy' extends beyond just the family structure, for although family structure may appear to be the best example of patriarchy, it is not the most important. Patriarchy is reflected in the very foundations of our social and political life as well, where it serves to inhibit the emergence of young people into the ranks of the leadership. In a period of rapid social movement, however, what is required is to liberate, not shackle, that generation.

This discussion, it must be added, by no means implies a delimitation of the 'younger generation' in terms of age in years, although this is important. Rather, the conventional term, 'younger generation' *(al-'anasir al-shabba)*, goes well beyond such a limited identification to include the intellectual character of the younger generation or the youthful mentality in keeping with the times, irrespective—if the matter so requires—of birth certificates. And yet, in our current state of development, the youthful mentality goes hand in hand with a young age. This should not dissuade us from attending to the exceptional cases that can sometimes be of great importance. Whether this applies to one faction or another of those who represent the youthful mentality, there are still undefined obstacles on the paths of both, exhausting, sometimes to the point of surrender. Given the chance, however, to overcome these obstacles, both sides find it difficult to transfer their newly acquired position to a generation that has all too soon arrived after them. One of the most obvious results of this is the acceptance of the principle that the holder of power remains as long as possible at the head of the power structure rather than exchange his position according to the dynamics of development and the promotion of men of the age in their continuous development on different levels of leadership.

Thoughts on Change and the 'Blind Language'   41

Again, we must add that what we mean by leadership is not at all the leaders of the state. The question is not, nor should it be, the question of an individual or group of individuals. The leadership is comprised of all those levels and functions practiced by humankind in a healthy and effective social order. In fact, the president of the state or the head of the party is the product of the whole collection of leaders present within the social and political body that he directs. It is incorrect to see it in terms of an individual. The change at the summit of the state is not at all change in the sense in which we understand the word here, since the collection of leaders forming the political pyramid is itself unsound, thus making it futile for us to ask that change at the summit respond somehow to our goals.

The issue behind this discussion is deeper than a mere formal movement and we cannot attend only to the superficies of forms and outward appearances. When we talk about change, we mean a profound change in the infrastructure of the social and political formation. It is this change that bestows on any president of a state, any party leader, or any organization's leadership, the ability, right, power, instrumentality, and authority to realize its goals and program. Thus when we say that the debility in understanding the younger generation's power leads to the acceptance of the principle that the holder of power in office for a long period of time forms within it an obstacle to those generations more in harmony with the developments of the age, we are in fact simply pointing to all of our apparatus, institutions, organizations, parties, administrations, and associations, in their political, economic, and cultural forms.

This phenomenon constitutes an invisible barrier obstructing the transference of our strong capacities for development onto the level of daily practice. This is precisely what we see embodied in the phenomenon of emigration and exile, for exile is a search not only for material wealth, but also for values. And it is precisely this too which makes us see the bureaucrats as older than the papers in their office archives, just as it prevents us from seeing younger faces in the seats of legal and executive power in a way that would reflect accurately the development that we are living.

What we are here calling a lack of enterprise and imagination and invention—not the capacity for such—is what is peculiar to the moment. It is the reason for the absence of any programs of ours for joining the spirit of the age, the absence of any administrative frameworks for keeping up with the rapid pace of movement in the society. It further nullifies the willingness on the part of organizations in our political life, whatever their form, to respond to and interact with the dynamism and capacities of the young.

At a first glance at images of organizations in different countries elsewhere in the world, it might seem that the younger generations there do not enjoy these privileges either, but such an image is incorrect in two important ways. First of all, the younger generations there have in fact seized their full opportunity in political and administrative institutions. And second, our own need, given the ups and downs of our intense and rapid development, to promote the younger generations into the centers of leadership is greater by far than the need of Western societies who do not face the enormous developmental gap between successive generations that we do. This fact leads us to another essential point, and that is the question of democracy.

The democratic institution is not just the translation of a parliamentary institution. Parliament is but one of the manifestations of democracy, not democracy itself. Democracy is a combination of equal opportunity, from parliament to the family, and continuous with the political, administrative, and cultural institutions that form the blood circulation system of a democratic situation. Any replacement of that 'blood circulation system' *(al-dawra al-damawiya)*, whether complete or partial, is itself an abuse of democracy. Only when our administrative, political, and cultural institutions are capable of spontaneously comprehending the youthful strength, its excitement, and influence, is there a democratic situation. The opposite has nothing whatsoever to do with democracy.

A new meaning is here added to our first point about 'patriarchy'. Our ability to understand the younger generation is in fact subject to our capacity for accepting its influence in our institutions and submitting these to a new, corrective, and growing comprehension. This ability is still limited. What we call 'technological underdevelopment' *(takhalluf tiknuluji)*, currently much discussed, is in fact in large part the result of wasting the ability of our younger generation. When the holders of power are unable to keep up with the age's rapid development, they prefer to keep closed the door of current accomplishments rather than relinquish their power because of their inability to keep up with the age.

This discussion does not, of course, mean that we are technologically advanced. It means: not only are we content with that lack of advancement, but we obstruct the potential for rapid change. As a result, those very capacities of ours that might form an important and basic beginning are lost without our really understanding why. The first accounts of highly educated young people obliged to emigrate warrant that we consider with alarm the massive accusation of our technological underdevelopment. And other unavailable data that might tell us just how many of our distinguished scientists work, or are obliged to work, in fields that have no relation to their specialization, would probably warrant that we consider this issue with an even greater sense of alarm. This age is witnessing a unique phenomenon, and that is that the overwhelming majority of groups that make up the scientific and technological corpus of the society is, as a result of the rapidity of development, a younger majority. Applying this maxim to our society and its intensifying speed of development, it is easy to see just how dangerous and basic the problem is that we are now facing.

Understanding this development requires of us an unusual capacity for agreement and an enormous capacity to replace traditional structures *(al-'itarat al-taqlidiya)* in order to keep up and evolve with it. Such an ability is necessitated by the twofold nature of the difficult race that we have embarked on. On the one hand, we are trying to overcome our own underdevelopment and, on the other, we are competing to catch up with the rapid movement of the age. The question is why, despite everything, this understanding has not occurred. Why, despite everything, has the younger generation not asserted its presence in the way required by this dynamic reality? Should not the replacement of the structures within which we move result necessarily from the growing speed of our development? The answers to these questions are in turn a question of time. Our society is really only in its birth phase and it would be unwise to believe that the movement of history will not assert itself in the end.

However, we must admit that the economic reality, and the political reality resulting from it, weigh atop this movement and prevent it from a real takeoff. It is hardly a coincidence that the whole region should be witnessing a series of attempts to determine this turning point with its different possibilities of success and failure, even bitter failure. Notwithstanding, these attempts—in varying ways—have become once more the captive of their own self-estimation, obstructing, at whatever level, the younger generation's constant, forward-directed, rapid movement. In the midst of these difficult birth-pains, at times violent and at others more tranquil, one phenomenon stands out for observation and analysis, a phenomenon that has spread in very similar ways throughout the region regardless of the different systems that prevailed. Ultimately, this was to be the inevitable result of all the contradictions concealed in and behind the numerous above-mentioned attempts in the past.

Over the last ten years we have witnessed the birth of what we might call a 'blind language' *(lugha 'amya')* in the region and nothing has been more operative in our daily life than this blind language. The most significant words lost all meaning. There was no longer any specificity and each writer had a private diction, using words according to a private understanding—an understanding that had no consensus and which thus meant nothing. The meanings carried by such conventional terms as 'revolutionary', 'Nasserist', 'socialist', 'justice', 'democracy', and 'freedom' appeared in innumerable writings that we would read every day and although it seemed—from just observing these words and their widespread dissemination—as if there was some consensus on their meaning, in fact, no one agreed with anyone else on their significance.

We need urgently to reevaluate these words, so that definite and meaningful specificities can be agreed upon. Such a step was similarly necessary for other peoples of the world at the end of the nineteenth century as they too stood at the threshold of an emergent age. The conventional terms have, however, become pure alienation for us and this mutual deafness leads only to a total absence of meaning in discourse. But the problematic has gone even farther than that and it has now become possible for someone to use language to conceal one's impotence, or to hide one's intentions. We now have a lore of blind language that has managed to empty discourse of any effective value, making it possible to employ words for contradictory aims at one and the same time.

Hiding behind a cloud of words is the basic weapon either for someone who feels impotent to realize goals or for someone who has no defined goal at all. Impotence and the absence of clear thinking, which themselves have become a kind of 'working strategy' *(istratijiyat al-'amal),* have buried us up to our necks in what might be called 'incantatory thought' *(al-fikr al-ghina'i)* that replaces clarity with sound and disguises the absence of a goal with ringing words that satisfy the emotionality in the depths of all of us without ever illuminating its vision. This blind language provides, in the final analysis, the sense of security for those who are frightened by change, the curtain of fog over the movement that they truly fear. Whereas the representatives of a certain class are greatly pleased to encourage this blind language that, under the veil of nationalism, they consider to be a healthy expression, it is, in fact, nothing but a shield to protect those who, by their economic and political influence, have been suppressing the beginning of the movement for change.

Might we not then, in accordance with our rejection of this exploiter class, call such encouragement itself the exploitation of language? This is, of course, possible, but only on the condition that we do not forget that the question of exploitation has two sides: the exploiter and the exploited. And if language is the means of the exploiter, what then can serve as the defense of the exploited? And if the exploiter goes beyond the exploitation of language used to obtain one's own objectives, then what is to be a strategy for the exploited? This is the operative side of the problematic that we are reviewing here, the side that focuses on the larger issue that we must now discuss. 'Blind language' has gradually deprived us of the ability to establish our own clear strategy for confronting the challenges that beset us on all levels. Given, on the most dangerous level, the enemy that confronts us, and given the clear and present danger, we must subject all our contradictions to the finding of a solution to that one main contradiction and its own well-defined strategy directed against us in unmitigated malice.

Ben Gurion, the chief architect and proponent of that strategy, has proposed the following plan:

> We must use military conquests as a basis for incontrovertible settlement and the creation of a new human, economic, cultural, and social reality that will force everyone to recognize it and take it into account. And the adherents of traditions and morals who attack our right to expand our borders to include the occupied areas, do they not understand that they are assisting the enemy who is still claiming those lands in our possession, one part of them with the consent of the United Nations and another without its consent? We must change the situation in those areas emptied [of Palestinians] through Jewish immigration and settlement. There is no excuse for defending the rights of the enemy lying in wait for us. For us he has no rights.

Ben Gurion wrote these words on the 20th of last October [1967], in the Israeli newspaper *Ha'aretz* where he unhesitatingly announced the Israeli strategy necessarily directed against us.

Thoughts on Change and the 'Blind Language'

In the face of such a clear goal and a logic that wants to use military conquest as a means of justifying settler colonialism, cancelling once and for all any rights for the other side, the 'blind language' engulfing us becomes more than a mere meaningless transitory phenomenon. It is a crime. It not only obstructs the arrival of a youthful vanguard, bringing new blood and influence with them, into the ranks of the leadership, but it also obstructs a clear view of the enemy and a recognition of the depth and breadth of the danger it poses, as well as the establishment of any firm strategy for confronting it and meeting its challenges.

None of this happened by chance or arbitrarily, but rather a series of interconnected links forms, in all of its small circles, the chain that obstructs our release. What we have been calling 'patriarchy' is really nothing but the necessary result of a feudal mentality, of a political feudalism and the logic of national capital. Nor is this patriarchy a psychological phenomenon except insofar as class itself crystallizes psychological phenomena. Furthermore what we have been calling 'blind language' is not so much a literary school as an intellectual chain whose links are forged on the anvil of narrow convention in order to impede rapid historical movement. The absence of a real working strategy, an absence that resulted from patriarchy and the blinding of language, is in turn a necessary result of the absence of a democracy appropriate to our present conditions and functioning as the 'circulation of blood' in our political body. This absence is not restricted to names alone, but arms itself here or there, in one case or another, with the blindness of language or patriarchy.

Going back over the parts of our argument, we come to the following conclusion: we are facing an enemy that brings with itself from the West the epitome of technology, scientific development, and an enormous capacity for assimilating the younger generations within the organization of its leadership, thereby utilizing not only one of the forms of democracy appropriate to its requirements and tasks, to the effective rapidity of current development and adaptation, but also using its natural and organic connection to the developmental movement of the age. The enemy has its own clear idea with its own strategic line, one that epitomizes much of the confusion and exposes all of the major contradictions erected, effectively and on a daily basis, between it and ourselves. The natural consequence of this circulation of blood is, from first to last, to redirect intellectual, political, social, and technological efforts to a clear and well-defined goal, with no waste and no frivolity.

For the Arabs, by contrast, historical circumstances have not facilitated the consolidation of the technological capacity promoted by the age. And to that we ourselves have added an amazing capacity for squandering not only our own scientific potential but even the very degree of development that this potential has, despite all the difficulties, managed to achieve. The traditional social structure of our political and economic organizations displays an unusual rigidity in its inability to admit our younger generations, to progress, develop, and transform.

Without the circulation of new blood, continuously, rapidly, and automatically, to the centers of power, not only was there an increased collapse of possibilities generally but an even greater separation as well from the age's developmental movement. This situation led naturally to a sanctification of the society's superstructure, itself a major impediment to the speed of change and transformation. Even in those periods when a relatively new power would take over, its ability to influence immediately came up against those broken bridges separating it from the society's infrastructure or base, in turn retarding the process of change.

Even with regard to democracy, whether it is called revolutionary democracy or traditional democracy, the result remained the same, that the social body's circulation system was only skin-deep and thus unable to circulate the blood properly. This then empties the 'dialogue' *(al-hiwar)* of everything that gives it its value and forces it into what we have been calling 'blind language' or what is more commonly called a 'dialogue of the deaf' *(hiwar al-turshan)*, not unlike the slogans of the parties and states in the region, whose constitutions, in and of themselves a matter for surprise, are astonishing for the number of contradictions they contain.

All these factors of course contribute automatically to the Arabs' lack of a working strategy, a lack that nullifies any capacity for redirecting their technological, intellectual, social, political, and even statistical, efforts towards more useful and less futile daily goals. The lack of such a strategy also annuls the capacity to organize the contradictions facing the Arab societies of the region, as well as any knowledge of how most appropriately to enlist these in resolving the largest and most immediate contradiction. Thus we fought our battle, so to speak, "without proper preparation," "without using our potential," "isolated from our capacities," and citing "startling technological underdevelopment," "rigid military and political traditionalism," and the fact that "the people didn't participate in their battle," and so on. Such formulas, and their repeated use, however, threaten only to express once again earlier situations and their unfortunate chain of circumstances. The very use of these clichés is itself a consequence that must be examined as such. Otherwise their use will become natural so long as their logic remains intact and inviolable.

The dispute between Ben Gurion and Levi Eshkol traces its origin back to 1917 and yet the two leaders managed to hang together in a single party organization until 1964, and even then neither Eshkol nor Ben Gurion closed off the question of annexation in 1967. Instead the 'circulation of blood' supplying the two parties with younger generations made for a direct synchronization with ongoing rapid developments. Directly after the June War, and at the height of the triumph, Yitzhak Rabin was removed as chief of staff of the Israeli army. In a period such as this whose speed surpassed the grasp of a single individual, the law prohibited a chief of staff remaining in his post for more than four years. At the time that Yitzhak Rabin left his position, the Israeli cabinet was determined to remain a cabinet of national unity combining conflicting groups sharply opposed among themselves. This conflict had to be subordinated to a calculated strategy for the next phase when the Israelis anticipated other developments.

These examples are not intended to be a systematic treatment of the enemy as a model, but to insist rather that what we have long been calling the 'distribution of roles' *(tawzi' al-adwar)* among the Israeli forces is not really so; it is quite simply an inevitability necessitated by a preplanned strategy that alone determines the duties and rights of each given phase. Thus the lack of a strategy of this sort on the part of the Arabs itself would lead to what we might call an 'error of judgment' *(khata' al-taqdir),* a judgment error that is certainly not a cause but a consequence.

This brings us to the following essential question: the issue, as we have said, is not that of changing the leadership since the leadership is in fact just one aspect of the problem. Rather, we must ask, how are we to go about modernizing our political and economic apparatus and our cultural institutions to make them effective enough to keep up with the speed of development in our society? The question places us at the crux of the issue, the issue of democracy, a term by which we understand, first of all, the rule of the people, by the people, and for the people, regardless of conventions used to undermine the word 'democracy'. We consider parliament to be but one feature of democracy, not democracy itself. And since by democracy we mean that circulation of blood, healthy and reinvigorating, that must reach every part and member of the social body, what is required of us is that we transform the democratic spirit into a daily practice at all levels.

The Arab world, in the context of its dialogue with democracy, has seen various experiments that merit examination: in one case there is parliament without freedom of the press and in another freedom of the press without a parliament; in still another case there is parliament but no parties, or else parties without a parliament; or there might be a parliament, parties, and freedom of the press without any of this being able to create a real democracy. Despite all this experimentation, the regimes still call themselves 'democracies'.

Where then is the solution?

It is wrong in fact for us to look for democracy in all these forms and opinions about its existence and non-existence, or about how many different appearances democracy has taken on in its parliamentary aspect, since we are also inquiring into democracy in its social and cultural dimensions. Furthermore, we are really asking that we look for democracy in its administrative and collective aspects, and, first and foremost, in its party aspect. The party itself is the consolidation of the democratic experiment. Thus, if the potential ability and qualifications of any party are measured by the circulation of blood in its body, we will see that the overwhelming majority of our parties suffer from an absence of democracy, both in terms of the apparatus of each of them and in terms of their relations with each other.

Within its own apparatus, the party founder assumes for himself the seal of sanctification and the small group around him forms the rampart against which the upward movement of the younger generation collides. Outside the apparatus, in its relations with other parties, accusation substitutes for dialogue, and willful defamation replaces mutual understanding. Inside the apparatus the leader's authority prevents the movement's growth and the fetishization of the role of the leader as irreplaceable is reflected in his own self-esteem when he makes of himself such an irreplaceable power. Outside the apparatus this absolute and positive self-esteem leads to a negative evaluation of others.

The social body might be compared to the human body in that each gland has its own function and that its well-being is endangered not just by a defect in one of these glands but also by a defect in its relation to other glands. As far as most of our parties are concerned, they are incapable, whether in their own internal organizational structures or in their relations with other parties, of creating a nucleus of real democratic spirit, and the absence of this spirit in turn impedes the crystallization of a clear strategy either for itself or in its conception of the role that other forces might appropriately play.

Party formation is an invaluable experience insofar as it instructs citizens as to the best means of playing a role of public responsibility. Within the party they acquire a new political culture and a new idea of political work, thus also enabling what might be called a 'democratic ethos'. Our parties have been incapable of realizing this indispensable task and of crystallizing within their own structures a political vanguard that could play a leadership role in the society, one that would at the same time both influence and be influenced by that society. This incapacity led then to a still more dangerous consequence, namely the incapacity of the parties to crystallize a strategy adequate to the dynamics of a society attempting either to express itself or to develop an alternative form that would replace the traditional ones that it has rejected. All of this results in two interconnected phenomena in our party experience: first, the multiplication of parties, and second, the inability to focus effective social forces.

In conditions of the kind experienced by our society, the absence of effective parties representing real forces is an incalculable loss, a destructive and horribly debilitating mistake with dangerous consequences resulting from it at all levels. There is no way out of this profound dilemma we are now experiencing except through party activism *(al-hizbiya)*, party activism in the true, effective, and productive sense, produced within an internal framework of established democratic relations, and of relations with others in a constructive and productive dialogue. These conditions of party activism cancel the unnecessary multiplication of parties which in themselves only reproduce the same previous mistakes and deficiencies rather than advancing the role of the party itself.

In their past experience our parties have taken the form of sectarian or clan or student groups, of undefined social forces and with unclear and indeterminate boundaries, that, taken together, recreate patriarchal structures within the party formation as well as in the form and content of its relations with other parties—quantitative accumulation rather than qualitative development. The sum total of these relations leads to the acceptance of the absence of a party strategy. The need for a quick understanding of the objective conditions as well as the desire to deal with these on a practical level are ignored. Although such experiences do not cancel altogether the inherent value of the party, they do require systematic study and critique in the direction of a total developmental practice.

In past years there has been a wide-reaching and interminable discussion on the issue of the single or multiparty system. In fact, no one criterion can be imposed, nor can any single paradigm be considered indispensable, since for every social condition there exist numerous reasons, motivations, and interpretations. Nonetheless, the groundwork remains first of all in the ability of these parties as a whole or of the single party individually to realize within their organizational structures and in their relations with other organized forces, a real circulation of blood that would make it a healthy phenomenon, one not trapped in some vicious circle.

The political party is one of the forms for organizing effective forces in a society but there are other forms as well that are capable of such organization. These are represented by the labor unions, including worker, peasant, and professional unions, or cultural institutions that, whether intentionally or not, function as the ground on which discussion is built. Whether the organization is a party, a union, or an association, its first priority should be to ensure the circulation of blood in its body. Its primary potential should be not for discussion, but for raising the level of understanding of what is young and new and how to adapt and interact with it. The problem in the region was never in the inconceivability of development, but rather that we did not use our developmental capacity to enhance our progress.

Our dilemma is not that we failed to implement our program but that we did not give ourselves the opportunity even to draw up a program. And our defeat was due not only to the traditional political, social, and economic forces fettering us, but to the fact that the alternative forces were more oriented towards refusal rather than constructing a new and comprehensive strategy. Furthermore our impotence was not so much an expression of our lack of qualification as it was the result of the prevention of new blood in our society from reaching its head and arms. The problem is not that we do not know, but that we do not permit those who do know to speak and to act. It is not that we are foreigners to the age, but that we have squandered and thwarted the younger generations who are themselves the bridge to the age.

The responsibility for all of this, as we have tried to demonstrate, is not limited to this or that individual, nor to a single system or organization, but is the responsibility of everyone to almost equal degrees. The entire region stands at the gates of a decisive historical turning point and there will be no victory in this confrontation except the victory of all, and no defeat that is not the ruin of everyone. Any objective assessment of the previous few years that the region has just passed through must demonstrate one thing at least, and that is that there is no one confronting the challenge more than any other, and no one can withdraw except at an enormous collective cost. Whatever the theoretical dispute that might have been engaging ideas about the unity of the region's destiny, that unity has never at any time in the past seemed stronger than it does now, following the humiliating defeat and facing what have become life and death challenges.

This idea imposes on Lebanon a number of tasks whose circumstances are themselves a kind of preparation for the fateful role Lebanon must play in confronting the big challenge certainly, but also in confronting the smaller challenges that collectively constitute its internal issues. The Lebanese role is made up of three basic components: national duty, historical commitment, and geographical standing.

From within the challenges contained in each of these three components, Lebanon stands at a historical turning point, whereby it might yet succeed in renewing its blood and moving forward with the age. This requires first of all a decisive clarification of priorities in the hierarchy of challenges making up the daily situation in the region, as well as a commitment to a program for meeting these challenges. This clarification should not happen as mere coincidence, or on the basis of spontaneous or automatic thinking, but rather by releasing the absorptive potential through free discussion, thus focusing the rapid developmental movement throughout the entire region and providing the necessary conditions for the crystallization of its effective powers.

The society must organize its discussion on the basis of definite strategic situations and give to the active social forces their full role in this discussion, its organizations and its parties. The movement of a healthy discussion must be such that it can create a form capable of absorbing and expressing the hidden potential of the people. The arteries for the circulation of blood in its body must reach as far as possible, deep and wide, connecting the given structures with the power to express the dynamism and vitality of development in our society.

In the present circumstances, national, historical, and geographical, the Lebanese situation might yet release the constructive potential of a courageous and responsible discussion, focusing the voices clamoring from one end of the Arab world to the other, and on the basis of this discussion, release its own specific potential as well. In Lebanon the fetters imposed by patriarchy could be abolished in order to give to the exuberant younger generations the opportunity to extend their dynamism and vitality, and their connectedness to the age, to the level of daily influence. Lebanon could extend the slogan 'national unity' *(al-wahda al-wataniya)*, in both form and content, from its purely sectarian character to its larger social, economic, and political character, and deepen the democratic spirit to the level of the circulation of blood, functioning in the parliament, in the parties and universities, in the cultural institutions and in the administrative centers, reaching even to the heart of family gatherings. Lebanon could open the eyes of language so that language is not just an expression of impotence, uncertainty, and incantation, but a clear vision of values and issues, and thus abandon the debate and discussion that have been so destructive of time, potential, and situation.

The Lebanese climate can be now perhaps critically important to a new dawn in the Arab dialogue, but only on the condition that we set free its full potential for understanding, effectiveness, and responsible commitment. While the spirit of critique after the defeat permeates the entire Arab world, it is not by chance that it should have had its first stirrings in Lebanon, even despite the many competing discussions, slogans, and intentions there. In effect, Lebanon is playing a part of its potential role, and it will doubtless play that role more fully as long as we can have faith in its possibilities for continuing, whatever the contending voices, to benefit the people.

All of this throws the burden of responsibility onto the shoulders of everyone, to differing—but nonetheless necessary—degrees. Responsibility rests on the shoulders of the younger generation, in its universities, its parties, and its families, to the same degree that it rests on the shoulders of the leaders in their sphere of influence, parties, families, and the centers of power that they enjoy. Responsibility rests on the shoulders of the intellectuals to be a conscious element rather than a blinding and vacillating one, to be an element of constructive commitment and not an element that sits back in its absolute rejectionism. Responsibility rests too on the shoulders of journalists and media people, responsibility toward the powerful weapon that they hold in their hands and for what comes of national duty, historical commitment, and geographical standing. And finally responsibility rests on the shoulders of the architects of state policy for building the domestic and foreign strategy required by the powers latent in the society and the younger generation representative of the blood that will renew that society and bring it to interact with the developmental movement of the age.

In the last quarter century, and as it enters the modern age, the Arab world has accomplished one of the miracles of development in history, and it has accomplished it on a land made muddy by more than five hundred years of oppressive underdevelopment. The Arab world has accomplished this miracle despite its rape by contrary forces surrounding it and working away at it from inside and outside in a series of fateful challenges that continue even now in difficult daily confrontations. Nonetheless our ambitions remain broader and greater than any retreat into silence. If there is any meaning to this at all, it is the meaning of worthiness.

The defeat came and this people discovered an extraordinary ability not only to reject it, but to reexamine its own account with itself. The opposition to its experience is harsher even than that enabled by a courageous critique. And if that critique was sometimes exaggerated to a painful degree, it was only to satisfy the yearning and ambitions to attain something greater and better. In this present and difficult experience, the Arab has added to his desire for steadfastness the desire for liberty and critical revision. The Arab was defeated in a deadly battle in which it was not granted to him to fight as he can and should. His desire for steadfastness and liberty, however, have not wavered, but have, on the contrary, acquired additional potential for firmness and yearning for the better, expressed collectively in the unusual awakening of a spirit of criticism and reexamination.

It would nonetheless be unwise for us to imagine that the Arab is finding full compensation in this critical awakening. Rather, this period of waiting, lived so tensely now, is not unlike that of 1949, or that experienced by the Russian people between 1904 when they were defeated by Japan and 1905 with their first revolution, to be followed ten years later by another revolution that changed the face of the twentieth century. What is happening now are only the labor pains of something great that will be born from the rubble of the defeat like a volcano born from under the cold ashes of a forsaken mountain.

The wound opened in a dead body causes no agitation, but what has rent *(anshaqqa)* a living body increases its potential for resistance. A hidden power in the depths is stirred and its capabilities are doubled in response. The wounded Arab body is moving. It is healing, preparing itself, resisting. Its senses are redoubled and it stands firmly on its feet, spanning a bridge of agony.

Notes

1 Faysal Darraj, "The Current State of Arab Culture," *Democratic Palestine* 33 (June 1989), p. 26.
2 Ghassan Kanafani's literary writings in English translation include: *Men in the Sun and Other Palestinian Stories*, trans. Hilary Kilpatrick (London: Heinemann, 1978); *Palestine's Children*, trans. Barbara Harlow (London: Heinemann, 1984); *All That's Left to You* (Austin: University of Texas Press, 1990).
3 In *Shu'un filastiniya* 12 (August 1972), pp. 8–18.
4 See especially "Secular Criticism" in *The World, the Text, and the Critic* (Cambridge: Harvard University Press, 1983), pp. 1–30.
5 Darraj, op. cit., p. 25.
6 Faysal Darraj, "al-Intifada: al-ibda' al-siyasi wa-l-dhakira al-sha'biya," *al-Hadaf* 962 (11 June 1989), pp. 40–41.

The Image of the City: Wounded Beirut

❖

Mona Takieddine Amyuni

The cities break up
The land is a train of dust
Only love
Knows how to marry this space.
—*Adonis*

Ils disaient que la ville rapide comme un fleuve
Est un lieu entre l'Homme et Dieu.
—*Nadia Tuéni*

I

The history of cities from all time has been one of upheavals of all types, whether geographic, climatic, or sociopolitical. Beirut, in particular, has been sorely tried. As Khalaf and Kongstad have noted, it has been "completely wiped out by a score of earthquakes and fires, threatened by plagues and famines, and ransacked and destroyed by successive waves of unfriendly invaders." And "it has survived all."[1] Kindled by this hope, my study of "Wounded Beirut" explores some city images with the following questions in mind: how have a few artists living in the city and writing about it reacted to the destruction of Beirut? What city images are molding our artists' sensibilities nowadays? Would one be able to draw out of the various texts originally written in Arabic and French some fundamental traits, some common basic city metaphors? Or, on the contrary, would one feel how the same facts may have opposite significations and values when integrated into different mental structures?

A comparatist approach will attempt to answer these questions on a provisional basis. It is not within the scope of this study to examine inherent differences of genre and language. The comparatist concept implies here an internationalist and a humanistic attitude towards literature, quite appropriate, I think, in a city which has traditionally been at the crossroads of languages, religions, and cultures; in a city whose artists are most often trilingual, broadly read and widely traveled, and who address themselves to a similarly sophisticated audience. The texts I shall examine partake of a "World Literature"[2] and have been strictly selected on their own merit, and for some intrinsic qualities which make them both reflections of a tragic decade in Lebanon, and of a universal urban experience.[3]

My essay focuses on a few works written just before the war in Lebanon and up to the current year, 1986, in which a few "urban dramas" are performed on and around the city-stage in an order of increased complexity and "multilayeredness."[4] The reading starts 'horizontally' with Tawfik Youssef Awwad's sociorealistic novel *Death in Beirut* where the city is brightly illuminated and clearly outlined. The city stage is 'vertically' constructed in Nadia Tuéni's poem "Beirut" in which the city polarizes all attention. There follows in Tuéni's "Consul's Garden," the dramatization of a particularly strategic sector of the city, the Kantari area, and a digging into the "Archives" of Beirut and her citizens' memory. The city is present–absent on Claire Gebeyli's stage. Her poet–narrator prays and supplicates in an attempt to bring together the fragments of a decimated city. Reference and cross-reference to images and symbols force the sensitive reader to apprehend Gebeyli's poetry "spatially, in a moment of time, rather than as a sequence."[5] Similarly with Elias Khoury and Adonis, whose "urban dramas" are rendered in surrealistic style, and are apprehended spatially as well. Beirut is transfigured into a mythic city in Khoury's fable, *Abwab al-madina (Gates of the City)*, while with Adonis's poem "Time," Beirut is the springboard for a cosmic voyage during which the poet dies the death of his city, and is reborn into a new state of being.

II

In Tawfik Awwad's novel *Death in Beirut*,[6] human beings, places, and things clearly stand out on a stage where many forces are gathering momentum, just before the anticipated explosion. The actors, here, vent their innermost feelings in dialogue, speech, harangues, public lectures, and articles in the most realistic of styles. The "roaring, noisy, grinding, millstones of Beirut" (p. 79) give their title to the novel while the city's nervous energy draws to it people from the whole of Lebanon and the Middle East. The novel thus mirrors various crosscurrents which clash in Beirut and build up tensions on all levels.

The drama takes place in a city buzzing with action, bedecked with jewelry, both enticing and cruel; similar to a femme fatale. Hamra street, for example, dazzles our young Shi'ite heroine, Tamima, freshly arrived from the south "with its bursting life and color" (p. 5). Awwad's Beirut is indeed the archetypal city which has always kindled peoples' imagination. Its accelerated rhythm intoxicates the people who seek it for higher education, freedom of speech, sexual adventures, jobs, power, and business. Hence collisions in interests, passions, ideas, while the young student–actors dream of changing things. The creation of the heroine Tamima is very successful. Bright, pretty, and independent, she is determined to live her life in Beirut and fulfill herself in a war, something that had been impossible for her illiterate mother.

Education is the ancestral tradition of Beirut.[7] Awwad's protagonists are young, bright, ambitious university students for whom the city means self-fulfillment and liberation. In fact, Beirut's wide-open doors allow the crystallization of many dreams other than Tamima's, which struggle to become reality. In the melting-pot of Beirut, generations, sexes, nationalities, classes, religious, and political ideologies clash in a manner reminiscent of the history of every city.

In Beirut, Awwad's actors perform their dramas before the city erupts and consumes them in its fires. Awwad's use of dramatic irony is certainly prophetic when he writes that "Beirut is boiling like a cooking-pot! Fires are stoked under the pots in all the Arab capitals" (p. 66).

The reader will certainly notice the recurring fire imagery in connection with the city since Sodom and Gomorrah. Beirut surely burns up Tamima. She exits from the scene defeated in her struggle to liberate herself, crushed by social forces too strong for an individual to confront alone. As the novel closes, Tamima's southern village is savagely bombed by the Israelis. Her rebellious temperament is not abated by her defeat in the city. She joins a group of Palestinian fighters in a common struggle against the enemy. Her private "urban drama" has fully equipped her for this ultimate engagement.

The city—emblem of the freedom to be—has surely a lethal hidden face. But Tamima would choose it at whatever cost. In depicting her, Awwad has drawn the powerful picture of a young woman ready to live and fight on an equal footing with men. It is significant to note that her young, male, fellow students acknowledge her as such, and love her for it. The sociorealistic novel has surely gone a long way in the Arab world since Naguib Mahfouz's *Midaq Alley*, published in 1947. In *Midaq Alley*, the great master of the Arabic novel creates a heroine similar in temperament and ambition to Tamima. Hamida's only choice, however, is to sell her flesh, whether in wedlock or as a prostitute on the streets of Cairo. *Death in Beirut* is written in the same vein as *Midaq Alley*, but the heroine here has had a chance to attend university and to have a job she loves. She is also ready to break through many socioreligious taboos. Her failure is but a stepping stone for other opportunities in the city.

The 'horizontal' reading of *Death in Beirut* leads thus to a rich chronological development of events in specific places in the city where all the urban elements are visible to the senses. A third-person point of view sheds light externally on facts and events, and internally into the characters' minds. Beirut shines with its thousand lures beyond the end of the story. Vital and cruel, it is the image of life itself for Tamima. It is worth noting in this context Awwad's accuracy of response to the historical conditions he objectively describes.[8]

III

Nadia Tuéni's poem "Beirut" forces us to move abruptly into a different register where the "accuracy of response" to the historical situation is modified by irony and political satire.[9] Tuéni sings the perenniality of her city whose multiple faces, thousand deaths, and thousand rebirths emerge, defying destruction. The poet cleverly superimposes the historical stages of her city in traditional alexandrine verse and highly stylized images. The architectural quality of the poem recaptures in an instant of time the deeply rooted polarities that have always been associated with the city:

Beyrouth
. . . .
Beyrouth des cents palais, et Béryte des pierres,
où l'on vient de partout ériger ces statues,
qui font prier les hommes, et font hurler les guerres.
. . . .
A Beyrouth chaque idée habite une maison.
A Beyrouth chaque mot est une ostentation.
A Beyrouth l'on décharge pensées et caravanes,
. . . .
Qu'elle soit religieuse, ou qu'elle soit sorcière,
ou qu'elle soit les deux, . . .
. . . .
qu'elle soit adorée ou qu'elle soit maudite.
qu'elle soit sanguinaire, ou qu'elle soit d'eau bénite,
qu'elle soit innocente, ou qu'elle soit meurtrière,
en étant phénicienne, arabe, ou roturière,
en étant levantine aux multiples vertiges,
comme ces fleurs étranges fragiles sur leurs tiges,
Beyrouth est en orient le dernier sanctuaire,
où l'homme peut toujours s'habiller de lumière.
(*Liban*, pp. 19–20)

Beirut
. . . . .
Beirut of the hundred palaces and Beryte of the stones,
Where people come from everywhere to build up statues,
Which make man kneel down in prayer and make wars roar.

The Image of the City: Wounded Beirut

> ....
> In Beirut in every house dwells a different idea,
> In Beirut every word is a parade.
> In Beirut one lays down thoughts and caravans,
> ....
> Whether she is a nun or a sorcerer,
> Or both together,
> ....
> Adored or cursed
> Blood thirsty or blessed with holy water
> Innocent or deadly,
> Phoenician, Arab, or anybody,
> A Levantine with multiple vertigos,
> Like those strange flowers fragile on their stalks,
> Beirut is in the Orient the last sanctuary,
> Where man is clad in the color of light.[10]

Nadia Tuéni's poem is rich with political overtones, as she situates her city in the midst of crosscurrents objectively described by Awwad. With high condensation and allusiveness, she refers to the worshipping of many idols, their breaking down in wars, the never-ceasing flood of people into Beirut's generous big heart which, as she puts it, is the last sanctuary of freedom in the Arab world.

In *Archives sentimentales d'une guerre au Liban*,[11] Tuéni frees her verse and constructs a three-part dramatic poem which projects the agony and death of her cherished "sanctuary" on the forefront of the urban stage. The verse quickly runs from past to present and future, while a narrator digs into the deep layers of the city as the title indicates. The "archives" surely unveil the cruelty of history, the vanity and solitariness of man, while the stage is set for the drama to take place. "Sentimental" and lyrical indeed is the narrator's interior monologue, which punctuates highly visual and condensed vignettes arranged like a musical suite. The monologue stands out in italics in the "Prologue," and at the top of each of the scenes of "The Consul's Garden," in contrast with the descriptive lines in roman type. Hence, the construction of several planes on the urban stage while death in the streets is dramatically projected onto the first level:

> Ils sont morts à plusieurs
> C'est-à-dire chacun seul
> sur une même potence qu'on nomme territoire
> ....
> une voix tombe: c'est le bruit du jour sur le pavé
> ....
> Alors
> ils sont bien morts ensemble
> c'est-à-dire chacun seul comme ils avaient vécu.
> (*Archives*, p. 11)

> They were several to die
> That is, each died alone
> on the same gallows called a homeland
> ....
> a voice breaks down: daytime is on the pavement
> ....
> Indeed
> they all died together, that is, each died alone as they had lived.

This scene is followed by a monologue which fuses impressions, dreams, nostalgia with the madness of men, while the narration starts in the first person:

> J'habitais la maison d'en face,
> face à la guerre et au Jardin,
> de morts plantés et de rosiers,
> ancêtres oubliés dans la dynamique d'une allée,
> dans un cube de mémoire.
> Sous le balcon d'un oeil, une moitié de corps,
> l'autre formant un angle sur le trottoir.
> Une moitié de corps, signe isolé sur ma fresque de haine.
> (*Archives*, p. 15)

> I lived in a house
> facing war and a Garden,
> planted with corpses and roses,
> forgotten ancestors in the movement of an alley
> in a cubicle of memory.
> Under the balcony of an eye, half a body,
> the other half at an angle with the sidewalk.
> Half a body, a single sign on my canvas of hatred.

Tuéni then moves to the "Consul's Garden" which is clearly located in the once-fashionable Kantari quarter of Beirut, halfway between the attractive Hamra street that had dazzled Awwad's heroine, and the city center. A strategic area, it has been badly destroyed during street fights—surrealistic contrasts between miraculously preserved houses with gardens next to leprous façades and crumbling buildings. Such are the bare facts of the Kantari area, transfigured into a cubist internal landscape with multiple perspectives:

> O jardin du Consul
> ....
> O jardin qui éclate sous la peau de l'été.
> Arbres de Kantari,
> Vous êtes la géométrie.
> Dans Kantari une maison,
> avec des portes autour du cou et du sang sur la tête,

des bouquets de gens aux fenêtres,
une lune dans le bassin,
. . . .
C'est le bal du Consul.
(*Archives*, p. 16)

O The Consul's garden
. . . .
O garden which bursts under the summer skin.
Kantari trees,
You are the geometry.
In Kantari a house,
With doors around the neck and blood on the head,
clusters of people at the windows,
a moon in the pool,
. . . .
It is the Consul's ball.

As Tuéni's spotlight floods the Consul's rose garden and ballroom, dissonant impressions and visions are filtered into the narrator's consciousness with harsh juxtapositions and syncopated rhythms. Time and space are telescoped here and internalized. What begins as the description of a scene becomes symbolic of the narrator's mind, with a perfect correspondence between the scene and the narrator's spiritual condition. In Tuéni's dramatic sequence, the Consul entertains his guests, then writes memos to his government while his Muse, a tall lady wearing long gloves, stands next to him on the balcony and plays with the map of the Middle East.

Opposite the couple, the narrator takes quick snapshots from a half-broken balcony, under which lie chopped-up men. A shock technique in cubist form powerfully operates in the midst of a city "white like a tomb." Irony, satire, and black humor punctuate the sequence of vignettes, while deep love for her city makes Tuéni's verse vibrate with renewed life. Beirut, she says later, is more of a city than Antioch or Babylon as it burns with passion and folly. A striking light imagery renders the mad rhythms of Beirut in Part II, "Folle Terre" (Mad land), a city she loves unto madness, as the title suggests:

J'aime
. . . . . .
ces cendres au goût de ville qui fut,
plus cité qu'Antioche ou même que Babylone;
ville chauffée à blanc par parole.
. . . .
J'aime
que l'on nomme cri un segment de lumière,
et nova, la folie.
(*Archives*, p. 55)

> I love
> .....
> these ashes that taste of a city which was
> more of a city than Antioch or even Babylon;
> a city turned white-hot by words.
> ....
> I love
> that a segment of light be called a shriek
> and nova, the madness of men.

A nova is a star which shows sudden and great increase of light and energy for short periods. In one compressed image, Nadia Tuéni seizes the essence of all cities which consume themselves in ever-recurring outbursts of energy and fire kindled, of course, by the madness of men. Once again, a surrealistic imagery projects multiple perspectives on the urban stage, while the poet dies of incoherence in the full glare of the sun: "Alors en plein soleil/je meurs d'incohérence/en éclats" (Then in broad daylight/I die of incoherence/splintered) (*Archives*, p. 31). When the poet digs into the archives of her city, the atavistic fights amongst men are bound to provoke rifts of the deepest sort, and this total collapse of comprehension.[12]

To sum up, the selection of detail in Tuéni's *Archives Sentimentales* is governed not by the logic of verisimilitude as in the case of Awwad's novel, but by the demands of the décor necessary to enhance the symbolic significance of the characters' drama, and the tragedy of their city.[13] A feeling of complete identification operates between the poet and her city: "J'appartiens à ma folle terre" (I belong to my mad land) (p. 61). Through the poem a sacred reintegration operates: "Aussi ai-je enfermé sous ma langue un pays,/gardé comme une hostie" (Therefore, I held tightly under my tongue a country,/ cherished like a host) (p. 17).

IV

Compassion and piety also dominate Claire Gebeyli's poetry.[14] Her poems are, on one level, the chronicle of Beirut at war. Precisely situated in time and space, her physical landscapes, however, are transmuted into the emotional landscapes of a poet who watches over her city, Sibyl-like. The mixture of elevated and journalistic styles, the juxtaposition of sordid and lyrical imagery, the broken rhythms, compel the act of writing to shoot upwards with an increasingly high intensity. The poet shifts graphically from frozen scenes to moving, leaping, flying ones until she endows her city with epic dimensions. We read, first:

> Sur chaque toit une attache
> Un cri dans chaque étoile
> Sous chaque bure une ville
> chaque veillée une naissance

Et le mal de ne pouvoir
dessiner une seule branche
(*Mémorial*, p. 35)

On every roof a bond
in every star a scream
under every coarse gown a city
with every vigil a birth.

And the aching inability
to draw a single branch.

The city is starkly delineated in this poem with a roof, a screaming star, an awaited birth, and the absence of greenery. The emotional texture conveys a kind of life sharply arrested, ready to leap, aching with expectancy, paralyzed by its inability to draw a single branch. The last two lines are arrestingly set off, the end has no punctuation, and the whole is built up on the antithesis between the awaited birth and the incapacity to draw a single branch.

The poem is an epigram chosen here to illustrate Gebeyli's symbolist technique in the whole of her urban poetry. An epigram is, by definition, a very short poem summing up, as though in a memorial inscription, what is desired to be made permanently memorable in a single action or situation. Gebeyli's consummate art ties in her epigram with the title of her collection, *Mémorial d'exil*. The existential feeling of loss and exile has traditionally recurred in urban literature, as if man had created a superb artifact, the city, and keeps on losing it. The poetry examined here certainly perpetuates this universal tradition.

In Gebeyli's epigram, the poetic imagery is emotionally unified around this feeling of exile. The emotion is perceived instantaneously. It transcends the boundaries of space and time and liberates the imagination. Ezra Pound's famous definition of a poetic image as "an intellectual and emotional complex in an instant of time"[15] comes to mind. Gebeyli's "memorial" is a memorial, indeed, for her wounded city, and for its people keeping vigil.

Gebeyli's poems are grafted on the daily events of her city. The difficulty of writing as one sits behind a desk in a room, in a city at war, is rendered in a frozen metaphor: "Une banquise glacée s'interpose entre le papier et moi, entre le monde et moi. Il n'y a plus de place pour un seul mot, une seule lettre" (A frozen ice-bank between me and my sheet of paper, between the world and me. There is no more room for a single word, a single letter) (*Dialogue*, p. 19).

Yet Gebeyli continues to suffer the pangs of labor, as she gives birth to vivid images of a dismembered city. She creates a series of dynamic images in a preliminary poem entitled "Portique," where she is liberated from her rigid position in the room of a house in Beirut. She runs wildly in the wind. The city dissolves through metaphors which swiftly succeed one another. The city is etherealized and weighs as lightly as the running feet in the wind, while the poet affirms her need to be involved and bear witness in her suffering city:

Portique

Il m'a fallu donner des noms
Il m'a fallu franchir ...
Semence égarée sur un verset d'yeux durs
déposée en chaton
sur une danse qui s'achève
La poitrine fendue brûlée
il m'a fallu redevenir partie
allonger les bras vers les lattes de lumière
courir le dos au vent
il m'a fallu écrire.
(*La Mise à jour*, p. 9)

A Porch

I had to name
I had to cross ...
over sown fields lost in the versicle of hard eyes
laid down cat like
on an ending dance
My breast is torn apart burnt
I had to be involved again
to stretch out my arms towards the thin strips of light
and run in the wind
I had to write.

When Claire Gebeyli writes of her wounded city her own flesh is lacerated. Nobody knows how it all started, she says in a poem entitled "Nul n'a su comment" (No one knew how). The city burst like entrails, the gates burn, and unending is the edge of barbed wire (*La Mise à jour*, p. 55). Time itself is chopped up, the week is broken like a broken bottle (*La Mise à jour*, p. 15), images of dislocation multiply. In "Un homme est mort" (A man is dead) for example, one reads:

Un homme est mort
Son temp s'abîme
feuillage qui lettre à lettre
s'effeuille
....
Les noms emballés
les cités
Le vécu grimpant
aux portes qui se déchaussent
....

Un homme est mort
de ses os
de ses serres
de sa taille
je fais mon sillage
(*La Mise à jour,* pp. 18–20)

A man is dead
His time disintegrates
A foliage which letter by letter
Sheds its petals
. . . .
Packed up names
Cities
Lived experiences encroaching
on broken doors
. . . .
A man is dead
With his bones
With his clips
With his waist
I trace my way

Finally Gebeyli dedicates a prose poem to her city written in a Baudelairean vein and quite different from Tuéni's highly stylized "Beirut." The 'vertical' reading of the former gives way to a poetic prose in which a city-goddess presides over the works of life and death in a continuous present. She watches the passage of seasons, years, women, and just carries on, recreating her life on a daily basis. Present and infinitive tenses, cumulative plurals, a play with obscure and shining images, political overtones inserted in an infinite timescale—all enlarge the urban scene, while the sand in the closing sentence equally covers up in neutral white-colored tombstones and cornfields:

Beyrouth
Ecrire pour Beyrouth . . .
   Telles des femmes voilées, les années écoutent aux portes, et les saisons, paupières baissées, frôlent ses débris, la soutane brûlée de ses murs. Seul le vent entre dans les chambres et parle bas sans que personne ne vienne briser son monologue.
   Ecrire pour Beyrouth . . .
   Le rivage calcaire du marché vide, les barbelés plantés dans le quartier souillé des dernières batailles, la bouche noire des galeries dans la falaise des ombres.

Des signes gravés dans les passages, creusés dans le corps des immeubles, la poussière grise pour dire la colère du feu.
Derrière une persienne deux prunelles sans larmes. Une voix lointaine égrène des prières. Un chat déplace, anxieux, un lambeau de sa proie.
Ecrire pour Beyrouth ...
Comme il importe peu que les vieux équipages installent leur soie sur cette ville perdue dans le malheur. Que la mémoire gérante déploie son or sur les écailles pour rendre coupable la plaie et humilier, par des regrets, la Capitale otage ...
Ecrire pour Beyrouth ...
Pour appeler encore, pour aimer vainement, pour se perdre et dormir dans ce vaisseau trahi par son chant et son plaisir de vivre.
Ecrire pour Beyrouth...
Sa robe de mille alliances, sa matière quadrillée et ses artères obscures, ses ordres dans la nuit, et la pierraille rougie chaque jour par la lumière.
Ecrire pour Beyrouth ...
Pour l'écouter revivre, vaquer à ses travaux du temps et de la mort, et dénier l'absence. Pour inventer ce sable qui, de son souffle égal, couvre d'une même blancheur la pierre des tombeaux et les champs de maïs.
(*Dialogue avec la feu*, pp. 52–53)

Beirut

For Beirut I write ...
Like veiled women, the years listen at your doors, and the seasons close their eyelids, touch your broken fragments, and the burnt soutane of your walls. Only the wind enters into your rooms and murmurs softly. No one interrupts its monologue.
For Beirut I write ...
The chalky side of the empty market, the barbed wire planted in the blood-stained quarters of the latest battles, the black opening of galleries on dark cliffs.
Signs engraved in passageways, carved within buildings, the grey dust which speaks for the anger of fire.
Behind a shutter two tearless eyes. A faraway voice says a prayer. A worried cat removes a bit of its prey.
For Beirut I write ...
How trivial it would be for old crews to fix their silks over this city sunk in misery. Let memory manage its gold over splinters, make wounds guilty, humiliate the kidnapped Capital, and burden it with regrets.

The Image of the City: Wounded Beirut

> For Beirut I write ...
> To call again, to love in vain, to lose one's self and sleep in this ship betrayed by its song and its love for life.
> For Beirut I write ...
> Her dress made of a thousand alliances, her checkered fabric, her dark arteries, her orders at night and her stones reddened each day by the light.
> For Beirut I write ...
> In order to listen as it comes back to life, as it attends to its chores with time, with death, with the denial of absence. In order to invent this sand which, in the same breath, puffs and covers up in identical whiteness the tombstones and the cornfields.

Thus the act of writing endows the city with an epic dimension,[16] inserting it into a universal type of life, of eternal duration, far beyond the immediate time and space of "Wounded Beirut." The tone of religious recollection and prayer, of course, consecrates the poetic act, as in the case of Nadia Tuéni.

V

Elias Khoury's Beirut is similarly transfigured into a strange mysterious city which hides behind tall doors. *Abwab al-madina (Gates of the City)*[17] is a parable rather than a novel—parable defined as a narrative used to typify a moral or spiritual truth which lies outside it.

We have witnessed so far a clearly delineated Beirut in Awwad's novel, both enticing and cruel, and a stately one in Tuéni's poem "Beirut," which later is narrowed down to one particular area where a surrealistic "death dance" is encapsulated in the "cubicle of a memory." We moved with Claire Gebeyli from the chronicle of a decimated city to a laborious city-goddess, in which the specific recedes and gives way to the universal.

Elias Khoury immediately sets the tone of the whole parable in the opening paragraph:

> He was a man and he was a stranger; he did not tell his story to anyone; he did not know it could be recounted; he believed as we believed in the same things; he was like us all and he did not know that what had happened could be told to any man. He was a man and he was a stranger.
> (*Abwab al-madina*, p. 6)

Thus starts Khoury's Beirut fable, though the city is never named. Similarly, his protagonist is not identified.[18] He is the Stranger who has traveled for a long time and who has endlessly turned around the tall doors of the city before he enters it. Once he is inside the city, a new search for its center starts, in dizzying circular movements. As a result, an accumulation of repetitive words and gestures creates a dream-like atmosphere which dominates Khoury's scenes. All cities seem to be captured on his urban stage, as all men are incarnated by this archetypal Stranger, brother to Kafka's K. or Beckett's Didi and Gogo. An atavistic imagery of the triangle of city–woman–death builds up in poetic prose the ritual of the search for a lost home:

—The city and women, I did not see a single man, said the man.
—The city is women, and the men drown in the sea.
(p. 73)

A return to the 'elemental water' is clearly illustrated here. It recurs in the novel until the final paragraph, where the sea submerges city and citizens. The plot is extremely simple in *Abwab al-madina*, and obviously of no interest to the author. His urban drama takes place on a circular stage which dispenses with any kind of verisimilitude. Khoury constructs myth-structures rather than a story, while his protagonist walks in and around the city in endless circles, soon joined by throngs of people who also walk round and round. These myth-structures seem to be 'improvised' or 'made up' by a narrator, as immediate responses to a situation which engulfs slowly and totally the walking Stranger, who has lost everything, including his memory. Hence the need for a narrator who follows him and tells us his story. The dreamlike atmosphere is intensified, heightened by a narrative discourse which seems to erase itself as it unfolds. Here is an example amongst many other similar passages:

The Stranger walked and walked. On his side walked another man. Next to the other man walked another one. And all walked towards the faraway city, and in the faraway city they lit a fire, and they die in the fire, and they are frightened in the midst of the fire, and they write a story in the fire which starts where it should end, and when it ends it seems as if it had never started.
(p. 8)

The errant Stranger is certainly the 'artist in exile' for he carries a suitcase full of papers, notebooks, and pens. He reaches the city after countless days and nights, and instead of being welcomed by many people, he finds himself absolutely alone behind its tall doors. The mythic structures cluster around a stone imagery of doors, walls, ramparts, and tombs which render as concretely as Claire Gebeyli's "frozen ice-bank" the artist's difficult search for meaning and self-expression in a fragmented city, in which steel and fire kill men every day. The artist's words become absolutely useless:

He only knew a few useless words, but they were his words; what would a man do with his words if they were useless? He did not ask the question for he walked and his words walked by his side and called each other by his side and fell like the dead leaves of an ancient tree.
(p. 7)

Finally, an old woman, Tiresias-like, lets the Stranger into the city and a new search starts as the Stranger loses his suitcase, his papers, and his pens. Even his memory is like dead flowers with a stale smell (p. 34). Such 'objective

The Image of the City: Wounded Beirut

correlatives' for the artist's plight are broadened when the whole population joins him in a new search for the king's tomb at the heart of the city. If this is found, the dead king would be restored, the stones would turn into living places and the city—the wasteland—would come back to life. Khoury alludes thus to the absolute necessity of finding the proper ruler for his city, if it should emerge out of the prevailing chaos.[19] Hence the central position of the king's tomb on Khoury's stage, in which he finally finds his notebooks and pens.

Artist and king are essential for the city to survive, although they are constantly sacrificed by the mob. Yet, slowly, the old woman multiplies into many women, and the population rallies around the Stranger. A collective weeping fills the scene, the smell of death is everywhere, and the terrified people decide to run away. In an oblique allusion to the departure of many Beiruti residents during the war, Khoury affirms the need to stay and not betray one's city:

—What will you do.
—We shall leave the city.
—Where to.
—We do not know.
—How do you depart and leave the tomb?
—I do not know. No.
—Are you staying?
—And you.
—And I.
—And I.
—And they and us and . . .
—We shall all stay, answered an old woman . . .
(p. 93)

The city doors disappear. Voices come out of the city's inner streets, people run away towards the sea or to faraway places where they walk in a wasteland full of marshes (p. 102). The stranger resumes his walk in infinite time and space. The dust multiplies until, suddenly, all burns up. Fire spreads into houses, doors, and faces. The Stranger's clothes burn and he sees himself far, far away, floating. He looks around him. He is at the center of the city. The center burns, the ramparts, the women, the tomb, the king's coffin—all burn up. Even the sea is aflame. What remain are weeping voices which come out of the entrails of the fish:

Then the sea came. The sea devoured the fire and spread across the city. The sea devoured the ramparts and spread over the doors. The doors collapsed and remnants of corpses floated over the blue deck and dark domes. Everything was floating. Nothing remained in the city except wailing voices coming out of the fish guts and up towards the place where no one can listen to them.
(p. 109)

Thus ends the book.

Khoury's fable is one thousand years old and will recur in another millenium, he tells us. Wallace Stevens beautifully expresses the operative function of metaphor when he says that "reality is a cliché, from which we escape by metaphor."[20] Elias Khoury's transfiguration of burning Beirut into the metaphor of this city without a name is quite effective. This Kafkaesque fable is written by an artist who has become a Stranger in his city, whose papers and pencils are but bits and pieces he finds in the tombs of dead kings. Nevertheless, he picks them up, which implies that he, like Claire Gebeyli, will continue to write in their city.

Exile and homelessness seem to be part and parcel of the urban experience. They are certainly more in focus in times of war. Yet a parable such as Khoury's could only be written in the city and out of city experiences. The condition of Beirut here, and the artist's own spiritual condition, are one, as in the case of Nadia Tuéni's narrator. The city defines the artist's soul. In the wake of Kafka, Khoury dismisses all but the design of his city, which is intimately identified with his own aching heart and his feeling of metaphysical estrangement.[21]

VI

The last work I shall consider is a poem by Adonis entitled "Time." The poem is dramatically pinned down to time and place since the poet informs us that it was composed in Beirut, between June 4 and October 25, 1982, the period of the Israeli invasion of Lebanon and siege of Beirut, in the so-called 'Peace for Galilee' operation. The intense spacio-temporal concentration, however, is so charged with emotion that, paradoxically, the poet escapes out of time and space and soars to intoxicating heights. He leaves behind him the narrowness of his individuality and place, and merges with the universe in the wake of many mystics.

The bare facts of life in Beirut during the Israeli siege were unspeakably horrible. The urban stage in Adonis's poem is first set in appropriate sordid-realistic fashion, with an accumulation of horror images in the Baudelairean vein of "La Charogne," or "Les Sept Vieillards" (both urban poems).

Time
Carrying the seeds of time, my head a tower of fire:
What is this blood sinking deep in the sand, what is this decline?
Tell us, O flames of the present, what shall we say?

The tatters of history in my throat,
On my face the victim's scars.
How unavailing has language become, how narrow the alphabet's
    doors.
....

—My brother is lost; my father demented, my children dead. Where shall I seek relief? . . . [22]

The haunting refrain of the walking poet, with his brain aflame, gives the poem an incantatory quality, while new wholes are constantly formed, fusing, as T. S. Eliot puts it, disparate experiences into an organic unity. The poet sets the sordid-realistic layer of his urban drama as paraphrased above, then he abruptly shifts to a surrealistic plane. The poet is a buffoon now, a madman who unveils the secrets of history. Nadia Tuéni's "archives" are transmuted, here, into a jewel-box and the marshland of prophets, while the multiple layers of history unfold through the magic of recitation. In the meantime, what has been called or has become a 'homeland' is only one moment that runs on the roads of time.

As with Elias Khoury, the poet's soul loses its memory; its heritage is deeply buried in the treasury of images, and he goes through a quasi-mystical experience. The soul plays games, draws a bird which is tied down to a boat and is tossed by the waves. The bird only hears screeching steel which tells it: "Watch the city's heart like a split moon tied to the navel of a ghoul of sparks." Examples can be multiplied to illustrate how the poet's fiery brain assimilates an increasingly wild imagery reminiscent of Baudelaire's lineage from Rimbaud to the great surrealists of our epoch. For these artists, poetry becomes a way to exalt life and go beyond man and the contingencies of history. Rimbaud's "dérèglement de tous les sens" (disordering of the senses) operates in Adonis's poem "Time," and the absolute seems to be conquered at the end of his voyage.

In this fashion, dismembered Beirut is transformed into the springboard of the poet who walks on it for a while—to heat up his brain, his nerves, all his senses—in preparation for taking off. One critic mentions that Apollinaire lived World War I in all its cruelty, but also as a kind of cosmic enchantment.[23] The reader of Adonis's poem feels that a similar "cosmic enchantment" seizes the poet's being. He leaves behind him the scattered corpses in the streets of Beirut, and flies further and further away from the earth, in dream and madness, until he merges with the universe. Hence the operative function of madness which "cleanses the doors of perception," as Blake put it, and liberates one from the prison of space and time.

In such a state, the poet's map is mad as well. Beirut is Sidon, and his hometown Qassabin, and many other cities. The whole world topples upside down; time and space incorporate all times and spaces. The city telescopes all other cities in that visionary instant; the poet also telescopes all men whose organs are huge battlefields. Adonis's "Bateau ivre" (Drunken boat) is propelled by titanic forces, his history is a precipice, and the poet's tryst a consumption by fire. His body escapes him, his face disappears in the mirror, while his blood splashes out of his veins. Thus, war in Beirut is mythicized as its violence is met with an accumulation of violent metaphors:

> Beirut enters into the death map
> Tombs like meadows, and torn-off limbs-fields.
> What does Qassabin pour into Sidon, into
> Tyre, and Beirut, which itself pours?
> What is this faraway thing approaching?
> What mixes this blood on my map?
> Summer has dried up and autumn hasn't come
> And the spring turned black in earth's memory
> Winter as if drawn by death: agony or hemorrhage
> an epoch which escapes from the vessel
> of determination and the hand of fate
> an epoch of divagation which improvises
> time and ruminates the air.
> (*Kitab al-hisar*, p. 11)

Nadia Tuéni's imagery of madness and dislocation reaches a climax in Adonis's "Time." The poet wonders:

> Madness? Who am I in this darkness? Teach me, guide me
> O madness
> . . . .
> I look for a name and for something to name,
> and nothing can be named.
> (*Kitab al-hisar*, pp. 13–14)

Thus, the act of writing is emptied of content in a blind time, a blind history, a primeval time, and a muddy history. The threads of the universe disintegrate, the roads lie, the shores betray man—how could one avoid being blown up by madness?[24]

A series of dynamic images with religious overtones prepare the climax of the poem. History is slaughtered in sacrificial preparation for a 'beginning' *(fatiha)*, a new body, and a new birth. The poet is the origin of water and the end of fire, the mad lover of life. Once again, the dialectics of fire and water, of life and death, operate:

> Saddle those wild winds
> history is slaughtered, the slaughter is but the beginning
> leave the slaughterer, the slaughtered and the slaughter as witnesses
> and bury me in the remains
> a ruin amongst ruins.
>
> Thus I draw wisdom from its source
> I shout: welcome my remains, welcome my defeat
> tomorrow death will extinguish me but I won't die
> tomorrow I shall go forth from light to another light.
> True, weaker am I than a thread yet nobler than a god.

> Thus I begin
> I embrace my soil and the secrets of its desires—
>   it loves the body of the sea, a love whose hands are of the sun
>   a body, the warehouse of thunder, the bower of tenderness
>   a body, a promise in which I lose myself
>   I emerge from this challenge a body
>   You men cover up with the compassionate rain the daisy's face,
> and let it be . . .
> (*Kitab al-hisar*, pp. 17–18)

The poet-seer ends with the affirmation of his difference, his separateness, and his uniqueness:

> Revealing to time the secrets of his love:
> thus he confesses:
> he is the dissenter, the rebel, the prodigal.
> (*Kitab al-hisar*, p. 19)

The poet has exploded language and forced the 'narrow doors of the alphabet' to reach out towards new frontiers.

VII

We have journeyed, in an order of increasing complexity and multilayeredness, from the reality of the "cooking pots" of Awwad's city which were preparing a bloody banquet about to take place, to the surreality of Adonis's rendering of his urban drama. Between the state of complete reconciliation of all opposites in Adonis's poem, and Awwad's objective rendering of his urban scene, images of dislocation and reintegration have recurred in the midst of the fires of Beirut. We noticed a major preoccupation with the artist's function in the city and the artist's feelings of complete identification with 'wounded Beirut'. The will to pick up pen and paper and carry on is affirmed in several ways as well. Through the word, the glare of images replace that of steel. In Khoury's fable, the circularity of his motifs assert the ever-recurring pattern of life and death in the city, while the symbol of the sea on the shores of Beirut suggests at the end the ebb and flow of history.

Gebeyli transmutes "Wounded Beirut" into a laborious mythic creature whose wounds will be healed in the process of active life. By day and night, Beirut assimilates all that stands in its way, and just carries on. Last year, a young group performed Gebeyli's *Dialogue avec le feu* in a theater in Beirut, shortly after it came out in a book. That night, shelling was heavy over the city, yet the audience flocked to the theater and listened in trance-like fashion to the recitation of Gebeyli's poetry, accompanied by music composed for the event. This was certainly one of those privileged moments in the history of all cities, during which the Aristotelian concept of catharsis was alive once again. Pity and terror were certainly purged out of the souls of the Beiruti citizens who witnessed on stage the ritualization of their war.

Moreover, a little later, a young theatrical group in France performed with great success Gebeyli's *Dialogue avec le feu* in several small cities of their country. The tragedy of Beirut has thus become for many people a symbol of the universal urban dramas mentioned at the beginning of this essay. In fact, Lewis Mumford expresses arrestingly the fact that "the most precious collective invention of civilization, the city, second only to language itself in the transmission of culture, became from the outset the container of disruptive internal forces, directed towards ceaseless destruction and extermination."[25]

Truly, "only love knows how to marry this space," when cities break up and the land is a train of dust. The city and language, the city and her spokesman, the artist, transcend violence and destruction. Both reconstruct constantly whatever breaks down: "Ils disaient que la ville . . . est un lien entre l'Homme et Dieu" (They said the city . . . is a link between Man and God). Yes, Tuéni had sensed it well. She becomes the prolongation of her own city. Her utmost receptivity absorbs the intimate vibrations of her "mad land" as she intently listens:

Folle Terre
II
Ecoute
. . . . . .
écoute: la ville blanche est un tombeau
. . . .
Ne crains ni l'amour ni la nuit,
. . . .
Ecoute.
Il y a sur ton ombre des chemins de quiétude
Absolue.
(Archives, p. 29)

Mad Land
II
Listen
. . . . .
listen: the city is white like a tomb
. . . .
Fear neither love nor the night,
. . . .
Listen
On your shadow are roads of
Absolute tranquility.

The welding of language and city leads to this magnificent state of absolute tranquility, of plenitude. Death becomes insignificant then:

Le futur de mon temps

....

J'appartiens a ma folle terre; je la crée par ma mort, et son visage brûle de mille regards plus incandescents que la faim.
Je ne suis libre que de sa permanence.

....

Je survis à ma propre poussière, et connais de mémoire le futur de mon temps.
(*Archives*, p. 61)

The Future of My Time

....

I belong to my mad land; I give it life when I die, and its face burns with a thousand eyes more glowing than hunger.
By its permanence I am free.

....

I survive my own dust, and bear in my memory the future of my time.

Her memory is her city's memory and it carries, as in the case of Adonis, all time, all space. It is the "memory of the race." In fact, the poet dwells in silence to sense better the pulse of the race:

J'habite le silence
pour mieux contrôler le pouls de la race.
(*Archives*, p. 63)

Notes

1 Samir Khalaf and Per Kongstad, "Urbanization and Urbanism in Beirut: Some Preliminary Results" in *From Madina to Metropolis*, ed. L. Carl Brown (Princeton: The Darwin Press, 1973), pp. 116–49. Two other sociological studies of Beirut are worth mentioning: Leila Fawaz, "Le Développement de Beyrouth au XIXe et au début du XXe siècle," and Salim Nasr, "Formations sociales traditionelles et sociétés urbaines du Proche-Orient: Beyrouth, Damas et Baghdad," in *La Ville arabe dans l'Islam*," sous la direction de A. Bouhdiba et D. Chevalier (Tunis: Imprimerie al-Asria, 1982), pp. 153–61 and 357–84.

2 For the concept of comparative literature as internationalist and humanist, see Cl. Pichois and A. M. Rousseau, *La Littérature comparée* (Paris: Armand Colin, 1967); for that of a 'world literature' inherited from Goethe, see Henry Gifford, for example, *Comparative Literature* (London: Routledge and Kegan Paul, 1969). The authors I discuss are certainly aware of what T. S. Eliot calls "the mind of Europe" and Paul Hazard "la conscience européenne," mentioned by Gifford, which they have expanded to integrate their own Arabic sensibility and culture.

3 The scope of this study compels me to ignore momentarily the two beautiful "Beirut" poems of Mahmoud Darwish, and the latest poetry of Khalil Hawi

and Nizar Qabbani, as well as some war novels by Hanan al-Shaykh and Nazik Yared, among others. I plan to deal with them later, in a larger study.

4 See Lewis Mumford's discussion of the "urban drama" in his brilliant book *The City in History: Its Origins, Its Transformations, and Its Prospects* (Harmondsworth: Penguin Books, 1961, 1973), pp. 136 *ff*. I have borrowed the concepts of "multilayeredness" and of 'horizontal' and 'vertical' readings from Erich Auerbach's *Mimesis: The Representation of Reality in Western Literature* (New York: Doubleday Anchor Books, 1957). Auerbach starts by drawing a superb comparison between the Homeric hero and the Biblical Abraham to set, in opposition, the two basic types of styles, realistic and symbolic, for the literary representation of reality in European culture.

5 Joseph Frank, "Spatial Form in Modern Literature," in *The Widening Gyre, Crisis and Mastery in Modern Literature* (New Brunswick: Rutgers University Press, 1963), pp. 8–9.

6 The novel [Tawfik Awwad, *Tawahin Beirut* (Beirut: Maktabat Lubnan, 1982, 1985)] quickly received public acclaim and was selected by UNESCO for its series of the most representative authors of their times. Translations in several languages are planned, the first of which, by Leslie Mcloughlin, appeared in London in the Heinemann "Arab Authors" series in 1976 as *Death in Beirut*. My excerpts are followed by parenthetical page references to the English translation. Tawfik Youssef Awwad was born in Lebanon and retired from his post as ambassador to Rome in 1975. His two early works *al-Raghif* (1936), and *al-Sabiy al-a'raj* (1939) made him a prominent writer in his own lifetime. He is broadly read in the schools and universities of Lebanon and the Arab world.

7 See Nina Jidejian, *Beirut through the Ages* (Beirut: Dar el-Mashreq, 1973), and on the subject of education in particular, p. 59 *ff*.

8 For this type of response, see Georg Lukacs's preface to his *Studies in European Realism; A Sociological Survey of the Writings of Balzac, Stendhal, Zola, Tolstoy, Gorki and Others* (London: The Merlin Press, 1972).

9 "Beyrouth," in *Liban, 20 poèmes pour un amour* (Beirut: Imprimerie Zakka Graphic Center, 1979), pp. 19–20. Born in Lebanon, Nadia Tuéni published her first collection of poems in French in 1963, and continued to write poetry until her premature death in 1983. She was awarded the Said Akl Prize in Beirut, and was recognized as one of the finest poets of the Francophone countries when she won the French Academy Prize in Paris in 1972. Her collected works are in press, and the excerpt quoted at the head of my essay is the first draft of an unpublished poem "Le Rêveur de terre," which will appear in the forthcomning *Oeuvres complètes* (Beirut: Dar Al-Nahar, Fondation Nadia Tuéni), p. 339.

10 This translation is mine, as are subsequent translations in the article.

11 *Archives sentimentales d'une guerre au Liban*, in three parts: I-Hier: Le

Jardin du Consul; II-Ensuite: Folle terre; III-Aujourd'hui: Le Futur de mon temps (Paris: Edition Pauvert, 1982). Page references in parenthesis follow excerpts. It is worth noting that the prologue was written in 1972, the first poem of "Le Jardin du Consul" in 1968, while the rest of the poems in the volume must have been written after *Liban* (1979) and up to 1982, the date of the publication of the volume.

12 See on the themes of madness, dislocation, and the poet's function, the beautiful essay by Jad Hatem "Poésie et violence: Etude sur les *Archives sentimentales d'une guerre au Liban* de Nadia Tuéni" in *Les Conférences de l'ALDEC: La Guerre du Liban au regard des sciences humaines*, (Beyrouth: Université Saint Joseph, Faculté des Lettres et des Sciences Humaines, 1985), pp. 73–89.

13 As Joseph Frank remarks of the cubist technique of Djuna Barnes in her novel *Nightwood*, in *The Widening Gyre*, op. cit., p. 31.

14 Excerpts from a few works by Claire Gebeyli are analyzed, followed by abbreviated titles and page references in parentheses: *Mémorial d'exil* (Paris: Editions Saint-Germain-des Prés, 1975); *La Mise à jour* (Paris: Agence de Cooperation Culturelle et Technique [A.C.C.T.], et Editions Saint-Germain des Prés, 1982), awarded the A.C.C.T. Prize in 1980; *Dialogue avec le feu, Carnets du Liban* (Paris: Le Pave, 1985; La Corde Raide, 1986). Claire Gebeyli is a naturalized Lebanese of Greek origin. A poet and journalist, she is in charge of the Developmental Program of the United Nations in Beirut where she has been living since her early twenties. Her *Dialogue* had appeared as a series of prose poems regularly published in the daily *Orient-Le Jour*.

15 Ezra Pound adds, "It is the presentation of such an image which gives that sense of sudden liberation; that sense of freedom from time and space limits; that sense of sudden growth which we experience in the presence of the greatest works of art." (*Poetry*, March 1913, as quoted in Joseph Frank, op. cit., pp. 9–10.)

16 Albert Beguin recognizes this epic dimension in some short works in our century and writes "Chez les Américains, ce n'est pas *Ambre* qui atteint à l'épique, c'est *Le Vieil homme et la mer*, c'est-à-dire une brêve anecdote, sans ampleur par elle-même lue en deux heures, mais qui laisse dans la mémoire du lecteur *l'expérience* incontestable d'une très longue durée et d'une vision de l'histoire humaine. Car ce qui compte, ce n'est pas la durée "réelle" du fait rapporté et le sens qu'il possédait avant de devenir un fait de littérature, c'est la durée que lui confère l'écriture, le sens qu'il prend, une fois entré dans cet autre univers où il commence sa vraie vie: *sa vie significative.* " (In "Le Roman Légendaire," *Esprit*, January 1954, pp. 133–39.)

17 A Lebanese journalist, literary critic, and novelist, Elias Khoury has several collections of critical writing, short stories, and novels, including *Abwab al-*

madina (Beirut: Dar Ibn Rushd, 1981; English trans. Paula Haydar, *Gates of the City*, Minneapolis: University of Minnesota Press, 1993).
18 For the theme of the contemporary protagonist as Stranger or Everyman, see Doris Enright-Clark Shoukri's interesting essay "Ontological Concerns in Twentieth-century Writers," in *Alif; Journal of Comparative Poetics*, no. 2 (Spring 1982), pp. 7–31.
19 Tayeb Salih's title *Bandarshah* (The city's king), comes to mind here. The Sudanese author has chosen it for a series of novels, two of which have already appeared: *Daw al-bayt* (1971) and *Meryoud* (1977). Salih explains his choice when he says in an interview with Hoda al-Huseyni conducted in Beirut, "I chose the title *Bandarshah* because our problem is the search beneath the city (or bandar), and secondly finding an appropriate formula to govern ourselves, i.e. the issue of the king (shah), in Ahmad Said Muhammadiya, ed., *al-Tayeb Salih: 'Abqari al-riwayya al-'arabiya* (Beirut: Dar al-'Awda, 1976), p. 220. Elias Khoury's quest for the city and the king is similar to Salih's preoccupation.
20 Quoted in Terence Hawkes, *Metaphor,* in "The Critical Idiom" series, (London: Methuen, 1972), p. 57.
21 As expressed in Irving Howe, "The City in Literature" in *The Critical Point: On Literature and Culture* (New York: Horizon Press, 1973), p. 42.
22 "Time" first appeared in Adonis's own literary journal *Mawaqif* ("al-Waqt" no. 45, Winter 1983) and later in a volume of collected poems, *Kitab al-hisar* (The book of siege) (Beirut: Dar al-Adab, 1985), pp. 5–6. See also Mona Takieddine Amyuni, "Adonis's 'Time' Poem: Translation and Analysis," *Journal of Arabic Literature* XXI (1991), pp. 172–82. A naturalized Lebanese, Adonis ('Ali Ahmad Sa'id) was born in Syria and has established residency in Lebanon since 1956; he now lives in Paris. One of the foremost poets and critics of the Arab world, he has regularly been invited to lecture on poetics and read his own poems in the most eminent academic institutions of the world. His poetry has been translated into many languages, and he has been awarded the International Prize for Poetry. The four lines quoted at the head of this essay are from *Yawmiyat hisar Beirut 1982*, in the translation of Abdullah al-Udhari, *Victims of a Map: Mahmud Darwish, Samih al-Qasim, Adonis*, (London: Al Saqi Books, 1984), p. 163.
23 Marcel Raymond, *De Baudelaire au Surrealisme* (Paris: Jose Corti, 1966), p. 230.
24 The critic Khalida Said has often written on Adonis's mystic trend and his use of "creative madness," (as with al-Hallaj, Blake, Nietzsche, Rimbaud, and Michaux, among others), which cleanses one's memory and innermost depths. See, for example, her excellent analysis of an earlier poem of Adonis in *Markabat al-ibda': dirasat fi-l-adab al-'arabi al-hadith* (Beirut: Dar al-'Awda, 1979, 1982), pp. 87–120.
25 Mumford, *The City in History,* op. cit, p. 67.

Brecht and the Egyptian Political Theater

❖

Mahmoud El Lozy

Without Marxist knowledge and a
socialist outlook it is impossible today
to understand reality or to use one's
understanding to change it.
—Bertolt Brecht

In his introduction to *Kumidyat Udib* (The comedy of Oedipus) by 'Ali Salim, the noted Egyptian drama critic 'Ali al-Ra'i recalls an incident that occurred at the theater conference held by UNESCO in 1966 in New Delhi. He quotes the advice of the representative of the German Democratic Republic on the subject of Brecht in the following terms: "Borrow from Brecht without reservation . . . take from him what you can . . . what suits you . . . and forget about the rest, of course."[1] In al-Ra'i's mind, Salim's play is a practical application of this advice in its treatment of a Greek myth.[2] In the case of Alfred Faraj's *al-Nar wa-l-zaytun* (Fire and olives), it is the playwright himself who in his preface recognizes and acknowledges the guiding influence of Brecht. The predominant feature of Brechtian theater that Faraj refers to relates to the relationship between the events of the play and the audience. Brecht, he says, "gave the audience the attributes of judge and referee. He presents the case to the audience from the platform of the stage dialectically with all its contradictions."[3]

It is rare to find two plays, written at almost the same time and performed during the course of the same theatrical season (1969–70), that derive their theatrical practice from a third party's theories, especially if these happen to have been met with considerable resistance for over two decades. As such, these two plays acquire specific importance for an examination and an evaluation of the problematics of assimilation by Egyptian playwrights and critics of one of the most influential theoreticians of the theater in the twentieth century.

'Ali Salim's *Kumidyat Udib* is indisputably an allegory of the Nasser period (1954–70).[4] The play's plot line follows more or less closely, and according to Salim's own evaluation and interpretation, the sequence of events that led to the shattering military defeat of 1967. In a broader context, it addresses itself to the question of democracy through a vehement attack on the "cult of personality" that characterized the Nasser regime. Salim's play is by no account a chronicle or a history play; it is a political allegory which tends to obscure, rather than illuminate, the nature of the conflicts peculiar to that period in Egyptian history. Many of the obscurities and contradictions in Salim's play can be elucidated by analysis of the tension between the playwright's conscious intentions and the ends realized in the play itself, as well as through the recognition of the fact that a radical shift has occurred in the playwright's intentions halfway through his work.

It is quite evident that the basic tragic elements of the Sophoclean model are absent in Salim's version. It is established quite early in the script that Oedipus is not in any way related to the royal family of Thebes. Oedipus did not kill Laius in this play, and though the latter was indeed murdered, it is suggested in the text that Jocasta may have instigated the murder. In any case, it is obvious that the murder of Laius is simply brought up to illustrate the conspiratorial nature of the Theban leadership. Salim also rules out entirely the incestuous relationship between Oedipus and Jocasta. Here she is not Oedipus' mother, and the action of the play does not touch upon its protagonist's quest for his origins. Nor is the play a parody of the Oedipus myth, for what may be perceived as burlesque elements in respect to Sophocles' play function only as isolated moments in the text and do not inform it as a whole.

Another major departure from the Sophoclean tragedy on the part of Salim has been to 'Egyptianize' the play. He has set the action in ancient Egyptian Thebes (now Luxor), and introduced new characters with Egyptian names like Oneh, Awaleh, and Horemheb (though retaining the original Greek names of the major characters). The distancing in time of the political allegory is undermined by shifting its action in space from ancient Greek Thebes to ancient Egyptian Thebes. One wonders if such theatrical games are responsible for ascribing a Brechtian influence to the play. Placing the action of contemporary events in some fictional past is contrary, if not antithetical, to the very basic premises of Brechtian theater. The notion of 'historification' that permeates Brecht's theoretical writings specifically emphasizes the 'pastness' of historical material to let the audience into an awareness that present conditions are themselves eventually bound to pass.[5] The political allegory set in a pseudo-historical period—a product of the playwright's imagination— implies the permanence of specific historical conditions. A nihilistic view of man's role in history is bound to develop from such a static world view, where the present and the future seem to be the mere reflection and repetition of a past that looms ominously over our heads.

Tiresias is perhaps the most disconcerting character in the play, so fraught with contradictions is his portrayal. Salim's failure at making Tiresias a dramatically coherent character is obvious from the outset. We are told quite explicitly that he is "the same Tiresias we know from ancient Greek literature; a seer" (p. 14). The evidence of the play suggests otherwise. There is certainly no need for a Tiresias endowed with prophetic powers once the original structure of the myth and its supernatural elements have been cast aside. As a matter of fact, Tiresias never makes use of his so-called prophetic powers at any point in the play. He is certainly not the Tiresias "we know from Greek literature." The opening and closing scenes suggest that he is merely a narrator—possibly another Brechtian element—who halfway through the play becomes heavily involved in the dramatic action and loses his earlier status. It is quite significant that Tiresias—the so-called voice of reason and soul of Thebes—should, in the second half of the play, identify himself with the Palace, while in the earlier scenes he stood among the people. When, in the final act, Tiresias returns to being a substitute for the people, we have difficulties accepting him as such.

Tiresias' second sequence in Act One, Scene One clearly reveals his function in the text as a mouthpiece of the playwright, as he directs our attention to the Sphinx as the symbol of an internal disease in the body of Thebes, namely corruption. We are furthermore informed by the all-knowing Tiresias that there is a "different riddle" to be answered from the obvious one put by the Sphinx. His objections to having Oedipus go by himself to confront the Sphinx ushers in the play's conscious "message"—the rejection of individual heroism. With the reappearance of the Sphinx in Act Three and Oedipus' advice to the population of Thebes that they themselves must confront the beast, a new process is set in motion. Oedipus initially wins the support of Tiresias. If we are to believe Tiresias at this stage, the Sphinx has now been reduced to a purely external threat. There is no mention here of the Sphinx "within." The people confront the Sphinx and are defeated. As Act Three, Scene Two comes to a close, Salim succeeds in reversing the entire premise on which the play is predicated. Tiresias advises Oedipus (again) to confront the people and tell them that no individual can save a city alone. Oedipus fails to make himself heard by the crowd, which goes on cheering him as if the second attack of the Sphinx had not occurred. The leadership of Thebes—exposed to ridicule through bitter satire to this point—is now aware and responsible, but it is the population that refuses to listen. This last scene quite conveniently lays the blame on the population for being unable to undertake any collective action against the Sphinx.

Confusion grows as Tiresias tells us in the opening of Act Three, Scene Three that he foresaw the defeat. After all, he was the one who urged Oedipus to address the population of Thebes. Tiresias then tells us that "it was necessary that Oedipus see for himself what fear does to people" (p. 120). The well-being of the city is ignored for the sake of demonstrating certain concepts to Oedipus! Either Tiresias or Salim is not aware that Oedipus' popularity was legitimately gained—as Act One demonstrates—and certainly not purchased at the price of fear.

With Oedipus' departure from Thebes, Creon undertakes an unsuccessful repetition of what Oedipus had done by confronting the Sphinx alone. This development is in direct opposition to the conscious message of the play on the subject of individual heroism. In the epilogue, Tiresias tells us that the price Creon paid was "the price for the people of Thebes to understand that it is necessary to die in order to live, and that by dying, man has nothing to lose but his fear" (p. 124). This seems to suggest that Creon's suicide mission was equivalent to a solution of the problem raised by the play.

Our protagonist—Oedipus—is equally laden with contradictions in character delineation and development, and these touch upon the very dramatic coherence of the play. Oedipus appears in the first scene as an intelligent and courageous young man. He succeeds in embarrassing Awaleh, the chief of police, in this opening scene and emerges as a dominant and shrewd adversary with whom the Theban leadership will have to contend once he becomes king—or so we are led to expect.

What remains unexplained is Oedipus' insistence on marrying Jocasta once he becomes king. The text indicates that becoming king of Thebes is quite a separate issue from marrying the Queen. Is Salim here merely following mechanically the traditional story of Oedipus? The answer is not clear, particularly when we realize that Oedipus and Jocasta are never seen together again. The lack of "intimacy" between them provides for a scene where Jocasta complains to Awaleh of the "lack of fervor" of her new young husband, but nothing develops from the relationship that serves the progression of the plot. It does, however, suggest that Oedipus has become something of a 'hermit', or an 'absent-minded professor' who never leaves his laboratory. That, in turn, could be an attempt on the part of Salim to absolve Oedipus from the excesses perpetrated under his rule. However, while it strengthens our perception of Jocasta as a neurotic and sexually frustrated woman (a stereotype guaranteed by twenty-five hundred years of theatrical history to arouse laughter), the Oedipus–Jocasta marriage fulfills no function in the development of the plot.

The manner in which Oedipus becomes king is worth mentioning. Because he has been 'elected' somewhat 'democratically' by the population, we expect certain radical changes to occur under his rule. Our expectations of such changes will be inexplicably frustrated. After returning safely from his first confrontation with the Sphinx, Oedipus is hailed king of Thebes as he is being carried by a jubilant crowd to the palace. Oedipus wants desperately to communicate something to the crowd, but he is unable to make himself heard. We never get to know what it was he wanted to say. Did he or didn't he kill the Sphinx? And how is it then that the Sphinx disappeared for quite a while before returning to Thebes? These are but a few of the many questions to which Salim never bothers to give an answer, however crucial these may be to the dramatic coherence of his play.

Our suspicion that all did not go well with the Sphinx is confirmed in the scene that takes place between Oedipus and his friend Kami. The latter witnessed the confrontation and knows something about it that could compromise Oedipus' new status. We cannot understand here why Oedipus closes his eyes to Awaleh's brutal disposal of his troublesome friend. Without apparent reason, Oedipus seems to have lost his previous interest in the internal affairs of Thebes. From an outspoken opponent of Awaleh's methods, he has become a silent accomplice who actually gives the chief of police his blessings to pursue a systematic repression of the population of Thebes. Even his response is confusing and contradictory when Awaleh asks him for a list of his political enemies so he can "deal with them." Initially we get the impression that Oedipus will no longer tolerate such actions. "I know of no such things as enemies of the regime," he tells Awaleh, "I only know of enemies of Thebes; and those are the ones you should concern yourself with. Your duty is to protect Thebes from harm" (p. 53). Up to that point we feel that Oedipus is determined to put an end to many of the practices of the old rule. Instead of our expectations being fulfilled in that respect, the scene ends with Oedipus dissociating himself from the issue and giving Awaleh a free hand to act as he pleases:

Oedipus: Awaleh, I have no time for such matters. You are expected to perform your duties efficiently; that is, you're in charge of the internal security of Thebes. You may go. (p. 54)

What Oedipus is saying here is directly at odds with his earlier statements. We may well ask ourselves why Oedipus didn't fire Awaleh. Why didn't he also fire Horemheb who had earlier come to him with manufactured evidence designed to prove that the new king was a "descendant of the Gods"? This scene also makes it quite clear that Oedipus is lying in Act Three when he tells Tiresias that he did not know what Awaleh has been doing.

Certainly a drastic change has occurred in the character of Oedipus between the first and the second scenes of Act One. At the end of the first scene we anticipate a power struggle between Oedipus and the Theban leadership, but these expectations are deceived. The shrewd and clever Oedipus of Act One, Scene One disappears, to be replaced by a reclusive Oedipus who spends most of his time in a laboratory. He has become politically naive, and we are left to wonder why or how these changes occurred.

Act Two reads like a satire of the creation, through media indoctrination, of 'cult leaders'. What is not made clear in these scenes, however, is the purpose of such indoctrination and what political goals it was meant to achieve. Except for Scene Six, Oedipus is conspicuously absent from this act. In that scene, his first wave of anger at finding out that he is being deified is subdued through the sophistry of his advisers into a tacit acceptance of his divine origins. He is certainly not the Oedipus we have seen in Act One. It would seem that he had become convinced that he has indeed killed the Sphinx. Thus Oedipus has become the prime victim of the 'cult of Oedipus' manufactured by the leadership. But we have been given no clues as to how or why this transition has occurred.

What Salim has given us, in fact, is a play which, however hard it tries to project a progressive outlook, really reflects a very narrow and conservative perspective. In other words, the political message rhetorically stresses the necessity for change, but only in terms of ideas (the creation of a 'New Man'); it is an abstract and idealistic notion of change. Indeed what Salim seems to be advocating carries more of a sense of continuity than of change, for his conception of it implies at the same time its historical impossibility.

Nevertheless, despite the lack of dramatic coherence, a political vision does manage to emerge. Salim's 'populism' collapses quite early on in the play and his distrust of the masses comes fully to the foreground as we reach the final act of the drama. After ridiculing what we inevitably recognize as the Nasser regime for nearly two acts (so familiar are the references), he succeeds through a clever trick in reversing the whole thrust of the play. After exposure comes containment. If change is to occur, as Act Three never tires of reminding us, it will come as a result of the political leadership's initiative, not from the oppressed masses. In other words, the ruling circles, now aware of their past errors, will reform their policies and mend their ways for the greater good of the very population they have been brutalizing for centuries (according to Salim's own premises as stated in the play). Salim has indeed succeeded in Egyptianizing the play, for his notion of class conflicts in history cannot even conceive that the pyramidal structure of power can be upset at all. His sharp satire of the 'cult of personality' phenomenon does not seem to grow out of concern for democracy, but, rather, from the bitter disappointment that accompanies the recognition that the great man he may have unconsciously worshipped was not so great after all. The final act of *Kumidyat Udib* is tinged with a romantic yearning for a new great man to replace the defeated one.

While Salim relied on the allegorical genre to express his views on the causes of the 1967 defeat, Alfred Faraj avoids all the temptations an elaborate dramatic charade may offer and faces his subject in the most direct genre available: the documentary drama.

In *al-Nar wa-l-zaytun*, Faraj covers what has been commonly referred to as the Arab–Israeli conflict from a perspective that links it to nineteenth-century European colonialism. The defeat of 1967 is not perceived as a cataclysmic disaster, but as a further step in the process of colonialism set up by European Jewish settlers in Palestine—a process that started well before the creation of the Zionist state in 1948.

The choice of the documentary genre indicates a desire to grasp the mechanics of history that led to a certain state of affairs with the aim of overcoming them by stressing people's roles in shaping their own history. The documentary genre as such developed in the aftermath of World War I in Germany—the European nation that had to undergo major reassessments in terms of its role in continental and world affairs. The names of Erwin Piscator and Bertolt Brecht are associated with that tumultuous period of German history. That first wave of a committed political drama was brutally crushed with the accession of the Nazis to power: fascism substitutes history with myth.

The documentary drama reemerged in the 1960s, in Germany again, through the dramatic works of playwrights such as Peter Weiss (*The Investigation*, 1965; *The Song of the Lusitanian Bogey*, 1967; *Discourse on Vietnam*, 1968; *Trotsky in Exile*, 1970), Heinar Kipphardt *(In the Case of J. Robert Oppenheimer*, 1964; *Joel Brand*, 1965); and Rolf Hochhuth *(The Deputy*, 1963), to name only a few. The documentary genre became the most prominent means of dramatic expression of progressive playwrights to denounce and expose the current or past practices of finance capital, whether in Europe or in the Third World.

By the late sixties, Egypt was still very much aware of itself as a Third World country, with all of the connotations that the term implies. It is therefore not surprising that a politically committed playwright such as Alfred Faraj should attempt to assimilate the documentary mode of dramatic presentation in his play on the question of Palestine.

Al-Nar wa-l-zaytun was written some time after the June War of 1967, in which the Sinai Peninsula, the Golan Heights, and what was left of Palestine, including Gaza, fell under Zionist occupation. The evidence of the text allows us to place the central dramatic event of the play, Abu-Sharif's story, as occurring some time after the 1967 war. The pro-Zionist demonstration in Berlin, for example, takes place in the days immediately following the war, and at a time when Abu-Sharif was probably still a student in Federal Germany.

In writing this play Faraj relied essentially on sources and materials from the Palestine Research Center in Beirut.[6] His research also took him to various military centers of Fatah, where he interviewed Palestinian fighters and refugees. Faraj confesses that he experienced some anxiety in his attempt to determine the most adequate dramatic form to present the Palestinian question. The first step, he says,

> is to choose a personal story of comprehensive significance of one of the victims or of one of the fighters in this cause. Then begins the writer's struggle with himself and with his thoughts to go beyond an artistic form that imposes the particular, when the writer's objective is to generalize. I confess to having lived with this anxiety, guarding myself from writing the story of one man, or of a group of men, when I wished no less than to present the story of an entire people. That is why I was attracted to the 'documentary' form of drama. 'Total theater' imposed itself on me, with its combination of expressive arts: drama, dance, singing, mime, and the eternal magic of the theater.[7]

Faraj is quick to add that he does not pretend that this form is the ideal one to present the Palestinian question, but, he adds, "I am certain that it is one of the most appropriate forms."[8] It is obvious that in its very genesis Faraj's play gets caught up in a web of eclecticism that threatens its very coherence, thereby undermining the specific effect it wishes to arouse amongst its potential audience. Identifying one's audience is another crucial criterion that shapes a particular work's structure of meaning. 'Total theater' and 'documentary drama' are not synonymous or interchangeable terms, nor is there necessarily any affinity between them and what we refer to as 'Brechtian theater'. Total theater can be and often is reactionary in content; documentary drama does not necessarily have to espouse a Marxian view of history, but Brechtian theater is first and foremost the translation of Marx's materialistic conception of history into a dramatic aesthetic. Though Brecht and Piscator collaborated for a while on a number of projects, their outlooks are quite different and they followed different paths in the respective developments of their artistic careers. Piscator was basically a theater director, while Brecht was simultaneously poet, playwright, actor, director, and theater theorist.

Brecht's theater is one form of Marxist theater; it is a dialectical theater. The various elements of a Brechtian production would be structured with the aim of producing the famous/infamous A-effect. "A representation that alienates," says Brecht, "is one which allows us to recognize its subject, but at the same time makes it seem unfamiliar."[9] This alienation is "designed to free socially conditioned phenomena from that stamp of familiarity which protects them against our grasp today."[10] The A-effect holds such a prominent place in Brechtian theater that one may venture to say that a dramatic work that does not seek to generate it does not belong in the tradition of its author. Whether Faraj's play belongs in the tradition of Brecht, as he seems to imply, will depend on its ability to generate the kind of alienation we have described.

Al-Nar wa-l-zaytun opens with a song addressed directly to the audience. The opening words ("the matter concerns you") are designed to draw the attention of the spectators and stimulate their awareness of the fact that what is happening in Palestine concerns us all. The song proceeds from an Arab dimension to an international one, climaxing with an invitation to join the ranks of the Revolution. At the end of the song three young people step forward and address themselves directly to the audience. These three characters do not remain mere announcers throughout the play, but often participate in the dramatic scenes and blend into the action after assuming different roles. Nevertheless, their principal function throughout the play is to supply the audience with a wealth of documentary information.

In their first scene the announcers identify their audience. After broadly sketching the colonial situation and the function played by citizens of Western colonial and imperialist powers in perpetuating the exploitation of the Third World, the announcers say, "As for the white person who is not possessed by devils, we present him—as we present people of all races—some Palestinian pictures" (p. 15).

And the purpose of presenting such pictures to these people is "to disturb them, not to comfort them." On the basis of this it becomes evident that the play supposedly addresses itself to a Western audience in 1970 that has presumably a potential for displaying solidarity with the Palestinian cause. And the place to reach that audience is none other than the National Theater in Cairo, in a production performed in Arabic! That Faraj actually believes that he is reaching this audience is evident from the following scenes, where he exposes (rather crudely) the myths of Zionist ideology that the average Westerner has been bombarded with for decades and has come to accept as 'objective' realities. Faraj supposedly carries out this process of demystification by letting Zionist ideologues themselves expose the racist and expansionist nature of Zionism.

Had Faraj carefully read Piscator he would have known that such a strategy does not produce any results.[11] His play actually addresses itself to a fictional audience—one that does not and cannot ever fill an auditorium. Furthermore, Faraj seeks to 'disturb' an audience that according to his own criteria would have been already sympathetic to the point of view he is trying to present. Unknowingly, Faraj is defeating his own utopian purpose.

The announcers become fedayeen as the opening scene comes to an end. We are now in a Palestinian camp where a group of young men and women are getting ready to launch a military operation against an Israeli munition factory. The fedayeen's leader's long speech—supposedly a briefing to the young fighters—is actually nothing but an awkward attempt at incorporating within the flow of the play the official Fatah position on the policy of armed struggle at the time the play was written.

As the fedayeen reach their stage of operations, we encounter for the first time the central character of the play, Abu-Sharif. He begins to emerge amongst the fedayeen as a high-strung and sensitive young man. "I don't know what the Zionists did to you or your family," the Leader tells him, "but I don't want to see you lose your nerve during the operation" (p. 23). The play shifts into a surrealistic mode as Abu-Sharif gets wounded in a direct encounter with Israeli forces. He dreams that he has returned to his family's house in Jerusalem and that he meets there with his childhood friend, a Jewish girl by the name of Nadya. In the course of this sequence, Nadya, who happens to be the soldier who wounded Abu-Sharif, puts on her military uniform, for she is an army reservist. As she finishes putting on her uniform, she becomes unable to recognize Abu-Sharif, and calls the police to have him arrested.[12] The arrival of the police blends, in Abu-Sharif's dream, with the massacre of Deir Yassin. The particular circumstances of Abu-Sharif blend with the collective national consciousness of the Palestinian people. At this point, an amazing transition occurs in the play. For, instead of returning to Abu-Sharif and the other fedayeen, the action shifts back to the announcers and to the 'documentary' mode of presentation, accompanied by short sketches and illustrations. In other words, Abu-Sharif's personal consciousness (his nightmare) has fused with the Palestinian collective consciousness (the Deir Yassin massacre), which is derived from a historical experience whose facts are presented to us through the 'documentary' mode of presentation. The play actually proceeds forward by means of two different modes of presentation: the dramatic and the documentary—Abu-Sharif's story and the historical facts presented by the announcers. A frail connection is established between the two modes of presentation by means of Abu-Sharif's dream sequences and reminiscences. The Deir Yassin massacre becomes the focal point from which the play proceeds—through interviews with various political forces, soldiers, refugees, etc.—to build up a documentary history of the events that led up to the Zionist occupation of Palestine, beginning with the Balfour Declaration of 1917, to the establishment of United Nations camps for Palestinian refugees fleeing Zionist terror.

We return after a long documentary sequence to Abu-Sharif and his comrades as they await the assault of Israeli forces. By association, the megaphone used by the Israelis to advise the fedayeens to surrender reminds Abu-Sharif of pro-Zionist demonstrations in West Berlin in the aftermath of the 1967 war. Apprehended at first by the police, he is then interviewed by a reporter who becomes an interrogator, as we are taken back to the time when he was put on trial by the Israelis. Again, at the end of this sequence, we do not return to our starting point, i.e. Abu-Sharif and the other fedayeens, but to more scenes in the documentary mode. By the end of that act we would have witnessed on parallel planes the development of Abu-Sharif's national consciousness as well as that of the Palestinian people towards the path of armed struggle.

We lose track of our protagonist for most of the second act, which opens with more songs, interviews, projections, etc. Largely, though, Faraj is preparing the ground for the events that lead up to and follow the Kafr-Qassem massacre, which will occupy the larger part of Act Two. We only return to Abu-Sharif, still agonizing, halfway through this act. The connection between him and the massacre is established in the final moments of his agony. As Abu-Sharif slowly sinks into a sleep of death, he dreams of going to his father's tomb to plant an orange tree his mother gave him. It is here that we learn that his father was one of the victims of the massacre. We now know at last the personal circumstances that led Abu-Sharif to join the ranks of the Palestinian liberation movement.

What Faraj has written is a rather peculiar type of documentary drama. Indeed, one wonders if *al-Nar wa-l-zaytun* can be said to belong to that genre at all. For Faraj has seemingly written a melodramatic revenge piece where the documentary aspects serve as a background that explains the attitudes and actions of the protagonist of the dramatic sequences. That explains his rather inconsistent and awkward attempts at incorporating documentary material through Abu-Sharif's delirious reminiscences and nightmares. Faraj's reliance on subjective time as a unifying factor that ties the play together as an organic whole is further evidence that the documentary element has been assigned a subordinate role. Chronological or historical time is a critical requirement where documentary drama is concerned, for without it we tend to lose the notion of causality in history. *Al-Nar wa-l-zaytun* cannot 'educate' or enlighten an audience politically or historically since it is written in such a way as to be intelligible only to those who are already informed.

Against the stated intentions of the text, the play is obviously meant for an Egyptian audience that in 1970 would have been overtly sympathetic to its author's political stance. In other words, Faraj's play does not rely on 'alienation' devices to communicate a social reality to its audience. On the contrary, *al-Nar wa-l-zaytun* merely reinforces existing attitudes and beliefs; it feeds and excites the nationalistic impulse, but the Arab social dimension of the conflict is swept aside. Its absence tends to simplify one of the most complex conflicts of the second half of the twentieth century. What about Arab–Arab conflicts and their repercussions on the Arab–Israeli conflict? In that respect, Faraj seems to have chosen to be on the safe side. Ironically, though, if performed today in Egypt, Faraj's play would appear more 'Brechtian' than it ever did when first performed. After ten years of Camp David, what Faraj's play has to say about the Arab–Israeli conflict will definitely seem 'unfamiliar' to an audience that has been trained into believing that the conflict had its roots in 'psychological obstacles' between Arabs and Jews. That is not necessarily a comment on the play; perhaps it is one on the level of political and historical awareness of today's Egyptians.

As written for a 1970 audience, Faraj's *al-Nar wa-l-zaytun* owes technically more to the influence of Piscator than it does to that of Brecht. The documentary passages and scenes are clearly designed to arouse intense emotional responses in the auditorium. One can see a production of this play easily sinking into a crude manifestation of the 'emotional orgy' Brecht so dreaded. The heavy reliance on complex technical means is not in tune with Brecht's theatrical vision with its emphasis on simplicity and economy. Nevertheless, despite its shortcomings, Faraj's play stands as one of the few attempts in the Egyptian theater to write plays with a sense of history and with a recognition of the need to grasp that sense and communicate it to a largely illiterate audience.

Almost twenty years after *al-Nar wa-l-zaytun* was first performed, the documentary drama has failed to make any headway on the Egyptian theatrical scene. To this day Faraj's play remains an anomaly, the beginning of what may have developed into a trend but was aborted by the ultra-reactionary onslaught of the 1970s on the theater. When history gets rewritten, the documentary is perceived as a subversive influence. Instead, the political theater followed the trend, set by the boxoffice success of Salim's *Kumidyat Udib*. Pseudohistorical and conservative in content, the dominant form of political drama today runs along the line of simplistic allegory; it confirms the inevitability and ineluctability of current conditions, social, political, etc. History is seen as Fate. The satirical aspect of Salim's political drama eventually reconciles the spectator in the auditorium to the dominant social reality by innocuously (and indirectly) ridiculing representatives of authority. Impotent laughter essentially protects the very system it ridicules.

Despite its numerous shortcomings, Salim's *Kumidyat Udib* represents a major point of transition in the development of Egyptian political drama. The crisis in thought among certain segments of the society in the aftermath of the defeat of 1967 is strongly reflected in Salim's play. This crisis, in turn, manifests itself in the play's artistic structure. It reflects the loss of a sense of direction as well as a desire to reevaluate the past in order to chart a path towards the future. Whether or not we agree with Salim's own evaluation and interpretation of Egypt's recent history, the play stands as a genuine attempt to depict some of the internal shortcomings and abuses that made the 1967 defeat a shattering reality.

The influence of Brecht on Egyptian theater has not gone much beyond theoretical and rhetorical enthusiasm. In practice, Brecht has been primarily sought as a source of inspiration for 'new' formalistic devices through the incorporation of songs, addresses to the audience, use of projections, etc. This distorting of Brecht is not peculiar to the Egyptian theater, for in that respect it bears much resemblance to the methods by which Western bourgeois dramatists and directors have appropriated Brecht. One could deduce that Brecht's theories have found their way to Egyptian critics and playwrights through secondary sources written largely by Western bourgeois commentators (legal Brechtianism?). On the other hand, the very class affiliation of these critics and playwrights may be responsible for this narrow and formalistic understanding of Brecht. The epigraph to this article indicates the starting point for a Brechtian theater in Egypt, should such a theater be at all desirable at the present moment.

Notes

1 'Ali al-Ra'i, introduction, *Kumidyat Udib* by 'Ali Salim, in *Masrahiyat 'Ali Salim* (Cairo: Maktabat Madbuli, 1976), p. 5. Pages cited in the text refer to this edition. Unless otherwise mentioned, all translations from Arabic texts are my own. See the entire translated play in Mahmoud El Lozy, "Four Egyptian Playwrights: Translations and Critical Essays," Unpublished Ph.D. dissertation, University of California, Santa Barbara, 1986, pp. 590–665.
2 Ibid.

3 Alfred Faraj, preface, *Al-Nar wa-l-zaytun* (al-Hay'a al-Misriya al-'Amma li-l-Ta'lif wa-l-Nashr, 1970), p. 7. Pages cited in the text refer to this edition. To my knowledge this work exists only in my own translation, of which I have only a first draft.
4 See Nadia R. Faraj-Badawi, "'Ali Salem: A Modern Egyptian Dramatist," *Journal of Arabic Literature* 13 (1981), p. 88.
5 See Bertolt Brecht, "A Short Organum for the Theater," in *Brecht on Theater,* translated and edited by John Willet (New York: Hill and Wang, 1964), p. 190.
6 The library was plundered by the Israelis in September 1982 during the invasion of Beirut. See Amnon Kapeliouk, *Sabra and Shatila: Inquiry Into a Massacre,* trans. and ed., Khalil Jahshan (Belmont, Mass.: Association of Arab-American University Graduates, Inc., 1984), p. 73.
7 Faraj, preface, *al-Nar wa-l-zaytun,* p. 3.
8 Ibid., p. 4.
9 Brecht, p. 192.
10 Ibid.
11 Erwin Piscator, *The Political Theater: A History, 1914–1929,* trans. Hugh Rorrison (New York: Avon Books, 1978), passim.
12 Ironically enough, this specific incident provides us with one of the rare Brechtian moments in the play, where action is determined by the character's social function. The situation itself appears to be heavily inspired by the Pope's dressing scene in Brecht's *Galileo.*

Naguib Mahfouz and the Sufi Way

❖

Hamdi Sakkut

I would like to explain from the outset that this essay is not concerned with the dervishes depicted in Naguib Mahfouz's realistic novels, like Shaykh Darwish in *Midaq Alley*, or Shaykh Mutwalli Abd al-Samad in *Palace Walk*. These characters, while they show possibly an indirect interest in the Sufi way, were mainly portrayed as part of the traditional neighborhoods described in these realistic novels. We are concerned here with the deeper, deliberate religious position taken by some characters in the novels which focused on this issue.

This position did not clearly appear in Mahfouz's work until the second part of the trilogy, *Palace of Desire,* and later in *Sugar Street*, when we encounter Kamal Abd al-Jawad going through an intellectual crisis. He has lost faith in everything and ceased to desire anything. He has lost faith in the way people around him lead their lives and has become skeptical and doubtful of their beliefs and practices. In short, he has become an outsider, as defined by Colin Wilson in *The Outsider*, published in London in the same year of the publication of *Sugar Street*.

As an example of Kamal's skepticism, in this monologue from *Sugar Street*, Kamal reflects on how his friend, Isma'il Latif, views his own articles:

> In the past, Kamal had rebelliously and stubbornly scorned such advice. Now he despised it, but did not rebel against it. Yet he wondered whether he should be disdainful, not because he thought the disdain misplaced, but because he worried at times about the value of what he wrote. He was even uneasy about his worry. He was quick to confess to himself that he was fed up with everything, and that the world, having lost its meaning, seemed at times to resemble an obsolete expression.[1]

Earlier in *Palace of Desire*, and in one of the most entertaining chapters, Ahmed Abd al-Jawad summons his son, Kamal, for the 'notorious' interrogation on his article explaining Darwin's theory. The father has just finished reading the article and is disturbed by its claim that men and apes are of the same species. The interrogation is, at once, long, sad, and funny. In the end the father asks, "Couldn't you find some other subject, besides this criminal theory, to write about?" Kamal then thinks to himself,

Why had he written this article? He had hesitated a long time before sending it to the journal. He must have wanted to announce the demise of his religious beliefs. His faith had held firm over the past two years even when buffeted by gales coming from two of the great poets and skeptics of Islam: Abu al-Ala al-Ma'arri and Umar al-Khayyam. But then science's iron fist had destroyed it once and for all.

'At least I'm not an atheist,' Kamal told himself. 'I still believe in God. But religion? . . . Where's religion? . . . It's gone! I lost it, just as I lost the head of the holy martyr al-Husayn when I was told it's not in his tomb in Cairo . . . and I've lost Aida and my self confidence too.'²

When his father asks him to correct himself, Kamal thinks, "What a good man his father was—wanting to get Kamal to attack science in order to defend a legend. He really had suffered a lot, but he would not open his heart again to legends and superstitions, now that he had cleansed it of them."

"I've experienced enough torment and deception," Kamal reflects.

Mahfouz ends the chapter with a description of what goes on inside Kamal's head:

He secretly promised his mother he would consecrate his life to spreading God's light. Were not light and truth identical? Certainly! By freeing himself from religion he would be nearer to God than he was when he believed. For what was true religion except science? It was the key to the secrets of existence and to everything really exalted. If the prophets were sent back today, they would surely choose science as their divine message. Thus Kamal would awake from the dream of legends to confront the naked truth, leaving behind him this storm in which ignorance had fought to the death. It would be a dividing point between his past, dominated by legend, and his future, dedicated to light. In this manner the paths leading to God would open before him—paths of learning, benevolence, and beauty. He would say goodbye to the past with its deceitful dreams, false hopes, and profound pains.³

This skeptical position, accompanied by loss of faith and of the desire for life on the one hand, and enthusiasm for science and absolute faith in it on the other, is also described by Samara Bahgat (before she turns from seriousness to absurdity) in *Adrift on the Nile*: "The major theme of the drama [referring to the play she is writing] is the Serious versus the Absurd. Absurdity is the loss of meaning, the meaning of anything. The collapse of belief—belief in anything. It is a passage though life propelled by necessity alone, without conviction, without real hope."[4]

She explains further:

> In order to simplify the issue I will say that mankind of old faced absurdity, and escaped it through religion. And today again, man faces absurdity; but how can he escape this time? It is pointless to entertain hopes of communicating with people in a language other than the one they use; and we have acquired a new language, which is science. This is the only language in which we can articulate greater and lesser truths.[5]

She adds:

> Let us look to the scientists for example and method. It seems that they are never trapped by absurdity. Why? Perhaps because they have no time for it! Perhaps also because they are permanently in contact with reality. Relying on a successful methodology of proven worth, they are not assailed by doubt or despair. One among them may spend twenty years solving an equation; and the equation will provoke new interest, and consume new lifetimes of research, and thus another firm footstep will be taken along the path of truth. The abode of scientists smells sweet; it is the smell of progress, of success. Questions like 'Where do we come from?' and 'Where are we going?' and 'What is the meaning of life?' present no temptation for them.[6]

The trust in science and the belief that it will solve the problems of humanity are also depicted in *Children of Gebelawi*, where the people aspire to salvation at the hands of Arafa, who symbolizes science and has caused the death of Gebelawi, who symbolized religion, or even divinity. The people then look to Hanash, Arafa's disciple, when he gets hold of Arafa's book.

People may suppose that Mahfouz lived for over ten years (the period between *The Trilogy*, published in 1952, and *Adrift on the Nile*, published in 1964) with the belief that science alone would realize the dreams of humanity. A more careful reading will prove that this was not the case. By the end of *The Trilogy*, we realize that the doubts of Kamal Abd al-Jawad are not limited to religion. He also doubts philosophy and science. Riyad Qaldas asks him about his view on the different philosophies he has reviewed in his articles in *al-Fikr* magazine, and Kamal answers, "I am a tourist in a museum where nothing belongs to me. I'm merely a historian. I don't know where I stand."[7] Qaldas then remarks that Kamal has shown special zeal in discussing materialist philosophy, and Kamal says, "My enthusiasm was sincere, but later I was troubled by skeptical doubts."[8] Qaldas asks him about other philosophies, and only gets similarly skeptical answers. At last, he says, "There's science. Perhaps it could save you from your doubts."[9] Kamal responds,

> Science is a closed world to those of us who know only its most obvious findings. Besides, I've learned that there are distinguished scientists who

question whether scientific truth matches our actual world. Some find the laws of probability perplexing. Others are averse to asserting that there is any absolute truth. So, I became even more tormented by doubt.[10]

Abd al-Aziz, an editor at the magazine, says laughingly, "Religion has taken its revenge on you. You fled it to pursue higher truths, only to return empty-handed."[11]

Kamal has moved from being an enthusiast of science and scientific solutions in *Palace of Desire* to a skeptic of religion, of science, and of everything, in *Sugar Street*. These doubts cause him suffering and confusion. He doubts the worth of life itself and considers suicide. He used to think that "his attachment to the troubled thread of life contradicts the awful doubts of his conscience." His soul—in the midst of this nightmarish whirlpool of doubt—yearns for "two contradictory ways: the Sufi way and that of sensuality"; in other words, gratification of both spiritual and physical needs. He manages to secure the gratification of his physical needs. This much is easy. But the spiritual needs, or Sufi ideals, are, he considers at this point, a form of "apathy and escapism."

This then is the position in the *Trilogy*. What about *Children of Gebelawi?* A careful reading of *Children of Gebelawi* will also reveal that the enthusiasm for science depicted in it was not absolute. It is true that the people in *Children of Gebelawi* expect salvation at the hands of Arafa (after he has killed Gebelawi), and at the hands of his disciple, Hanash, after Arafa's death, but this should be interpreted with the understanding that the novel attempts to recount the history of religion and present a view of the people's attitudes towards it. The author here takes the role of historian and attempts to present an objective image of what happened historically. It is evident that the scientific discoveries led to a contraction of the role of religion, and that they overwhelmed most people, making them enthusiasts of science, who expected it to fulfill their dreams. However, they soon realized that they were wrong, particularly after the realization that science is used to create weapons of mass destruction and to support tyrannical rulers. This is what *Children of Gebelawi* depicts. It shows the people's expectations of Arafa, or science, and their disappointment when he and his book become 'pawns' of the *fettewa*, the thug who wants to control the alley. Arafa, therefore, aids tyranny and dictatorship, until he himself is killed by the *fettewa*. When Arafa dies, people hear that his book has fallen into the hands of his disciple, Hanash, and that Hanash is planning to take over the alley. It can be seen, therefore, that there is only a faint hope that science will be a road to reform and to human welfare.

This faint hope of salvation at the hands of Hanash is not much different from the hope of salvation at the hands of the religious figures awaited by certain groups. Mahfouz here is merely trying to depict the real history of humanity using symbols and allegories, as he does in the preceding chapter, which presents the appearance of prophets and their reception by their own people. Furthermore, Arafa himself regrets killing Gebelawi and realizes his immense offense to the neighborhood; thus he intends to use his magic to revive him. This symbolizes the search for a religion with a more scientific idiom, as Samara Bahgat also suggests in *Adrift on the Nile*.

Thus, in both *The Trilogy* and *Children of Gebelawi*, Mahfouz shows skepticism towards both traditional religion and the usefulness of science. In the first work, there is an inclination towards Sufism, and in the second, a semblance of hope for a new religion, which is convincing to a generation brought up on scientific discourse.

The later works of Mahfouz, as well as his personal statements, have further demonstrated that Sufism was his chosen way. In an interview with Ahmed Hamroush, published in a newspaper following the serialized publication of *Children of Gebelawi* in the newspaper *al-Ahram*, Mahfouz said that he called for "socialist Sufism," and explained that he meant to call for an "aspiration to God," which cannot be accomplished unless individual life is freed of sins and evils. "As long as there is exploitation, then the exploiter is evil, the exploited is miserable, and their relationship is one of hatred and resentment. There cannot be an aspiration towards God in this case."[12] This is what he expressed on a theoretical level.

After 1960, Mahfouz wrote a short story, "Zaabalawi" (1961), and two novels, *The Search* (1963), and *The Beggar* (1964), which deal with the same issue. In all of these allegorical works the protagonist is attacked by the "ailment that has no cure" (in the words of the principal character in "Zaabalawi") and tries to find therapy or salvation through the search for God, or the achievement of Sufi ecstasy. The experience of Omar al-Hamzawi in *The Beggar* is a good example of what is akin to a Sufi experience. Omar suffers from an ailment without a cure, the ailment of alienation, the same ailment from which Kamal suffered before. He abandons his house and family, and wanders about aimlessly, trying to forget his ailment. One night he goes out to the desert before dawn:

> He parked the car along the side of the deserted road and got out. The darkness, unrelieved by ground lights, was particularly dense, unlike any night he could remember. The earth and space itself seemed to have disappeared and he was lost in blackness. Raising his head to the gigantic dome overhead, he was assaulted by thousands of stars, alone, in clusters, and in constellations. A gentle breeze blew, dry and refreshing, harmonizing the parts of the universe. The desert sand, clothed in darkness, hid the whispers, as numberless as the grains of past generations—their hopes, their suffering, and all their last questions. There's no pain without a cause, something told him, and somewhere this enchanted, ephemeral moment will endure. Here I am beseeching the silence to utter, for if that happened, all would change. If only the sands would loosen their hidden powers, and liberate me from this oppressive impotence. What prevents me from shouting, knowing that no echo will reverberate? He leaned against the car

and gazed for a long time at the horizon. Slowly it changed as the darkness relented, and a line appeared, diffusing a strange luminosity like a fragrance or a secret. Then it grew more pronounced, sending forth waves of light and splendour. His heart danced with an intoxicated joy, and his fears and miseries were swept away. His eyes seemed drawn by the marvelous light, out of their very sockets, but he kept his head raised with unyielding determination. A delirious, entrancing happiness overwhelmed him, a dance of joy which embraced all earth's creatures. All his limbs were alive, all his senses intoxicated. Doubts, fears and hardships were buried. He was shadowed by a strange heavy certitude, one of peace and contentment and a sense of confidence, never felt before, that he would achieve what he wanted. But he was raised above all desire, the earth fell beneath him, like a handful of dust, and he wanted nothing. I don't ask for health, peace, security, glory or old age. Let the end come now, for this is my best moment.

The delirium had left him panting, his body twisted crazily towards the horizon. He took a deep breath, as if trying to regain his strength after a stiff race, and felt a creeping sensation from afar, from the depths of his being, pulling him earthwards. He tried to fight it or delay it, but in vain. It was as deep rooted as fate, as sly as a fox, as ironic as death. He revived with a sigh to the waves of sadness and the laughing lights.

He returned to the car and drove off. Looking to the road dispiritedly, as if addressing someone else, 'This is ecstasy.' He paused before continuing: 'Certainly, without argumentation or logic.' Then in a more forceful voice, 'Breaths of the unknown, whispers of the secret.' Accelerating his car, he asked, 'Isn't it worth giving up everything for its sake?'[13]

Omar does abandon everything to capture a similar moment once again. He roams the wilderness and fields, but he never reaches his goal.

This failure, with which *The Beggar* ends, is what leads to disappointment with the Sufi way after the earlier disappointment with the scientific way. This disappointment may explain why Anis and his friends resign themselves to the state of alienation and resort to their hashish-smoking sessions and daily socializing in the houseboat to escape it in *Adrift on the Nile*, the work which followed *The Beggar*. The hashish-smokers' sessions are an intelligent technique to express Anis's penetrating thoughts and philosophical inquiries in the guise of a drug-addict's ramblings. However, the technique, unfortunately, escapes many readers who find the story to be only a collection of nonsensical remarks made under the influence of hashish. At best, they see political and social commentary in the smokers' remarks, but they miss the fact that Anis and his friends are concerned in the first place with philosophical questions like 'Being' and the 'mystery of death'. Their concerns go beyond the mundane ones of most people; in fact, they even believe that people escape from facing major problems by concerning themselves with minor ones, such as employment, marriage, politics, etc. Samara Bahgat says to Mustafa Rashid, "You are using the absolute to escape from your responsibilities" (p. 96). His answer is that "people use their responsibilities to escape from the absolute." Samara Bahgat also suggests that her play should revolve around "non-oriented" protagonists, like Anis and his pals. In reply, Khalid Azzuz says, "But these also have their artistic problems. . . . They live without any beliefs, wasting their time in futile pursuits in order to forget that they will soon turn into ashes and bones and nitrogen and water; and at the same time they are worn down by a daily life that forces upon them a certain kind of desperate and—to them—meaningless seriousness."[14]

Anis Zaki is, perhaps, the most sophisticated, profound, and perceptive character in any Arabic novel. His unique insights and poetic reflections reveal extensive knowledge of the world and pinpoint ironies and contradictions in different historical epochs and their contemporary analogues with their political and social dimensions. As his mind wanders at one point, he says to himself, "And when a light like the light of these embers blazes in the heavens, the astronomer says that a star has exploded, and in turn the planets around it, and everything has been blown to dust. And one day the dust fell onto the surface of the earth and life sprang from it . . . And after all that, they tell me: 'I will cut two days from your salary!'"[15]

On another occasion,

> thoughts clashed in Anis' head. Thoughts of the first battles of Islam, of the Crusades, of the courts of the Inquisition. The deaths of great lovers and philosophers, the bloody conflict between Catholics and Protestants, the age of the early Christian martyrs. The founding fathers' voyage to America, the death of Adila and Haniya, his dealings with the street girls; and the whale that had saved Jonah, and Amm Abduh's job, divided as it was between prayer leading and pimping. The silence of the last watch of the night, which he could never describe; and the fleeting, phosphorescent thoughts that glowed for an instant before vanishing forever.[16]

When the director asks him how he has managed to write a report with a pen which has practically no ink, he wonders, "How indeed. How did life first creep into the mosses in the cracks of the rocks, in the ocean depths?"[17]

It is important to note that these characters' positions do not change throughout the novel. To the contrary, the change happens to Samara Bahgat, the serious journalist, who comes to the houseboat eager to change the others.

The profound and utter despair soon gives way to Sufism and Sufi ways in novels like *Qalb al-layl* (Heart of the night), *The Harafish*, and *The Journey of Ibn Fattouma*. In these novels, hope centers on Sufism as a way out of the spiritual emptiness suffered by twentieth-century intellectuals, and as a consolation for the weak and the wretched in human society.

In *The Journey of Ibn Fattouma*, the protagonist travels to different lands: the abode of the Orient, the abode of perplexity, the abode of the arena, the abode of security, the abode of sunset, and the abode of the mountain. This journey allegorically exposes different parts of our world and different governmental systems. It views them all as falling short and unable to offer people what they aspire to: peace, happiness, and security. The traveler compares the conditions of his own society to those of others (each land of those mentioned represents a state or society), and finds his land to be the worst of all, except for a Third World police state, symbolized as the land of perplexity, where everyone and everything is enslaved for the protection of the "God," who presides over the state, where deceiving slogans abound, and where innocent individuals are detained for the slightest of suspicions.

From this perspective, *The Journey of Ibn Fattouma* reminds us of the play *al-Farafir* by Yusuf Idris, even though the issue is treated from a different viewpoint. *Al-Farafir* has a pessimistic end, which implies that the master–slave relationship will persist till the end of life, and even after that, ruling even the planetary worlds, while *The Journey of Ibn Fattouma* ends with the approach of Ibn Fattouma to the abode of the mountain, "the abode of utter perfection," which is apparently the state of fulfilled Sufis, who live in peace, purity, harmony, and happiness. This society does not have any of the ills earlier seen by Ibn Fattouma in his long journey, and which reminded him of parallel ills in his own society and in different times in history. The abode of the mountain offers the ideal life, which no dominant system in the present world is able to offer. Thus this Sufi abode offers a solution of 'salvation' for humanity on the social level, while in works like "Zaabalawi" and *The Beggar*, individual salvation is offered. In other words, the Sufi way offers salvation for both individuals and social orders.

In all these works, the story always ends when the salvation is about to be achieved, but is never actually realized. "Zaabalawi" ends when the protagonist, awakening from his sleep, discovers that Zaabalawi has actually come to him, but has departed; he does not know when he will find him again. *The Search* ends when the protagonist is waiting for his father, who will, if he arrives, save his son from a hanging. *The Journey of Ibn Fattouma* ends as the protagonist is setting out to climb the mountain while thinking of himself, his family, and his society, as well as what he may encounter that may prevent him from returning. He decides, then, to give his travel notes to the head of the caravan to deliver to his family and society, and to devote an entire notebook to his observations in the abode of the mountain, should he be able to visit it and return back. The novel closes with the following:

No history book makes any mention further of this traveler.
Did he complete his journey or did he perish on the way?
Did he enter the land of Gebel? How did he fare there?
Did he stay there till the end of his life, or did he return to his homeland as he intended?
Will one day a further manuscript be found describing his last journey?
Knowledge of all this lies with the Knower of what is unseen, and what is seen.[18]

The question remains whether Mahfouz stands on the frontiers of the Sufi world, because the Sufi world "exclusively belongs to its people," as stated by Sayyid al-Rawi, protagonist of *Qalb al-layl*. Does it follow, then, that the Sufi experience on the individual level cannot be depicted because no one who has lived it could or wanted to portray it in the concrete, realistic, and tangible language of our world, thus making it comprehensible and accessible?

Does Naguib Mahfouz, on the social level, leave out the definition of "the abode of utter perfection" and abstain from supplying us with information that goes beyond its general description because he is primarily concerned with *defining the road leading to it*, and because he envisages this new 'utopia' to be the analogue of 'paradise'—of which it suffices for us to know that in it we shall be fulfilled?

"Knowledge of all this lies with the Knower of what is unseen and what is seen."

Notes

1. Naguib Mahfouz, *Sugar Street*, trans. W. M. Hutchins and A. B. Samaan (Cairo: The American University in Cairo Press, 1992), p. 44.
2. Naguib Mahfouz, *Palace of Desire*, trans. W. M. Hutchins, L. M. Kenny, and O. E. Kenny (Cairo: The American University in Cairo Press, 1991), p. 336.
3. Ibid., p. 339.
4. Naguib Mahfouz, *Adrift on the Nile*, trans. Frances Liardet (Cairo: The American University in Cairo Press, 1993), p. 92.
5. Ibid., p. 93.
6. Ibid., p. 93–94.
7. *Sugar Street*, p. 94.
8. Ibid., p. 94.
9. Ibid., pp. 94–95.
10. Ibid., p. 95.
11. Ibid.
12. *Al-Jumhuriya*, 8 January 1960.
13. Naguib Mahfouz, *The Beggar*, trans. K. W. Henry and N. K. al-Warraki (Cairo: The American University in Cairo Press, 1986), pp. 87–88.
14. *Adrift on the Nile*, p. 118.
15. Ibid., p. 59.
16. Ibid., p. 85.
17. Ibid., p. 4.
18. Naguib Mahfouz, *The Journey of Ibn Fattouma*, trans. Denys Johnson-Davies (Cairo: The American University in Cairo Press, 1992), p. 148.

The Mythmaker: Tayeb Salih

❖

Ahmad Shams al-Din al-Haggagi

Myth is not synonymous with imagination, lies, or illusions; neither is it equivalent to reality. To those who believe in it, myth is undoubted reality and a fact. Lewis Spence has defined mythology as "the savage's science, his manner of explaining the universe in which he lives and moves."[1] However, mythology goes beyond that to include religions of ancient, modern, and contemporary people, preliterate and postliterate. In short, myth is humanity's belief in the world of metaphysics.

'Mythmaker', in the context of this study, does not mean the creation of a new religion or formation; no single individual is capable of that since myth is a communal belief formed by peoples' experience in nature and in the universe. What I mean is that the author of *The Wedding of Zein*, Tayeb Salih, is able to use myth in his work and employ it as a means of conveying the universality of human experience.[2] He conveys precisely his own lived reality with its creeds and beliefs as they really are. In that, he was preceded by the Greek tragedians, who depicted in their plays the beliefs of their society through a number of myths colored with their own vision of reality. *Oedipus Rex* by Sophocles, for instance, was a new reality that went beyond the world of myth or Greek beliefs. Yet it was colored with the author's own conception of the myth, thus becoming a new product of his making. Hence, the Greeks were highly convinced of Oedipus because—to them—it was religion, history, and reality.

What Tayeb Salih does in *The Wedding of Zein* and "The Doum Tree of Wad Hamid" is not entirely different from what Sophocles did in *Oedipus*, except that he does not have to reconstruct a myth since he has access to the extensive Sudanese and Arab folk heritage, with its belief in *awliya'* and saints and their miracles. Sufis constitute an independent world, and they have a great influence upon the social life in the city, the countryside, and in the oases. There is hardly a village along the Nile valley without a *wali* (saint) sought by the people for his blessings.

Tayeb Salih uses the living myth of Sudanese society and bases two of his works, *The Wedding of Zein* and "The Doum Tree of Wad Hamid," on it. Here he depicts popular myth in all its dimensions, collecting its detailed parts into a harmonious unity, and thus becoming a mythmaker.

The story of *The Wedding of Zein* conveys to us the world of Zein's village. The author does not mention the village's name in this story because it seems he wants it to be 'any Sudanese village'. However, he specifies it in two other novels, *Bandarshah* and *Meryoud*, as Doumat Wad Hamid. The author is right not to mention the name of the village in the *The Wedding of Zein*; this makes his readers recognize this village from their own experience rather than his. The world of Zein's village is full of life and juxtapositions. Zein is the center of this world: a world in which Zein lives, a world that is close to Zein, and a world that is far away from him. He is the focus, clarifying the main lines of the village's world.

The character of Zein is drawn as an enraptured dervish with all the familiar characteristics of a *wali* (saint), as known in Arab villages. This character, generally and specifically, is quite puzzling. Zein has two dimensions: the dimension of the mindless dervish, who is lost to and unaware of the surrounding world, thus incurring its scorn. The other dimension points to a serious man, who undertakes deeds of which the strongest in his village are incapable. He is singled out among them, yet he is one of them. These two dimensions stand juxtaposed: the distraught Zein versus the serious Zein.

The image of Zein differs from that of the village people. His is a strange birth, in the manner of mythical heroes whose births are accompanied by strange events and miracles. Horus, the ancient Egyptian god, was born as a result of a sexual relation between his mother and his dead father. Buddha, Zoroaster, and Jesus were all born to virgin mothers. In folk epics, Abu Zeid's birth came as a result of his mother's specific wish: he was as black as the bird she saw overpowering the other birds. Popular beliefs concerning al-Sayyid al-Badawi refer to him as having been born with a complete set of teeth and the ability to speak. Because of the strangeness of such a phenomenon, the child was examined to determine if this was a divine miracle or Satan's work. It was proven that the miracle of al-Badawi's birth was indeed a gift from God.

The birth of Zein is also accompanied by a miraculous event. Whereas newborns "meet life with screams, with Zein, however, it is recounted—and the authorities for this are his mother and the women who attended his birth— that no sooner did he come into this world than he burst out laughing."[3] This kind of birth, then, marks a change in the usual norms of children's births. The laugh accompanies Zein afterwards, for he continues to laugh all his life; the village responds to this laugh until it became a part of it.

Zein's appearance is strange in comparison to other men as he is different in his physical formation. "His face was completely hairless, with neither eyebrows nor eyelashes, and on attaining manhood no hair had sprouted on his chin or upper lip" (p. 34). The character of Zein baffles the village people, and very often they look upon him as unbalanced. Children crowd around him, and he throws stones at them. He pulls a girl's dress one time, prods a woman's waist or pinches her thigh another time. These actions never allow the villagers to take him seriously. Zein, however, is capable of true moments of seriousness that appear when faced with love.

Love kills Zein when he is young, before reaching manhood. The girl who kills him is Azza, the Omda's daughter. One day, amidst a crowd of men the Omda had mobilized to work in his field, he cries out, "Hear ye, O people of the village, O kinsfolk, Azza the Omda's daughter has slain herself a man. Zein is slain in the courtyard of the Omda" (p. 39). People are surprised at what Zein says because it is quite serious, all the more so because he says it in front of the Omda himself. However, relief from the tension comes when people burst out laughing, not taking him seriously. Even the Omda, known for his sternness, shares in the laughter. He begins afterwards to exploit Zein and gives him "any number of arduous tasks which would have defeated the jinn themselves" (p. 40).

This is one side of Zein's image, which puts him on the level of the disabled and mentally deficient. Arab villages classify this kind of human being into three types: one is associated with God, and selected by Him; the second is Satanic, selected by the devil; and the third includes diseased people with no supernatural powers involved.

Where does Zein stand in relation to those? The story demonstrates from the beginning that he is related to supernatural powers, which caused a change in his physical formation. This happened as a result of an accident. Zein's mouth had a full set of pearl-white teeth, as his mother says: "When he was six, she took him one day to visit some relatives of hers; at sunset, passing by a deserted ruin rumored to be haunted, Zein had suddenly become nailed to the ground and had begun shivering as with a fever. Then he let out a scream. After that he took to his bed for several days, and on recovering from his illness, it was found that all his teeth had fallen out—except for one in his upper jaw and one in the lower" (p. 33). In folklore, wastelands are usually inhabited by spirits, and it seems that these spirits were chasing him. Did Zein communicate with this evil underworld and give in to it? Of course not. The story does not link him in any way to the underworld; to the contrary, it presents him as a dazed dervish, alienated from the rest of the world. Scorn and laughter with him or at him are the only contact points with this world. His image is that of one who is relieved of his legal and religious duties, as the Sufis say. He is one of the 'enraptured' who are unable to wake up to the realities of the world around them; their religious duties are waived.

Country people are able to differentiate clearly between the insane and the enraptured. Arabs have connected jinn with madness, and Sufis connected God with the state of rapture, for God here is "the One who enraptures by means of His affection."[4]

Sufis do not disagree concerning the enraptured person, while those who do not believe in Sufism condemn him as mad. A Sufi was once asked, "How are you with the Lord?" He said, "I never shunned Him ever since I have known Him." He was then asked, "When have you known Him?" He said, "Ever since they started to call me mad."[5] A verse is attributed to Sidi Ahmad al-Badawi in their defense: "The secret of their madness is noble—Reason itself lies prostrate at its portals."

Here, according to Sufi belief, there is no separation between the seen and the unseen worlds. Whereas the non-Sufi or non-religious person sees the world of the mind as the material world and considers the unseen world imaginary and irrational, the Sufis see the whole world as one unit. The world of the mind and that of the spirit mix because the mind penetrates into the world of the spirit and meets with it to form one unit. Mind alone cannot reach a knowledge of this world, and so it needs divine aid. Abu Bakr al-Sabbak, one of the major Sufis, once said, "When God created the mind, He asked: 'Who am I?' It was silent; God then adorned its eyes with the Light of Divine Oneness, so it opened its eyes and said, 'You are God and there is no god but You.' For the mind would have never known God except by means of God."[6] From here comes the variance in the villagers' attitudes towards Zein.

The Sufis identify three types of the enraptured: the non-Wayfaring Ecstatic (*majdhub ghayr salik*), the Ecstatic Wayfarer (*salik majdhub*), and the Wayfaring Ecstatic (*majdhub salik*).[7] We now ask: to what type does Zein belong? The story determines Zein's image not as a wayfarer along the path of God who is struck afterwards by rapture. He is also not the Wayfaring Ecstatic who is already on the path to God. He appears to be of the first type: the non-Wayfaring Ecstatic, who was described as "one whom the Truth [God] has chosen for His Intimacy and has purified by the water of His Sanctity."[8] What does Zein lack, then, to become the Wayfaring Ecstatic? "He is the one who is enraptured, who then practices the Way and arrives at the destination; this is the best kind of all."[9] There is a long path that Zein must follow before becoming the Wayfaring Ecstatic. He needs an awakening, and the leadership of a guide to lead him to this Way.

Zein has not gone to the mosque yet, and there is no reference to his praying in the story. He appears as one living within God's realm, unified with Nature, and relieved of legal and religious duties. There is another side to the image of the enraptured alienated Zein concerning the values in his society. He appears to be the villager's living conscience that never stops carrying out the noblest of social duties, though in an unconventional manner. The image of Zein develops along two parallel axes:

The axis of the enraptured who is alienated from the village's reality

The axis of one who is vigilant in reforming the village's wrongs

On the first axis, Zein appears unaware of the customary social situations, such as offering condolences in funerals, or being vigilant concerning people's mistakes and calling them to account—as a self-defense mechanism to protect social status. He is also unaware of customary religious situations, such as going to the mosque for prayer. As for the second axis, he is aware of his role in the village as a messenger of love and mercy.

Zein has impeccable taste in beauty. He only loves the most beautiful girls in the village, the best-mannered and most pleasant of speech. No sooner does Zein start talking about his love for a girl than she becomes the talk of the whole village and ends up marrying a distinguished young man. "Love, first of all, would strike at his heart, then would be quickly transferred to the heart of another" (p. 42).

Zein's love for girls is not denied to him by society, for he poses no danger, has no evil intents, nor is he of bad conduct. His aptitude and capacity for love make him look at a girl, and he "would be overcome by something that was perhaps love. His innocent heart having succumbed to this love, his thin legs would carry him to the far corners of the village, running hither and thither like a bitch that has lost her pups, his tongue continually singing the girl's praises and calling out her name, so that ears were soon cocked and eyes on the lookout. Soon, too, some handsome young man's hand would stretch out to take that of the young girl" (pp. 42–43). Zein plays an important role in this conservative society that does not provide opportunities for young men to meet girls, and thus he becomes "a broker, a salesman, or a postman" for love (p. 42). Mothers know about this role of his and begin to use him; every mother wishes that Zein would fall in love with her daughter so that her name may be uttered by him, "for such a girl was guaranteed a husband within a month or two" (p. 44).

Not only the women, but also the men realize Zein's importance in this area. Mahjoub, one of the village's men famous for his firm and stern position on behalf of traditions, does not get angry when Zein asks to marry his daughter. He answers him seriously and firmly as if he really means what he is saying, "I promise the girl to you—right now before all these people here. After you've reaped your wheat and gathered up your dates and sold them and brought the money, we'll make the wedding celebration" (p. 37). Naturally, Mahjoub does not mean a word of what he says, but he wants Zein to extol his daughter until the village's young men—who trust his taste—hear about her, thus guaranteeing her a suitable husband.

The position of the village people concerning Zein's relationship with their daughters confirms that they view him as one in a state of unconsciousness. He does not harm a girl when he speaks of her, thus there is no fear of him. In that he resembles Shibli when he entered upon Junayd and his wife. When she tried to cover up, "Junayd said to her, 'Shibli has no interest in you, so stay put.' He continued to address him until Shibli began to weep, and so Junayd said to his wife, 'go cover up, for Shibli has awakened from his unconsciousness.'"[10] To the people of his village, Zein appears to be in a state of self-effacement, and whoever is seized by effacement has "no knowledge, nor mind, nor understanding, nor feeling."[11] The state of unconsciousness and effacement that befalls the Sufi prevails in Zein's relations with the village people. He does not return to an awakened state except on encountering certain kinds of people; his world is actually a circle (of which he is the center), and that circle divides into unconsciousness and awakening.

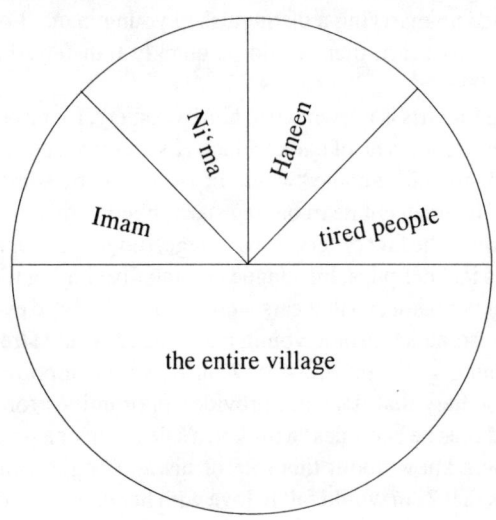

Unconsciousness – Awakening
Imam, Ni'ma, Haneen, the tired people – The entire village

Zein awakens with the tired and worn-out of his village, for he does not forget his role and his constant and spontaneous desire to help them. Zein also awakens when he meets three people: Haneen, Ni'ma, and the imam of the village's mosque. Yet, this awakening of his differs from his awakening when he is with the tired people of the village. His encounter with these three exercises a great influence on his movement and elicits a different response from him. The encounter with any one of them turns into a particular influencing factor and the responses are totally different.

The world of Zein's awakening uncovers the whole village. Zein has numerous friendships with persons whom the villagers regard as abnormal and crippled, such as Deaf Ashmana, Mousa the Lame, and Bekheit who was born deformed with no upper lip and a paralyzed left side.

Zein feels compassion for such people and does not lose his awakening when the matter revolves around them. If he sees Deaf Ashmana approaching from the field bearing a heavy load of fire wood on her head, he carries it for

The Mythmaker: Tayeb Salih

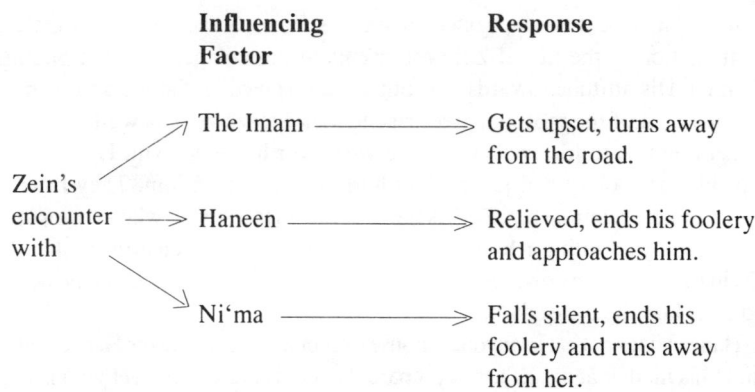

her with a playful smile. So afraid of people is she that if she comes face to face with anyone, man or woman, she becomes utterly panic-stricken, as though they were wild beasts. Yet she enjoys Zein's company and gives him her sad, dumb laugh that resembles the clucking of hens.

Mousa, whom people call not by name but the "the lame one," is a very old man who suffers when walking, and for whom life is an irksome and arduous trial. He had been a slave of a wealthy man in the village, and when the government gave the slaves their freedom, Mousa stayed on with his master, who had shown him great kindness, and provided for his needs. When the master died, his wealth was inherited by his son, who threw Mousa out. Overtaken by old age, Mousa found himself destitute, without a family or anyone to look after him. Zein reaches out to this man who takes shelter in the wastelands at night and scavenges here and there by day. Zein "built him a house of palm branches and provided him with a nanny goat in milk. In the morning he would go to inquire how he was and after sunset would come with his garment bulging with dates and other sorts of food, which he would lay before him. Occasionally, he would bring along an ounce of tea, a pound of sugar, or a little coffee" (p. 46).

In his awakening, Zein extends to the core of the village, carrying out the duties the village should have performed for these men. Between Zein's unconsciousness and awakening, the village stands puzzled at the contradiction, which it has failed to understand. From the villagers' point of view, he is a dazed, ill-mannered, or ill-bred dervish. During the state of his awakening, people are still amazed and unable to explain that huge store of goodness in Zein, so they give it a supernatural, non-rational interpretation: perhaps he is one of God's prophets, or an angel sent down by God in lowly human form to remind people "that a great heart may yet beat in one of concave breast and ridiculous manner such as Zein" (p. 46).

Zein is quite baffling to the village; it can find no explanation for him. He does all that is good, then retreats into unconsciousness when he shatters the intensity of their feelings by calling out, "O kinsfolk, O people . . . I am slain"

(p. 46). Thus he becomes once again a subject of scorn and laughter. Contradiction in the life of Zein represents to the villagers a never-ending dilemma. His attitude towards two other men, Haneen—the blessed man—and the imam of the mosque, gives rise to their amazement as well.

Zein returns to his awakened state whenever he meets with Haneen; he stops his tomfoolery and jesting and hurries to embrace him. They have a special mutual relationship. Zein is the only one in the village whose company Haneen enjoys, smiling at him kindly when he sees him and chatting with him. If Zein runs into him down the road, he embraces him, kisses him on the head, and calls him the blessed one.

Haneen does not eat in anyone's house except Zein's, who takes Haneen with him to his mother and asks her to prepare dinner, tea, or coffee. Yet who is this Haneen who returns Zein to an awakened state when meeting with him? The story presents a picture of him the way the villagers see it. He is a pious man, wholly dedicated to religious devotion. "He stayed six months in the village praying and fasting, would take up his pitcher and prayer-rug and wander about in the desert, disappearing for six months then returning. No one knew where he went" (p. 44).

People's view of him is not something unusual in a Muslim society, for he is considered one of the Sufis. His description fits that which is usually attributed to Sufi men: "They are people who abandoned the world, and so left their homelands and deserted friends to wander about in the lands. They lived without food or clothes and obtained nothing out of this world except what is not possible to leave out, such as covering their nakedness and alleviating hunger. And because they left their homelands, they were called wanderers."[12] The man who devotes himself to worship lives in the village only six months, carrying nothing but his pitcher and prayer-rug. He is conscious of what he does, and his return to the village constitutes a state of awakening in which he presents to his people an example of piety.

But what does Haneen do during the six months in which he is absent from the village? No one knew what he eats or drinks, for "he carried no provisions on his long journeys" (p. 44), and like all ascetics, he "thinks of no means of subsistence other than God."[13] This picture, therefore, makes him one of the Wayfarers, though it is not clear whether he is an Ecstatic Wayfarer or a Wayfaring Ecstatic. People's opinion shows that he has traversed many stations along the Sufi Way, reaching the highest degree in sanctity.

Sufis had drawn up an inner world opposing the outer world. They have their own government tending to the world's affairs, and Haneen—according to the people's description of him—stands within the highest ranks of this government. Sufis agree that the Spiritual Pole is the one situated at the top. A complete picture had been drawn of this government, although there is some disagreement among Sufis concerning the number of stations in this council. Chart a, taken from al-Qaysari,[14] and Chart b, from al-Amili, depict this government in graphical form (see pp. 108–109).[15]

This world surrounding the Pole's orbit does not increase or decrease. If one of them dies, another from the following rank in line replaces him.

These are not all of God's *awliya'* (saints), for there are also Disciples and Trustees who are called *malamatiya* (those who draw blame upon themselves), ascetics, servants of God, and scholars, present at every time and place. Their number is not constant; they increase and decrease, all under the ordinance and rule of the Pole.

And there are saints who do not fall within the Pole's circle. Among them is the Perfect Man, "the person who has matured to the extent of complete perfection in the sciences of *shari'a* (religious law), the Way, and Truth, because he has reached a rank requiring him to perfect others."[16] The station of such perfect individuals is equivalent to the "Pole's station except for the Caliphate; they have dissented from his rule, receiving directly from God— Glory to Him—divine secrets and meanings, contrary to those under the Pole's ordinance who receive only from him."[17]

It is noteworthy that most people associated with the inner caliphate of the Pole are known by cosmic names. The Pole is the center of this caliphate and may be called "The Help." "The Help" can also be one of three immediate followers of the Pole. In that case, he becomes the helper of people in their affairs. As for the two imams (leaders), one is to the right of the Helper, viewing the *malakut* (the Angelic World) and the Hidden World; and the other is to his left, viewing the reign and the Visible World.

As for the Pillars, they are geared to the universe's four main directions. The Substitute is the Pole's substitute in one of the seven districts. The Guardian of Liturgy is the Keeper of the Inner Name. The twelve men are the sovereigns over the twelve astronomical signs and whatever cosmic events are associated with them. The ninety-nine are the manifestations of God's names, thus they are directly linked to the universe; and the world, until its very end, is never without them. If God wills the destruction of the world, He will destroy them, keeping the Pole as the last one, followed by the apocalypse.[18]

If people have placed Haneen in a higher Sufi rank, then where is his rank in this cosmic orbit? The villagers say that Haneen in his unconscious state accompanies the wandering saints who control the universe and tend to its affairs. They also relate strange stories about him: "One swears that he had seen him in Merowi at a particular time, while another swore he'd caught sight of him in Karma at that very same time, though a distance of six days' journey separates the two places" (p. 44). These stories show that they place him in the rank of the Substitutes, for they are capable of substitution. "No one travels away from his station, unless he leaves a body in his image, so that no one would know he is gone; this is the meaning of substitute."[19]

Accordingly, it was not strange for Zein's mother to put it about that her son is one of God's saints, because of his friendship with Haneen. This relationship is a private one that draws people's attention since they could not

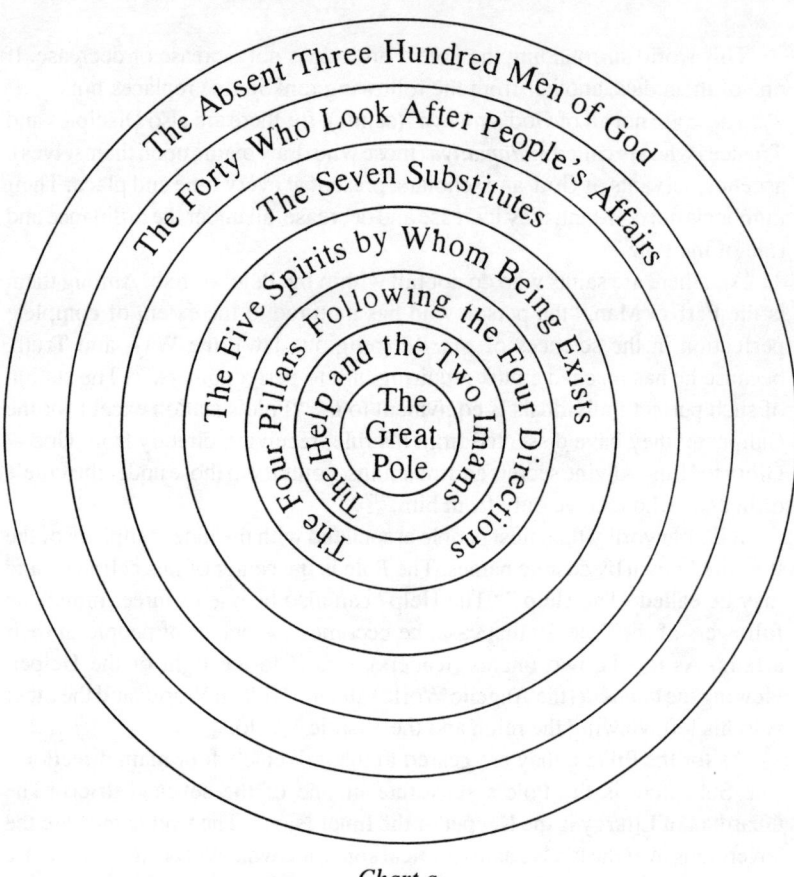

Chart a

explain it. Zein returns to his awakened state when he sees him, and they talk and laugh for hours. When the villagers try to know from Zein the secret of this friendship, he only answers, "Haneen is a man blessed of God" (p. 45).

Thus, the relationship takes the form of a certain cosmic secret, a subject that Sufis usually refrain from discussing with ordinary people. Theirs are virgin secrets denied to deluded people.[20]

Zein's attitude towards Haneen resembles that of a *murid* (disciple) towards his master sheikh. This kind of attitude is not demonstrated by Zein towards anyone else. In fact, he shows a different attitude towards another man in the village, the imam of the mosque. His attitude vis-à-vis the imam is the opposite of that towards Haneen.

Zein is never provoked by anyone in the village as much as he is by this imam, who stands in opposition to Haneen in Zein's scale. Haneen is on the positive side and the imam is on the negative side. Haneen represents pure truth, while the imam represents falsifying religious law, hence turning into a

The Mythmaker: Tayeb Salih

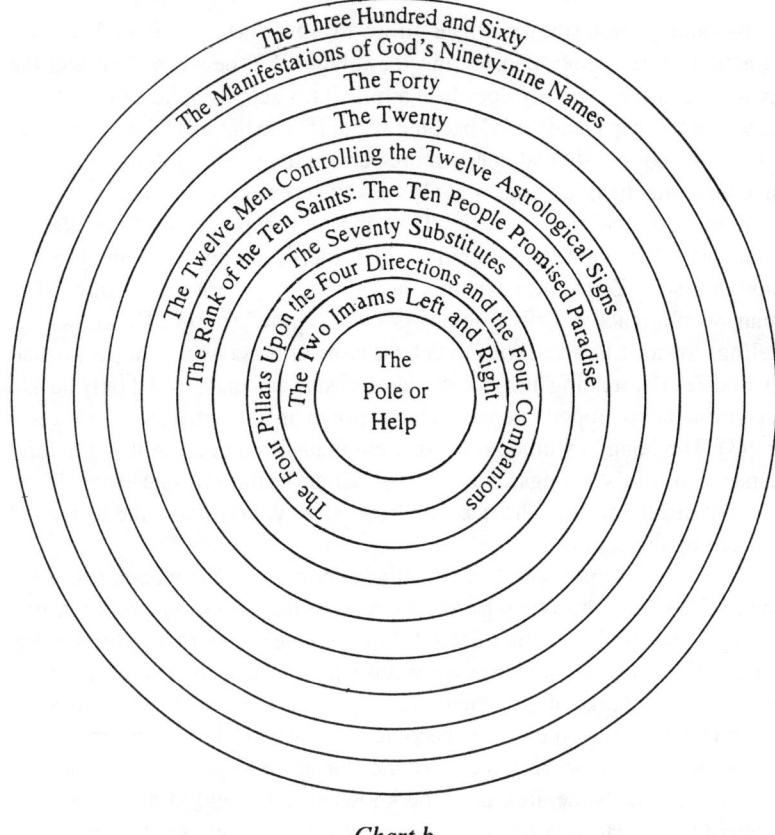

Chart b

representative of hypocrisy. Zein experiences the world between Haneen and the imam. A cosmic power attracts him to Haneen and attracts Haneen to him; the same force repels him from the imam and the imam from him.

Haneen ←── force of attraction ──→ Zein ←── force of repulsion ──→ Imam

It seems that Zein is right in his attitude, for there are numerous contrasts between Haneen and the imam. Zein's relationship with the imam may appear as contradictory to his nature, since Zein's life is full of love and he never hurts or hates anyone, with the exception of the imam. When Tayeb Salih mentions that he hated the imam, he precedes the statement with the word 'perhaps': "The Imam was perhaps the only person Zein hated" (p. 93). Why does Tayeb Salih use the word "perhaps" rather than omitting it? Is it to soften the effect of putting the term 'hate' beside Zein? Does he worry about creating a contradiction between the character of Zein—whom it seems he deeply loves—and attaching the term 'hate' firmly to him? Yet the word 'perhaps' has no actual impact when considering the relationship between Zein and the imam, because Zein really does hate him. All his actions indicate this. Thus, the words 'perhaps' and 'only' become an attempt on the part of the author not to deny the possibility that one or more persons are hated by Zein; they must have an antithetical relationship to his cosmic connection.

Zein treats the imam rudely: "If he met him approaching from afar he would leave the world clear for him.... His mere presence at a gathering was enough to spoil Zein's peace of mind and start him cursing and shouting. The imam would react to Zein's outbursts with dignity" (p. 93). He knows his feelings towards him and tries to defend himself by saying "that people had spoiled Zein by treating him as some one unusual and that [...] if only he had been brought up properly he would have grown up as normal as anyone else" (p. 93). The imam's attitude towards Zein is justified because it is a natural response to Zein's feelings about him, for he may be the only one in the village who ignores the imam. The question now is: why does Zein take that stand concerning the imam?

Zein here is expressing the collective sentiment of the village about the imam. The village, however, for special reasons does not make known its real attitude towards him because it needs him. As one villager who clings to the old traditions says, he is a "necessary evil" (p. 92). He is the village's scholar and the one in charge of implementing religious law. He spent ten years at al-Azhar University and returned to become a teacher to little boys, the mosque's imam and leader of prayers, reciter of the Qur'an, and the one who writes out marriage contracts; he appears to be knowledgeable and in touch with the depth of things. However, his knowledge of religious law is only superficial, and his relations to the villagers expose his abuse of this law. He is the only one, according to the villagers, who has no definite work to do (no field to cultivate and no business to occupy him), but lives off teaching children for a set fee collected from every family—a fee grudgingly paid. He is never interested in what interests the villagers,

> not being concerned as they were with the time for sowing wheat and the ways of irrigating it, fertilizing it, cutting and harvesting it. He was not interested in whether the corn in Abdul Hafeez's field was a good crop or a bad one, whether the watermelons in Wad Rayyes's field were large or small, what the market price was for an ardeb of beans, whether the price of onions had fallen, or why the season for pollinating the date palms had been delayed. He had by nature an aversion to such matters, and because of his ignorance of them he was also contemptuous....
> He also did not like the village people, for he used to chastise them harshly in his sermons as though avenging himself on them with an outburst of words of exhortation about the Judgment Day and punishment, Heaven and Hell-fire, disobedience to God and turning to Him

in repentance—words that passed down their throats like poison. Each would leave the mosque after Friday prayer boggle-eyed, feeling all of a sudden that the flow of life had come to a stop. Each looking at his field with its date palms, its trees and crops, would experience no feeling of joy within himself. Everything, he would feel, was incidental, transitory, the life he was leading, with its joys and sorrows, merely a bridge to another world (pp. 88–89).

Despite all these preachings, the imam himself is not a model of goodness or piety. His is the lower hand that takes from the villagers, living off their hard work. During the month of Ramadan, he dines in the houses of the wise folk among them, each one inviting him over once, giving him the skins of the animals they had slaughtered. If one of their sons gets married, they give him a fee in cash, together with a cloak or piece of cloth. Moreover, a monthly salary is collected for him by the people of the district. He takes while they give; the reason for taking as well as the taker himself are not convincing. The villagers split into clearly divided camps in relation to him: one of the camps is composed mostly of sensible-minded established men who attend all the prayers in the mosque and treat him with reserved affection. The second camp comprises seven very influential men, who possess real authority and take charge of social affairs in the village. They don't pray; one of them only goes to the prayers once a month for a visit with the purpose of inspecting the mosque's building and of giving the imam his salary. They don't respect him but refrain from verbally abusing him as much as they can, remaining courteous and civil. The third camp is made up largely of young men under twenty, educated people, rebels, and the lazy who find it difficult to perform their ablution at dawn during the winter. They pay no heed to a man whose business it is to remind people of death, and so they are openly antagonistic to him.

Zein comprises a camp all on his own, for he does not care about this man whose job is to take from others and to use religious law as a means for profit. Zein here stands alongside truth in confronting hypocrisy and with the religious law in confronting its falsification. Since Zein stands opposite to the imam, it is not surprising then that no link whatsoever appears in the story between Haneen and the imam. The only connection between the two happens as a result of an incident involving Zein and a young man from the village called Seif ad-Din.

Seif ad-Din is considered the opposite of Zein. Just as Zein represents goodness or the forces of light in the life of the village, Seif ad-Din represents evil or the forces of darkness in it. They have no mutual relationship, except in contrast. Zein never acts against Seif ad-Din; to the contrary, it is the force of evil that initiates the attack against the power of goodness to destroy it. It is natural for the forces of darkness to begin the aggression against the forces of light. During the wedding celebration of Seif ad-Din's sister, Zein comes with his usual jesting and foolery. Seif ad-Din doesn't like Zein's behavior and hits him on the head with an axe. The strike gives him a large wound close to his right eye and to his chest, and his trousers are blood-stained. Zein is taken to Merowi Hospital where he stays for two weeks.

He returns from Merowi to meet with his friends; these are the men who tend to the social affairs of the village: Abdul Hafeez, Taher Rawwasi, Abdul Samad, Hamad Wad Rayyis, Ahmed Isma'il, Sa'eed, and Mahjoub, the head of the group. They are between the ages of thirty-five and forty-five, except Ahmed Isma'il, who is twenty, and is one of them due to his sense of responsibility and manner of thinking.

Zein usually spends most of his time with this group which hates the imam. Zein's relationship with them is quite unique, for he recognizes the power of good in them and thus feels comfortable in their company. As for the group itself, its members consider him one of their major responsibilities. They are bent on keeping him away from problems, and if he faces a certain crisis, they get him out of it. They know about him more than his mother does, taking care of him and watching over him from afar. He also loves them and knows them well, while they love him and do not know him. Their love for him is mixed with sympathy and mysterious compassion.

Zein sits down with them joking about the time he spent in Merowi Hospital. While he smiles at them and they at him, and with Zein's smile widening during the chatter, the light from a large lamp is reflected on his teeth. Suddenly he jumps, as though stung by a scorpion. All his friends dash to stop him, but he is quicker. In a flash, he has seized hold of a man, raised him high in the air, and thrown him to the ground. Then he tightens his grip on his throat. This man is Seif ad-Din himself.

Everyone falls upon Zein trying to stop him. One of them seizes hold of his right arm, another his left, a third takes him by the middle, and a fourth by his legs. A fifth man bites him on the back. As for the sixth one, Mahjoub, he starts to curse when he does not know what else to do. The unusual supernatural strength that invests Zein's body makes them all helpless, for Zein is stronger than all of them put together: "Amidst clamor they heard a snorting sound emanating from Seif ad-Din's throat and saw him striking out at the air with his long legs. One of them shouted, 'He's dead; he's killed him'" (p. 62).

Zein has a lean body, but he also possesses unusual supernatural strength. All the inhabitants of the village "knew that this emaciated body concealed an extraordinary superhuman strength" (pp. 61–62). not within the normal capacity of any man. The village knows about it not from his dealings with its men, but rather from his contact with other natural forces. Once he seized a wild calf (which provoked him in the field) by the horns, "lifted it from the ground like a bundle of hay," then threw it down, breaking its bones. Also, "in one of his fits of excitement, he had torn an acacia bush up by the roots as through it were a stick of maize" (p. 61). Zein hasn't used this power against a human being before, but at this stage of his life he has to do something with this power in order to enter the world of the village.

The laughing, unconscious Zein moves to perform a serious deed and use his superhuman strength to put off the fire of evil in the village and overcome the forces of darkness. At this decisive moment, Haneen's voice suddenly rises "calm and serene above the hubbub: 'Zein the blessed, may God be pleased with you'" (p. 62). Zein has to release his grip and Seif ad-Din falls limply to the ground.

It is not that Zein returns to an awakened state because he was never really unconscious. In fact, the moment he grabs Seif is for him a moment of complete awareness of Being. The voice of Haneen exercises control over this awakening. While no one can stop Zein, Haneen's voice does. This voice is a surprise for everyone, as is "the sudden immobility of Zein. It was as though there had been a wall in front of them that suddenly collapsed" (p. 62). After a short while, they remember Seif ad-Din, who had lost consciousness, and so they all bend over trying to bring him back to life. Then they also remember Zein and see him "sitting on his backside, his hands between his knees" (p. 63), in all politeness like a student before his sheikh or as an obedient son intimidated before his father. In the meantime, Haneen places his hands with extreme tenderness on Zein's shoulder, the tenderness of a master sheikh or a father. He was talking to him in a firm voice, but affectionately: "'Zein, blessed one of God, why did you do it?'" (p. 63).

This moment is necessary in Zein's life in order that Haneen might perform the role of his teacher-guide. Zein, the non-Wayfaring Ecstatic, who possesses a tremendous supernatural force, had to control these powers and direct them well. No one was to undertake this task but the sheikh himself. People of the Sufi Way believe that a *murid* (disciple) does not arrive at higher stations without a sheikh (master). These masters are physicians of the hearts. If a physician is ignorant of a certain illness, he will harm the patient with his wrong cure, for he will not know the nature of the illness or its dangerous symptoms and thus may assign food or drink in contradiction with it. If a master knew that the "disciple someday will abandon this Way, he would forbid him to enter upon it; if, on the other hand, he was certain that the disciple will persist and reach the goal, he would then give him spiritual nourishment."[21]

The Sufis drew up a lineage of this Way which ends with the Prophet (Peace be upon him). This image, taken from the life of the Masters of the Way, explains the relationship between Zein and Haneen. Haneen's role and his very presence was to return him again to being a responsible person and to present him to the whole society. He would also return Zein's power to its proper place.

Zein fills the life of his mother and that of the whole village with happiness; wherever he went,

> like a restless soul, he had no fixed abode. Whenever, though, a
> wedding party was being held, you'd be sure to find Zein there; neither

cold nor raging storm at night, not even the swollen Nile at the time of its flooding, would keep him away. With rare sensitivity his ear would detect women's ululations from miles away, at which he would throw his robe over his shoulder and hurry off as though drawn to the source of the sound. (pp. 55–56)

Seeing Zein, people would know that some wedding party was being held in the neighborhood. At the wedding, Zein would leap and then land in the dance circle: "Suddenly the place would quicken into life, for Zein would have imbued it with new vigor." As for the people, the minute they see Zein coming from afar, they would greet him: "Welcome! Welcome! Join in the company!" (p. 56).

Seif ad-Din stands at the opposite side. He is disobedient to his parents and commits what the village calls 'grave offenses'. When there is a proper social situation, Seif ad-Din always becomes a factor of anxiety and grief. Whenever he goes, evil and corruption follow.

Seif ad-Din is the son of Badawi, the jeweler, who had built up a fortune in less than twenty years out of his own hard work, partly in lands and estates, partly in commerce along the Nile, and partly in the form of gold worn by his wife and daughter in jewelry covering their necks and arms. Seif ad-Din was brought up an only son among five daughters. Everybody pampered him until he was spoiled, and his father died displeased with him. This boy brought him great unhappiness: "He had spent a lot of money on his education," but he failed. "He had set him up in the village in a business," which went bankrupt within a month. "After this he had put him into a workshop to learn a trade, but he had run away." Then "he succeeded in having him appointed as a junior government employee," but reports came to the father "that his son was spending all his nights in a wine-shop and was seen at office only once or twice a week," and was threatened with dismissal. The father therefore had him return to the village, completely disappointed in him, "having sworn he would keep him imprisoned in the fields his whole life long, like a man in bondage" (pp. 67–68). Indeed, Seif ad-Din spends a year working in the fields, yet without abandoning his evil ways which kept increasing day by day. He knows all the places of liquor and frequents the girls who used to make it. Their straw houses built on the edge of the desert are a place for pleasure-seekers. The villagers call it the "Oasis," and Seif ad-Din knows the road to it very well.

One night, Seif, reeking of liquor, comes home to his father, who is on his prayer-rug after performing the evening prayer. He announces that he is in love with Sarra, one of the Oasis girls. His father flies into a rage, hits him, and swears that he isn't to spend another night under his roof. This conduct causes the father great pain, and he "passed the rest of his life like a man stricken with some infirmity. Pain bit into his heart, and his face became as thin and emaciated as a consumptive's. He used to say that his son had died; when sometimes, by a slip of the tongue, he mentioned his son, he did so as though he had in actual fact died" (p. 70). The boy lives after that a reckless life with prostitutes, exposing himself to all sorts of accusations. He is even accused once of killing a man in Port Sudan and is almost hanged until they find the real murderer. Then the father dies the death of all good men, as Muslims believe, in the month of Ramadan, in the final third of it—on his prayer-rug after having performed the special Ramadan prayer. He dies without writing up a will to cut his son off from his inheritance.

Before the mourning days were over, Seif ad-Din marches in on people with no luggage whatsoever, dirty and with ruffled hair. He greets no one, and all eyes avoid him. Then he begins his usual role of squandering his father's fortune and turns out Mousa the Lame, whom his father had taken care of. Zein promptly takes him under his care as if he always had to rebuild what Seif destroys in their society.

Seif lives an unrestrained life, spending a month in Khartoum, a month in Cairo, a month in Asmara, only returning to the village to sell some land or dispose of a crop. The whole village regards Seif ad-Din as a type of person alien to their way of life; his deeds are nothing but immorality and sinfulness, and he completely loses people's trust. Contrary to Zein, who is welcomed in every house, Seif finds all doors shut in his face. Even those closest to him do not trust having him in their homes lest he seduce their daughters.

The people are annoyed with Seif ad-Din from the beginning and with the Oasis he used to frequent: "In their displeasure . . . [they] burned it down, but it returned to life like the alfa plant that will not die. Though the villagers drove away those who inhabited [it], tormenting them in a variety of ways, they soon got together again, like flies alighting upon a dead cow" (p. 69). On one of his visits to the village, he finds his sister's marriage in progress, and Zein is there breathing life into it with his usual gaiety and raillery. Seif imagines him to be something akin to himself and strikes him with an axe. It does not end there, for he quarrels with the bridegroom who would have changed his mind if not for the intervention of the wise men of the village. In the last week of the marriage celebrations, Seif invites a group of his friends, and "tens of strangers whom no one had ever seen before descended upon the house: brazen women, and men with lascivious glances, vagabonds and insolent boors, who came from who knows where" (p. 73). Now that the situation has become intolerable, the villagers find themselves bound to do something: "About thirty men with stout sticks and hoes in their hands, locking the doors behind them, gave a good beating to all the intruders, and the best hiding of all they gave to Seif ad-Din. Then they threw them out into the street" (p. 72). All these tribulations happen while Zein is in the hospital.

Zein returns from the hospital in order to act and root out this evil. Because Zein stands in the camp of goodness, he has to destroy the evil represented by Seif, this evil which the village was unable to stop or curb. When he sees Seif, he moved towards him invested with the supernatural power that almost killed him, if it hadn't actually done so. The act is violent, typical of the character of Zein, for great love is usually accompanied by a great act. This action is directed at Seif; it represents the awakening of Zein, so as to be the village protector against these evils. The man who fills the village with joy has to return it once more to these joys by overcoming this evil, or rather ending the life of the man who fills his village with unhappiness and darkness. A confrontation must occur for him to stop.

Experienced Seif → confronts → pure, untouched Zein

Then the situation changes:

Pure, untouched Zein → confronts → experienced Seif

Or:

Experience → confronts → innocence

And:

Innocence → confronts → experience

The real picture is:

Evil → confronts → good

And:

Good → confronts → evil

Both are violent.

Haneen arrives at the critical moment of confrontation to present his pupil with the Sufi experience: if you love the world, you have to reform it by means of love as well.

Zein returns to his awakening, for he must now use this supernatural power granted to him in a new manner. He has traversed the first stage of the non-Wayfaring Ecstatic to the stage of the Wayfaring Ecstatic, who endures people's problems and solves them.

How does he solve them? Here lies the role of Haneen. It is not, therefore, a coincidence for him to appear at this moment. His whole presence in the story is no coincidence; rather it functions within a certain cosmic arrangement and has a distinct role: to stop Zein from killing Seif, to teach him how to confront

The Mythmaker: Tayeb Salih 117

evil, and to introduce him to his society. Haneen takes Zein aside and speaks to him in a firm voice that is also affectionate: "Zein, blessed one of God, why did you do it?" (p. 63). Haneen is in fact providing a cosmic introduction of Zein to his society, for Haneen is the mature man who has already traversed this stage. Haneen begins to joke with Zein and asks him about what he has done in the wedding of Seif's sister. Zein answers, "His sister had her eye on me. Why did they want to marry her off to that good-for-nothing fellow?" (p. 63). Ahmed Isma'il, one of the six men who witnessed the incident, cannot help laughing. His laughter is tinged with mockery and scorn for Zein, but Haneen ignores it and says in a more gentle and tender voice, "All the girls are after you, blessed one of God. Tomorrow you'll be marrying the best girl in the village" (p. 64). Haneen asks Zein to make up with Seif; he rises without hesitation and apologizes to him. Seif ad-Din also apologizes to Zein and kisses his head, then seizes Haneen's hand and kisses it. The six men come along; each silently takes hold of Haneen's hand and kisses it, while Haneen says in his soft gentle voice, "God bless you. God bring down His blessings upon you" (p. 65). Then he rises and takes up his pitcher. Mahjoub hastens to invite him over to his house, but Haneen gently refuses. Clasping Zein's shoulder with the other hand, they both make off into the darkness. Zein is now the chosen man, and that night means an end to Seif ad-Din's work and a beginning to Zein, a new beginning of what follows the crossing over.

In the view of his society, Zein has crossed over the stage of childhood and adolescence to manhood, and—according to Sufis—from the stage of the non-Wayfaring Ecstatic to the stage of Wayfaring Ecstatic. Haneen introduces Zein to his society in the image of a blessed one and associates him with the miracle of bringing Seif ad-Din to life, or at least preventing his killing. When Zein seizes his throat and chokes him with his hands, the men cannot stop him, and one of them screams, "He's dead; he's killed him" (p. 62). Some of them are firmly convinced that Seif ad-Din is indeed dead and has fallen lifeless to the ground. Seif himself later confirms this and says that he was really dead. The coming of Haneen represented a miracle because he was the only one who could control Zein's action and stop what the village might have called a murder, judging by outer laws. On the other hand, Zein considered it an act of ridding the village of the forces of evil.

Haneen arrives to undertake three tasks simultaneously: to stop a crime, to teach Zein self-control, by turning him into the Wayfaring Ecstatic, and to introduce him to his society. Haneen, in presenting Zein to society, is not doing something new, for there exists a general and universal cosmic system, in which the role of the Guide is initiating the person with the superhuman power. This phenomenon occurs in the lives of the majority of prophets and many saints and *awilya'*.

When Moses came of age, God granted him wisdom and knowledge as heavenly gifts without any human interference. He also granted him superhuman strength, beyond the reach of any other man, which caused him unintentionally to kill an Egyptian: "And he entered the City, at a time when its people were not watching, and he found there two men fighting—one of his own people, and the other of his foes. The man of his own people appealed to him against his foe, and Moses struck with his fist and killed him. He said: This is a work of Satan, for he is an enemy that manifestly misleads."[22] Moses knew that killing the man was the devil's work, that is, this superhuman strength was misused and so he asked forgiveness for his deed. He ran away to Madyan, and there met a man cognizant of God. Some sources maintain that he was a prophet from God, namely Shu'ayb, with whom Moses lived for ten years.[23]

These years constituted a learning period for Moses so that he would become qualified and prepared to undertake his mission later. He did start on his mission after leaving Shu'ayb. "A fire appeared to him, when he saw it, he took it for real fire, yet it was from the light of God—a special light that extended from the heavens down to a great boxthorn tree."[24] "When Moses had fulfilled the term and was traveling with his family, he perceived a fire in the direction of Mount Tur. He said to his family, 'Stay here, I perceive a fire; I hope to bring you news or a firebrand that you may warm yourselves.' But when he came to the fire, he was called from the right bank of the valley from a tree in hallowed ground: 'O Moses! Verily I am Allah, the Lord of the Worlds.'"[25]

John the Baptist performed a role, similar to that of Shu'ayb, in the life of Christ, for he also introduced him to the people. It is mentioned that while John was baptizing the people, the Jews were thinking that he might be Christ. "John answered them all: 'I baptize you with water; but he who is mightier than I is coming, the thong of whose sandals I am not worthy to untie; he will baptize you with the Holy Spirit and with fire. His winnowing fork is in his hand, to clear his threshing floor, and to gather the wheat into his granary, but the chaff he will burn with unquenchable fire.' So, with many other exhortations, he preached good news to the people."[26]

So John did not only announce the coming of Christ, but he also gave him precedence over himself in front of the public whom he was baptizing. Christ had come to him to be baptized, but John prevented him saying: "'I need to be baptized by you, and do you come to me?' But Jesus answered him, 'Let it be so now; for thus it is fitting for us to fulfill all righteousness.' Then he consented."[27]

When John baptized him, "the heavens were opened and he saw the Spirit of God descending like a dove, and alighting on him; and lo, a voice from heaven, saying, 'This is my beloved Son, with whom I am well pleased.'"[28] It was not only John who helped Christ in his self-recognition—that divine voice as well made the whole process complete. When John died, Jesus left Nazareth for Galilee and began to preach faith to the people.

Muhammad also heard this voice from Gabriel, saying to him, "O, Muhammad, you are the messenger of God."[29] Muhammad's experience—as well as the experience of his people with divine revelation—was limited, so he needed certitude to come to him from outside the heavenly realm, from a human. Waraqa ibn Nawfal played this role when the prophet and his wife Khadija went to him. After the prophet told him of what he saw and heard, he said, "This is the Law that descended upon Moses ibn Umran."[30]

Muhammad recognized himself by means of Waraqa ibn Nawfal; he realized the meaning of this revelation and that he was the awaited Prophet. The conversation that went on between them, though brief, contains a prophecy concerning the future of the Prophet and the Message. It was related by the Prophet that Waraqa said, "'I wish I could be alive when your people turn you out.' I said, 'Are my people going to turn me out?' He said: 'Yes, no one has ever brought something like what you are bringing to the people without incurring animosity. If I were to live to this day, I would strongly support you.'"[31] Hence, Shu'ayb, John, and Waraqa all performed the role of introducing these prophets. It also happened very often in the Sufi world that a sheikh (master) introduced his disciple to the people. Tayeb Salih relates such a situation between Hasan ibn 'Isa ibn Dau al-Beit and Sheikh Nasrullah Wad Habib.

This Hasan is the father of al-Taher Wad al-Rawwas, one of Zein's friends. The village disagrees over his lineage, and it was once said that he used to be a slave. Yet the villagers all agree that he was a pious saint of God; his friendship with Sheikh Nasrullah Wad Habib began when he was a young lad over fifteen and under twenty. It may be that he was wandering far in the open space to worship and practice humility. In fact, God only knows, since he was not visible in the village—as if not present in it at all. One day in the study ring of Sheikh Nasrullah Wad Habib after the Dawn Prayer (for this was his habit, to stay for an hour after Dawn and Night Prayers guiding people and answering their questions), suddenly the sheikh falls silent and his face changes. He then shouts loudly, "Come to us Bilal, come to us Bilal!" The people do not understand what the sheikh wants. All of a sudden, a man, as if struck by heavenly revelation, says, "The sheikh means Hasan." The man tries to describe Hasan to the people until the matter is clear to them, and they all shout, "Hasan, O God, O God . . . the slave?" At that moment, Sheikh Nasrullah, in a semi-unconscious state, speaks to them, "By God, if you knew about him what I know, your hearts would be shattered and you would be stricken with terror and confusion. He has seen, heard, and reached stations which hearts yearn in anguish to attain. By God, if Bilal had asked God, He would have granted him; and if he requested of the Truth Himself—may He be exalted—to make you sink into the ground, He would do it." The sheikh utters those words in a voice that strikes his audience with fright, then he calls out to Bilal once more. People swear that the minute Sheikh Nasrullah Wad Habib finished calling, they heard a voice shouting at the mosque's door: "Here I am at your service; here I am at your service." Hasan, who was named Bilal ever since that day, enters covered with the dust of traveling, a long wooden rosary around his neck and a piece of leather in his hand. He bends over the sheikh's feet, kissing them and sobbing: "Here I am at your service; here I am at your service." The sheikh helps him up, embraces him and kisses him on his cheeks and between his eyes, then says to him with tearful eyes: "Why, brother, do you go so far away from me? Haven't you and I suffered enough? Treat yourself gently, my dear one, for you have come to occupy a rank that but few of the humble lovers have attained. I run and scarcely keep up with your dust."[32] Bilal weeps hard until he almost expires and keeps repeating, "Master, do not say such things. You are the Axis [Pole]. You are master of the time and I am your servant and your slave."[33]

Haneen's going with Zein to his house is not a compliment from the master but rather a necessity. After Zein's violent action with Seif, it is necessary that the master have a private meeting with his disciple. What can the master say to the disciple or vice-versa? There is no doubt that between master and disciple there are certain secrets which they do not talk about in front of people. This private talk is extremely important to the future of the disciple—for the non-Wayfaring Ecstatic to become whole, a Wayfaring Ecstatic. The story does not reveal this conversation or any other that took place in private between Haneen and Zein. Yet a talk takes place between Bilal and Sheikh Nasrullah in the story of *Meryoud*, which may come close to what went on between Haneen and Zein. The sheikh says, "O Bilal, you are the slave of God just as I am the slave of God. We are brothers in respect of God. You and I are like specks of dust on the kingdom of God, may He be glorified. And on the day when a father will not be compensated for by his son, it is possible that your scale will outweigh mine in the balances of the Truth, may his majesty be exalted. My scale outweighs yours in the balances of the people of the world, but your scale, O Bilal, will outweigh mine in the Balance of Justice. I, Bilal, run like a thirsty camel in order to attain a drop from the Cup of the Presence, while you, Bilal, have drunk to the full. You have heard and you have seen; you have crossed and you have passed over; and when the voice called you, you said yes."[34]

Haneen introduces Zein in words and action. He always calls him "Zein, blessed one of God" (p. 63), and asks him once, "Zein, blessed one of God, why did you do it?" (p. 63). He also follows the first phrase with, "May God be blessed with you."

The question shows his disapproval of Zein's action in overcoming evil this way. In other words, this means the sheikh's disapproval of the disciple's action. And when Mahjoub says to Zein with contempt, "Who would marry this imbecile?" (p. 64), Haneen feels offended for his disciple and gives Mahjoub a stern look at which he trembles with fear to the extent that he spontaneously corrects himself and calls Zein blessed: "Zein's no imbecile, Zein's a blessed person." Haneen leaves them, and seizing Zein's hand, he announces that his dinner is to be at the house of the blessed one (pp. 64–65).

There are unknown secrets between them, and the six men who witness the event are left in a state of shock and disbelief, looking at each other and shaking their heads. It seems that the word "blessed" is not enough confirmation of Zein's heavenly position, so it is necessary that it be followed by an action to support it. For, when Haneen calls out "God bless you all. May God bring you His blessing" (p. 76–77), it is as though supernatural powers in the heavens had answered in one voice "Amen" (p. 77). After that, miracles happen to them and to the village in quick succession. This is a sign from Heaven that Zein is indeed the "blessed" man in the village, for whom the miracles take place. Haneen dies shortly after the incident, after he completes his role and finishes the task. Blessings encompass the whole village. The first miracle comes with the change in Seif; he sincerely repents following this incident as though born anew. The following morning he goes to his mother, kisses her head, and weeps lengthily before her. He then brings together all his paternal and maternal uncles, repents and asks forgiveness before them. As an assurance of his repentance he takes all that remains of his father's fortune from his own charge and makes his senior uncle a trustee over it, until he becomes wholly fit for carrying out his responsibilities. He also starts frequenting the mosque, and goes to Mousa the Lame to ask his forgiveness. Finally, he makes a resolution to perform the pilgrimage. The man's social image is completed by marrying his cousin. Seif's return to the circle of society is the great lesson Haneen teaches to Zein. Haneen destroys evil in the whole village by returning Seif to the community. Though Seif does not follow Haneen's spiritual way and turns instead towards the imam, Haneen is not as concerned about what specific path Seif takes as much as with Seif's return to the community. Seif would not take the spiritual direction anyway. In fact, his inability to see the spiritual path makes him stand out in Tayeb Salih's *Bandarshah*—which depicts a time subsequent to that in *The Wedding of Zein*—in which he has left the imam, turned to politics, and is about to become a representative in Parliament. He "oscillated between being on the right path and being astray,"[35] but he never returned to his old ways and became like any other ordinary member of the society.

As for the remaining seven men who witness the incident and who receive Haneen's blessing, they also see one miracle after another. The village had never experienced such an auspicious and fruitful year as "Haneen's year," as they begin to call it. That year, the government permits the village to cultivate cotton, the price of which soars to an unprecedented level, until the profits of one of the incident's witnesses alone, Mahjoub, reach more than a thousand pounds. For no particular reason, the government also sets up a large army camp in the desert two miles from the village. So the benefits from supplying the army with vegetables, meat, fruit, and milk, and the prices of the village's agricultural products rise considerably. The government also decides to build in their village a large hospital, a secondary school, and an agricultural school, which enhance the state of prosperity. Furthermore, only two months after Haneen's death, the government also decides to organize their lands into a large agricultural project, and so some lands receive water that they had not seen for ages.

The villagers are struck by what happens to their village—one miracle after another—and they ascribe it all to Haneen and his relationship with Zein. However, an important event arrests their attention even more than all those miracles: Zein's marriage. Zein, the dervish—whose proximity never threatened the maidens and who was trusted by their parents—is to marry the most beautiful girl in the village: Ni'ma, his cousin. Only three people object to the marriage, each for a different reason.

The first one is Amna, who is not on good terms with Ni'ma's mother, and yet has to go to her and request her daughter's hand in marriage to her son Idris. Idris is fond of Ni'ma. However, the mother tells Amna "that Ni'ma was still a minor and not of marriageable age. And here they were marrying her to this boorish dolt of a man—Zein of all people. Amna felt that the marriage was an intentional affront directed against her personally" (pp. 49–50). The second person is the school's headmaster. Like Amna, he feels that a personal affront has been directed against him. He had asked for Ni'ma's hand in marriage, and her father rejected him because of his age. When he hears of the girl's engagement to Zein, he can't work and is surprised that Ni'ma's father would marry her to a dervish who is unfit for marriage (p. 84). The third person is the imam; he finds here an opportunity to make known his disdain of Zein, the only man in the village the imam really fears because he cannot take him under his wing or subdue him. While he is capable of attacking his opposers in his sermons because they transgress religious and social traditions, he cannot attack Zein on any grounds except to inform Ni'ma's father that he isn't a man for matrimony (p. 103).

As for the rest of the villagers, no one pokes fun at this, but they shake their heads, and wonder further as if they had been expecting such a matter after Haneen's incident. They regard the wedding as a fulfillment of Haneen's prophecy that Zein was going to marry the best girl in the village (p. 64).

Ni'ma's marriage to Zein is quite the natural thing, for she is the most suitable woman to become his wife. She was prepared by means of a cosmic power to be the *wali*'s (saint's) wife. Ni'ma was within the realm of Zein's awakening; she was one girl about whom Zein never talked or joked, and whenever he saw her approaching, he would return to an awakened state, stop his foolery and jesting, and run away from her path (p. 47). She used to be jealous and hate it when he joked with women. She found him once joking as usual with them, so she chided him saying, "Why don't you give up this nonsensical chatter and go off and get on with your work?" (p. 47). Zein never made a reply, but regained his awakened state, stopped laughing, lowered his head in shame, and stole away from the women.

The Mythmaker: Tayeb Salih

Ni'ma is quite a unique girl in the village. She is the only girl to go to the Qur'anic school to learn reading and writing, praying, and reciting the Qur'an. Something inside her makes her different from the rest of the girls. She used to dream about a great sacrifice, not knowing at her young age the exact nature of this sacrifice, yet she knew somehow that she would undertake it someday. She used to experience a strange sensation when reading the Chapter of Mary (in the Qur'an). She also felt close to the prophet Job and upon reaching the verse "and we restored unto him his family, and as many more with them, through our mercy," she would feel a great elation. She was attracted by the idea of a wife supporting her husband, and would picture Rahma (Mercy) to herself as a woman of rare beauty, dedicated to the service of her husband.

Ni'ma grows up with this feeling until she reaches sixteen years of age and her mother begins to talk to her about the men proposing to her. They are all well-disposed men of esteemed social status—the rich, the educated, and the handsome. Ni'ma rejected them all.

Her family realized that she may have been keeping a secret from them. Her father was angry at her once because she refused a suitable young man for no reason. He was about to slap her but suddenly stopped. Her father sensed that the girl was neither disobedient nor rebellious, but that she was destined by an inner counsel to embark upon something from which no one could deflect her (p. 54).

This mystery deep inside of Ni'ma concerning the man she would marry is encompassed by the word "fate." It is a mystery that is linked to a cosmic secret which she herself is unable to discern. When she thinks of marriage, she feels that it will come unexpectedly and unplanned, just as God's divine decree falls upon His servants—just as people are born, fall ill, and die. Just as the Nile floods its banks, storms rage, date-palms produce their fruit each year, wheat sprouts, rain pours down, and seasons change, so would her marriage be: a destiny preordained on a tablet by God before she was born, before the Nile began to flow, before God created the earth and all that is on it.

She felt that her marriage would be "a great responsibility placed upon her shoulders." She never dreamed like other girls "of the knight who would tether his steed outside the house one evening and come in and snatch her off from amidst the family, fleeing with her far away to magical worlds." She does not know who her man will be. He "might well be already married with children and would take her as his second wife; he might be a handsome and educated young man; or yet a farmer from among the ordinary folk of the village, with cracked hands and feet." And who knows; he could be Zein (pp. 53–54). She has a special feeling towards Zein, and used to observe him from afar in his "horseplay and raillery" with her angry yet beautiful eyes (p. 47). Unlike the rest of the village's women, she takes him seriously just as he takes her seriously, like no other girl in the village.

Zein, the man qualified to continue the role of Haneen, is in need of a woman like her, prepared to have a message. Her message is that of the wife who is also the protector of her husband, who can provide him with emotional stability in order to perform his heavenly role within his society and to be transformed from the dazed, enraptured figure to the awakened one.

The Islamic tradition endows marriage with great value, for it is a completion of the other half of one's religion. In that, it differs from Christianity, which honors virginity and most of whose saints are monks. It is true that some Sufis did not marry, but this is not the pattern. Tayeb Salih narrates in *Meryoud* that a woman fell deeply in love with Bilal, and not knowing what to do went complaining to Sheikh Nasr. He counseled Bilal to marry her; his reply was, "O master, I would sacrifice my life for you, but there is no secret about the circumstances of your humble servant that is hidden from you. I am walking in the paths of the people of the Presence and yet you order me to do the actions of the people of this world."[36] The sheikh did not accept his disciple's opinion because there was a divine wisdom behind this love. He told him,

> O Bilal, to walk in the paths of union is like ascending in rugged mountain tracks. The wish of the Truth is obscure, O Bilal; the love of certain servants is from the love of God, and this poor woman loves you in a way that I do not find is of the kind of love of this world's people, and it may be that the truth has sent her to you for some purpose of His. Perhaps He, glorified be His wish, wants you to test the extent of your own love in the balance of this poor woman's love for you. Either you recover and your journey is interrupted, or your thirst for the cup of Eternal Love is increased when He, be He glorified and exalted, will have accomplished His wish by subjecting you to His ultimate will.[37]

Bilal submitted to his sheikh and married her, but only for one night, then took his sheikh's permission to release her.

Bilal here is different from Zein. Bilal is a Wayfaring Ecstatic with moments of awakening. He also goes through moments of effacement. Zein, however, is a non-Wayfaring Ecstatic, whose moments are all moments of effacement. Hence, in the time of his conversion to a Wayfaring Ecstatic, he needs to deal with society in the form of a marital relationship.

Hawwa, the woman who was attached to Bilal, is also different from Ni'ma. She loves to joke, is pleasant of speech, and is openly adorned. There is a little flirtation and explicitness in her manner of talking, which leads many to pursue her. However, the woman refuses and stays away, not accepting any of them in lawful or unlawful relations. When she falls in love with Bilal, she starts to pursue him during his prayers and worship. Hawwa represents temptation to Bilal, and so his marriage to her is a test of his piety, as the sheikh told him, "Either you recover and your journey is interrupted, or your thirst for the cup of Eternal Love is increased." Bilal does go through the experience successfully; as for the woman, her marriage to Bilal is a new experience out of which she emerges an ascetic. She refuses to remarry and "applied herself

The Mythmaker: Tayeb Salih

to bringing up her son [from Bilal], doing so with that devotion known only to single-minded Sufis."[38] She greatly differs from Ni'ma, who did not represent a temptation to Zein, but stability and wholeness.

The girl begins to discern that gradually, for when Zein used to cross her mind, she would experience "a sensation of warmth in her heart, of the kind a mother feels for her children. Intermingled with it was another feeling: of pity. She would see Zein as being an orphan in need of being cared for. In any case he was her cousin, and there was nothing unusual in the fact that she should feel concern for him" (p. 55). All those feelings prepare Ni'ma to turn with all her being to Zein, to believe that he is her man, and that she is prepared to be his wife. In that case, no power would be able to stop her from making the decision.

The decisive moment comes when Zein returns from the Merowi Hospital, where he stayed for two weeks as a result of Seif's blow. Zein returns with a clean face and shiny white clothes. When he laughs, people do not see in his mouth the usual two teeth, but rather a set of teeth in his lower jaw. It is as if Zein had become another person. Ni'ma looks at him and finds him not lacking in handsomeness (p. 58). She begins to look upon him as a real man, and so the situation develops towards marriage.

The village relates stories about this marriage. Among these stories is one about the girl seeing Haneen in her dreams, who had said to her, "'Marry Zein. The girl who marries Zein won't regret it.' On waking up next morning, she told her father and mother, who came to a unanimous decision" (p. 107). Another story held that Zein is the one who proposed to Ni'ma and that he ran into her on the road, so he asked her, "Cousin, will you marry me?" She said, "Yes." He went to his uncle to talk to him, and he accepted (p. 108). A third account tells of Ni'ma finding Zein in a gathering of women with whom he was flirting and joking: she "glared severely at them and said: 'Tomorrow all of you will eat and drink at his wedding.' She went to speak to her father and mother, who had both given their consent" (p. 107).

These three accounts demonstrate the general opinion in the village concerning Zein's marriage: one of them refers it to Haneen; another makes Zein fully conscious and aware of what he says when he proposes to his cousin; the third story capitalizes on the feeling of sympathy.

At any rate, the three accounts can be credible but they are not true. The truth is that Ni'ma after Haneen's death became fully prepared to be Zein's wife. His role in the world of the spirit, which he inherited from Haneen, could now begin. The girl has decided with obstinacy and independence, which are in keeping with her character—and perhaps because of sympathy for Zein or the desire for sacrifice— to marry him. In any case, this does not exclude the possibility that a hidden force is driving her towards Zein.

It is natural that Ni'ma is the one to propose to Zein and not the vice versa; he is her choice and she wants to defend this choice against any opposition.

When the imam informs her father of his opinion concerning Ni'ma's marriage to Zein, she not only tells Zein of what the imam said, but tells him of what will happen in the future, as if he did not know it: "On Thursday, they'll marry me to you. You and I will be man and wife. We'll live together and be together" (p. 103).

What Ni'ma does makes the men blessed by Haneen, and those close to Zein, respect her even more. One of them comments that she is like no other girl and that she will keep Zein "on the straight and narrow all right" (p. 104). All the men agree that she is the girl Zein needs to guide him, relieve him of the responsibilities of daily life, and lead him on towards new life.

The day of the wedding is a new day in the history of the village. It is like a celebration for the whole village, not just for Zein's marriage—it is a celebration of his new life as the true successor of Haneen. Joy prevails in all the houses of the village, and all of its sons participate in the festivities, even those who were hurt by the marriage. Ululations come out of Zein's house, started by his mother, then shortly all her neighbors, friends, family, and relatives join in. And so does everyone who wished her well (pp. 106, 108–9). Not a woman is present who does not ululate at Zein's wedding; even Amna ululates from extreme annoyance (p. 109). Dumb Ashmana also ululates in joy. People come from everywhere to celebrate Zein's wedding. "The Koz bedouin flocked in to the feast, racing each other on their camels.... The Talha people came along to the very last man.... People came from up the river and people came from down the river. People came across the Nile in boats, and others came from the fringe villages on horses, donkeys, and in lorries.... The town's merchants came, as did its government employees, its notables and leading men. There attended too the gypsies who camped out in the forest" (pp. 111–12).

The story does not mention whether these people were invited or came on their own. However, they appear as if driven to come on their own, not just for a wedding but to witness a special celebration for a man with a special place in their hearts. In fact, the party looks like a *mawlid* (saint's festival). "The whole quarter heaved in its every nook and cranny, and the houses filled up with visitors. There was not a house in which a party of people was not being put up [... such as] the Headmaster's house ... and that of the Cadi" (pp. 109–10).

Joy fills the whole area and invigorates all the guests. Men beat the drums, waving their hands, shaking sticks and swords, and the Omda fires some shots in the air. That day is filled with contradictions: the slave-girls of the Oasis sing and dance; sheikhs recite the Qur'an in another house; singers beat on drums in a third house; and young men get drunk in a fourth house. The story describes this wedding as a collection of celebrations, not just one (p. 113). It may appear as if it is contradictory for all this to occur in the celebration of the crowning of a new saint. However, the reality is that the scene itself makes of the wedding a *mawlid* holiday, a birth anniversary of a saint in the traditional manner. Everyone finds a place in it, for the saint never rejects anyone.

A glance at the singing that goes on that night reveals it as a real night for a saint. This is the love lyric the singer Fattouma sings:

> The luscious dates that early ripen
> Steal my sleep and my thoughts quicken. (p. 113)

or:

> The girl who made Gushabi her home
> All night long for her I yearn. (p. 114)

These love lyrics do not greatly differ from Sufi love poetry, and so this singing becomes a form of *sama'* (mystical concert). And when Zein spontaneously enters the dance floor to dance, he is actually performing mystical movements to the tunes of the *sama'*. Fattouma sings the praises of Zein:

> Speak, O tongue, goblets of praise bring forth.
> Charming Zein the town a scene of merriment has made. (p. 112)

Fattouma praises a saint who has brought joy onto his village. It is also natural that the chanter should sing the praises of the Prophet:

> Blessed be he who takes his provisions and journeys
> In the plain of Fereish, seeing the beckoning banner,
> To visit Hussein's grandfather. (p. 117)

People's eyes fill with tears, and some break into sobs, especially those who had performed the pilgrimage and visited Mecca, Medina, and the other places described by the chanter. He continues to chant:

> Blessed be he who takes his provisions and urges on his camels
> And who, reaching the plain of Fereish, calls out for joy on seeing the banner.
> He visits Hussein's grandfather.
> Before him raisins, figs and watermelons, they spread—
> And cups of wine, "Go ahead and drink," they said
> When he visits Hussein's grandfather. (p. 117)

The wedding is a genuine mystical occasion in the life of a Sufi, as well as an occasion in the life of the whole village, revealing to the people themselves their own world. They change from dance to praise and from praise to dance; their feet moving on the dance floor, and their enthusiasm running high. They experience a moment of silence, and then in the circle of praise they live the yearning of love and have tears in their eyes. These juxtaposed states can only occur in the celebration of a saint's birthday.

After all this, do the people fully realize who Zein is, or do they still consider the event an ordinary wedding? The story shows that since Haneen had stopped him from killing Seif ad-Din, the people do begin to realize Zein's true status. The mention of Zein and sainthood had occurred at the beginning of the story in association with his mother: she had made it known among the people that her son was a pious saint of God, and this statement is reinforced in the story with the mention that "this belief was strengthened by Zein's friendship with Haneen" (p. 44). Haneen himself is presented to us in no uncertain way as a 'true saint'. The story also depicts Zein's friendships with those considered by the village as abnormal, who are in need of Zein. Finally, when Haneen comes to stop Zein from killing Seif, there remains no doubt whatsoever that there is a special cosmic link between them.

When Zein looks at the imam during the writing up of the marriage contract, the story indicates that perhaps he feels uneasy by these looks. Immediately following this, the story in an informative statement confirms that the imam knows that deep within Zein there is a glimmer of light, for "everyone knew that Zein was a favorite of Haneen and that Haneen was a holy man who would not frequent the company of someone unless he had perceived in him a glimmering of spiritual light" (p. 94). Haneen's control over him when he hit Seif is the strongest proof of that. This incident becomes a tale to be related by the men who witnessed it. Perhaps the most important incident that has the greatest effect on them is the marriage of Zein. Everyone realizes that this marriage is no trivial matter but a universal cosmic affair. And when the Headmaster who was opposed to the marriage says that "Zein is a dervish who shouldn't be marrying at all" (p. 81). Abdul Samad responds with profound conviction, "You should, sir, be careful when talking of Zein. He is a man blessed of God and was a friend of that devout man Haneen" (p. 82).

The situation is made crystal-clear at the night of Zein's wedding, and the cosmic link between Zein and Haneen, as well as the future role of the former, also becomes evident. In the middle of the celebration Zein disappears from sight, as Mahjoub notices, and so he asks his friends, but they don't know where Zein is. They begin looking for him, though without attracting anyone's attention. They search everywhere, for they still believe that Zein could well forget anything, even the matter of his own marriage. They look for him in the desert that lies opposite the quarter, and some of them head towards the fields, right up to the Nile's bank. They enter the houses, going through them house by house; they look under the trunk of every date palm, every tree. There remains only the mosque, though never in his life had Zein entered it. They go to look there, but in vain. They lose all hope: he must have taken off, but where to? They do not know whither he could have escaped, for the image of the dazed Zein was still alive in their minds. "Suddenly an idea struck Mahjoub. 'The cemetery!' he shouted. They did not believe it. What would Zein be doing in the cemetery at that time of night? But when Mahjoub went off ahead, they followed him" (p. 119). The fact that Mahjoub thinks of the cemetery as a probable place demonstrates his implied admission and recognition of Zein as a true saint. Mahjoub is the most rational of them all and has little faith in miracles and saints.

He has to see for himself, and the other men with him as well, the kind of relationship between Zein and Haneen after the latter's death. It seems that when he thinks of the cemetery as a place that Zein would resort to, he is implicitly admitting the position of saints as well as accepting the new reality of Zein's character. Mahjoub's relationship—as well as his friends' relationship with Zein—is one of sympathy. Now, however, he realizes that when he gives Zein sympathy, he is really not offering him much because he receives from him love and blessedness.

The men arrive at the cemetery and hear a faint sound of sobbing coming from the large mysterious and forbidding tomb in the middle. Mahjoub walks up to the figure of Zein bent over Haneen's grave. Mahjoub asks him, while the others stand watching in bewilderment, why he is there. This is the kind of bewilderment they had felt about Zein all his life. Zein's presence here is a manifestation of loyalty to his master sheikh and a wish to have him physically there that night. Zein here is in full awareness of Being, and when he goes out with them he is also fully conscious.

Tayeb Salih is careful to depict Zein that night "like a cock—indeed, as resplendent as a peacock" (p. 112). The clothes that the villagers give him— the white caftan and green sash—demonstrate their awareness of the entire situation. He stands amidst them, with a long crocodile-leather whip in his hands. The crocodile had appeared before Seif lost consciousness: "He saw a vast crocodile the size of a large ox with its mouth agape; the crocodile's jaws closed upon him, then came a wave so large it seemed like a mountain and plunged the crocodile down into a vast bottomless pit" (p. 66). The crocodile is a symbol of fertility among the people of the Nile valley, as well as a source of bounty and a good omen. People put it stuffed in front of their shops. It is also one of the ancient Egyptian deities representing the Nile. Thus, the figure of the crocodile had attacked Seif ad-Din, the evil-doer, to show him the punishment he would get if he persisted in his evil. Its skin in the hand of Zein is a whip that Zein can wield as he wishes.

These images are enhanced further by the ring on Zein's finger which he wears that night. The ring has a ruby stone in the form of a snake head. The snake, which is not poisonous, represents to the masses the protecting Saint, and to some it is the Spiritual Pole. Zein has now fully introduced himself to his society.

He returns to the dancefloor and leaps high in the air, landing right in the middle, with his face still wet with tears. He looks as though he is truly responding to the Sufi *sama'* with certain dance movements. The place bubbles with excitement, Zein having transfused into it new energy, yelling at the top of his voice, "Make known the good news! Make known the good news!" (p. 120). It is as if he grants all—the pious as well as the sinner— blessedness and security. Tonight, he is in control of their spiritual world.

If the myth of the saint is completed by this wedding, does this mean that Zein's life's story comes to an end? Tayeb Salih does not need to talk about him after his marriage, for he has told his life's story when talking about Haneen.

At this moment, Zein is living the life and treading the way of Haneen—in fact he is Haneen himself. The myth of a saint in the stage prior to the crossover is put under the name of Zein, while his myth after the crossover can be put under the name of Haneen.

The myth of the saint from his birth until his death is depicted in the story of *The Wedding of Zein*, yet the story does not show how the saint dies and how people received the news of his death. The author has clarified that side of the myth in the story *Meryoud*, in which he relates the death of Bilal, the *wali* (saint). This picture is perhaps the most cheerful picture ever drawn of death.

After the death of his sheikh, Bilal gives up making the call to prayers and going to the mosque, and he disappears from sight. Then, one day, the people awake to his voice calling out from the minaret of the mosque, a voice that those who hear it describe as being like that of a conglomeration of voices coming from diverse places and bygone ages. Wad Hamid trembles at the vastness of the voice that begins to extend and grow bigger, to grow higher and wider, as though it were some other city in some other time. Every one of them rises from bed, makes ablutions, and hurries off to the source of the voice, as though the call that dawn were meant for each one alone. As they stand ready for prayers, they see Bilal wearing a shroud. The mosque is crammed with a great concourse of people, inhabitants from the village and people from outside. It is a remarkable event. As he used to do in the days of Wad Habib, he starts the prayers with the words "God is great," then takes his place to lead them in prayer. He does not stand in front of them as the sheikh used to do, but takes his place among them in the center of the first row, dressed as he was. He recites the "Chapter of the Forenoon" in a joyful voice, the verses coming out as radiant as clusters of grapes. After prayers he turns to them with a happy, glowing face and says farewell to them, asking of them that they should not carry him on a bier but on their shoulders and that they should bury him alongside his sheikh, Nasrullah Wad Habib, while leaving between the sheikh and him such space as the dictates of respect and reverence demanded. After that he stretches out on the ground by the prayer niche, utters the avowal of faith, and asks forgiveness of God, while the people look on in awe and astonishment; then he raises his hands as though shaking hands with someone and yields up his soul to its Maker. They bear him off, from that place in the mosque, to the cemetery, and they say that so many people walk in his funeral procession it is as though the earth had opened up and spilt them out. They bury him, as they relate, at sunset.[39]

The matter does not end there; rather, the full cosmic picture of the saint's death is only completed at the moment of praying over his body. The image of Sheikh Nasrullah comes to everyone's mind, and people mention that the person who led the prayer was indeed similarly dignified, though his face was seen by no one. However, most of them said it was as if he was indeed Sheikh Nasrullah Wad Habib. Did the sheikh come back from the world of the spirits

The Mythmaker: Tayeb Salih

to pray for his disciple? "They narrated that there was not a man that witnessed the death of Bilal who did not wish his own soul might be snatched away at that very instant, for he had made the taste of death in their mouths to be as that of honey."[40]

The world of the spirits, according to the Sufis, is a hidden world. A Sufi's life does not end with his death, for another side is born with the saint's death, namely, his role in 'formation'. He is linked to changes in natural phenomena, which science is unable to explain. By the villagers' own admission, miracles have happened in succession, the simplest of which is snowfall in a hot desert area. The new 'formation' took place through the process of fertility. Sterile women bore children; cows and sheep gave birth to twins and triplets. The continuity of the saint's role after his death in renewing fertility gives his grave a holy status in the world of the living.

The story here depicts the saint's shrine as the largest shrine in the cemetery, whereas the picture of such a prominent shrine was not emphasized in the story of *The Wedding of Zein*. The author has focused on that point in "The Doum Tree of Wad Hamed." The story narrates the beliefs concerning the saint's grave, for when a saint dies, his life's story may get lost and nothing remains of his legacy except his shrine. In Egypt's as well as in Sudan's countryside, there are numerous shrines of saints whom people sanctify without knowing anything about their particular lives. The story of Haneen and Zein may develop into a myth representing a general framework of this saint's life. He must have revolted for the sake of his religion and chosen the place of his death, as happened in the story of "The Doum Tree of Wad Hamed." If the place chosen by the saint is barren, then the miracle will be a certain new 'formation' as a manifestation for the living. Hence, the Doum Tree becomes like a supernatural, mythical eagle spreading its wings over the village. It hasn't been planted by anyone, and most probably it grew by itself. No one remembers how it grew in a rocky land elevated from the shore.[41] The 'formation' is not only confined to this tree, but also the whole village, with its people, water wheels, and habitats coming full-fledged out of the earth. It was a complete wasteland before the sheikh arrived.

There is a widespread belief among many Muslims that the saint's soul after his death remains active and influential in society. It can answer the needy

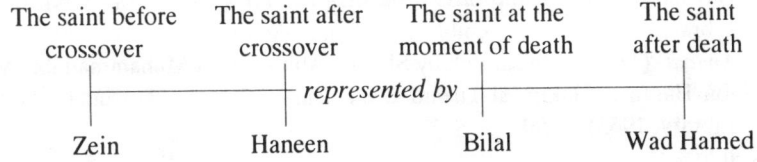

The saint before crossover	The saint after crossover	The saint at the moment of death	The saint after death
	represented by		
Zein	Haneen	Bilal	Wad Hamed

and cure the ill. The narrator in "The Doum Tree of Wad Hamed" mentions that they go to the Doum Tree and ask for the help of Wad Hamed. There once was a woman whose throat was swollen and who was bedridden for two months. She had a fever, but got out of her bed before dawn and in difficulty went to the Doum Tree of Wad Hamed and stood beneath it. Unable even to stand up, she yelled, "O Wad Hamed, I have come to you to seek refuge and protection— I shall sleep here at your tomb and under your doum tree. Either you let me die or you restore me to life. I shall not leave here until one of these two things happens."[42] The woman continues her story: she curled herself up in fear and was overtaken by sleep. Midway between wakefulness and sleep, she "heard sounds of recitation from the Qur'an and a bright light as sharp as a knife-edge, radiated out, joining the two river banks, and she saw the doum tree prostrating itself in worship. Her heart throbbed so violently that she thought it would leap up through her mouth. She saw a venerable old man with a white beard and wearing a spotless white robe come up to her, a smile on his face. He struck her on the head with his string of prayer-beads and called out: 'Arise.'" The woman swears that "she got up she knew not how and went home she knew not how. She arrived back at dawn"; it was clear that she was completely cured.[43]

This pattern clearly exists in popular belief, and Tayeb Salih has in fact molded it out of people's actual beliefs. The result is an accomplished literary representation of a saint based on folk myths.

Notes

1 Lewis Spence, *An Introduction to Mythology* (London: George G. Harrap Co., 1921), p. 12.
2 The universal nature of mythic structures has been advocated by a number of prominent folklorists and anthropologists, notably Carl Gustav Jung and Claude Lévi-Strauss.
3 Tayeb Salih, *The Wedding of Zein and Other Stories*, trans. Denys Johnson-Davies (London: Heinemann, 1969), p. 33. All citations from the novel are in parentheses within the text.
4 Abu Bakr Muhammad ibn Ishaq al-Bukhari al-Kalabadhi, *al-Ta'arruf li-madhhib ahl al-tasawwuf* (Knowledge of the doctrines of people of tasawwuf), ed. Arthur John Arberry, (Cairo: Al-Khanji, 1933), p. 3.
5 Ibid., p. 40.
6 Ibid., p. 39.
7 Haydar al-Amili, *Kitab nass al-nusus* (The book of text of texts), ms., Library of People's Assembly in Tehran, taken from notes of *Khatm al-Awliya'* (The seal of saints), by Shaykh Abu Abdalla Muhammad ibn Ali ibn Hasan al-Hakim al-Tirmidhi, ed. Isma'il Yahya, (Beirut: Catholic Library, 1965), p. 507.
8 Ibid.
9 Ibid.
10 Abu Qasim 'Abd al-Karim al-Qushayri, *al-Risala al-qushayriya* (The qushayri epistle) (Cairo: Dar al-Kutub al-Haditha, 1972), p. 265.

11 Ibid., p. 252.
12 Al-Kalabadhi, *al-Ta'arruf*, pp. 5–6.
13 Ibid., p. 65.
14 Al-Tirmidhi, *Khatm al-awliya'*, pp. 504–5.
15 Ibid., p. 495.
16 Ibid., p. 505.
17 Ibid., p. 495.
18 Ibid., p. 505.
19 Ibid.
20 Al-Qushayri, *al-Risala*, p. 309.
21 A. U. al-Hujwiri, *The Kashf al-Mahjub*, trans. R. A. Nicholson (Leiden: Brill, 1971), p. 55.
22 A. Yusuf Ali, *The Holy Qur'an* (Lahore: Ashraf Press, 1934), XXVIII: 15.
23 Ibn al-Athir, *al-Kamil fi-l-tarikh* (The complete in history) (Beirut: Dar Sadir, 1965), vol. 1, p. 177.
24 Ibid., p. 178.
25 *The Holy Qur'an*, XXVIII: 29, 30.
26 *The Holy Bible* (Revised Standard Version) (New York: Meridian Books, 1962), Luke, III: 16–18.
27 *The Holy Bible*, Matthew, III: 14–15.
28 *The Holy Bible*, Matthew, III: 16–17.
29 Ibn al-Athir, *al-Kamil*, vol. 2, p. 48. See also Ibn Hisham, *al-Sira al-nabawiya* (The life of the Prophet), introd., commentary, and ed. Taha Abd al-Rauuf Sa'd, (Cairo: Maktabat al-Kulliyat al-Azhariya, 1978), vol. 1, p. 222.
30 Ibn al-Athir, *al-Kamil*, p. 49.
31 Ibid.
32 Tayeb Salih, *Meryoud*, ms. trans. Denys Johnson-Davies, p. 63.
33 Ibid., p. 63.
34 Ibid., p. 57.
35 Tayeb Salih, *Bandershah*, ms. trans. Denys Johnson-Davies, p. 18.
36 Tayeb Salih, *Meryoud*, p. 65.
37 Ibid.
38 Ibid.
39 Ibid., p. 58.
40 Ibid.
41 Tayeb Salih, "The Doum Tree of Wad Hamid," *The Wedding of Zein*, trans. Denys Johnson-Davies (London: Heinemann, 1969), p. 6.
42 Ibid., p. 11.
43 Ibid., p. 13.

Opaque and Transparent Discourse in Sonallah Ibrahim's Works

❖

Ceza Kassem Draz

When Sonallah Ibrahim's first 'novel', *The Smell of it,* appeared in 1966, it was banned by the censor and, though it was already printed, the novel was confiscated from the printshop by the police; only a few copies were saved and those were distributed to friends. The general criticism leveled at the novel, not only by the authorities but also by sympathetic readers, was that it was improper, strange, confusing; readers were disoriented by this novel that seemed to be quite innocent on the surface. It related the perambulations of an anonymous narrator in the streets of Cairo after his release from prison in no more than a hundred or so pages. *The Smell of it* represents a break in the history of Egyptian narrative. Relating his experience upon reading the novel, Yusuf Idris succinctly describes its impact on him in his introduction to it:

> This is not a novel but rather, let us say, a slap, a cry, a strong awakening moan that almost stirs terror. The real hero in this novel is a general overwhelming feeling which has no name. The author himself does not name it and I feel embarassed myself trying to find a name for that general feeling that Sonallah has carved, created and introduced into the scope of art and literature. It is not a feeling of strangeness or disgust or loss or rebellion or desire for tenderness or yearning for existence. It is a different feeling.[1]

In this passage Yusuf Idris, a sensitive writer and perceptive literary critic, has given us the germ of what may be called avant-garde art. Firstly, it negates the traditional forms—"this is not a novel"—and, secondly, by negating the traditional forms, it defamiliarizes reality and evokes in the reader a different feeling, an experience that is quite unprecedented; so much so that there is no name for it, no word that could describe it, not even a neologism; it remains perforce unnamable.

The rejection of traditional forms implies the rejection of the society that produced these forms, and the aim of this rejection is to awaken the reader to a new reality or, at least, to the necessity for a new reality. Avant-garde literature in Egypt is a literature which is deeply rooted in the social reality, a literature which is *engagée,* and aims at criticizing reality as much as—if not more than—at expressing it. Within the last twenty years, the role of this avant-garde literature has been one of contestation and an overt critique of the repressive social order.

The paradoxical situation of the avant-garde writers was their confrontation with the 1952 Revolution in Egypt that was to realize their dreams and fulfill their expectations. The failure of the Nasserist revolution to create the ideal society these writers were dreaming of brought about a deep feeling of frustration and triggered an era of suspicion, a suspicion not only of the traditional forms and traditional society but also of the present society and its self-expression in language. The gap that existed between the traditional forms of fiction and reality was similar to that existing between society and its self-expression in a discourse which claimed to be the discourse of truth, while it was in reality a discourse of mystification and deceit; words did not mean what they were meant to mean. It is my assumption in this paper that the new writing of the avant-garde was motivated as much by the negation of this discourse of truth as it was by the negation of traditional forms of writing. What it was negating was the fiction of language as much as the language of fiction.

To present an analysis of a negative text we have to contrast it with the text it negates in order to elucidate the broader articulations of that negation. There is no doubt that Sonallah Ibrahim's *Najmat aghustus* (The star of August), which appeared four years after *The Smell of it* and developed further those traits which characterize the latter, could be contrasted with the novels of a traditional novelist like Naguib Mahfouz, but the process of negation becomes more overt and significant when we contrast *Najmat aghustus* to a text that claims to be true to reality but *which is* actually fictionalized. The process of mystification is more active when the reader is confronted with a text that claims to represent truth than when he is confronted with one that admits to being fictive. The mechanisms of what Marie-Laure Ryan has called "the principle of minimal departure"[2] are here suspended; the self-defense mechanisms against illusion are restrained; the process of allegorical interpretation accompanying the reading of fiction is cast aside and the reader presumably submits unconditionally to a sense of mystification, or at least this is what he is meant to do since these texts' underlying assumption is that the reader is in a way infantile and credulous, incapable of making the distinction between fact and fiction.[3]

Najmat aghustus was conceived as a negation of a text written by Sonallah Ibrahim and two other writers: Kamal al-Qilish and Rauf Mis'id. The three writers went to visit the site of the Aswan High Dam in the summer of 1966, the year following the diversion of the Nile that was to witness the last flood of the river; on their return they wrote a *reportage* of their visit. The text, published in 1967, entitled *Insan al-sadd al-'ali* (Man of the high dam) aimed at presenting firsthand information from eyewitnesses on the work of erecting the High Dam.

The reportage or documentary is the prototype of what we might call the discourse of truth; it refers to an extra-textual reality which may be verified. The text aims at a correlation between signifier, signified, and referent; it does not aim at creating an alternate possible world as in fiction but at reproducing the real world as it is.

I would like to argue that, in their work, the authors have consciously or unconsciously worked towards the mystification of their readers by processes familiar in the discourse of fiction, and that the novel *Najmat aghustus* is, in a way, generated negatively by this text. It is a demystification of the language of *Insan al-sadd al-'ali* which one might call the 'pre-text' and, by demystifying the language, it defamiliarizes the reality that it presents whereas the pre-text was aiming at a more profound familiarization and acceptance. It seems as if there were an interchange between the two texts, perhaps even an exchange of personality: the fictive discourse becomes factual while the factual discourse becomes fictive. One could even call it a split in personality: the public discourse is mystifying while the private discourse of art is demystifying.[4] The text and the pre-text center around the Aswan High Dam: an object of great magnitude and of an even greater controversy in all possible contexts, an object around which intersected tensions and vital issues, major struggles and confrontations.

The Aswan High Dam was the point of confrontation between man and nature. It was a climax of the long line of direct struggles between the Nile and the people of the valley of the Nile and thus entered into the realm of modern mythology. The Aswan High Dam was also, in the arena of modern life, the point of confrontation between man and machine. It meant the shift of a whole society from an agricultural stage to an industrial one. The very crux of these two confrontations is that they center around the process of change as the result of struggle.

The Aswan High Dam was, on the other hand, one of the arteries of the 1952 Revolution. The project was started in October 1952, three months after the coup d'état in July 1952, and was completed in 1970, the year of Nasser's death. It thus became the focus for the concentration of a number of forces, among which we can cite the industrialization of Egypt which would entail the transformation of the country from a poor, underdeveloped, agricultural society into a rich, technologically advanced, industrial one. The industrialization process was presented as a battlefront of equal importance to the military battlefront against Israel and imperialism.[5]

During the two decades involving the process of the erection of the High Dam, it came to symbolize a number of cultural, social, political, and even industrial *sèmes*.[6] The High Dam became the symbol of the will of a people, the self-sacrificing capacity and power of a people, the self-determination of a people, the inspired and charismatic leadership of Nasser, the mobilization of a people, the establishment of socialism, the possibility of establishing humane cooperation between countries, a unified and homogeneous society, the struggle against imperialism, the advent of prosperity, the ascending forces of history, the conquest of nature.

This list of what one might call the *sèmes* of the High Dam as symbol is by no means exhaustive. The mythical discourse that was woven around the High Dam grew as the process of construction proceeded and the discourse itself attained the proportions of its gigantic object. But, in a way, the discourse itself replaced the object, thus blurring the vision and distorting reality. The High Dam became the emblem of the Nasserist revolution and Nasser's death was reflected on the emblem that represented him. The High Dam became the nucleus around which de-Nasserization was undertaken, the greatest achievement of all times was debased, belittled; it was described as a blunder, a mistake; it ruined the environment which had not been properly studied and, besides, it had not solved the problems it was supposed to remedy, had not fulfilled the promises and—above all—was a disappointment. The battle had been lost on all fronts. The year 1967 saw Egypt's military defeat and, with Nasser's death, the High Dam—as symbol—crumbled.

Sonallah Ibrahim belongs to the generation of the High Dam builders. They set all their hopes on it; it stood as the personification of what they believed in. They were truly fascinated by it. The High Dam provided that generation with the feeling of fulfillment and of 'building' as well as a sense of direction leading towards social and economic transformation. However, the 'text' of the High Dam, the mythical discourse that had been woven around it, and which the builders helped weave, was a means of mystification. The ideology of the 1952 Revolution informed such texts. Side by side, for over twenty years, and standing in opposition, were the High Dam and the text of the High Dam.

In turning now to our two texts, the reportage *Insan al-sadd al-'ali* and the novel *Najmat aghustus,* I would like to analyze the ways in which the first text creates an object of mystification while the second creates a discourse of demystification. This is actually achieved by processes of familiarization on the one hand, and defamiliarization on the other. Sonallah Ibrahim has, in his novel, recreated the High Dam; in a way, he has disentangled the object itself and reinstated it in reality. Art is truth, while reportage is deceit.

Both texts are structured on the model of the journey and might each be entitled 'Itinerary from Cairo to Abu Simbel'. The journey as a structural element is recurrent in literature and may have different functions. It is a mode of discovery of an unknown world; it is the major mode of *dépaysement*; the character is dislocated, removed from his natural, familiar, secure environment and placed in a new, unfamiliar, alien environment. In this alien locus he experiences transformations, changes; he discovers himself, and with the discovery of a new world external to himself he discovers a new self. The journey is as much an exploration of a new internal world as the exploration of a new outer world.

A. The 'Pre-text'

In the text of the reportage the main function of the journey—the function of *dépaysement*—is canceled; the dislocation effect is annulled by a process of familiarization: the unfamiliar is described in terms of the familiar. The main device that is used is personification. As the title of the book indicates—*Insan al-sadd al-'ali* (Man of the high dam)—the text tends to reconcile the object and the subject. It establishes a relationship between the subject (Man) and the object (the High Dam). The relationship is set in the grammatical structure of the genitive possession—*idafa*—that links the two substantives: Man and the High Dam. In this structure, the first member of the genitive construction—the *mudaf*—is, on the one hand, determined by its annexation to the second member—the *mudaf ilayhi*—and, on the other, it becomes the possessed while the second member is the possessor. In this context, the genitive of possession likewise conveys the idea of agency and production as in the syntagm (linear syntactic succession) "the novel of Sonallah Ibrahim," where the genitive construction entails both possession and production. That Man is, therefore, owned and is also a product of the High Dam; if Man has built the High Dam, the High Dam has also built this new man, a 'humane' new man. The High Dam has, in this context, a humanizing power, for the word *insan* (human) has all the connotations of all the values attached to human compassion: civility, kindness, benevolence, spirituality. It is also opposed to the word *hayawan* (animal) which is antithetical to it.

The process of personification and humanization governs the text from its opening stanza which is a poem by the well-known Egyptian poet 'Abd al-Rahman al-Abnudi entitled "Ode to the High Dam":

I feel that the arm of the High Dam
Needs some of my blood.[7]

The exchange of blood between the poet and the High Dam humanizes the Dam as the Dam had humanized man.

The first chapter of the book, entitled "The Marketplace," introduces the reader, who has started his journey by opening the book and reading the first page, into an all-too-familiar locus—a locus of popular festivities and human interchange. The narration is introduced through the second person pronoun,

Opaque and Transparent Discourse 139

which indicates a hearer and a message implicating the reader in an act of communication and involving him in the situation described. It moves him to engage himself in the dialogue and to immerse himself in the situation. It is used as an invitation addressed to the reader by the narrators to accompany them on their voyage of discovery. But, from the very start, the narrators are careful not to dislocate their fellow travelers; they start from the familiar and guide them carefully to the unfamiliar:

> For a moment it will seem to you that you are entering a familiar world similar to that of the little cities scattered along the green stretch of the valley from the north to the south ... but you will open your eyes in amazement when you confront the new city of Aswan ... this new city of Aswan is the site of a battle between the river and the city, between the old city and the new city.[8]

However, the narrators feel that though they are introducing their readers into a new world, they must first reassure them that deep inside the new Aswan still lies the old Aswan, and that nothing has in effect changed:

> The heart of the city has not changed since the days of the pharaohs. In those days the city was called Suwant meaning *al-suq,* the market. The dark granite has proven that it is—till now at least—stronger than the machine.[9]

What is valorized in this text is permanence as opposed to change. The narrators are here emphasizing the perennial value of Aswan as a city that has managed to survive from the times of the pharaohs to the modern era, and is still surviving the battle against industrialization.

The process is reiterated when the travelers reach the site of the High Dam itself: "It is as if you were suddenly entering one of the popular quarters of Cairo."[10]

It seems that the narrators are careful at every step to reassure the reader that what he is about to experience is not different from what he has experienced before. The process of familiarization is achieved through a number of tropes, mainly metaphors and similes, based on anthropomorphism. What could be closer to the reader than his own body? Aswan is humanized and is equated with man himself. At the end of the day "Aswan puts her head on her arms of granite and sleeps as if nothing in the world was worth being awakened for."[11] Also, the road leading to the High Dam "sweats during the daytime, but at night it stretches and opens its infinite heart to you and sighs with you."[12]

Not only are the city and the road anthropomorphized but the machine is likewise transformed into human form. The trucks returning from a day's work are compared to wounded soldiers returning from the battlefield waiting to be attended to in the hospital (the garage) while others are convalescing, and still others, after being cured, are awaiting their orders to return to the battlefield.

The process of metaphorization which binds setting (city, road) and man, object (machine) and man, also extends into another dimension, namely, present and past. The High Dam is compared to the pyramids and to the Sphinx, and the concrete that is poured daily into the constructions is described as a daily meal offered to the High Dam which devours it as the Sphinx devoured its victims. Sidqi Sulayman, the minister of the High Dam, is compared to a pharaonic statue which has just been rescued from one of the temples of Aswan: "an ancient dark giant of the color of the stone and the hardness of granite." The valorization of the present in terms of its resemblance to the glorious past is still another process of familiarization. However, this process is, at the same time, a means of mystification. As Michel Le Guern has shown in his study of metaphor,[13] the referential function of language, the function that refers the discourse to the context of reality which is external to both the speaker and the hearer, is attenuated when metaphorization is used, when we pass from the literal meaning to the figurative meaning. Metaphor is used also in the traditional mode, to wit: for adornment, liveliness, elucidation, or agreeable mystification. And it is this last function that is at work in the text of *Insan al-sadd al-'ali*. Metaphor is used to transform reality from what it is to what it is not, mainly by changing what is not agreeable or not acceptable into something agreeable; by transforming a reality which is alien and novel into a reality which is familiar and everlasting. It is a freezing process which is used in those types of discourse which aim at blocking the process of transformation and motion.

The transformation of reality is further emphasized by another trope, hyperbole, which is used to amplify reality and thus anchors an image of it albeit a distortive one.[14] Hyperbole is a figure which is, in a way, mathematical: it adds value or dimension to the object. It is obvious that the High Dam by its very nature invites such a trope. But in the text of *Insan al-sadd al-'ali* the trope overflows from the object itself to permeate all the other semantic fields of the text. The semantic field in which the contamination manifests itself most clearly is the field of human action. Action is amplified into heroism and the outcome of the struggle is presented as victory and exemplary achievement.

At this point, the two main axes around which the text is structured emerge: the axis of figurative language and the axis of the dynamics of the text, that is, the resolution or non-resolution of the tensions in the text.

The axis of figurative language is used, as has been previously mentioned, to blur the reality of the object. The discourse that results from this use is highly opaque. According to Todorov, an opaque discourse is opposed to a transparent discourse in that

> the discourse without figures of speech is a completely transparent discourse and thus non-existent. Then the figure of speech appears as a drawing imposed on this transparency, a drawing that permits for the first time apprehension of the discourse in itself and not as a mediator of significance. The true character of the discourse that is called today poetical makes it opaque as clothes on an invisible body and allows it to be seen for the first time.[15]

Although I tend to disagree with Todorov in his equation of opaque and poetical discourse, I do agree with him as far as his distinction between opaque and transparent discourse in their relation to their referent goes. The opaque discourse calls attention to itself and effaces the referent; the transparent discourse tends to efface itself in order to establish the referent in its place. I also agree with him on the role of figurative language in the making of opaque discourse. Language, in this instance, creates a fiction, becomes a fiction severed from its referent, and stands as a construction in its own right.

The opacity of the text of *Insan al-sadd al-'ali* stems from another process aside from the use of figurative speech, namely, from the presence of the subject of the enunciation in the discourse.[16] In a way, the speaker forces his subjectivity on the hearer who has to obliterate his own and adopt that of the speaker. The narrators are creating a narrative situation in which the reader has to identify with their point of view. The narrative that started with the second person singular shifts to the first person plural. In a way, the reader is tempted to assimilate himself to the group, to the 'we' and to become part of the community created by the narrators in their text; the High Dam's society is the society where the 'I' melts in the 'we'. The nature of this collective subjectivity is of an affective type; the text abounds in what Pierre Guiraud has called "locutive messages"[17] expressing the comments, judgments, and feelings of the narrators. The locutive dimension of the text blurs its predicative dimension so that the primary message of the text—its denotative, objective significance—is totally taken over by a connotative, subjective significance. The reader is immersed in the affective 'we' identity and loses the critical perspective of individual rationality.

I would like to pursue this argument a step further and add that the dissolution of the individual 'I' and its integration into the collective identity of the 'we' is a way of solving the alienation of the 'I' and its isolation. This is also achieved in the text by the resolution of all the tensions of the narrative and adds to the mystification, since no narrative can reach this type of resolution except in a utopian world or in a comic narrative mode where all tensions are resolved without leaving any residue. The world of the High Dam is presented as an ideal possible world, a utopia where man and machine live happily every after. All tensions are solved: man has conquered nature, he has forced the machine to submit to his will. There is a perfect leveling of the social tensions; the High Dam was able to create a perfect model to which all the individual 'I's had to conform: ministers, engineers, workers, Egyptians, Russians, Sa'idis, proletarians, even capitalists all undergo transformation and conform to the model. The merging of all these elements into a harmonious whole is extended to language; the utopia has a language of its own, in this case, a language peculiar to the High Dam: a composite of Arabic and Russian.

The world of the High Dam is the perfect world. If we analyze the syntagm *al-sadd al-'ali,* we notice that the connotations attached to the first element, *sadd* (obstacle, obstruction, barrier, barricade), are discarded while the connotations of the second element, *'ali* (high, elevated), are put to full use and could be considered the main paradigm around which the text is structured. The root *'lw* implies the semantic field of perfection, elevation, loftiness, and the derivatives from this root comprise signifieds such as: sublime, exalted, outstanding, etc. Furthermore, the root *'lw* is a composite of the syntagm: *al-mathal al-a'la* (the ideal) and thus an equation is posed, i.e., *al-sadd al-'ali = al-mathal al-a'la*.

Also the world of the High Dam is not an independent possible world grafted on the larger Egyptian society, but acts as a synecdoche. The part is equivalent to the whole and the general conclusion of the narrative is that the High Dam is my country: *al-sadd baladi*. The reader is led on a journey to utopia that has lulled all his suspicions; a journey of illusion and delusion from which he has to be awakened.

B. The 'Text'

Three years after the publication of *Insan al-sadd al-'ali,* in the year of Nasser's death in 1970, Sonallah Ibrahim's novel *Najmat aghustus* (The star of August) appeared. It is, in its own right, the inversion of the text that had preceded it, and negates all the devices of mystification that prevailed in the official discourse. By using defamiliarization, the novel was aiming at restoring the referents in place of their signifiers and also at dismantling the symbolic apparatus that stood between the reader and reality.

The first question that comes to mind is that of the interpretation of the novel's title. What is the "Star of August?" What does it represent? What does it symbolize? The star appears only at the end of the novel—on page 225—and does not stand for anything but itself:

> At 7:30 the only star appeared. It seemed to me that it was moving west. Then it stopped. I thought of rising and asking someone about it. The Rayyis must know it. Maybe it was Sirius which used to appear to the Ancient Egyptians at the time of the flood or maybe it was the famous Big Bear that guided navigators and wanderers. But I did not have the energy or the enthusiasm to rise and I felt that any answer I would get would not change matters.[18]

The narrator's process of thinking about the star he sees in the sky on an August night is the matrix around which the text is structured. The experience of the vision of the star is an immediate one and the different interpretations are rejected one after the other as useless; even the proper names that could identify the star are of no consequence. The star is apprehended in itself, in its physical existence. Objects are to be presented without mediation. The text then tends towards the immediate presentation of the physical world, a physical world that stands for its own sake and is not interpreted, and the question arises: should we interpret it at all?

Opaque and Transparent Discourse

On the first page of the novel, the narrator boards the train that is to take him from Cairo to Aswan. Sitting behind a closed window he sees people standing on the platform; he cannot hear what they say.[19] He does not try to guess what they are saying or to understand what they are doing; he remains at the surface of the physical world and does not try to penetrate beyond this surface.

The text of *Najmat aghustus* is as resistant as the windowpane, and as transparent. It is resistant because the reader is not allowed to penetrate the surface of the physical world; what the narrator presents to him is only what can be apprehended by the senses. Thus, the text has no depth; there is nothing beyond the world of objects. On the other hand, the text is as transparent as the windowpane; it exemplifies what has been described as transparent discourse: it is systematically stripped of all tropes[20] and tends towards a type of innocent and neutral discourse which Barthes has termed "writing degree zero" where language effaces itself to let the referent emerge in total 'objectivity'. It is also transparent in the sense that it is severed from the subject of the enunciation. The various functions of language are set aside to allow the referential function, and the referential function only, to be assumed by the text. The text is taken over by the referent to such an extent that it becomes iconic, i.e., it becomes a diagram of the object.

The overall structure of the novel tends towards an iconic representation of the High Dam. It could be represented in the shape of a step pyramid:

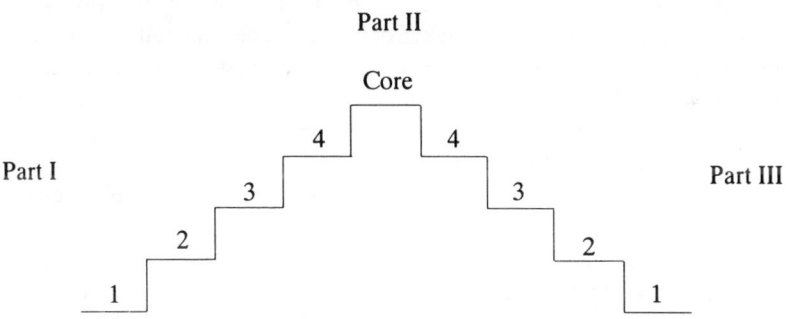

The first part, divided into four chapters numbered one to four, describes the various steps of the High Dam's construction:
1. Excavating.
2. Blasting.
3. Moving.
4. Dumping.

The subject of each one of these operations is a piece of equipment:
1. Excavators.
2. Dynamite.
3. Bulldozers.
4. Dump-trucks.

The second part of the novel covers only thirteen pages and consists of an uninterrupted interior monologue.

The third part reproduces the four operations of the first part, but in descending order, and describes the dismantling of the Nubian temples.

The diagram of the novel is similar in form to that of the High Dam: the first part represents the upstream face of the dam while the second part represents the impermeable core and the third part the downstream face. The High Dam is to emerge in its objective reality. The general structure of the novel reestablishes the High Dam as an object as opposed to the High Dam as a signifier. The iconic structure of the novel creates a distance between the reader and the object: the object as an independent part of reality that exists outside the apprehending self. This distance is a process of defamiliarization which has become one of the characteristics of modern art.

The subject does not identify with the object but remains detached from it, empathy is canceled and the self becomes alienated from the object. The defamiliarization is further corroborated by the nature of the actants[21] in the novel and their relations. The machine is one of the actants of the novel and the textual space occupied by the machine is as extensive as that occupied by human actants. The presence of the machine as an autonomous actant places two constraints on the text: first, it implies a mechanical causality that dehumanizes the text; and, second, it cancels internal space. The machine functions only in external space and does not possess any 'interiority' or subjectivity. The machine is the model of all the other actants: all are described in terms of their outer appearance. The narrator has no way of penetrating into the internal space of the other characters; the text is stripped of all psychological analysis—only what can be apprehended by the senses is presented. The human as well as the physical world remain uninterpreted. The windowpane stands between the narrator and the other characters as it stands between the reader and the text. The world of *Najmat aghustus* is dehumanized.

The narrator himself is dehumanized, his subjectivity is suspended. He presents himself to the reader as he presents the other characters. He describes his actions from the outside as though he were an automaton. In the train, the narrator—who is not named throughout the novel—describes his minutest gestures in closing the door of the compartment: "I got up and went to the door, turned the metal handle; it turned in my hand. The door opened towards me. I closed it again and secured it with the hanging metal chain. I returned to my place by the window."[22]

Though narration is conducted in the first person singular, what emerges from the text is a subject devoid of subjectivity. The narrator introduces himself as a 'you' not as an 'I'; as any other self would have apprehended him from the outside and not as a self-conscious subject. He does not analyze himself or conduct any introspection; he does not comment on his actions as he does not comment on the other characters' actions. By canceling his interiority he destroys the basic characteristic of the 'I', namely the continuity of consciousness.[23]

This type of narrative is diametrically opposed to the interior monologue technique where only the internal space is presented in the text. In objective narration, only actions and gestures are presented; reality becomes somehow the sum of external relations. The feeling of defamiliarization is amplified when the physical gestures which are not part of consciousness are described by the subject himself. Also, a person describing outer reality does not include himself in his perception: he perceives but does not perceive himself perceiving, unless the ego of the subject is split. Thus, the process of defamiliarization is achieved by transforming an unreflective consciousness into a reflective one.

What is the nature of the actions and gestures which are described? These are mainly minute actions and small gestures that make up the core of one's daily life. Verbs such as: I woke up, I went to sleep, I entered, I came out, I lit a cigarette, etc., are repeated over and over again. Behavior is analyzed into its smallest components and recorded in its minutest details. This is, for example, how the narrator describes drinking a sip of water in the train's compartment:

> There was a small rack next to the window on which there was a tumbler; below was a faucet of water and a metal panel which I pulled down out of the wall. It was converted into a basin. I filled the glass and raised it to my mouth. The water was warm, and I contented myself with only one sip. I let the water from the faucet collect in the bottom of the basin until it became full. Then I pushed it back into its place in the wall. I listened to the sound of the water as it drained towards the outside.[24]

It becomes obvious that seemingly quite unimportant events, such as drinking a sip of water, acquire an exaggerated importance. Ortega y Gasset has noted that in order to dehumanize it is not necessary to alter the inherent nature of things, it is enough to invert the order of importance and create an art in which events of minimal importance in life loom up monumentally in the foreground.[25]

The uneasiness generated by the novel is in part the outcome of a process of defamiliarization at work in the text, but it is also generated by the coercive power of the text. It is quite obvious that the transparency of the text is not as innocent as it seems. Internal space is not totally canceled: it is repressed. The residues are created by the tensions at work on the surface of the text and these are not resolved or dissolved. Rather they are transferred from the surface of the text to its depth. Sonallah Ibrahim has presented this dichotomy between surface level and deep level by creating a totally new form in the novel. We find more than one level of narration. First, we find the mainstream of the narrative, or the surface level, which deals with the construction of the High Dam in bold print; second, we find the undercurrent of the narrative, or the deep level, in small print. The surface level seems to pressure the deep level, repressing it in such a way that one can sense the repression work in both the size of the text (always a small one-paragraph text) and in the size of the print. The undercurrent of the narrative—or deep level—consists of the narrator's dreams on the one hand, the interior monologue that forms the second part of the novel and represents the impermeable core of the dam, and on the other, those independent subtexts which are inserted in small print (repressed form) at various points in the mainstream of the narrative. The connection between the subtexts and the surface level is absolutely fortuitous and totally unmotivated by the text, there being no obvious connection between the mainstream and the subtexts. The reader is disoriented and does not find any logical or narrative causality in these shifts. The only motivation is the complete rupture between internal and external space; between public and private life, between perception and self-consciousness. The dichotomy is actually the result of the work of censorship at both the individual (dreams) and collective level (social and political critique). The subtexts represent the repressed dreams of society; they revolve around four axes: art, social conflicts, the totalitarian state, and the cult of personality.

At this level of his novel, Sonallah Ibrahim creates another iconic diagram, that of coercion. On the surface is a neutral, transparent, innocent discourse aiming at presenting reality in its objectivity but, at the deep level, this transparent discourse seems to conceal a turmoil of coerced forces: art as a subversive force that has to be repressed, unresolved social conflicts, the tyranny of the totalitarian state, and the cult of the personality. The coercive discourse does not ultimately eliminate other discourses, it only represses them. In *Najmat aghustus* the surface discourse is made meaningful by what it omits rather than by what it includes.

Arabic literature is at a crossroads. The issues that face literature today are above all epistemological. Literature is the privileged, perhaps even the main medium of knowledge: knowledge of the world and knowledge of the self. In societies where truth is concealed, distorted, and repressed, literature's function becomes the revaluation of this truth and its disclosure. The modern Arab writer has become the bold ad hoc spokesman of society. The result is a literature immersed in everyday problems and directly linked to the media of information and communication, so much so that literature has replaced the channels through which day-to-day knowledge is transmitted and has become, in some cases, the only truly genuine if not immediate expression of the pressing problems of society.

Notes

1 All translations are mine, unless otherwise noted.
2 For an analysis of "the principle of minimal departure," see M.-L. Ryan, "Fiction, Non-factuals and the Principle of Minimal Departure," *Poetics*, vol. 9, no. 4 (August, 1980), pp. 403–22.

3 See T. Ben Jelloun, "Le désarroi du monde arabe et les refuges de l'histoire," *Le Monde Diplomatique*, February 1981.

4 This fact may be attributed to the role of censorship since the reportage on the Aswan High Dam was a journalistic text submitting to the governing ideology, while the artist feels a greater freedom in his writing of fiction. It may also be attributed to self-censorship, which shapes behavior in public life.

5 The financing of the Aswan High Dam changed the course of Egyptian foreign policy when the World Bank refused to advance the loan and Egypt turned to the Soviet Union in 1952.

6 'Sème' in the terminology of the semantic analysis of a lexical unit is the minimal unit of signification and cannot have an independent realization. Thus, one would say that the symbolic signification of the High Dam is the sum total of all the individual semantic traits or components which are *sèmes*.

7 Sonallah Ibrahim, Kamal al-Qilish, and Rauf Mis'id, *Insan al-sadd al-'ali* (Cairo: Dar al-Katib al-'Arabi, 1967), p. 3.

8 Ibid., p. 11.

9 Ibid., p. 15.

10 Ibid., p. 39.

11 Ibid., p. 16.

12 Ibid., p. 29.

13 See M. Le Guern, *Sémantique de la métaphore et de la métonymie* (Paris: Larousse, 1973).

14 For an analysis of hyperbole, see Abu Hilal al-'Askari, *Kitab al-sina'atayn* (Cairo: Matba'at Muhammad 'Ali Subaih, n.d.), p. 238.

15 T. Todorov, *Littérature et signification* (Paris: Larousse, 1967), pp. 117–18.

16 The bipolar concept of transparency and opacity used in the linguistic analysis of discourse notes the presence or absence of the speaker in relation to his discourse and from the point of view of the hearer. In the case of absolute transparency, the speaker effaces himself completely. At the opposite extreme, the text will be deeply marked by the subjectivity of the speaker.

17 P. Guiraud, "Modern Linguistics Looks at Rhetoric: Free Indirect Style," in *Patterns of Literary Style*, ed. J. Strelka, (University Park: Pennsylvania State University Press, 1971), pp. 77–89.

18 Sonallah Ibrahim, *Najmat aghustus* (Cairo: Dar al-Thaqafa al-Jadida, 1976), p. 225.

19 In *Le Mythe de Sisyphe* Camus uses this image to show the absurd situation par excellence.

20 The author informed me that he rewrote the first chapter of his novel thirteen times in order to strip it completely of all metaphors, similes, and other tropes. This technique has been termed "dénument" and is a distinctive feature of Camus' *The Stranger*.

21 I use the term "actant" after A. J. Greimas in his *Sémantique Structurale* to convey the concept of an abstract narrative role that could be assumed by

a number of more concrete occurrences. However, no complete actantial model is attempted here, since it does not serve the purposes of my analysis.
22 Sonallah Ibrahim, *Najmat aghustus*, p. 10.
23 E. Benveniste, "De la subjectivité dans le language," *Problèmes de linguistique générale* I (Paris: Gallimard, 1966), pp. 258–67.
24 *Najmat aghustus,* p. 10.
25 See Ortega y Gasset, *Velasquez, Goya and the Dehumanization of Art,* trans. A. Brown (London: Studio Vista, 1972).

Force and Transitivity: Bayram al-Tunisi and a Poetics of Anticolonialism

❖

Marilyn Booth

When Mahmud Bayram al-Tunisi (1893–1961) sailed from Alexandria in late 1919, bound for twenty years as a political exile in France, Tunisia, and Syria, he left behind an audience of readers and listeners who had already become avid consumers of his compositions. This young writer was banished for the political effectiveness and the popular reach of his writing, for he had joined the growing ranks of those for whom political activism centered on mass education through a popular-satirical press—following the path of 'Abdallah al-Nadim and others. Bayram (as he is known in Egypt and therefore as I will refer to him throughout) faced exile as a result of his activism.[1]

In exile, Bayram went on writing. During the early 1920s, his major forum was the newspaper *al-Shabab,* published in Cairo by 'Abd al-'Aziz al-Sadr.[2] Over the second half of the decade, he wrote for *al-Funun,*[3] an arts review published by Ahmad Kamil al-Hilli, also in Cairo. In both, Bayram published a variety of prose and verse offerings, in colloquial Egyptian Arabic and in various renderings of a modern literary idiom. The result was a sharp and ongoing satirical critique of Egyptian society, an analysis of European society as viewed at close range by an outsider on the economic margins, and a barrage of verse commentary on political events and actors in Egypt and elsewhere.

Bayram was not an original thinker. The political significance of his oeuvre lies in the specific ways in which these texts convey ideas and concerns of the time, and the ways in which they communicate confusions as well, for it is not as easy to extract a consistent political point of view from his works as the general thematic treatments which characterize 'Bayram studies' would suggest.⁴ Situating his corpus within the ideological constructs of the time will require much more specification and definition: detailed analyses of linguistic structures, study of the interrelationships of meanings and concepts, attention to the interplay of individual texts within one production context, and study of the shifts from one period of production to another.⁵

At the center of Bayram's commitment to didactic writing is a concept of audience-becoming-actor which is manifest in the deictics of the texts. Equally, this concept defines the linguistic field within which the texts are shaped and the particular conflicts which they construct. Bayram's oeuvre adheres—in form as well as focus—to the concrete terms of familiar experience and everyday communication in the community from which and for which he wrote, on the basis that this is the ground on which political and ideological battles occur. This concept as a foundation for creation and communication is exemplified well in a comment on the usefulness of "philosophers" implicit in a poem of Bayram's which lauds the efforts and achievements of Mahatma Gandhi:

> A philosopher, and your speech does not fail
> All your philosophy is in your loom.⁶

فيلسوف ما يخيبش قولك   كل كلامك فى نولك

Bayram's philosophy, too, is in his loom, and it is in the specific weave of his products that we find it.

This essay takes up features of certain poems from the 1920s which focus on European activity in Egypt and surrounding nations. First, I will note certain dominant textual features, particularly the interplay of poetic framework, subject–verb–object structures, and semantic relationships in two poems both published initially under the heading "'Ala-l-arghul." I will suggest how the themes of opposition, exclusion, force, and passivity dominate—through the specific deployment of language—these texts' construction of the global and regional politico-economic circumstances of the early 1920s. Second, I want to suggest how such structures are expanded through imagery found in certain other poems with the same subject—specifically, those published as "il-Fahl yidrab bi-l-qulla yutlub istiqlal," "Ihtilal Suriya," and "Aah ya Sudani." Third, I will discuss the poems "A'uzu bi-llah" and "'Ala-l-rababa (Lagnit Milnir)," noting how the dominance of an "us–them" polarity is modified according to subject and circumstance.

Limits of space preclude a broader sampling of poems or a fuller discussion of levels of expression in each poem. The fact that I pay little attention to phonology does not mean that I regard this level as unimportant; the emphasis in one section on syntactic–semantic relationships and in the other on imagery does not mean that these are separate or independent elements. A longer study would deal more fully with the interplay of all levels of expression in each poem as a unity.

I. Syntax and Dominance

Throughout Bayram's corpus runs a notion of community and exclusion—although the boundaries of each shift across texts and over time.[7] Boundaries are drawn most clearly in poems published in the 1920s which focus on the political scene in Egypt and specifically the relationship between a community defined as 'Egyptian' or 'Muslim' or 'Arab' and one defined as 'European'. The dominant relationship is one of opposition, but not of balance, for one pole is more powerful—more *active*—than the other. We find an active/passive, actor/acted upon, powerful/powerless dichotomy in which the relation agent–verb–object defines a certain direction and force of activity.

In one of numerous poems entitled in early publication "'Ala-l-arghul" (On the reedpipe), probably published first in *al-Shabab*,[8] this opposition concerns the process of European encroachment upon peoples and places to the east. As the poem's title suggests, it echoes forms drawn from the heritage of orally composed and transmitted sung composition in Egypt. Generally, it employs the "style of accumulation" typical of oral composition.[9] More specifically, the poem is constructed on the form of the *mawwal/marduf*, a tripartite structure in which each stanzaic unit (*maqta'*) builds upon the previous one.[10]

The opening consists of a series of 'aah's, an expression in this context of tribulation, plaint,[11] and resigned sorrow:

The first is aah	الأوله آه
The second is aah	والتانيه آه
The third is aah	والتالته آه

The series of 'aah's structures a cumulative narrative in which successive *maqati'* add to and build upon the core statements of the first proper *maqta'*, which follows the opening and is known as the *farsh* (foundation, basic furnishings). This occurs through two types of accumulation:

1. Accretion: modification through repetition of the core statement with additions strung onto it, which further specify and describe the core statement.

	A (*maqta'* I)	A+D	A+D+G
Opening	B (*farsh*)	B+E (*maqta'* II)	B+E+H (*maqta'* III)
('aah's)	C	C+F	C+F+I

2. Complementarity: new statements attached to the series of 'aah's. These refer back in significance to each element of the previous series (*farsh* and accretions), commenting on and evaluating those elements. This sort of *maqta'* is known as a *ghita'* (cover), and 'completes' the statement of the *farsh*. Traditionally, one *ghita'* completes the *farsh*, but in the poems discussed below, there is a further *ghita'*.

A 2	A 3
B 2 (*maqta'* IV)	B 3 (*maqta'* V)
C 2 (*ghita'*)	C 3 (*ghita'*)

In "'Ala-l- arghul," the *maqta'* following the opening consists of three core statements, each made through a verbal sentence structure in which the references of the pronominal subject of each line emerge through the narrative context, while the objects of the verbs describe colonized space:

الأوله شطبت تونس من الاسلام
والتانيه تحكم بلاد الهند والاهرام
والتالته حطت على حكم العراق والشام

The first, she effaced Tunis of Islam
The second, she rules the countries of India and the Pyramids
The third, she alighted on the rule of Iraq and Syria[12]

The verbs of each line suggest both action and state, emphasizing thereby the result of each action. At the same time, there is a movement from defined action in the past to stress on the present. The perfect verb of the first line suggests through the tense completed action and connotes irreversible finality and complete destruction. The second, an imperfect, acts as a past continuous where action has been established but is continuing in the present. Semantically, the line moves beyond the previous line's description of control through violence and negation to one of control through political power. The third parallels the second in signifying also a certain type of control: political rule. It parallels the first in suggesting a completed action, but this action results in a continuing state. The duration of *hukm* remains undefined—thereby stressing the continuing effect of the verbal phrase. This verb phrase, *hattit 'ala* suggests 'gentle' action (alighting over), a significance which becomes more dominant with the accretion of descriptive terms, as we will see shortly.

The objects/recipients of each action progress eastward in geographic location and forward in time according to the event which initiated the action: the formalized occupation of Tunisia by France, 1881; the occupation of Egypt by Great Britain in 1882 and the declaration of the British Protectorate; the institution of mandatory control by the French in the Syrian province of the former Ottoman Empire and by the British in Iraq (instituted in 1920 and formalized in 1922). India, further to the east and an earlier object of British imperialist control, is linked in this and other poems to British designs in Egypt.[13]

The second *maqta'* is one of accretion (A+D). The first 'aah' extends the reference to the Maghreb as object/recipient of action with respect to French colonialism (*wi-gazayir*, referring to al-Jaza'ir, Algeria). The second adds a prepositional phrase qualifying the verb, and spelling out the means of rule ("She rules... with gestures/signals") as does the third ("with ammunition"). The qualifiers of the two lines are in contrast: *bi-ashayir*, control achieved through the simple giving of an oral order or even a gesture versus *bi-dhakhayir*, attainment of rule through force, corresponding to the verbs *tuhkum* and *hattit 'ala-l-hukm*.[14]

Force and Transitivity 153

The third *maqta'* is one of further accretion (A+D+G):

الأوله شطبت تونس من الاسلام وجزاير طواها البين
والتانيه تحكم بلاد الهند والاهرام باشاير وغمزة عين
والتالته حطت على حكم العراق والشام بذخاير وطيارتين

The first, she effaced Tunis of Islam and Algeria—painful separation submerged her
The second, she rules the countries of India and the Pyramids with gestured orders and the wink of an eye
The third, she alighted on the rule of Iraq and Syria with ammunition and an airplane or two

In the first line, result is expressed through a metaphoric expression drawing on a metaphoric field familiar in folk narratives (*tawaha il-bayn*, "separation submerged, hid, enfolded her").[15] In folk *mawawil*, the referential meaning of *bayn* also takes on an extended meaning of suffering derived from enforced separation. Here, the phrase refers immediately to the closest object (Algeria) and probably refers to the more pervasive French control (cultural as well as political and economic) which Algeria experienced. Yet the process of accretion creates further links; as in the previous unit Algeria as second object of the verb was linked to the Tunisian experience, so in this one the object pronoun of *tawa* may take as antecedent "Tunis" as well as "Gazayir." There may be an implicit linkage between the folk metaphor's suggestion of hardship and hurtful separation on the one hand, and the effacing of Islam—the cultural and spiritual system of the colonized area—on the other.

In the second line, the definition of means is given further emphasis and specificity, as "the wink of an eye" extends the significance of "gestured orders." Not even verbal orders are necessary to achieve and maintain control over the objects, it is suggested; rather, all that the controlling power must do is to give an indirect indication of what it wants. Here, weakness, passivity, and a willingness to be co-opted are imagized as characterizing the objects. This enhances the contrast between object and agent of action further, supplementing the unidirectional action of the verbs. In the third line, also, "two airplanes" cement the role of "ammunition," but the phrase also suggests that indeed not much armed force has been necessary to achieve control, for the use of the dual in colloquial Egyptian Arabic signals "a little" or "a few." The phrase also enhances the metaphoric use of *hattit 'ala*. Not only do the airplanes, the ammunition (and the control) alight from above, but the dual stresses yet again the ease of the exercise. In these lines, the strength of the subject plays against the weakness and passivity of the object; both are placed in the foreground. It is implicit, then, that neither pole is solely responsible for the result. The subjects are targets of attack—but the objects are the target of criticism, of that provocatory presence which Bayram established in the pages of *al-Shabab*.

The repetition of verbs through these stanzas underlines the actor–acted upon dichotomy, as the named colonized/ruled areas remain in object status. In the next *maqta'*, one of complementarity (A 2, B 2, C 2), or in other words the first *ghita'*, this sequence is interrupted momentarily. The spotlight (and subject position) moves to the objects and the crux of their perceived weakness is explicated:

الأوله لما كل المسلمين صارت خدم وعبيد

The first, when all the Muslims became servants and slaves

The verb (*sar*, to become) is one of equivalence more than action; moreover, the line is given the subordinate status of a supporting explanation referring back to the first 'aah' of the expanded *farsh*. Thus, the dominant agent–verb–object parallels of the *farsh* are not reversed by this intrusion, but rather complemented. The reference is broadened, though: descriptively, this is an explanation of the reasons leading to the alleged "effacing" of Islam in Tunisia and Algeria but it expands that reference through naming "all the Muslims" and thus percolates through the other objects named—*bilad il-ahram*, Iraq, and al-Sham.[16] Here, the weakness of the objects which has emerged in the previous stanza is made specific, as both a material and a moral submission is suggested. At the same time, the use of *sarit* suggests that the imbalance has not always existed. It is a reference to the historical might of the Islamic *umma* which the author poses against the present weakness of the community. Again the provocatory note emerges; cannot reference to the past become a blueprint for the future?

The second line of this *maqta'* returns to the unnamed agent and repeats the verb *hatt*, this time in plural perfect form:

والتانيه حطوا بيناتهم قشلاقات فارت بنار وحديد

The second, they placed barracks between them, boiling over with fire and iron

The line refers in the first instance to Egypt (and India), objects of the second 'aah', in its description of London's continuing control over colonized or occupied areas through the reminder and threat of military force in place. But the object of the preposition is also unnamed, also plural: the line suggests the collapse of discrete agents, and separate objects, each into one pole. In the *ghita'*, each 'aah' is no longer dominantly a reference back to the parallel 'aah' of the previous stanza. Rather, its references touch and permeate each other, just as the various manifestations and agents of capitalist and imperialist European control do, and just as the conditions of the controlled interact, each set representing in the end a single pole of the conflict.

The third 'aah' introduces the economic element of imperialistic control and also shifts the third-person narrative to first person, as the narrator includes self and addressee(s) in the controlled group, by implication:

والتالته اسعارنا فى سوق الغنم بارت نهار العيد

Force and Transitivity

The third, our prices in the sheep market went to nothing—and on the feastday

Again, the merging of separate references is evident. Referentially, of course, the line sets up another inescapable contrast, for it is on the feastday that the selling prices of sheep should be at their highest.[17] *Barit* parallels *sarit,* establishing a sense of movement, suggesting that the situation has not always been as it is now. The reference to "feastday" links the line back to Islam as the community's shared point of identity, once mighty, now perceived by the narrator as weak.

The final *maqta'*— a further *ghita'*— summarizes, evaluates, and judges, as the underlying provocatory note continues to sound:

والتـــاريخ مـــعلوم   الأوله امــه خــيــبــه
مــن بــلاد الــروم   والتانيه جات ضربه صايبه
والكلام مــفهــوم   والتالته قول جاتنا نايبه

The first, a ne'er-do-well nation   and history is well known
The second, came an on-target blow   from the nations of the *rum*
The third, say "to hell with us"   and the expression is understood

Again, the collapse of the separate 'aah's is clear. The specific objects of the poem's *farsh* have been subsumed first into "all the Muslims" and then into "a ne'er-do-well nation" (or, community, specifically of Islam—the *umma*) in which the narrator and addressee(s) are included. The reference to history returns us to the transformed status of the *umma* which the use of *sarit* has already implied. This is enhanced further in the next line with the reference to *rum*, which brings together the subject/agent references of the *farsh*. *Rum* (Greek, Greek Orthodox) is a metaphor for Europeans, but also a synecdoche for 'Christians' and finally it yields a historical connotation: the Crusaders.[18] The qualification of "the blow" as *sayba* suggests that in another time and place, such directed blows were *not* on target. History has witnessed a switch in subject position: it is this historical consciousness (which runs throughout Bayram's corpus) that moves the poem from descriptive narrative of a present situation to analysis of its development—and to provocation.

It should be noted that the movement from *farsh* to *ghita'* has marked a transition from expansion to contraction.[19] The expanded description of each line of the *farsh* and accretions (second and third *maqati'*), is channeled into a set of summary statements, moving from explanation and evaluation in the first *ghita'* to unequivocal conclusion and judgment in the second *ghita'* which invokes the historical background.

If we summarize the verbal structures of the poem, we find that out of fifteen lines (each of which is a complete statement), eleven are proper verbal sentences with initial verb (nine of which are the repeated verbs of the *farsh*). All imply contextually a member of the collectivity "nations of rum" as the agent, performing an action upon "Tunis," "Gazayir," "Bilad il-hind wa-l-ahram," "il-'Iraq wa-l-Sham."[20] The other verbal statements—where some element of the latter community/communities acts as agent—consist of a verb of being (line 13) and an intransitive verb with downward/negative semantic force *(barit)* (line 15), both of which, as noted, strengthen the theme of historical change—for the worse with regard to the subject. The imperative with embedded self-directed oath, which ends the poem, is directed to this subject/object, collectively, in a negative and inclusive evaluation which permits no equivocacy. The syntactic structures of the poem construct and underline a one-way direction of action; semantically, the dominant verbs suggest force and control while the accretion of adverbial phrases also suggest the ease of controlling the objects. The thematic force of the poem emerges in its syntax and choice of lexicon. The actor–recipient, active–passive dichotomy—as much as a particular historical referential field for narrative—is the fundamental axis of the poem.

Another composition built upon the same framework of expression—and also titled "'Ala-l-arghul" in early publication[21]—shows a similar interplay of syntactic structure and a particular vector informing a web of relationships. This poem focuses on the historical arena of British–Egyptian relations in the early 1920s, specifically taking three historical moments as the referential framework of narrative. Both the linear chronological progression from one event to the next and the interweaving of the three aspects of the relationship which they represent emerge through the expectations set up by the compositional framework, the 1–2–3 organization whereupon each *maqta'* through either accretion or complementarity builds upon and transcends or broadens the previous one.

The three historical moments are: first, the popular expression of resistance to the British presence in Egypt and to the failure of negotiations for independence, which erupted in 1919; second, the Milner Mission (announced in November 1919, present in Egypt from December 1919 to March 1920) in which Lord Milner was dispatched by the British government to lead a commission of inquiry into the circumstances and consequences of the mass resistance; third, the Declaration of 27 February 1922 which offered Egypt a nominal separation without abolishing any of the basic sources and channels of British control in the country.

Examination of syntactic relations and lexicon in the *farsh* reveals a directional emphasis similar to that of the last poem:

الأوله بالبنادق سكتوا الثوار

والتانيه جا اللورد ملنر يربط الاحرار

والتالته تصريح فى فبراير واصله هزار

The first, with rifles they silenced those who revolted
The second, Lord Milner came to bind the free
The third, a declaration in February, and in truth it's jesting.

Force and Transitivity

In the first line, neither pole of the relationship/opposition is mentioned with specific reference to spheres of national identity—British or Egyptian— or to the poles of colonizer and colonized; the actor/subject of the first line is implied through the context.[22] The object of the first line consists of the rebels, acted upon through a verb which conveys semantically a smothering dominance, an ability (and desire) to cut short the revolution:

الأوله بالبنادق سكتوا الثوار

The first, with rifles they silenced those who revolted

A parallel structure initiates the second 'aah' (line 6), where the plural implied agent of line 4 is concretized through a synecdoche (Lord Milner), and the transitive verb phrase (*ga . . . yurbut*) echoes the decisive stopping power suggested by the transitive and intensive *sakkitu*:

والتانيه جا اللورد ملنر يربط الاحرار

The second, Lord Milner came to bind the free

The object noun signifies a conception of the Egyptian community and the foremost representatives of that community's struggle for freedom (linking the line back to *is-suwwar*) in contrast with the actual circumstances of that community under occupation. But at the same time, it may carry double, ironizing significance, punning on the name of the political party formed in opposition to the Wafd. This party (*Hizb al-Ahrar al-Dusturiyin*), the Liberal Constitutionalist Party, was not formed until after the February Declaration (it was officially founded in October 1922). Arising from differences between Sa'd Zaghlul and the other founders of the Wafd, it was a political grouping which represented a more cautious line and which Bayram lashes elsewhere as self-interested, out of touch with the populace, and liable to compromise with the British either tacitly or actively, as we will see later.[23] Prominent leaders of this group were ready to accept the Declaration's contents.

The nominal structure of the third 'aah' suggests a fait accompli: the event of the February 1922 Declaration:

والتالته تصريح فى فبراير واصله هزار

The third, a declaration in February, and in truth it's jesting

The verbal noun *hizar* makes an equivalence which sums up the narrator's evaluation of this progression of historical events (following Zaghlul's lead that the Declaration was traitorous to the nationalist cause).[24] The vertical structure of components in the unit, through the linking power of the end rhyme, shows a digression from *is-suwwar* to *il-ahrar* and finally to *hizar*.

```
(humma)           ──→ sakkitu      ──→ is-suwwar
  (representative)                       │
il-Lurd Milnir    ──→ ga ... yurbut ──→ il-ahrar
  (result)                               │
Tasrih fi fibrayar ←──────────────── wi-asluh hizar
```

Accretions in the next *maqta'* extend the emphases of the basic 'aah's.

الأوله بالبنادق سكتوا الثوار ومدافع اهم فاضلين
والتانيه جا اللورد ملنر يربط الاحرار ويترافع عن الغالبين
والتالته تصريح فى فبراير واصله هزار ومش نافع وقولوا آمين

> The first, with rifles they silenced the rebels
> and cannon—well, they still remain
> The second, Lord Milner came to bind the Ahrar
> and put the case of the conquerors
> The third, a declaration in February
> and in truth, it's jesting and to no benefit, so say 'amen.'

In the first line, the force of *sakkitu* is emphasized further as the means of action are named, and their permanence is suggested. In the second, as Lord Milner has "bound" the object, he fulfills his mission—to "legalize" the British presence in a sense; the use of terminology with a legalistic echo (*yitrafi' 'an*) resonates against the epithet *il-ghalibin*, which suggests victory through force. In the third, the evaluation of the Declaration is followed by a plural imperative: the only active response possible is a collective utterance of finality and despair, yielding the sense that events will not work out as the speaker would wish.[25]

The second set of 'aah's—complements rather than accretions, comprising the *ghita'*—expands upon the reference to forced action through the use of 'legalistic' or at least pacific means, even as it represents a contraction from description to evaluation. The diction and syntax extend the active/passive, powerful/powerless dichotomy through the vocabulary of victory and plunder. The evaluation of the events and circumstances described in the *farsh* is, in this case, framed as rhetorical questions (in the first and second lines of the *maqta'*):

الأوله مين يمزق حـــجــــة   الـطـالـب فـى ديـن مـطـلـوب
والتــانيـــه مين بس يمنـع   سلطة الغـالـب عن المغلوب
والتـــالتــــه تسلب ولكن   قـال لنا السـالب انا المسلوب

> The first, who shreds the document of the demander in a debt demanded?
> The second, who bars the authority of the victor from the vanquished?
> The third, she plunders but the plunderer said to us 'I'm the plundered'

"The seeker" refers us back to the collectivity of *is-suwwar*, the unsuccessful attempts of the Wafdist leadership to negotiate independence in London, and the uncompromising stance of Zaghlul. The (silenced) demand has the formal backing of a mandate from the people but still cannot overcome the *ghalibin*—as the diction of the extended *farsh*'s second 'aah' is repeated and the *suwwar/ahrar* now become "the defeated," as postwar promises of the allies are seen to be a sham. In the third 'aah', the motif of force sanctioned through legal/diplomatic process is underlined as the plundering subject *(il-salib)* tries to claim the status of the wronged object *(il-maslub)*. The vocabulary of plunder clashes with the narrated attempt by the British and their local allies to establish the legality of a unilateral declaration which ensured continued British control over four points: Egypt's foreign alliances, an ongoing military presence in Egypt, continued immunity for foreigners from local laws, and the status of Sudan.

The final group of 'aah's—a second *ghita'*, which is a further contraction—offers a set of statements which declare outcomes or evaluations of the series of events that have framed the *farsh* as well as advancing an indirect comment on the first *ghita'*. The same dominant structure of acting subject/ acted upon object with the same referents is again found, again with a pronominal plural subject in the first line:

الأوله بالسهوله ضيعوا ارواح

The first, with ease they wasted souls

The second line metaphorizes Lord Milner as the *ghul* (ghoul) of folk belief, not only a *ghul* but the son of a *ghula*, Mother England:

والتانيه غول ابن غولة جار علينا وراح

The second, a ghoul son of a ghoul bore down upon us and left

The third statement—a nominal structure as in the third lines of the previous units—evaluates the fact of the Resolution and once again invokes an audience with a second-person reference—a warning of things to come, as *mizah* recalls *hizar* and posits a sardonic judgment, possibly shading into a rhetorical question to the addressee, upon the course of events:

والتالته هى المهوله تلتقيها مزاح

The third, it's the one to dread—you find it a jest . . .

The combination of a specifically directed and dominant agent–verb–object structure and a lexicon of terms recalling force and seizure establish the dominant tone, direction, and "message" of each poem.[26]

II. From Syntax to Image

The language of force, dominance, and pillage is not employed only in those poems which invoke, describe, and judge political events in a direct and topical manner. This language also intersects with a dominant image found in Bayram's corpus, and particularly in poems published in the 1920s, as we find Egypt imagized as a woman. In the poems which celebrate Egypt's wealth and fertility, and which communicate the narrator's longing for Egypt from an enforced distance explicitly noted, the image is that of the nurturing mother or the beloved who is yet beset with ills. However, in those poems which treat the relationship between *bilad ir-rum* and *ibn/bint il-balad*, the image is that of a weak, passive, and mournful woman, subject to strong-arm, implicitly or explicitly male, treatment. The motif of legalized rape captures her situation—as suggested, for instance, in "il-Fahl yidrab bi-l-qulla yutlub istiqlal."[27] This poem was first published in *al-Shabab* between 1921 and 1923. In it, as in "al-Isti'mar," Egypt's occupied status is linked to British activities in India, for Egypt stands "directly/on the road to India." Egypt is personified and addressed in second person as a female:

مالك شهقتى على العالى   ياللى مـــــــــالك زند
مالك يا واقفه طوالى   فـى طـريــق الـهـنـد

What ails you, that you sob so, out loud. You who have no forearm
What ails you, O one standing directly on the road to India?

Paronomasia links the woman's resigned state and her lack of power, through the double use of *malik* as, first, the query "what is the matter with you?" and, second, a negation of the possessive *lik (ma-lik zind)*. Her lack of a "forearm" suggests both physical weakness and lack of a "protector"—Egypt's sons and perhaps its daughters too, although the image of "forearm," particularly in the context of this poem, suggests a physical strength traditionally associated with male spheres of conduct. She is capable only of lamenting her state "out loud" but not of backing up complaint with action. But her fate is cemented by geographical position, emphasized by *tawali*, which signifies physical placement ("directly") but may, secondarily, also suggest temporal duration ("always"). A stationary situation is suggested by the active participle *waqfa*.[28] The subject's weakness is indicated further in the next line, where the active participle is one, semantically, of submission:[29]

يا مسلمه المسيو المالى   يفـــــــــرك بالـعند
والقطن ينضاف عالغله   جـــــــــوا بيت المال

You who submit to Monsieur Moneybags
As he impoverishes you with a will
While the cotton is added to the grain
Inside the state treasury

Here, the status of active subject shifts to "Monsieur Moneybags" whose rape is an economic one; the force of his action is fortified through the qualifying prepositional phrase *b-il-'ind* (deliberately, with stubbornness). The use of a European term to describe the European interloper is a frequent device in Bayram's writings which suggests that the invasion is not only one of political force or economic pillage but also of cultural (linguistic) imposition. Here, the term also serves to emphasize the gulf between the two subjects, Egypt/woman and the "monsieur," the one powerless and the other armed with financial vigor.

Force and Transitivity

And from the start, Egypt's rape by "Monsieur Moneybags" *(il-misyu il-mali)* is linked by association to the ongoing accumulation of national wealth in agricultural products through monopolization inside the state coffers.[30] At the same time, the term *bayt il-mal* has an Islamic pedigree, and perhaps suggests that the foreign presence is set against not only the state (Europe–Egypt) but also against the community of faith (Christendom–Dar al-Islam).

It is only now that we see a possible rival to the "monsieur" emerge, in a line which becomes the repeated refrain of the poem:

الفــــحل يضـــــرب بالقله   يطلب اســـــتــــقـــــلال

And the stallion strikes with the waterjug
Demanding an independence

The term *il-fahl*, the stallion, is a common metaphor for the strong and sexually potent male and also for the celebrity or well-known persona.[31] Here, it is probably a reference to the nationalist spokesperson Sa'd Zaghlul. The *qulla* (traditional pottery waterjug) conjures the colloquial expression *kasart waraah qulla* (literally, "I broke the *qulla* behind him"), said after one has expelled an unwanted, undesireable individual from one's presence. Indeed, this expression was used as a rallying cry during the events of 1919 with regard to the British. But how far will this carry the *fahl?* The rape is occurring simultaneously with a nationalist rhetoric which, it is suggested, may represent no more than an active and virile image, an appearance which masks ineffective speech.

The poem goes on to note the means by which the woman "with no forearm" can be controlled: the threat of force, the police apparatus, and coercion through the preferential allocation of scarce goods are accompanied by a legal system mainly concerned to "impound the cooking-pot/and bring the auctioneer." The *halla* (cooking-pot) is a concrete image for the fundamental possessions of daily life (suggesting that the foreign rulers are stripping Egypt even of her basic implements of existence, are stripping even the poor).[32] It is only the rapist who can work the legal system with success, and through co-option of the local bureaucratic structure. Again, it is not just the British who are invoked: "the auctioneer" (and "the judge") may well refer to those Egyptians who were taking a more cautious line (and one, it is suggested here and elsewhere, which is linked to individual self-interest) than that of Zaghlul.

Egypt cannot even complain without being immediately quashed: any expression of dissatisfaction on the part of "the woman" brings the variety of means articulated in the first poem discussed above to bear on the objects— armed force (Qantara was a major British military base), pitiful bribes, the allure of material acquisition on credit (a reference to Egypt's foreign debt):

وان قلتی یاخــــواتی یانا   ینضـــــرب تلیــــفــــون
م القنطره للشــفـــخـــانه   یحـــــضــــر الكركـــون
بالبــسكویت والجــبــخـــانه   والحــــاجــــات البــون
والخــــرق ینســــد بفله   والـزعـل ینــشـــــــال

And were you to say: 'Aah' sisters 'aah'. A telephone call would be made
From [remote] Qantara to the donkey pen. The police arrive
With biscuits and ammunition. And the things on credit
And the hole is blocked with a cork. The anger is siphoned off

Further lamentation brings no help; seeing merely "the shadow of the whip" silences the potential resister. As in "'Ala-l-arghul," and foreshadowed by the presence of the sequestering judge, it is clear that legal documents are no use. We find a similar image and diction in this poem:

والحجة تصبح مهريه	ممتليه خروق
Full of rips and tears	The document becomes worn out.

In this poem, the dominant structure—which establishes the power relationship, suggests the dichotomy of active and passive, and provokes the question of responsibility—is not so much a transitive verbal structure but rather elaboration of an image through the second-person address to Egypt, personified—an elaboration supplemented by her syntactic position as the object and recipient of action.

A brief look at two other poems shows the same strategy. The motif of legalized rape surfaces more than once in Bayram's poems on imperialist activity in the region: Egypt, occupied, has her equally oppressed sisters. The conflation of sexual metaphoric imagery and the suggestion of possibilities for economic exploitation marks the opening of "The Occupation of Syria,"[33] as a French lexical invasion foreshadows the story:

يا جانطى خالص يا طريه	يام الضفاير يا شاميه
وكلمينى عن الرمان	خوخك بكام ردى عليه

O braid-tressed maiden, Syrian woman
　Very *gentille* tender one
What price are your plums, give me an answer
　And tell me of your pomegranates.

As in "il-Fahl"[34] the dominant tone established from the start is that of sorrow and despair, in the context of reminiscenses of better times—*ayyam afrahik* may refer either specifically to weddings or more generally to happy days.

شبعنا عض فى تفاحك	يامـا فى ايام افراحك
ومحوطاه بزبيب لبنانى	ايام ما كان سنك ضاحك

Ahh, the days of your wedding feasts
　How we satiated ourselves on your apples
In the days when your teeth showed in laughter
　And you surrounded them with Lebanese *arak*

Force and Transitivity

But recent history—the internal decay of societies—is brought in subtly to bear, as the breakdown of territorial resistance is suggested through a sexual metaphor for "the last bastion" of resistance:[35]

واصل ترباسك خسران

And at base your bolt is in ruins

The only possible result is the passivity of acceptance, as legal means are constructed to justify the rape and "monsieur" has his way:

خاتم الخطوبه فى صباعك   جاب هولك المسيو بتاعك
حطى دراعه فى دراعك   وخشى وياه البستان

The engagement ring on your finger
  Was brought by your *monsieur*
Place his arm in yours
  And with him go into the orchard

As in "il-Fahl," territorial and economic occupation are seen to have an ulterior motive—European expansionism has its own logic:

دخل وصدد فى حماكى   ونيته فى اللى وراكى

He entered and stretched out in your sanctuary
  His goal is that which lies behind you

And the conclusion is one of hopeless mourning, wherein "the foreigner" is the agent of the action and thus of the result described in the poem:

يا حلوه فين ورد خدودك   وفين معاصمك ونهودك
يعنى الخواجه نحل عودك   وصبحك حالك عدمان

Sweetheart, where's your cheeks' bloom
  Where are your wrists and your breasts
I mean, the foreigner has emaciated your figure
  Till you've reached a state of nothingness

Another sister—or neighbor—is chided for her inaction, in the context of the fraught issue of unity between Egypt and Sudan, one of the Wafd's demands.[36] But as "the female neighbor" (Egypt) rouses Sudan, late in the day though it be, a note of hope and positive action is sounded. Like Egypt, Sudan wears a *khulkhal* (anklet), familiar traditional adornment of the Egyptian/Sudanese peasant woman or of *bint al-balad*. Its quality as a gift is undermined, however, as it symbolizes the recipient's possession by another—the *khulkhal* here is a sign of betrothal or marriage. But not only that—it represents a deception and a cheapness which belies any notion of respect or regard. Rather than being composed of true precious metal, it is merely plated, hiding a baser material beneath. The *khulkhal* becomes a means of restraint, as it becomes a metaphor for occupation and control, a weight to drag the woman down. It is a burden ill-concealed below the shining silver of an offered "gift."[37]

والخلخال اللى جالك مطلى   على س‍ـــــــــوم اصلى
لا يـخـلـى رجـلك ولا رجـلى   تــــــــــــرف تــنــدار

And the anklet which came to you is plated
Claiming to be real [silver]
It allows neither your foot nor mine
The ability to turn away.

Egypt then addresses her southern neighbor, chidingly, as *maksurit il-raqba*, (broken-necked, powerless). This addressee's situation is even worse, it seems, than that of "you who have no forearm." She counsels Sudan to "learn to pluck the goose/and how to play at butting"—or how to become an agent rather than an object of action. Thus may she end Egypt's "scandal" and her own—situations linked intimately, in the eyes of the nation.

III. Unidirectionalism Tempered

The "'Ala-l-arghul" poems discussed earlier, offering the language of violence and defeat, may well have been published first in *al-Shabab,* the first following the dashed expectations of 1919 and the second in the bitterness following the announcement of the February 1922 Resolution. In these poems, the note of passivity and hopelessness dominates, constructed through the agent–verb–object structure and the imagery, and accompanied by the hint that it is not only the invader's might but also the passivity of the invaded which is to blame. But the language of violence, unidirectional force, and rape set against weakness and ineffective nationalist rhetoric (for instance, in "il-Fahl," first published no later than 1923), begins to shift. In the address to neighbor Sudan, the tone of hopelessness is tempered and indeed challenged by the speaker's call for arousal and action, thus suggesting a transition from despair at the active/passive dichotomy to anger which carries a positive note of action.

A similar shift is found in other poems from the mid-1920s, although it will require further efforts to establish a firm dating of Bayram's poems in order to trace such shifts precisely—and of course the complexity of vision and artistic expression in the corpus precludes any absolute periodicization. The conception of a dichotomy remains: two poles locked in combat, one of which through its power and activeness as agent is winning. Yet, a different note sounds. For example, if we look at a poem published in October 1924 in *al-Shabab*,[38] (thus, towards the end of Zaghlul's ministry, and just a month before the assassination of Sir Lee Stack), we find that the opening is a direct address in which a hortatory tone emerges through the use of the introductory interjection *ala*:

الا البلاد ياولاد مالها مقلوب حالها

What of the country, lads, what's the matter? It's all topsy-turvy

The speaker goes on to provide an interpretation: Egypt is not only asleep, but fast asleep *(shib'it tashkhir)*. The two poles of conflict are set in contrast almost

Force and Transitivity

immediately, recalling the diction of poems already discussed, although there is a note of challenge in the characterization of *bilad ir-rum* as *il-bilad il-dun*, "the low (base) countries:"

اما بلاد الدون ربحت مصر اندبحت

As for the base countries, they've profited; Egypt has been slaughtered

These countries, the narrator notes, "are behind us with the cane/and the cudgel until they've worn us down and we've become donkeys." The focus grows more specific, centering on entrepreneurs in Egypt, especially European ones, and particularly bakers. The attack through epithet suggested by *il-bilad il-dun* is resounded as "bakers" are described each and all as "boor, dullard/his ear closed tightly at the time of crisis . . . ." But the opposition of *ribhit/indabahit* is recalled through specific description:

طحن البلاطه وسكتنا يالله امتكنا وحطها فى قعر التكنه وخلطها شعير

He ground up the tiling and we remained silent, disgrace upon us
He put it in the bottom of the *takna* and mixed it with barley.[39]

Balata may refer to paving tiles or stones. Taking this general sense, the expression *ga'id 'ala-l-balata/il-hatta il-balata/il-hadida khaduh* may be significant. In other words, the very lowest and poorest material and physical perch (*'ala-l-balata/'ala-l-hadida*, broke) is destroyed by this sort of entrepreneur. But more specifically, in the poem's context, *balata* may refer to a circular object made of red brick on which bread is baked inside the traditional oven. If the *balata* is broken, bread cannot be baked. Or, *balata* could refer to a grinding stone. Taking both possibilities, this line suggests the destruction of local means of production by the (foreign) entrepreneur—while the local populace does not even protest. Not only that—the ground-up stone is used, it seems, to adulterate Egypt's bread. *Takna* (stand) may refer to the oven itself; placing these ingredients in its bottom may suggest surreptitiousness as well as careless and unappetizing production methods. It is interesting that the entrepreneur is described as using (taking over) the local traditional means of production; both the physical and the economic nutrition of the Egyptian poor have been taken over and destroyed by the entrepreneur.

This situation elicits an oath connoting both helplessness and disgust, and further attack on *il-arwam*[40] by means of insulting epithets drawing on animal imagery. This device is found often in Bayram's poetry, and earlier in this poem an animal epithet familiar in the colloquial is employed with reference to "us" (*il-himir*). All builds to an insult carrying particular force in its reference to an animal not touched by Muslims:

اعـوذ بالله دى الأورام ولادى الأغنام   اللى ما ينجح فيها كلام الا بسواتير
ما حد حقه الحرق بجاز غير الخباز   وقلع عـينه بالمخـــراز ابن الخنازير

> God save me from this! Are these foreigners or sheep
> With which no speech succeeds but the chopper
> No one deserves burning by kerosene but the baker
> And poking out his eye with an awl—son of pigs

The opposition between poles is sounded in the juxtaposition of *halak* and *amlak*:

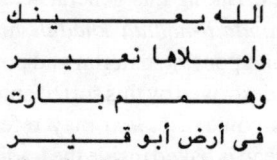

> On the day people become poverty-stricken, ruined
> He builds estates

But the call for action which sounds through the attacks above is specified as the narrator calls his countrypeople to awaken and notice the sources of worsening circumstances, which he suggests (as in previous poems) are not only brought from outside but self-inflicted through ineffective leadership and apathy. This invocation is followed by a series of imperatives which transform the attacks already made into a battle-call. These are set against a reminder of passivity which has led to successful foreign military action in the past:

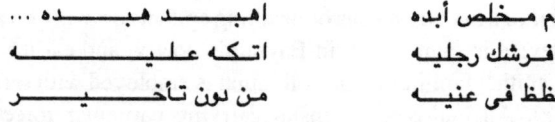

> Put the pistol in your right hand
> God give you aid
> And make us a company, by your faith
> And fill it with clamor
> For in it [Egypt] cooking-pots have boiled over
> And cares have gone to nothing
> And devilish vultures have flown
> Into the land of Abu Qir

Signs and representatives of the foreign invasion lead to another series of imperatives, intersected by an echo of a popular proverb[41] and recalling the earlier diction by which "bakers" were attacked:

اسمع كلام مخلص أبده   اهبد هبده ...
من مد فى فرشك رجليه   اتكه عليه
بالحيل وبظظ فى عنيه   من دون تأخير

> Listen to sincere words, and begin
> Strike a real blow ...
> The one who has stretched out his legs in your bed
> Press upon him
> With strength and poke your finger in his eyes [make him pay]
> Without delay.

Force and Transitivity

The tables are turned; it is now "the European" who is soft and easily crushed:

صنف الأوروباوى مرخرخ بـــشـــت مـــلـــخـــلـــخ
من شخطه والثانيه يسخسخ ....

The European type is flabby
A tottery Ganymede
From one loud oath or two he faints

And the portrait of the Egyptian, now awake, is in contrast, as the usually negative adjectives *tilim* and *barid* take on positive connotations:

والمصـــرى واد جن مـقـــارد وتـــــــلــــــم بـــــــارد

And the Egyptian is a jinni-like lad, clever as a monkey
Blunt and cold

In this poem, the transition from one-way to two-way direction, supplemented by imperatives and epithets which lash and tear down the interloper as they build up the pole of 'us', moves the opposition of forces onto a plane of active combat. The linguistically structured agent/object, powerful/powerless dichotomy begins to break down. The 'us' versus 'them' polarity is not guided here by a one-way verbal direction.[42]

Nor is this polarity always defined according to an 'Egyptian' versus 'foreign' standoff. As a Wafdist strongly loyal to the leadership of Sa'd Zaghlul, Bayram was harshly critical of forces opposed to the Wafd—particularly those, as I have suggested, which took a more conciliatory stance towards the British, a perspective which he links frequently with the power of personal economic interests.[43] Seven months before the poem discussed above was published, a poem had appeared in *al-Shabab* which took a retrospective narrative glance at the internal political situation in Egypt from 1919 until the first parliamentary elections of January 1924 in which the Wafd gained an overwhelming victory.[44] In this poem, the agent–action–object structure is submerged in a standoff of agents; the narrative shifts back and forth from one pole of conflict to the other. These agents are both Egyptian; the entrance of the (external) agent that was dominant in "'Ala-l-arghul" is implied to be catalytic but it is not central to the conflict which structures the narrative. Published in *al-Shabab* under the heading "'Ala-l-rababa," this poem is constructed upon another compositional form drawn from the oral culture: a folk epic, a framework which the poet had already employed in *al-Shabab* to narrate and comment upon the Greek–Turkish hostilities of a few years before. As in any epic, there are heroes and there are knaves. The traditional invocation to the Prophet, coupled with an invocation to *Misr al-sa'ida*, opens the way for introduction of the heroes in the diction of tribal identity and for introduction of their adversaries as well, defined simply and from the heroes' point of view as "the enemies." As the conflict takes shape, the identity of "the enemies" as the spectre which the heroes must and can overcome is given sharper focus, one which puts the audience unequivocally on the heroes' side, for their adversaries are characterized through an uncomplimentary descriptive animal epithet. The subject–object referents of this line parallel those of the introduction a few lines earlier; in both, the heroes are the agents of action and their adversaries are the objects and recipients of the action:

ركبت بنى زغلول تزيح الأعادى ...
حاشت بنى زغلول كلاب البوادى

Bani Zaghlul rode, to drive away the enemies . . .
Bani Zaghlul held back the dogs of the desert

But the victory—or holding action—does not go unchallenged:

ومين يحوش الكلب والكلب جايع

And who holds back the dog when the dog is hungry?

Thus is the second pole of the conflict introduced and the narrator's sympathies established, with the use of debasing animal imagery. But this rhetorical question, which ends the initial introduction of the narrative situation and characters, and precedes the more specific development of the narrative, also extends the metaphoric field of the "dogs of the desert." "The dog" is wild, roving, and hungry; it may refer both to the immediate enemies of Bani Zaghlul and to the hovering ally of these enemies, a linkage which is made in the terms of economic interests:

دخل السفير ملنر على مصر شارى   قالت بنى الأحرار حدانا البضايع

Ambassador Milner arrived in Egypt buying
Bani Ahrar said: 'We have the goods.'[45]

The enemy's interest and alliance is underlined further but at the same time his advance is checked somewhat by a negative, as an allusion is made to Zaghlul's call for a boycott of the Milner Mission, a call to which *most* of the populace responded firmly:

لم يلتقى ملنر خلاف المنادى   امير بنى الاحرار فى مصر بايع

Milner met none except the auctioneer
The Amir of Bani Ahrar is selling Egypt

As the alliance between the agent/occupier and the Liberal Constitutionalist leaders (al-Ahrar) is defined as one of shared interests vested in the language of commerce, "Bani Ahrar" emerge not only as the local representative of foreign interests but also as the main adversary which "Bani Zaghlul" must fight. Polarization is further defined with reference to the human context in which the conflict takes place; the term *ashraf* with its religious connotations takes on an ironic sense and the flight of "the nobles"—whether a physical or a metaphoric one—is contrasted to the situation within Egypt, bringing to mind the opposing images which the political parties had at the time—the Ahrar as *hizb al-dhawat* (party of the aristocrats) and the Wafd as *hizb al-fallahin* (party of the peasants—and, by extension, the urban poor):

واتغربت اشرافنا عن ديارهم ...
واتيتمت أطفال ...

Our nobles have become estranged from their homes...
traveled west
And children have become orphaned . . .

Animal imagery returns as the focus shifts to another battleground, the election, imagizing the conflict as one between wild beasts with clear symbolic identities. "The lions"—Bani Zaghlul—become clearly distinguished from their opponents, "the hyenas." The contrast in their interests with regard to the populace is brought out sharply not only through the images but also through apposition and invocation to a broader constituency. "The lions" are coupled with an invocation—"O folk"—while "the hyenas" are described as "eaters of human flesh."

فى الانتخابات ياناس بانت اسودها   من أكـــالين لحم الأنام الضـــبــــايـع

In the election, O folk, her lions were sorted out
From the voracious eaters of human flesh—the hyenas

The "tribe" invoked ("O folk") calls for its leader:

صاحت بنى زغلول ألا يا سعده

Bani Zaghlul cried out: 'Verily O Sa'd.'

The contrast between the two continues to structure the narrative through dialogue; Bani Ahrar's response pits violence against the recognized procedures of electoral process. Declaring their intended methods, the Bani Ahrar substantiate the narrator's epithet for them as "the eaters of human flesh":

قالت بنى الاحرار نحارب بسيفنا

Bani Ahrar said: 'We fight by our sword.'

Bani Zaghlul's reply, in turn, shows the heroes upholding the principle of legal/constitutional process.[46] Moreover, it links the notion of electoral process to a sanctified struggle through the choice of diction:

قال الأمير زغلول دى حرب الشرايع

Amir Zaghlul said: 'This is war according to law.'

Thus, the side of Bani Zaghlul is placed firmly on the side of the law—whether constitutional or divinely ordered. Further sanction is suggested in the passage's echo of the poem's opening invocation, where the Prophet is characterized not only as "the one sent" but also as *il-muntakhab* (the elected, the chosen). And the poem is marked by other oppositions which echo terminology familiar to listeners of folk epics. The poem ends with a direct address that reverberates back to that of *akkalin il-lahm*, preceding an oath and a challenge which presumes the victory of Bani Zaghlul and notes the grounds of its struggle:

يا آكلين الحق رحـتم فى نايبـه   والحق ده ينعـاد ولو كـان ضـايع

O eaters of right (truth), go to hell
That right (truth) will be returned even if it has gone astray

The poles of conflict here are shifted from *rum* versus *'arab* to forces within Egypt itself—seen as hero versus allied villains, wherein Lord Milner (synecdoche for the British government) is *éminence grise* rather than ghoul. The back-and-forth movement between poles of the conflict as agents of action—Bani Zaghlul and Bani Ahrar—is in contrast to the unidirectional dominance of a single class of agents acting upon a single class of objects.

Thus, both in poems taking internal political circumstances in Egypt as their referential focus, and in those which make links between Egypt's experiences and those of other peoples, the framework is one of opposition between exclusive groups, although the specific poles of opposition vary, as does the definition of community according to the conception of what is most threatening to Egypt's autonomy. And the terms and context of opposition are concretized through the interplay of verbal structures with this shifting definition of conflicting poles.

Further work on dating the corpus will help to clarify the shifts and silences in one writer's political vision of Egypt. This will also aid in tracing the development in Bayram's writings of an identification, between a community defined as 'Egyptian' (with shifting reference as to what 'Egyptian' includes and what it means) and other communities, based on more than the shared circumstances of external control. This emerging identification will characterize Bayram's topical political poems increasingly from the mid-1930s, influenced not only by changes in the internal balance of forces in Egypt but also by the growing popularity and potency of ideas of Arab nationalism and Third World solidarity.

Notes

1 I am indebted to 'Abbas Ahmad Labib for his critical reading of an earlier draft of this article, and to Mahmud Amin al-'Alim for his comments. I am also grateful to Nelly El-Aref for her help.

For a biographical sketch of Mahmud Bayram al-Tunisi, focusing particularly on his activities in journalism before and during exile, see Marilyn Booth, "Egypt in its Own Words: Mahmud Bayram al-Tunisi (1893–1961) and the Literature of Vernacular Expression (1920–1934)," Ph.D dissertation, Oxford, Michaelmas 1984, chapter 1. Particularly useful for the early period are the works of 'Abd al-'Alim al-Qabbani (*Mahmud Bayram al-Tunisi, 1893–1961,* Cairo: Dar al-Katib al-'Arabi li-l-Taba'a wa-l-Nashr,

1963) and Muhammad Kamil al-Banna (*Bayram al-Tunisi kama 'araftuhu*, Cairo: Matabi' al-Sabah, 1961, and *Mahmud Bayram al-Tunisi: qitharat al-adab al-sha'bi*, Tunis: al-Dar al-'Arabiya li-l-Kitaba, 1980).
2 On *al-Shabab*, see Booth, chapter 1, and pp. 338–39.
3 On *al-Funun*, see Booth, chapter 1, pp. 340–42, and comments throughout al-Banna's earlier book.
4 Most of the treatments of Bayram's life and career give copious excerpts from his corpus according to broad thematic division. The numerous articles which have been written on him tend to focus on various life experiences, often illustrated by passages of *zajal*. (There has also been a tendency to read first-person references in the poetry as unmediated references to an authorial autobiography rather than as appropriate metaphoric usages.) A recent study which focuses on the formal organization of the *zajal* corpus falls into the same approach by describing sets of poems briefly, according to categories of human images. See Yusri al-'Azab, *Azjal Bayram al-Tunisi: dirasa fanniya* (Cairo: al-Hay'a al-Misriya al-'Amma li-l-Kitab, 1980).
5 Much groundwork remains to be done before it is possible to attempt any definitive study on Bayram's oeuvre. No edition of his poetry exists which provides original published texts and publication data; much of the prose which appeared in the 1920s and 1930s has never been edited and republished.
6 From "Gandhi," republished in *al-A'mal al-kamila li-Bayram al-Tunisi*, vol. VII (Cairo: al-Hay'a al-Misriya al-'Amma li-l-Kitab, 1982) (hereafter, *al-A'mal*), 21–24.
7 Work in progress includes tracing the varying use of certain key terms through the oeuvre, linking them horizontally and linearly according to the situating of the poems and prose works themselves in a specific historical and production context to the extent possible (terms such as *umma, watan, gom, balad/bilad, ibn/bint al-balad, misr/misriyin, rum/khawaga/urubbi;* the slippage between *Arab* and *Muslim* as labels of community).

I am grateful to 'Abbas Ahmad Labib for calling to my attention the work of Marlin Nasr, who has traced key usages in the speeches and writing of Gamal 'Abd al-Nasser. While her approach to semantic linkage would need to be modified in important ways as a model for the study of didactic poetry, her construction of fields, linkages, networks, and oppositions is a starting point for this sort of textual analysis. See Marlin Nasr, *al-Tasawwur al-qawmi al-'arabi fi fikr Jamal 'Abd al-Nasir, 1952–1970: dirasa fi 'ilm al-mufradat wa-l-dalala* (Beirut: Markaz Dirasat al-Wahda al-'Arabiya, 1981).
8 Bayram began publishing this form in *al-Shabab*. I suspect that this poem was published there first, although it will be impossible to establish this until a full run of the publication is located. The earliest publication of the

poem I have found is "Il-Bayramiyat: 'Ala-l-arghul," *al-Funun* II, no. 81 (6 May 1928), p. 10. Republished in *al-A'mal*, vol. VI (Cairo, 1980), pp. 111–12, under the title "al-Isti'mar."

9 Nabila Ibrahim, *al-Dirasat al-sha'biya bayna-l-nazariya wa-l-tatbiq* (Cairo, n.d.), p. 280, quoted in al-'Azab, pp. 278.

10 The term *marduf* refers to this structure, suggesting the device of successive completion or complementarity. See al-'Azab, p. 276. As Rushdi Salih explains it, the structure supports "presentation of a problem (qadiya) . . . and then the solution to this problem." (Ahmad Rushdi Salih, *Funun al-adab al-sha'bi* [Cairo: Dar al-Fikr, 1958], part 1, p. 81).

11 For an example of this compositional form, characterized as a *shakwa* (plaint), see Salih, part 1, pp. 82–83. For a description of Bayram's use of this form, see al-'Azab, pp. 275–82. Al-'Azab notes that Bayram composed nine *mawawil mardufa;* I have found two additional examples in *al-Imam*: "'Ala-l-arghul: al-tigara wa-l-sina'a" vol. 31, no. 3 [3 Sept. 1933], p. 3); "'Ala-l-arghul" (vol. 31, no. 7 [1 Oct. 1933], p. 18). Bayram used the heading "'*Ala-l-arghul*" for other types of *mawawil* published in *al-Imam* as well.

12 The use of *al-ahram* (the pyramids) as a symbol for Egypt, which imagizes the pharaonic heritage, invokes past power and glory; thus it contrasts with Egypt's present status as passive, occupied object. The use of pharaonic images is frequent in the corpus, particularly in poems from the 1920s, and suggests attention to the call for Egyptian (as opposed to Arab or Islamic) nationalism popular at that time (for a good example, see "Tut'ankhamun," *al-Shabab*, vol. 6, no. 112 (18 March 1923), republished in *Muntakhabat al-shabab*, vol. 11 (Cairo, 1923), pp. 16–17, and in *al-A'mal,* vol. VI, 17–18.) But in Bayram's corpus, it coexists with other available frameworks for identity and solidarity—one of the ideological tensions, or at least multiplicities, in his oeuvre which call for further investigation.

13 In the early corpus, India represents a consciousness of the linkages between the machinations of Europe in the Arab–Islamic lands and elsewhere. References to other non-Arab lands or peoples are sparse. This suggests that a consciousness of community with other non-European peoples/nations was limited at this point in the oeuvre to expression of the common experience of colonization/occupation by European powers. For the historical period in question, a link based on the negative experience of common oppression rather than on a positive identification is not surprising. (For other references to India, see "il-Fahl yidrab bi-l-qulla yutlub istiqlal," discussed below; "Qanal" republished in *al-A'mal*, vol. VI, pp. 136–37).

14 These notations of types of control contrast further with the reference to Islam in the first line of the *farsh;* the action described there emphasizes a process of cultural control through obliteration of the system of belief and legal organization of the occupied object.

Force and Transitivity 173

15 *Tawa* echoes a verb often coupled with *bayn*: the phrase *tawahu/ha al-bayn* is found in folk narratives.

16 The reference to *bilad al-hind* (the lands of India but also of "the Hindus") recedes into the background through its non-inclusion in the general identification made in this *maqta' (kull al-muslimin)*, and the next *(umma khayba)*. See note 13.

17 The subjection of local commodity prices to external forces is represented graphically: even on a feastday when each able Muslim is expected to slaughter an animal in thanksgiving, and thus when the market is tight, the prices that local products command are reduced to nearly nothing (either through price control, external flooding of the market, or local poverty which leaves the population unable to purchase—or consequently to eat, or celebrate the feast). But *ghanam* is used elsewhere in the corpus as a metaphor for human groups as passive and unthinking. (See "*A 'uzu bi-llah*" where the term is put into juxtaposition with *al-arwam*.) And the action of slaughter *(dhabh)* which is implicit in the image of *ghanam* on the feastday may not be irrelevant. As so often in Bayram's corpus, the line invites multiple interpretation.

18 See for example the contrast between *ibn al-'arab* and *bilad al-arwam* in *"Kharima yiqbad wi-yhassal,"* republished in *al-A'mal*, vol. V (Cairo: al-Hay'a al-'Amma li-l-Kitab, 1977), pp. 65–69.

19 See al-'Azab, p. 279.

20 The verbal clause *tawaha al-bayn* in line 10 further pinpoints the same elements as objects.

21 Like the previous poem, this was probably published first in *al-Shabab* not long after the February Resolution was announced. The earliest publication of it which I have found is "'Ala-l-arghul," *al-Funun*, vol. II, no. 80 (29 April 1928), p. 3. Republished in *al-A'mal*, vol. VI, pp. 19–20, under the title "Tasrih 27 fibrayir."

22 Thereby allowing some ambiguity: throughout the corpus are to be found harsh attacks on those segments of the Egyptian ruling elite who cooperate either actively or tacitly in the maintenance of the British presence; here, these elements may well be implied as an adjunct to the main implied agent as drawn out in the rest of the poem, the British. For such attacks, see "In kunt tut 'ankh amuni—ahuwwa da al-matlub," *al-Funun*, vol. II, no. 54 (16 Oct. 1927), p. 7, republished in truncated form as *"Khebit al-kifah" (al-A'mal*, Vol. VI, pp. 23–25: "Kilam al-gidid fi-l-sikka al-gidida," *al-Shabab* vol. VII, no. 201 (7 Dec. 1924), p. 1, reprinted as "Fi-l-sikka al-gidida" *(al-A'mal*, vol. VI, pp. 49–50); "Di 'amlitak 'amla sakhifa," *al-Shabab* vol. VII, no. 171 (4 March 1924).

23 Sa'd Zaghlul, leader of the Wafd and popular hero for his leadership of the nationalist resistance to British control, was in exile for the second time while the constitution and unilateral declaration were in preparation. 'Adli Pasha Yakan was asked by the king to form a government, and was the

target of a Wafdist campaign of vilification which several of Bayram's poems express from a Wafdist point of view (see "Istiqlal 'Adli Basha," republished in *Diwan Bayram al-Tunisi,* vol. II, Cairo, 1947, p. 32; in *al-A'mal,* vol. VI, pp. 40–42 as "Istiqlal 'Adli; Awamir 'Adli," republished in *al-A'mal,* vol. VI, pp. 45–48.

24 *Asluh,* which suggests the basis, foundation, or origins of something, also acts in the colloquial mode as an expression of emphasis and explanation: 'in fact', 'actually'. While this is the primary usage in the context of this line, the original meaning should be seen as a secondary, and significant, sense. This sort of double echo can be found frequently in Bayram's corpus, and is often meaningful in creating an ironic twist.

25 The statement may also be directed sardonically to the English, in the context of the fulfillment of their goals, and to the Egyptians who supported the Resolution.

26 The diction in which pharaonic and twentieth-century (A.D.) history are brought together in "Tut 'ankh amun" poses a corresponding interplay of oppressive action vs. passivity. This was published in *al-Shabab,* vol. no. 112 (18 March 1923).

27 Republished from *al-Shabab* in *Muntakhabat al-shabab,* vol. II, pp. 38–40. Republished in *Diwan Bayram al-Tunisi,* vol. II, pp. 28–29 with the title "al-Sawra al-misriya 1919: il-Fahl yidrab bi-l-qulla yutlub istiqlal" and in *al-A'mal,* vol. VI, pp. 13–14 under the title "Tariq al-hind." Both of these later republications are missing the final two stanzas of the *Muntakhabat* version as well as several minor modifications. Al-'Azab erroneously gives the occasion of this poem's composition as "the 1936 treaty" (al-'Azab, p. 242).

28 In later publication this becomes *wag'a,* 'falling', 'situated', which does not emphasize the personification of the addressee quite as *wagfa* does.

29 *Radya,* 'content with' in later texts, yields a slightly different tone.

30 This may be a reference to the government's panacea for falling cotton prices, from 1921: buying the excess up without actually making needed changes in the structure of agricultural commerce. See Jacques Berque, *Egypt: Imperialism and Revolution,* trans. Jean Stewart (New York: Praeger, 1972), pp. 418–19.

31 There may be a second image suggested here, *qulla* as the camel gullet. This would mean that *fahl* is also the camel, both beast of burden and proud symbol of Bedouin endurance and self-reliance. It would suggest that the *fahl* can do no more than vent his exasperation, though the threat of rebellion sounds through the idiom: when the *qulla* (camel's gullet) begins to move and expand, one gets out of the camel's path. The conflation of the images of stallion and camel suggest virility, renown, endurance, and impatient strength. The lack of an article to define 'independence' suggests that the nationalist's rhetoric is equally undefined: what sort of an independence? *Il-fahl* could also possibly refer to 'Adli Yakan, Zaghlul's adversary who carried out unsuccessful negotiations with Lord Curzon in London in 1921,

as prime minister. If so, the irony of the epithet becomes stronger, and the suggestion of ineffectiveness greater: Yakan was no nationalist hero as Zaghlul was.

32 Elsewhere in the corpus, the *halla* becomes a double-entendre as it imagizes the womb in the context of sexual intercourse, particularly outside of marriage. An echo of that signification implants itself here, particularly as there is a suggestion throughout the poem, becoming dominant in the penultimate stanza, that the raped subject can have no recourse to the law. See the final stanza of "al-Baladi tagir diqiq," *al-Shabab* vol. VI, no. 152 (23 December 1923), p. 1; "al-Sayyid wi mratuh fi misr," *Muntakhabat al-Shabab* vol. III (1925) (published serially in *al-Shabab* vol. VI, 1923), p. 10.

33 "Ihtilal Suriya," *al-A'mal* vol. VII, pp. 59–60. Kamil al-Banna claims that this poem was composed "at the time (*'inda*) of the French occupation," (al-Banna, *Mahmud Bayram al-Tunisi: Qitharat al-adab al-sha'bi*, p. 88). The text itself suggests that this was composed considerably after the act of occupation. *Khukh* in Shami colloquial Arabic are plums; in Egyptian colloquial Arabic, they are peaches.

34 For similar imagery see "Istiqlal 'Adli Basha" (references in note 23). On *bint il-balad* in the corpus, see Booth, pp. 163–69 and 239–41; al-'Azab, pp. 157–72.

35 See for example its use in "Bi-l-baladi," *al-Sa'iqa* vol. 42 no. 90 (22 July 1937), p. 10; republished as "Hamid 'Ashur" in *al-A'mal*, III (Cairo, 1976), pp. 138–43. Here, as in "'Ala-l-arghul," *'asl* may serve both to emphasize and to describe the foundation, here, of the bolt.

36 "Ah ya sudani," *al-A'mal*, VII, pp. 55–57.

37 See also "Istiqlal 'Adli Basha" (references in note 23) for the image of the *khulkhal*. For slightly differing interpretations of the *khulkhal*'s significance in this poem, see al-'Azab, p. 171, and Booth, p. 239 n248.

38 Untitled poem published in *al-Shabab*, vol. VII, no. 192 (2 October 1924), p. 1; republished as "A'uzu bi-llah," *al-A'mal*, vol. VI, pp. 35–39. See al-'Azab's general comments on this poem, pp. 184–85.

39 *Yalla ihtikna* (literally, 'disgrace upon us'): phrase said when the speaker sees something amiss but cannot say or do anything about it directly.

40 *Arwam*, broken plural of the collective *rum*. Throughout the poem are found clear references to foreign enterprise and foreign military activity; this polarity (Egyptian–European) is the dominant if not the sole one in the poem.

41 *'Ala gadd lihafak midd riglak*. See Ahmad Taymur, *al-Amthal al-'ammiya* (Cairo: Markaz al-Ahram li-l-Tarjama wa-l-Nashr, 4th pr.,1986), p. 327.

42 The staccato rhythm of the poem enhances the poem's force as *tahrid* (provocation). Certain other poems in the corpus exhort the Egyptians to become active in no uncertain terms. But it is not always clear when they were written. It will require a much broader sampling of the original texts,

in their original context of publication, to advance hypotheses about the directions which dominant structures in Bayram's oeuvre take over time and how they work within the specific historical conjunction of the time of writing.

43 This is one of the points on which a certain double vision in political outlook emerges through the texts. While certain texts suggest a recognition that the goals of the liberal nationalist leaders (whether Sa'dist or Ahrar) might not extend to include the needs and best interests of most of the Egyptian populace, there is at the same time unequivocal support for the Wafdist political line. Another crux is the support, at once, of a nationalist Egyptian line and a pan-Islamic line.

44 The poem was published just two months after the election; given the time necessary for Bayram's contributions to reach his publisher through French–Egyptian postal connections, one may assume that it was composed not long after the election. "'Ala-l-rababa," *al-Shabab* vol. VII, no. 161 (24 February 1924), p. 1; republished as "Lagnit Milnir," *al-A'mal,* vol. VI, pp. 26–28.

45 Elsewhere in the corpus, Bayram uses the active participles *shari* (buying) and *bayi'* (selling) in a colloquial metaphoric sense signifying, respectively, valuing someone *(shari)* and betraying or letting someone down *(bayi')*. This signification may form a secondary echo in this poem. (See the narrative *mawwal* "Umm Khalil" *(al-A'mal,* vol. III, pp. 133–37).

46 As did the Bani Ahrar. In fact, the Wafdists had boycotted the Constitutional Committee and the setting up of the parlimentary system in the view that to participate in it would be an admission of acceptance for the February 1922 Declaration.

Experimentation and the Institution: The Case of *Ida'a 77* and *Aswat*

❖

Samia Mehrez

The cluster of poets who formed and continue to maintain the two major poetry groups of the seventies in Egypt, *Ida'a 77* (Illumination 77) and *Aswat* (Voices), are perhaps the most important participants in the elaboration of a new experimental poetic movement in the country. Together, these poets' politico-cultural experience and poetic production provide an exemplary means for understanding the developments and transformations within the poetic movement in Egypt, the forms of its articulation and expression, as well as its general reception in the critical and intellectual milieus inside and outside Egypt.[1]

It is important to note that these poets first imposed themselves as a significant presence in the cultural arena as groups and not as individuals. It is through collective organization that they sought to challenge the existing literary critical establishment and unsettle the dominant aesthetic values of their time. Together, Ida'a 77 and Aswat provide a wideranging and longstanding experience in becoming part of what the literary critic Sabry Hafez has called an "alternative culture."[2] Even though they are known as two groups, with two separate lines of publication, the affinities and collaboration between the poets allow one to deal with them as different manifestations of the same phenomenon, or similar answers to the identical problem.

This cluster of poets does not represent all those who wrote during the seventies. Rather they represent an important part of an experimental movement in modern poetry in Egypt that coexisted and still coexists with other more traditional and more conventional trends. The history and development of this cluster of poets is the history of attempts to create an alternative outlet for experimental poetry in face of the institution. Despite the individual differences between them (whether those be ideological or aesthetic) it was clear to them that they had a common goal to defend and that it would be best defended with group strategy.

This article will focus particularly on the conditions that shaped and defined the emergence of Ida'a 77 and Aswat (whether those be political or cultural) and these poets' position within the cultural environment in Egypt today. The need for collective organization is always proportionate to the change being sought. Hence we will pose the question: what are the kinds of changes advocated by these poets which lead them to recognize the necessity for collective action in face of the institutions? How effective has group organization been in altering, even to a minimal extent, the face of the literary establishment? Needless to say, the weight of the institutions which support and propagate the dominant aesthetic values will eventually have an effect on the development and forms of opposition. This will lead us to explore the constraints, if not the limits, of group action in a country where legitimacy still derives from institutional acceptance and consensus.

Unfortunately, it is beyond the scope and general thrust of this article to deal with the poetry itself. However, we hope that the reader will establish a dialogical relationship between some of the general statements made here, concerning the characteristics and poetics of this movement, and some of the more textually oriented pieces of this collection.

To speak about the poets of the seventies *(shu'ara' al-sab'iniyat)* as the poets of Ida'a 77 and Aswat are often loosely labeled, is to speak about them as part and parcel of an entire generation of young intellectuals and artists who lived through this period. For Egypt, the decade of the seventies is doubtless a turning point which initiates some of the major political and ideological changes since 1952. As such it is equally a landmark for the downshifts which occurred in the intellectual and cultural climate of the country. The generation that came to maturity during these years considers itself the sole heir to defeat; it witnessed the first one in 1967 and from then on has seen a succession of them. If the fifties and sixties were the years of the elaboration of a national project, then the seventies witnessed the aging and final death of that project. If the fifties and sixties were the years of confrontation, independence, and pan-Arabism, then the seventies were the years of compromises, individual solutions, and isolation, beginning with Sadat's visit to Jerusalem, and culminating in the Arab boycott of Egypt. Gone were the years of 'socialism', centralization, and national culture and in set the years of 'democratization', privatization, and the culture of consumption. Simultaneously the generation of the seventies witnessed the exodus of a significant number of intellectuals (among whom were journalists, creative writers, and literary critics) and the influx of petro-dollars; the gradual folding of serious cultural periodicals and the mushrooming of the *Infitah* projects.

Ironically, all these bleak elements combined were to provide the impetus for change and for the emergence of an alternative. This alternative culture in a way exploited the empty slogans of 'democratization' and made its way in the very heart of the dominant culture of consumption. Groups of Egyptian intellectuals banded together to resist the increasing prohibitions on writing and the commodification of thought by producing their own non-periodic journals and cultural reviews and by taking turns in financing and publishing each other's work. By so doing, they were able to propose and elaborate, in the midst of this defeatist period, new cultural and aesthetic values and establish new ways of communication that guaranteed freedom of expression and publication.

Perhaps the absent mother of these non-periodic publications in Egypt is *Gallery 68*, the first independent and effective cultural journal, established after 1967 by Edwar al-Kharrat, Ibrahim Mansur, and Ahmad Mursi. It is in the aftermath of this successful experiment that the "stencil" revolution of the seventies (as the period is often referred to, given the means by which these journals were printed), flooded the Egyptian cultural market with alternative literature: *Ida'a 77, Kitabat, Aswat, Misriya, al-Nadim, al-Kurrasa al-thaqafiya, Kafnun, Khatwa,* and others.[3] Varying in lifetime, and overlapping in interests from the more generally cultural to the more specifically literary and poetic, these stencil publications represented a resistance to and contestation of the dominant aesthetic values as well as the official state-run publishing outlets.

Two of the most noticeable groups that have made a lasting imprint, where experimentational poetic production is concerned, are *Ida'a 77* and *Aswat*. Both groups were formed exclusively by poets who dedicated their efforts not only to writing and experimentation in poetry, but also to theorizing "the new poem," and hence elaborating its new criticism. One might ask the question why the urgency of groups that are composed exclusively of poets, especially that such an effort is not unprecedented in the history of Arabic poetry? From the Mahjar, emigré poets in the Americas, the Apollo group in Egypt, to *Majallat shi'r* in Lebanon, Arab poets have formed united fronts, independent of other forms of artistic creation, in order to change, if not completely subvert, the institution of Arabic poetry. The very fact that such exclusively poetic groups continue to emerge is indicative of the weight of the institution of Arabic poetry that still perhaps requires collective confrontation.

Unlike the Arab novelist whose recent, borrowed, and therefore flexible tradition of novel-writing dates to the beginning of the twentieth century, the Arab poet has to contend with a tradition in poetry that predates Islam. In fact, Arabic poetry is the only pre-Islamic institution that is legitimated by Islam. As such, Arabic poetry is more of an institution than the institution itself!

Hence the coupling of the words 'experimental' and Arabic poetry' seem at first contradictory, especially that our morning newspapers in Egypt still present us with examples of contemporary poetic creation that sound like mediocre pieces from the museum of medieval Arabic poetry.

The blatant coexistence of the modern and traditional up to our very day reveals two realities at once: first, the weight of the institution of traditional Arabic poetry that, approximately fifteen centuries later, continues to reproduce itself; second, the fact that various manifestations of the institution of traditional Arabic poetry are supported and protected by other institutions, both political and cultural, equally opposed to change and equally bent on reproducing themselves.

Given the Egyptian reality since the seventies and the increasing conservatism that has occurred since, it is no surprise that experimentation in poetry would be considered, as one of the poets has phrased it, "more dangerous than Israel itself." These words exaggerate to a point of absolute clarity the relationship between the cultural and the political: the conservatism of the one will be matched by the conservatism of the other, whatever challenges the status quo (on any level, whether political or cultural) is bound to be eliminated, or at least marginalized.

When asked to speak about his generation, Rif'at Sallam, one of the poets of Ida'a 77, does so by juxtaposing his generation's political and cultural experience against that of the generation that preceded it:

> The beginnings of the formation of this generation extend further back in time: I mean the June 1967 defeat, the death of Nasser and the 'peace initiative'... etc. All this was enough to account for the intellectual and cultural difference between this generation of poets and that which preceeded it. The earlier poets had witnessed the July revolution and what was called the socialist laws, the construction of the High Dam, and various national victories. As for our generation, it was destined to live through the defeats not the victories. We belong to the generation that kindled the 1972 demonstrations, the generation that witnessed and endured the first detentions in the seventies. At the same time many poets and intellectuals of the preceding generation were in sympathy with the regime, they were even appointed to its ministries.... This blatant contrast between a generation that enters the ministry and another that enters detention camps reveals part of the difference and distance between the political, social, and cultural making of the generation of the seventies and that which came before it.[4]

Despite the broad generalizations that may mark this self-representational portrait of the generation of the seventies, Rif'at Sallam's words remain significant because they outline the parameter of the problem. This is the war of generations and their relationship to power and with the establishment. Sallam's juxtaposition of the "ministries" against the "detention camps" reinforces the weight of the institution which alone has the power of according legitimacy. One does not have too many options: you either enter the institution or you do not count. Hence, the necessity of confrontation and resistance, which in the case of this group of poets has taken more than one collective form.

In a group interview session conducted with some of the poets, Walid Munir, one of the poets who has participated in both Ida'a 77 and Aswat, described the poetry groups of the seventies as corporations with one basic common interest, inside which there are various perspectives but where individuals will cooperate, each having a share, given the larger general interest of the corporation.[5] This metaphor is indeed very telling not only because it is drawn from the lexicon of the post-*Infitah* reality in Egypt, but more significantly because it says something about the very nature of these groups, their internal dynamics, and the individuals who form them.

A close look at the group of poets in question will show that they all belong, even though many have rural origins, to the Egyptian urban middle class. They all hold university degrees ranging from philosophy, literature, and journalism to accounting, pharmacology, and psychiatry. They all lead the double existence, so familiar to Egyptian writers: morning employees, evening poets—the only way to secure the regular income which allows them to be poets. They had met either as colleagues on university campuses or at the poetry readings organized by the poet Sayyid Higab in the Arab Socialist Union during the years 1973–75, in the context of the literary review *al-Shabab*.

Two features characterize this cluster of poets of the seventies: first, they are all (except for one) *fusha* poets, i.e., all their poetic production is in classical Arabic. Despite their openness towards and support of *'ammiya* (colloquial) poets, they themselves have had no creative attempts in 'ammiya, and therefore still maintain the classical dichotomy of fusha/'ammiya. The second feature is that they count no women poets among them. These two features merit two lengthy studies, in and of themselves, considering that we are dealing with an experimental group that is opposed to the status quo.

In the early and mid-seventies, the point at which they started publishing, they went to the institution. Some published in *al-Katib* when the poet Salah Abdul Saboor headed al-Hay'a al-'Amma li-l-Kitab (the General Egyptian Book Organizaion), others in *Sanabil*—a monthly cultural review—which was founded and edited by the avant-garde poet Muhammad 'Afifi Matar, while others still published in various literary magazines inside and outside Egypt.

A look at the dates of the publication of their first individual poems and their respective first collections of poetry provides an explanation of the urgency of collective action and group organization. For example, Muhammad

Sulayman, one of the more senior poets in the group (b. 1946) published his first individual poem in 1971, his first collection of poems appeared through Aswat in 1980; 'Abd al-Mun'im Ramadan's (b. 1951) first individual poems were published in 1972, his first collection appeared in 1981 and again through Aswat; Gamal al-Qassas (b. 1950) started publishing individual poems in the mid-seventies, his first collection appeared, through Ida'a 77, in 1984. These intervals between the first poems and the first collections are indicative not of the individual poet's productivity, but rather of the difficulty these poets had in placing their production. The same institution that was willing to grant the space for an individual poem was unwilling to recognize the authors as individual poets with individual collections. Hence, almost all of the first collections by the poets of Ida'a 77 and Aswat have been published either by the respective groups or in some cases, at the poet's own expense. Not only were they denied the legitimacy bestowed by publication through the institution, but because not all their work was available in print, they were also denied the legitimacy bestowed by serious criticism. Muhammad Sulayman from Aswat deplores their generation's publishing situation and casts his words (again) in a comparative framework with preceding generations:

> We are the generation that was destined to carry what it has written to the critics. We have to make the material available, in person.... The poet Salah Abdul Saboor, for example, did not have this problem. His work was published when he was in his thirties. As for us, all our work remains in the drawers.[6]

And indeed, a comparison between the published and unpublished collections of poems, not to mention individual poems or critical studies, will show an average ratio of one to two. It is obvious therefore that one of the main reasons for the creation of Ida'a 77 and Aswat was these poets' desire to become individual poets. To work within a group, yes, but to equally work towards their respective individual poetic projects.

The first poetry group to be formed was Ida'a 77. It was established in 1977 by the four young poets Hilmy Salim, Rif'at Sallam,[7] Hasan Tilib, and Gamal al-Qassas. Ida'a 77 has a long and rich history of fourteen issues published at irregular intervals over a period of approximately ten years (the first issue appeared in 1977 and the fourteenth was published in 1986). It is interesting to compare the price of the first and last issues: the first one sold for ten piasters and the last one for one Egyptian pound, which leads one to conclude that Ida'a 77's initial budget (LE100) must have also increased substantially. This is more than just a fleeting detail since it is the poets themselves who financed this independent project and had to bear the burden of the inflation even as their social lives and social obligations changed over the years.[8]

Despite its internal organizational and administrative problems, irregular appearance, and inconsistent publication quality, Ida'a 77 has succeeded in becoming one of the landmarks of the seventies. Ida'a 77 boasts of having published more than one hundred poems by Egyptian and Arab poets besides the works of its editorial board. Moreover, the founding editorial board has seen several additional members over the years: the poets Amgad Rayyan, Magid Yusuf (the only 'ammiya poet in the group), Muhammad Khallaf, and Walid Munir. Besides the collectively signed editorial introductions, and the poems themselves, Ida'a 77 counts several heated debates, theoretical pieces, and critical essays by members of the group and other noted Egyptian scholars, which focused on the role of poetry in society, the relationship between the poet and revolution, the relationship between poetry and reality, etc. Alongside this major collective project there was another that guaranteed more extensive publication for the members who did not monopolize the pages of their review. As a group, they paid equal shares to publish each other's respective collections of poems.[9]

Two years afer the establishment of Ida'a 77, another group of poets collaborated to form Aswat. Like Ida'a 77, the poets of Aswat held weekly poetry readings and debates, and maintained close ties (whether through publication or debate) with the first group. However, unlike Ida'a 77, Aswat, which began its activities in 1979 and comprises the poets Ahmad Taha, 'Abd al-Mun'im Ramadan, Abdel Maqsud Abdel Karim, Muhammad Sulayman,[10] Muhammad 'Id Ibrahim, and Muhammad Badawi, focused its energy on publishing the individual collections of its members, as well as other publications which the members deemed important.[11] It is only in 1988 that the same group published the first issue of their collective non-periodic review, *al-Kitaba al-sawda'*, which has yet to be followed by a second issue.

The thrust of *al-Kitaba al-sawda'* and its difference from the issues of Ida'a 77 are indicative of significant developments in the strategies of the group's self-representation. This new publication seeks to define itself not so much by talking about itself, as did the editorial introductions of Ida'a 77, but rather by establishing a genealogy to which the experiment belongs, or with which it dialogues. Besides the texts of the poems, which are strategically located in the middle, *al-Kitaba al-sawda'* opens with a graphic rendition of the situation of the intellectual in general and the poets of the seventies. In particular it includes "The Impossible Grip," a reproduction of a painting by the surrealist Egyptian painter of the forties Ramsis Yunan which depicts a human head being crushed by the tight grip of two hands. The issue continues to unfold other significant filiations of the group: an article on the poet Adonis, a chapter from Taha Hussein's controversial book on pre-Islamic poetry *Fi-l-shi'r al-jahili*, the text of Diwan Ibn Arus in 'ammiya, translations of poems by the Salvadoran poet Roque Dalton and the Egyptian francophone poet and intellectual Georges Henein.

Even though the two groups of poets have developed their respective projects and agendas at different points in time, their experiences have never closed in on the group to which they belong. The pages of Ida'a 77 bear witness to this cooperation, as do the joint readings and debates organized by the members of the groups, both in Cairo and in the provinces.

It is both interesting and significant to note that the experience of this cluster of poets is framed by two non-periodic publications: Ida'a 77 and *al-Kitaba al-sawda'*. On the one hand, this apparent return to the beginning, more than ten years later, is crucial because it continues to inform the poet's marginal position within the Egyptian cultural context. On the other hand, the contrast between the two publications, as means of self-representation and articulation of the poetic movement, is instructive because it provides us with a spiral (therefore open), rather than circular (hence closed) movement. Over a period of ten years, these poets move from the youthful manifesto-like language of self-representation of Ida'a 77, to a thoughtful attempt at placing this experimental movement in poetry within an earlier Egyptian context that testifies to modernism, and unconventional thinking and writing. We move from the urgency of theorizing rupture and legitimating difference to that of locating and presenting a harmonious alternative context through which some kind of continuity could be established. It is through this spiral movement which begins with Ida'a 77, and ten years later leads to *al-Kitaba al-sawda'*, that one can read an important aspect of the history of experimental poetry in Egypt since the mid-seventies.

One of the most pressing objectives of the poets of the seventies was to alter collectively the dominant view of poetry that reigned in Egypt during the fifties and sixties: poetry as a functional art at the service of 'the people', of nationalism, and revolution with all the requirements of exteriority, clarity, and directness indispensable to such a function. As Hilmy Salim put it:

> The poetry of the seventies eliminated the 'revolutionary' understanding that dominated during the fifties—that understanding which established a direct link between the role of poetry and art in general as agitators of the people, stimulators of collective power and what follows this definition as regards artistic characteristics such as foregrounding the progressive content and neglecting the aesthetic dimensions. This understanding which reigned over the fifties and sixties was expressed and supported by several prominent poets and critics. . . . It was crucial to eliminate this understanding which was expressed by Mahmud Amin al-'Alim when he said that Salah Abdul Saboor was a melancholy poet in a country that was building the High Dam and establishing Socialism.[12]

What is being contested and redefined in the above passage is the relationship between the poet and the revolution. The passage essentially rejects the modern counterpart to the function of the medieval Arab poet: the spokesman of the tribe, and singer of its glories. For the poets of the seventies, the role of the poet as a revolutionary is defined by the extent to which he revolutionizes his own medium: the poem itself. To be a miltitant poet is to contest the authority of the Arabic literary tradition, to dialogue with it without reproducing it, to benefit from predecessors without being enslaved by them, to free oneself from the tyranny of the Arabic language with its sacred rhetoric and metrics, to destroy the myth of the 'Arab ear', to rebel against the easy structures and ready-made genres in Arabic poetry, to problematize the immediacy of the image, to question the poet's relationship to reality, to eliminate the dualism of form and content, and to delete the boundaries between literary genres. This for them is the true revolution.

Indeed, the need to break away from the dominant aesthetic values in Arabic poetry, whether those be located in the poetic work itself or the literary critical establishment that supported and reinforced the role of the poet as spokesman of the tribe, did not occur in vacuum. Similar battles had already been fought. Whether we choose to think in terms of the distant past—'Umar ibn Abi Rabi'a, Abu Nuwwas, Abu Tammam, al-Hallaj, and al-Niffari to mention but a few figures—or the more recent past—the Diwan school (1921), the Apollo school (1932), the Mahjar poets (1920/1933), the Taf'ila movement (1947), and *Majallat shi'r* movement (1957)—all have been and still are manifestations, at different junctures, of the struggle between the traditional and the modern, the hegemonic collective values and individual freedom of contemplation and expression.

Hence it is quite natural that the first editorial introduction of Ida'a 77, written in a manifesto-like style, should echo other rebels especially in its articulation of the role of art and its relationship to reality, the relationship between the poet, language, and the revolution, the contested dualism of form and content, etc.

Art is an aesthetic experience of reality and cannot mechanically reflect it. Rather, Art creates, through figurative expression, a symbolic world, parallel to reality. . . .

The relationship between the poet, the people and the revolution cannot, given this understanding, be measured by the number of people who assimilate or understand his poetic work. Rather this relationship should be measured in terms of the poet's success in remolding his people's aspirations by using and refining his people's medium and historical experience. According to this understanding all other models which sacrificed poetry for the sake of slogans must fall. . . .

Indeed, genuine poetry always includes, among other things, the genuine slogan. But the genuine slogan never includes genuine poetry.[13]

The poet of the seventies no longer wished to be "an alert doctor who puts his finger on the ailing area," as the Egyptian critic Raga' al-Naqqash once put it. The poet is not just one self, but many, contradictory and complex. His role is to articulate these multiple selves, within the poem, through internal dialogue, and multiple—even conflicting—voices. He no longer erased his individuality to foreground the collective; rather he began writing the collectivity through the individual self.

Such an understanding of the role of the poet in society brings this cluster of poets much closer to their senior Egyptian contemporary, Muhammad 'Afifi Matar, whom they predominantly consider one of the most prominent innovators of the modern Arabic poem in Egypt. Indeed, through his poetry, Matar, who for several years had lived in Iraq, represents the poet as individual against the tribe, i.e., against its dominant aesthetic values, a position which places him in direct opposition to another of their senior contemporaries, Ahmad Abdel Mu'ti Higazi. For the poets of Ida'a 77 and Aswat, Higazi represents the modern counterpart to the medieval Arab poet par excellence, for he is the "foremost bard" of the Nasser regime. Because this is a position that they reject, Higazi's work has been targeted with criticism by more than one of these poets.[14] For them, accepting to play the role of bard is by necessity accepting to compromise with the institution and the authority, in whose services the bard places himself.

Hence, their refusal to be the voice and consciousness of the collectivity stems not only from their understanding of poetry, but from their understanding of politics as well. But to refuse to play the role of bards does not at all mean that they are oblivious to the reality that surrounds them. Their early poems on the 1967 defeat, their poetry on the fall of Beirut, collected in a special issue of *Ida'a 77*, and their poems to the children of the Palestinian Intifada, besides other works which are more obliquely political, all are testimonies to their involvement in the real.[15]

Just as they reject the relationship between the poet and the tribe, and the hegemony of collective values over individual creative freedom, they reject Arabism in the sense of sameness that erases individual specificity. It is not surprising that the insistence on difference be so blatant in many of their pronouncements. Indeed, it is only logical that a generation that has witnessed the eclipse of the pan-Arab project should seek refuge in specificity and difference. Even though they are Arab poets who share the general problems of the modern Arab poet, they are ultimately Egyptian poets whose solutions to these general problems will certainly be specific. Their constant insistence on difference is often misinterpreted as 'regionality'. Because they foreground the idea of an Egyptian poem, an Egyptian language, and an Egyptian modernism, they are accused of 'separatism'. However, this need to individuate the modern is in perfect keeping with the general shift from the collective to the individual, and in absolute harmony with their disillusionment with and alienation from the Arab nationalist project. 'Abd al-Mun'im Ramadan put it succinctly:

> I am one of those who are deeply disturbed by the idea that there is one
> Arabic language—what we have been taught at school. I believe that

there is an Egyptian Arabic language—a language I dream of realizing, even as I fail to do so. I hope that this dream will come true: an Egyptian poetic language in which we write poetry. This vision has a direct relationship with my understanding of nationalism.[16]

And indeed, like other Egyptian poets before them, starting with Louis Awad's experimentation in *Plutoland* (1947), they have been able to remold their poetic language by simplifying it, by using the spoken dialect, not simply on the lexical level but on the structural and figurative levels as well. Their concern with an Egyptian poem has reinforced their sense of a poetics of place and space that is specifically Egyptian: history and mythology, the Nile and the countryside, the mundane Cairene street and the familiar coffeehouse.

The resistance to the authority of an Arabism that erases specificity in culture in general, and poetry in particular, is part and parcel of these poets' resistance to the stale reproduction of the Arabic literary tradition *(al-turath)*. It is important to remember that when the poets use the word *turath* they do so to signify that which has been institutionalized over time and has become representative of the dominant official Arabic culture. For these young poets such a *turath* is synonymous with the tyranny of conformity which, in order to continue to dominate, will by necessity exclude all attempts at experimentation and innovation. As such the Arabic literary tradition becomes another authority that needs to be challenged.

Perhaps the most extreme negation of *turath* is articulated by Abdel Maqsud Abdel Karim, one of the poets of Aswat:

> I am free. I tell myself that I am the first poet especially at the moment of writing.[17]

This exaggerated metaphoric rendition of the relationship between the poet and *turath* captures the size of the rebellion against inherited hegemonic structures and aesthetic values. Hilmy Salim from Ida'a 77 recasts the same idea in the following words:

> No doubt we are the sons of preceding generations. But our real role as children must manifest itself in the destruction of what they have built. Then begins the process of reconstruction.[18]

Even though there are distinctively different renditions of this process of destruction/reconstruction in the poems of Ida'a 77 and Aswat, there is no doubt that generally speaking these poets problematize the question of rupture *(qati'a)*/continuity *(tawasul)*/deviance *(inhiraf)* throughout their work. From the poems of Hasan Tilib which establish a constant dialogue with the mystical tradition, the idea of play within the poem, the exploitation of the musicality of the word, to the poetry of Rif'at Sallam that takes a critical stance from Tradition: once satirical, once affirmative, to the poetry of Muhammad 'Id Ibrahim, which smears its face, defames its idols, and desecrates its authority, we have a multiplicity of positions that all constitute various relationships of destruction/reconstruction.

One of the crucial aspects of the process of destruction/reconstruction is located in these poets' work on the formal aspects of the Arabic poem. For them, the poem is its own law. In stipulating this, the poets destroy the sacredness of Arabic prosody and metrics to go even beyond the barriers of the more lenient *taf'ila* (foot) composition that still remains metrically restrictive:

The poem is its own law. As such it concerns itself solely with its own internal organization. Hence it creates its own musical laws that emerge from its internal movement and structure.[19]

Even though some of the poets in both groups continue to use metrical composition in their poetry, there is a noticeable move from the mixing of prose and poetry towards the adventure of the prose poem. For many of them, the prose poem is the epitome of liberation from the authority of the Arabic literary tradition, for it does not obey any rules external to itself or preexisting before its composition. Its rules and regulations are different: they begin with the poem itself, that is, from the internal juxtapositions in the poem, the mixing and confounding of genres, the structure of the poetic image, and the very rhythm of a continuously invented language that defies the ordinary and the familiar.

This perpetual process of destruction/reconstruction indicates that these poets reject the easiness of the ready-made and the authority of the officially accepted and respected. It also locates their work with others who have stood ouside the hegemony of Tradition in general: the Kharijite poets, the Sufi poets, the Symbolists, the Surrealists, in short all those who reshaped the relationship between the poet, the poem, and the world.

Perhaps one of the most consistently positive and sympathetic of the critics towards the experimental movement in poetry during the seventies has been Edwar al-Kharrat. A writer himself, and a founding member of *Gallery 68*, the mother of non-periodic publications in the post-1967 period, al-Kharrat could understand these poets' acute sense of rebellion against the institution and the already established. In an attempt to distinguish the experience of *shu'ara' al-sab'iniyat* (the poets of the seventies) from others who were writing concurrently, al-Kharrat came to their rescue with an alternative name that embraced them under the seemingly larger yet effectively more exclusive umbrella of "the new sensibility."

In one of his more recent articles on these poets, al-Kharrat defines "new sensibility" by opposing it to "conformist sensibility," i.e., that sensibility which in reproducing the already made supports the dominant cultural, social, and political institutions. For him the term "new sensibility" represents a basic shift in the vision of the relationship between the self and the world which is ultimately translated into a shift in the techniques and modes of artistic expression. Defined as such, those who write in this "new sensibility," whether they write prose or poetry, rebel against the prevailing historical political and cultural realities. As such they become heralds of an alternative reality. For al-Kharrat, the "new sensibility" in poetry is best represented by the work of the cluster of poets who form Ida'a 77 and Aswat.[20]

What al-Kharrat provides us with as readers and critics alike, as he proceeds to define this new sensibility, through a reading of the accomplishments of these poets, is a way of entering the world(s) of experimental poetry. We are to expect the unusual, the unfamiliar, even the shocking. The "new sensibility" places demands on the readership to develop new ways of confronting the poetic text, of deciphering it, of appreciating it. It actually demands a new critical idiom in order to be able to speak about it. Al-Kharrat's words represent a kind of warning to the average Arab reader whose expectations from a poetic text are bound to be unsettled when confronted with such experimental poetry.

How then does the institution or the dominant literary establishment, more generally, greet this "new sensibility" in poetry? Unfortunately, whether it be inside or ouside Egypt, this experimental movement is met with various degrees of rejection: from outright banning to subtler forms of containment and marginalization.

Consider for example the opening and closing lines of the following article, published recently in an Egyptian newspaper by the well-known cultural columnist, Galal al-'Ashry, where he uses, as his lead, the pun on the Arabic word *hasasiya* which can mean either sensibility, sensitivity, or allergy:

> *Al-Hasasiya* (allergy) is one of the widespread sicknesses of our time
> .... The strange thing is the Satanic attempt to uproot this sickness from among others in order to use it in the clinic for cultural diseases and distribute it among the various writers .... Stranger yet is the addition of the word *al-jadida* (new) to the word *al-hasasiya* in order to form the expression: '*al-hasasiya al-jadida*' (new allergy) . . .
> So those of you who are plagued with *al-hasasiya al-jadida* (new allergy/new sensibility) get yourselves a cure from this illness before we are infested with the summer diseases of this year.[21]

Despite the apparent lightness of the piece, its implications, we believe, are rather grave. Here, the very attempt to deal with the new is denigrated and the new itself is transformed into a sickness that needs to be cured. If in the early seventies political action sent this young generation to detention camps, then in the mid-eighties their artistic creations seem to merit them a sick-house! Here, precisely lies the point of intersection between the political and the cultural: if you threaten the dominant political practices you are detained, and if you threaten the dominant aesthetic values you should be 'put away'.

The theme of sickness that borders on madness runs through the history of this experimental movement in poetry as a means of marginalizing and delegitimating. In a series of articles, written as late as the mid-eighties by the noted literary critic Raga' al-Naqqash, one of the leading proponents of the free verse movement in Arabic poetry during the fifties and sixties, we witness the same campaign. Al-Naqqash begins one of these aricles by telling us about his friend, the poet Amgad Rayyan (Ida'a 77), whom he has known for ten years and whom he used to consider "a talented poet":

> During my last and brief encounter with the poet Amgad Rayyan I felt that he still possessed his purity and his Upper Egyptian good raw material ... but I was violently shocked when I read some of his new poems which he gave me.... I was confronted with an abstruse literary specimen which, in reality is but a kind of *eccentricity* that does not express any level of experience, vision, or anguish. Besides, on a literary level it does not represent a clear cut object with characteristic features that we can name in literary critical terminology. It is neither poetry nor prose nor is it a third form in between. It is a deformed and immature literary object devoid of art and life.[22] *(My italics)*

It seems that somewhere along the line, between the first time they met and the date of al-Naqqash's attack (1985), Amgad Rayyan, the "talented poet," did something drastically wrong! He wrote something that was "neither poetry nor prose," he fell "victim to Adonisism," he used words that "have no origin in the Arabic language," and even if they did, "they are hateful." As for rhythm, al-Naqqash finds it "completely alien to Arabic prosody," and finally he characterizes the text as "dim" and incapable of "moving our emotions and our dreams."

The above is obviously a lexicon of medieval critical idiom that is trying to read an experimental poem. But this is not the most serious charge against the passage. For us, the most serious problem wih this passage is its accusation of eccentricity. Amgad Rayyan is mad! His poetry is "eccentric" and "deformed" and, therefore, needs to be "put away." Such is the ultimate logic of this criticism and, hence, its ultimate danger.

Since indeed these poets are mad, the institution and the dominant literary establishment at large need to take measures to protect the poets against themselves. In order to deal with deviant behavior, of which the works of these poets seem to be symptomatic, one must use strategies of containment and/or correction, in extreme cases, complete banishment. The example of the treatment of these poets on the pages of *Ibda'*, the cultural periodical published by al-Hay'a al-'Amma li-l-Kitab since 1982, is a case in point. Most of the poets of Ida'a 77 and Aswat have published with this periodical. However, they are predominantly placed in the rubric *tajarib* (experiments) which is printed back to back with the rubric *shi'r* (poetry). Even though the word is of the same root as *tajrib* (the verbal noun which means experimentation), the word *tajarib*, which is the plural form of the unit noun *tajriba* connotes a one time trial, a single occurrence. There is of course a very subtle element of containment in this: the institution does provide the space for the "experiment," so it cannot be accused of overtly marginalizing. However, the very compartmentalization that occurs within the issue is, indeed, but another way of labeling, and another form of marginalization.

With the same logic the poets are "corrected," especially when they violate what 'Abd al-Mun'im Ramadan from Aswat has called "the trinity of prohibitions": politics, religion, and sex. It is interesting to note that when the editor in chief makes suggestions for cuts in the poem, especially when the cuts are for religious or sexual reasons, censorship is renamed: protection. The institution seeks to protect the poets from dominant values: for example, the conservatism of Islamic fundamentalist groups in the country. Hence, it advises them, for their own good, to make cuts in their poems. One anecdote, from a handful, will suffice to illustrate this situation.

Muhammad Sulayman of Aswat presented to the editor of *Ibda'* a poem that started with: "Qul huwa al-nilu ahad" (Say there is but the Nile, the One), a direct adaptation of the Quranic verse: "Qul huwa illahu ahad" (Say there is but Allah, the One), with the word *Allah* replaced by *nilu*. This line constituted not only the opening, but also the refrain of the poem. In order to have the piece published in *Ibda'*, the poet accepted the deletion of the opening line to the poem (so that it does not attract too much attention) with the promise that it would appear internally, as a refrain.[23] Needless to say the balance of the entire poem suffered as a result. But then the poet's deviant behavior was corrected and contained!

However, these anecdotes of correction and containment in a state-run periodical come to confirm the actual political reality in Egypt in general. In this respect, they are somewhat expected and understandable. What remains truly revealing, and unexpectedly patronizing, is the treatment the poets of the new sensibility received on the pages of *al-Karmal*, published by the General Union of Palestinian Writers and Journalists, in a special issue on *Literature in Egypt Today*.[24] The dossier that was prepared by Edwar al-Kharrat, and which comprised a collection of poems by the young Egyptian poets, was "corrected" by a member of the editorial board, Salim Barakat, himself a poet! Some poems were missing lines, others were missing whole sections, and others still were touched up to correct what the editor deemed metrical faults in poems which, in fact, deliberately broke away from the meter. "If they [i.e., the poets] all received partial amputations," says al-Kharrat, "then Muhammad 'Id Ibrahim suffered complete butchery."[25] The latter poet's only contribution was simply deleted from the dossier!

The politics of correcting and banishing poets, even in *al-Karmal,* one of the most open and pluralistic of the Arab publications, is perhaps the most telling of the limits of experimentation and the real crisis between poetic generations and artistic sensibilities. The poets of Ida'a 77 and Aswat are still considered by the dominant literary establishment to be "eccentric" hence they continue to be contained. To these politics, Mumammad 'Id Ibrahim, who still does not exist for the institution, would probably respond as he did in a slightly different yet equally taxing situation:

You place your hand on my vision
A veil
You do not emerge
After ravishing the veil
Kill me
I kill you
And all between us is blocked.[26]

Ironically, one of the important sources for the budgets of Ida'a 77 and Aswat is the honorariums given to the poets for their publications in local and Arab periodicals. In fact, these honorariums in many instances represent a supplementary source of income for the employee/poet. This situation sets up a dualistic existence for almost all the poets, one which borders on schizophrenia: simultaneously to write for the establishment and abide by its rules and write outside it to challenge and subvert these same rules.

Given the financial constraints of the poets, as well as the difficulties of distribution and limitations of space in non-periodic independent publications, how do the groups Ida'a 77 and Aswat envision the future of their collective effort as alternative outlets for experimental poetry? Has their interaction with the institution and their agreement to deal with the dominant literary establishment unsettled, even to a minimal extent, the hegemony of consensus? Or has it, on the contrary, taught them to impose self-censorship on their own poetic production whether they write within or without the boundaries of the institution?

The core of the problem is obviously the weight of the institution and the dominant literary establishment and sensibility, inside and outside Egypt and vis-à-vis which the experimental poet is constantly either acting or reacting. However, one cannot overlook the fact that a substantial part of the problem falls equally on the shoulders of the members of the poetry groups themselves. More than ten years after the establishment of both groups there still remains a division of opinion among the members, as regards a unified position in face of the institution (a division that seems to be increasing, in correlation with the recognition the respective poets have gained, as individuals, through their relationship with the institution, whether as poets or as employees).

For example, Hilmy Salim is a journalist in *Adab wa naqd*, the literary review published by the Tajammu' Party (National Progressive Rally). True, it is an opposition party but it represents an institution all the same. Given his own position within that institution, it is no surprise that he would be willing to strategize from within it:

I have no complex vis-à-vis the cultural institutions. They are official, traditional, at times even hostile to intellectual and artistic innovation. However, I believe that these institutions are our institutions: they

belong to us and we must use (not refuse) any space available within them so long as it does not require an artistic or intellectual compromise on our part. . . .
Anyhow, working with these institutions (partially or strategically) does not eliminate the persistence on constructing an independent path (completely strategic) in culture, art and poetry.²⁷

Hilmy Salim's position towards the institution is reiterated by other poets who have essentially the same links to the institution. For example, Walid Munir, a member of the secretarial board of *Fusul*,²⁸ who has published two poetry collections in 1985 and 1988, respectively, through the institution *(al-Hay'a)*, like Hilmy Salim, does not see a solid wall separating his work from the establishment:

> I believe that with some intelligent interaction, it is possible for the creative writer to contain the institution as much as it contains him.²⁹

To this, a poet like Gamal al-Qassas, whose only published collection is available through the collective effort of the members of Ida'a 77, would probably respond:

> Yes, we may be able to gain a step or two, but only by adopting the perspective of the institution.³⁰

'Abd al-Mun'im Ramadan, today considered one of the leading poets in Aswat, is perhaps a case in point. He has published quite noticeably with *Ibda'*, yet considers the institution a space "filled with traps" for new talents. After several poems published in *Ibda'*, his attitude is apologetic, for he recognizes, and so do some of his critics, the compromises (which are essentially a kind of self-imposed censorship) he has made to be in that periodical:

> . . . and the more you hang on to [them], [i.e., state-run periodicals] the more you have to bend over, and bending over frequently deforms the body and destroys taste.³¹

However, Ida'a 77 and Aswat are still there. If indeed there is a sense that Ida'a 77 in particular will not be resurrected as a non-periodic publication, because of a general sentiment that it itself was becoming an institution which published work simply to produce an issue, the members of the group that formed it are still willing to consider other forms of group organization.³²

But even if Ida'a 77 were to fold, Aswat has just published *al-Kitaba al-sawda'* to remind younger poets, perhaps, that group organization remains the answer, that the movement is indeed spiral and not circular. If such a statement sounds romantic, one has only to reconsider the accomplishments of these two groups and read them against the first editorial statement of Ida'a 77 written some thirteen years ago:

> We know that the distance between ambitions and actions is great. But we also know that it will diminish, little by little, with candid hard work. We are not ashamed of the dream. For dreaming is a noble element in revolution.³³

Notes

1. Apart from existing publications, much, if not most, of the material which informs this article has been gathered through several lengthy interviews with the main poets of the movement together with their answers to a questionnaire that sought to illuminate several crucial issues: their understanding of experimentation and the extent to which it is reflected in their poetic texts, the internal dynamics of the movement itself, the relationship between the individual poets, their position vis-à-vis the literary establishment, and the position which they occupy in relation to the preceding and succeeding poetic generations. All translations in the article are mine.
2. Sabry Hafez, "Irhasat al-taghyir al-thaqafi fi misr," *al-Jumhuriya* (Iraqi daily), 7 May 1985.
3. For a more detailed discussion on the non-periodic journals of the seventies see Amgad Rayyan, "Les revues non-périodiques dans les années 70," Bulletin du CEDEJ, no. 25 (premier semestre, 1989), pp. 117–21.
4. This quotation is part of the poet Rif'at Sallam's comments during the debate organized by Edwar al-Kharrat with the poets of the seventies for a special issue of *al-Karmal*, no. 14 (1984), on *Literature in Egypt Today*, p. 294.
5. My interview wih the poets of Aswat, Cairo, February, 1990.
6. Muhammad Sulayman, first group interview with Aswat, Cairo, February 1990. Attending were the poets 'Abd al-Mun'im Ramadan, Abdel Maqsud Abdel Karim, Muhammad 'Id Ibrahim, and Walid Munir.
7. After the second issue of *Ida'a 77* there occurred an internal division between the founding members of the group which essentially brought into question the role of *Ida'a 77* as a poetic publication. The appearance of the third issue of the review coincided with President Sadat's visit to Jerusalem. Even though the group opposed the visit and condemned it, a long debate occurred over the nature and tone of the issue's editorial introduction, which was to be written by Rif'at Sallam then approved and signed by the other members. Sallam's introduction was too militant for the group's self-conception, and because no compromise could be reached, he eventually left the group and started *Kitabat*, a more general cultural review which, like *Ida'a 77*, was independently funded. Despite this rupture however, Sallam has maintained close ties with the members of both Ida'a 77 and Aswat.
8. When the two groups were first formed, all the poets were single. Except for one, today they are all married and with children. In the interviews conducted with them, this detail became relevent in relation to budgetary considerations for their non-periodic publications. It becomes an equally important consideration for the division of time and division of labor between them.
9. *Ida'a 77* issued *Khisam al-warda* by Gamal al-Qassas, *al-Sama' wa qaws al-bahr* by Mahmud Nisim, *al-Abyad al-mutawassit*, by Hilmy Salim, and *Sirat al-banafsij* by Hasan Tilib. Some of the other published collections by the poets were individually financed.

10 Muhammad Sulayman is no longer part of the core group of Aswat but maintains very close ties with the group and still participates in financing their projects.
11 Aswat issued *A 'lana-l-farahu mawlidahu* by Muhammad Sulayman, 1980; *Azdahimu bi-l-mamalik* by Abdel Maqsud Abdel Karim, 1980; *Tawru al-wahsha*, by Muhammad 'Id Ibrahim, 1980 and *al-Hulmu zill al-waqt al-hulmu zill al-masafa*, by 'Abd al-Mun'im Ramadan, 1981.
12 Hilmy Salim is one of the founding poets of Ida'a 77. This statement was made in a debate organized by Edwar al-Kharrat in *al-Karmal*, no. 14 (1984), p. 293.
13 Unsigned editorial, *Ida'a 77*, no. 1 (July, 1977) pp. 1–4.
14 See for example Muhammad Badawi,"Ka'inat mamlakat al-layl," *Fusul*, volume 3, no. 2 (January, February, March, 1983). See also the articles by Ahmad Taha and 'Abd al-Mun'im Ramadan in the first issue of *al-Kitaba al-sawda'*, Cairo, 1988, pp. 3–23.
15 See *Ida'a 77*, no. 9 (January, 1983), a special issue on the Lebanese civil war.
16 This is a comment made by 'Abd al-Mun'im Ramadan during my interview with the poets from Aswat: Muhammad 'Id Ibrahim, Abdel Maqsud Abdel Karim, Muhammad Sulayman, and Walid Munir, Cairo, February, 1990.
17 My group interview with Aswat, Cairo, February, 1990.
18 Hilmy Salim, answer to questionnaire, Cairo, 1990.
19 Muhammad Badawi, debate in *al-Karmal*, no. 14, p. 301.
20 Edwar al-Kharrat, "Lamahat 'an shi'r al-hasasiya al-jadida fi misr," *Majallat al-shi'r*, Cairo, October 1989, pp. 6–22.
21 Galal al-'Ashry, "Marad al-hasasiya al-jadida," *Majallat al idha'a wa-l-tilifizyun*, July 28, 1986.
22 Raga' al-Naqqash, "La sh'ir wa-la nathr," *al-Sharq al-awsat*, March 23, 1985.
23 My interview with Aswat, Cairo, February, 1990.
24 See *al-Karmal*, no.14.
25 My interview with Edwar al-Kharrat, Cairo, March, 1990. This information about the special issue of *al-Karmal* was provided by both the poets and Edwar al-Kharrat himself. Eventually the poets published a statement protesting the masacre that had befallen their texts.
26 Just recently Muhammad 'Id Ibrahim was accused of poetic theft and of plagiarizing an ancient Egyptian poem (*al-Hayat*, March 10, 1990). Lina Tibi, the author of the article in *al-Hayat*, recounts that she had come accross Ibrahim's "stolen" poem in the double issue of *Mawaqif* (59–60). Tibi had translated the same ancient Egyptian text into Arabic, based on Ezra Pound and Noel Stock's English translation from the Italian which was among the texts included in *Women Poets* (Penguin, 1988). Tibi explains that the poem she had recognized as "stolen" had been published in

Mawaqif with three other pieces as part of a section titled "Teachings," all signed by the Egyptian poet Muhammad 'Id Ibrahim. Even though three of these pieces she had not seen before, she suggested, in her article, that they too may have been "stolen" by the poet from some other source. What Tibi does not tell the reader is that the same issue of *Mawaqif* included some twelve poems by Ibrahim, and that the "Teachings" were the appendix to a longer poem titled "Events are not Excuses." Muhammad 'Id Ibrahim responded to Tibi's accusation, in the following issue of *al-Hayat*, reminding her that what he did was called "adaptation" and that modern literary criticism has for some time now renamed the process, which Tibi referred to as "plagiarism," under the heading of "intertextuality." In his response, Ibrahim recognized that the piece in question was indeed his rendition of the ancient Egyptian poem, but proceeded to explain that it constituted one short section in a much longer appendix to his poem "Events are not Excuses." His use of that particular ancient Egyptian poem, he argued, was one way through which he could dialogue with the specificity of his own time, space, and traditions. He ended his own defense with the lines I have translated in the article from the poem that had been under attack.

27 Hilmy Salim, answer to questionnaire, Cairo, 1990.
28 *Fusul* is the journal of literary criticism published by al-Hay'a al-'Amma li-l-Kitab.
29 Walid Munir, answer to questionnaire, Cairo 1990.
30 Gamal al-Qassas, answer to questionnaire, Cairo, 1990.
31 'Abd al-Mun'im Ramadan, answer to questionnaire, Cairo, 1990.
32 These comments were made during two interviews: one with Mahmud Nisim and Gamal al-Qassas, the other with Hasan Tilib and Amgad Rayyan. All poets are from Ida'a 77.
33 Editorial, *Ida'a 77*, no 1, July 1977, p. 4.

Shukry Ayyad

❖

On Criticism and Creativity

Ferial Ghazoul: You have written both criticism and creative literature. Do you believe that they stem from two radically different abilities? Will you comment on the rupture between the two activities in the Arab world?

Shukry Ayyad: Criticism, as a scientific discipline, could be 'creative', as any scientific work is creative. I mean the sense, sometimes the thrill, of discovery, the sudden light that is thrown on things, that makes them suddenly significant. Add to this the nature of the thing discovered. It is a deeper human reality. That is why I consider criticism as a science, and at the same time an art or a literary genre; not partly one and partly the other, or sometimes this and sometimes that. Criticism which is lacking either in scientific approach or in artistic feeling is simply bad criticism.

However, there are significant differences between the two processes. Criticism starts with a few main ideas, even if you are planning to write a whole book. Many problems are left to be solved on your way. In creative writing proper the incubation period is much longer; you do not start writing until you have solved all the chief problems of form: you have chosen your genre, your tone, your point of view, your type of sequence, etc. When you are actually in the process of writing, you seldom think of what you are writing now, or what you are going to write next. Words flow with natural ease. If they seem rather recalcitrant sometimes, then it is you who are showing resistance. You should stop writing and only take it up again when you feel an inner compulsion to do so.

The main thing, when you are writing both criticism and creative writing and cannot resist either temptation, is to watch out for the right mood for each of them, and not to mix them up. For, although they stem from the same source, and hence, generally speaking, the same aesthetic effect, their production must follow two distinct procedures.

Some sort of antagonism is bound to appear between critics and creative writers as separate groups, especially when the function of criticism is not sufficiently clear. If creative writers consider critics as salesmen, whose main job is to promote the new literary commodity, then it is no wonder that the critics will be inclined to act as judges, and sometimes as hangmen. This describes the attitudes of most critics and most creative writers all over the Arab world.

Ceza Draz: In some of your introductions you denied that you "had a theory." Was it a 'trick' or have you never been able to embrace a theory? Perhaps you believe that a critic should not subscribe to one theory? Can a critic reach his full maturity without having arrived at a global theory, which would embrace his particular 'views'?

Shukry Ayyad: I am still skeptical about this word 'theory'. If this means that I have not yet reached my mature stage, then I pray to God that I never reach it. What is a theory? A theory is a system of thought, and I prefer thinking as a process. Mind you, I am not trying to be modest; on the contrary, I believe that no honest thinker would admit to having a theory, or has ever done so. Thinking is a passion, just like artistic creation. As for me, I will never surrender this love of mine for the mere purpose of being called a theorist in textbooks. However, you may have noticed me trying to systematize, at times even categorize, my thinking. How else can you ever hope to understand, and thus to accept this whole mess of a world around us, not just literature? No, I will never agree to put myself, of my own free will, into the straitjacket of a theory, however tempting this word might be.

However, there is more than one meaning to this unfortunate word. The more common, especially with us, and this one that I have rejected just now—have always rejected, in fact—is a contemplative view of a certain field, characterized by generality rather than validity. This means that it will be open to much bias. But we are starting to speak of 'theory' in another sense. 'Theory of literature' stands for the basic principles of a science of literature; in this sense it is not the theory of one person: it is a systematized, organized, objective approach to literature. It means simply a methodology of literature, with nothing individual or idiosyncratic about it. This 'theory of literature' is being worked out by many scholars from various backgrounds, disciplines, and cultures. I most humbly attach myself to this army of scientific workers.

From the standpoint of the 'theory of literature', particular 'views' as such, mine as well as any other person's, are of very little value. They simply record the impressions or reaction of one particular reader. Any real significance they might have must rely on the methods and techniques followed by the critic, in terms of his scientific approach. I have to stress this point, because all attempts at scientific approach in criticism are always challenged by more traditional, subjective critics on the grounds that such and such a view about such and such a work of literature had been expressed before, and did not gain by being put in the scientific (or, according to them, pseudo-scientific) garb of technical, difficult language. This ignores completely the use of scientific method. What we hope to construct is a tool by which any reader could understand and appreciate more of the given work of literature than he would have without its use. In other words, we aim at the efficacity and validity of the tool. As for views, even the most universal ones, everybody knows that they can pop up as easily and unheedingly as the most common words in ordinary speech.

Abdel Moneim Tallyma: Modern stylistics points to a wide, unexplored horizon in the work of ancient Arab linguists and rhetoricians. Can you suggest some of the possibilities involved?

Shukry Ayyad: Contemporary stylistics, as you know, has moved away from the purely descriptive method of Bally and his disciples, as well as from the purely intuitive approach of the German school, represented by Spitzer and Auerbach, to a more unified appraisal of the speech act, benefiting from the adjacent disciplines of semiotics and the pragmatics of language. Arabic rhetoric was pragmatically oriented from the very beginning: the addressee almost rules the whole field, governing the speaker's use of his language to emphasize, evade, or simulate. Let me remind you of what our rhetoricians have to say about the use of emphatic articles when the addressee is denying or hesitant; the use of the period when the preceding sentence raises a question in the addressee's mind; blaming the addressee for his neglect by making a statement which he already knows, and is known to know. The list can be extended to any length you desire. As for the semiotics of language, the enquiry was started by al-Jahiz, as far back as the ninth century, but it has not been developed since, as far as I know. Only some hints might be noticed here and there, like al-'Askari's mention of a particular characteristic of poetic language, viz., that meanings which would be shameful or embarrassing to mention in prose or in common language, such as those referring to the speaker's extreme suffering because of love (especially if such a speaker be a man of high standing), are freely stated in poetry.

However, I would like to stress that nothing can be gained by merely pointing out resemblances. There is a core of Arabic rhetoric, connected with the core of the Arabic language itself, which needs to be revealed before the real possibilities of this rhetoric, in terms of future research, can be shown. This means that Arabic rhetoric should be studied in its totality and against the background both of Arab social life and Arabic creative literature. This is a task which nobody, as far as I know, has undertaken yet.

Abdel Moneim Tallyma: We would like to raise with you the question of literary historiography. How do you visualize a history of Arabic literature? Should it follow a time sequence, whether of social periods or political eras, or would you opt for another classification: types and traditions, for example, or maybe regional and vernacular characteristics?

Shukry Ayyad: It is a trite saying now that a literary history should be a history of literature (i.e., of creative writing) and not of something else. Neither should it vie with general history in treating everything under the sun. This means that a history of Arabic literature must start by defining what is considered 'literature' and what is not. This might seem simple, but it is not. Histories of Arabic literature now in use have no place for historiography, travelogues, or philosophical treatises, let alone folk poetry, folk tales, and folk legends. This means that they give a very imperfect picture of Arab creativity. Then comes the problem of classification. I believe that Arabic literature constitutes a unity, with several recognizable and definable focal points which have established and developed its artistic traditions. Of course more than one focal point may exist at the same time. Thus, our classification will be more or less temporal, its basis being the literary producer, not as an individual but rather as a corporation or a fraternity, following its literary vocation to cater for the needs of a certain community. Any kind of ramification in this basic classification is permissible. 'Peaks' such as al-Mutanabbi or al-Ma'arri will not suffer; on the contrary, I believe that they will benefit a great deal when the interaction of their personalities with both the environment and the tradition becomes more evident.

Abdel Moneim Tallyma: It is believed in some academic circles that Arabic literature is particularly hospitable to comparative studies, by reason of its long history and close ties with other world literatures, ancient, medieval, and modern. In the light of your study of the Aristotelian *Poetics* in Arabic culture, what further studies in the field of comparative criticism would you suggest to the younger generation of scholars?

Shukry Ayyad: I would like to add that the study of Arabic literature, ancient, medieval, and modern, suffers from the lack of competent comparative studies. Whole areas have been left practically untouched, in spite of their vital importance in the history of world culture and the development of modern Arabic thought. I mention three major subjects:

1. The relation of pre-Islamic culture with Persian culture on the one hand, and Hellenistic culture on the other, both through the kindred Aramaean culture. It seems that immediately before Islam, Persian culture was quickly infiltrating the Arab peninsula, both from the northeast through the Kingdom of Hira, and from the south through Yemen, which was then a Persian protectorate. Islam revolutionized the whole situation, linking Arabic culture, or rather restoring its more ancient ties, with the culture of the eastern Mediterranean. I propose this statement as a working hypothesis, but much research has to be done before proving or disproving it. Its significance, in either case, can hardly be exaggerated.

2. The impact of Arabic on European medieval culture. The role of the Moorish culture has been widely recognized. This is a field with which I cannot claim to be familiar; besides the study of Asín Palácios on the possible Arabic sources of the *Divine Comedy* there is practically nothing else that I can mention. I know that our colleague Amina Rachide, has continued research on more or less the same lines. Our Hispanic scholars should know better. But I

doubt that there is much of note being done in this field. I would like to point out, more particularly, the possible influence of the Arabic poetic theory (based on the Arabic translations of and commentaries on the Aristotelian *Poetics*) on early classicism, as well as of Arabic poetic techniques, and Arabic art generally, on the Baroque movement. What is more important, however, is the whole cultural atmosphere in fourteenth- and fifteenth-century Europe. The question of cultural contacts should not be individual cases represented by particular persons or books. All sorts of details betraying such contacts should be particularly collected and analyzed. The reason for the importance that I attach to this subject is not pure national pride: I believe that the fourteenth and fifteenth centuries were one of the crucial moments of history, when East and West met on a very grand scale, both on the field of battle and in the institutes of learning, to part company for a long time afterwards, each following a different path. Their encounter in modern times, bedeviled as it is with prejudices on both sides, calls for a patient and minute study of that earlier period, when the rising Western culture was able to draw at least some of its elements from the Arab culture, which was embarking on an era of stagnation.

3. The influence of modern Turkish (and, to a lesser extent, modern Persian) literature on the literary revival in Arab countries. The first protagonists of this movement were familiar with Turkish letters and, indeed, the whole Turkish scene, which witnessed an important trend towards modernization. Direct contacts with the West only came later. No serious study of al-Barudi, Shawqi, or al-Zahawi—to mention only some of the more important names—could be attempted without first clearing the question of their contacts with Turkish cultural life before the Kamalist era.

Ceza Draz: There is a block *(azma)* in criticism, in creativity, in culture. Is all this 'blockage' peculiar to the Third World or is it common to both East and West? Is humanity seeking a new formula to deal with reality? If this is so, can you see any signs that such a formula is actually emerging?

Shukry Ayyad: I would like first to draw your attention to some of the psycholinguistic problems involved in your question. In Arab countries we refer to this 'block' as an *azma* which means 'crisis', 'stress', as well as a dearth of something. The same word is used for material goods as well as cultural values. The Anglo-Saxons, I think, will speak about 'problems', the French will probably prefer 'problématiques'. Who knows how the Germans, the Russians, the Chinese, etc., will express the same situation? I think that the heart of the problem lies here. There is a general feeling that the situation is one and the same; but there are so many ways of looking at it; and, consequently, so many solutions, or attempts at a solution. And indeed the situation, although identical in itself, is relativized in each case. Let us say that each people sees only the part that is closest to them. And there is no real effort, that I know of, being made to get at the 'formula' you are mentioning. It is not simply that the whole thing has become like an enormous jigsaw puzzle, there are too many emotional attitudes, biases, and prejudices involved on all levels: class, national, personal.

The only hopeful sign is that the younger generation—especially the 'literary' minded, those who are more inclined to the study of the humanities—have a keen, urgent feeling of the situation. Naturally enough, their reactions are hectic, outlandish, sometimes even suicidal. Most of them are politically minded. This is also natural; who can avoid politics nowadays? But to be concerned with 'culture' is to go to the deeper layers of politics, to cut yourself off from the daily concerns and practices of politics, which they are unable to do. Of course I am not advocating any 'ivory tower' attitude—I think that this notion is completely exploded now, if it ever had any validity.

Exploded also are the assumptions of the New Criticism, which were blindly adopted here by some university professors. Structuralism too has virtually surrendered its claims about the purely formal nature of art, since it developed a deeper concern with semiotics.

You can speak more about the 'literariness of literature' without forgetting its role in social change—or social stagnation as the case might be. However, writers of the younger generation—I speak particularly of Arab writers—have not completely shaken off the false attitudes of pure formalism. I don't even think that they have been bold enough to raise the question squarely or seriously. They go on experimenting gratuitously with form. At best they believe that a cabalistic form will hide them from the censor's eye. Their vision is blurred by scenes of degeneration and collapse, while their mastery of the Arabic literary language and the basic techniques of writing is too shaky to give this vision—limited as it is—its full, possible effect. I believe that the fault is not theirs; it is rather the members of the older generation (my generation), who were, perhaps, better equipped to deal with these difficult problems, but who have been satisfied, generally speaking, with adopting whatever 'theories'—social or critical—they were able to lay their hands on; and turning out novels, plays, and short stories, in the hope that they will be acknowledged, at last, as 'world' writers.

Call it what you like: block, crisis, or problem. I consider it a case of moral cowardice.

Ferial Ghazoul: You have worked in several parts of the Arab world. What would you like to say about cultural interrelations—particularly in the literary field—between these countries? What do you suggest for strengthening them?

Shukry Ayyad: I know that there is a general dissatisfaction with the actual conditions of literary exchange in the Arab world. Arab writers in North Africa may have a stronger reason to complain, but even in the Arab countries of the East, which have always been closely connected, literary contacts are rather weak. Usually they take the form of festivals or conferences, which serve the purpose of bringing poets, dramatists, or critics from all over the Arab world together, but cannot be expected to have a lasting effect or establish a common set of norms.

The movement of New Poetry, alias 'free verse', may be mentioned as an exception. But I think that most people—I mean most discriminating readers—will hesitate to affirm that it has established different norms for Arabic poetry. This is not to underestimate its effect, nor to accuse free verse, as a technique in writing poetry, of superficiality or ineptitude. What I mean is simply that the contacts between the exponents of the movement were, perhaps, too infrequent to encourage its growth. I don't know of one conference, seminar, or panel discussion which was devoted to a discussion of the New Poetry, its claims and problems. With the exception of the group of the quarterly *Shi'r* in Beirut, all the exponents of New Poetry, whether poets or critics, worked in isolation. The movement flourished for some time thanks to the attention given to it by some literary editors in key positions; now it seems to be withering for the same reason. This is just one aspect of the problem. The weak ties between people working in the same literary field cannot be considered as the only, or even the main reason for the ephemeral appearance of such a movement as that of New Poetry; on the other hand, the effects of those weak ties are not confined to poor development of literary movements that spring up, more or less independently and sporadically, in different Arab countries. Regional jealousies and suspicions often supported by political feuds between different Arab regimes, have more far-reaching effects in hampering the free flow of literary materials throughout the Arab world. At the same time, the neglect of purely literary contacts, which would be established and developed by such relatively free organizations as universities, literary societies, etc., redounds both to the general weakness of literary research and production, and to the lack of interest in literary matters shown by what is considered to be an educated public.

The whole situation in the world of letters is one of anarchy. However, I can see in this same anarchy signs of an exceptional vitality. I believe that the excessive, unchanneled, almost feverish movement we notice today in all—literally all—parts of the Arab world is bound to crystallize into some more durable trends. It is impossible, of course, to make any reliable forecasts as to how this is going to happen or what direction it would take. I can be sure of only one thing: new literary norms are imposed by people with a new outlook. Only creative spirits can transform the reigning chaos into significant unity.

Nancy Witherspoon: In 1931, Ibrahim 'Abd al-Qadir al-Mazni, in *Ibrahim the Writer,* said, "I appear differently to myself every day . . . I change every hour, every moment." Does this state of flux and reaching for identity still reflect the Arab character today?

Shukry Ayyad: The mere fact that you are raising this question points to the actual existence of such flux. Still, there is a big difference. Half a century ago, what you call "reaching for identity" meant preoccupation with one's own feelings, realization of one's potentialities. What I notice now is a preoccupation with one's orientation. There are two burning questions: Where to belong? What to seek? It is not just flux that we see—and experience—today; it is a general feeling of instability; a curious mixture of euphoria and desperation. But I don't consider this as a bad sign. I am inclined to compare it to the state of nervous tension that precedes the creative moment in an artist's life. Something is bound to emerge out of this chaos; something truly, solidly original. And I believe that this time it will lead to more social cohesion.

Nancy Witherspoon: Over half a century ago, Yahya Haqqi, in *The Saint's Lamp,* showed how Egyptians resorted to superstition, while a scientist or intellectual might accommodate them by accepting the superstition, incorporating it into practice. Later Abd al-Salam al-'Ujayli, in his short story "The Dream" was still pointing this out, portraying a schoolmaster who reconciles himself to the villagers' superstitions. Is this tendency to reconcile oneself with false beliefs still expressed by the younger generation of writers in the Arab world?

Shukry Ayyad: The younger generation of writers has grown up in a completely different atmosphere. There is no need to go into details. Suffice it to say that the problems that harry them are not those of a backward population whom they want to arouse from its stupor, but rather their own predicament in an alien world. Thus they do not put up a fight against superstition. They are more inclined to draw some strength, some will to live, from the obscure forces treasured in the huge mass of the people. Hence the ever-growing interest in folklore, the mythical flavor of much of their writing. This might be one of the reasons for the gap that exists between the younger and the older generations.

Nancy Witherspoon: Some Western writers have suggested that the extremist Islamic attitudes towards the West are principally due to the nineteenth-century colonial aggressions in the Middle East. Are there any literary Arabic works which would clarify this or other causes for current tensions against the West?

Shukry Ayyad: You may consider it a question of colonial aggression, but I think it is more than that. The impact of Western culture on Arab life and values had been a major theme in modern Arabic literature since the early days of the Arab renaissance, which preceded the advent of colonial rule. We cannot go into details now, but I would like to mention that something like a Magna Carta was obtained by the population of Cairo from the Turkish pasha and his Mamluk partners, some ten years before the French occupation, which lasted only three years. That is why there has always been a sort of ambivalence towards the West. On the one hand there is a keenly felt need to learn from the West; on the other hand there is doubt, fear, and distrust. The last attitude was strengthened by the failure of the West to remedy its own faults, the high price that had to be paid for material progress. Al-Hakim's *Bird from the East* is but one example of the disillusionment of an essentially pro-Western writer when he comes to grips with the realities of Western civilization. Naguib Mahfouz expressed a similar dichotomy in his famous trilogy. *The Season of Migration to the North,* by a younger writer, Tayeb Salih, presents the meeting of East and West as a tragedy for both. However, it seems that nobody in the West paid any attention to the dissatisfaction of Arab intellectuals until the desperate moves of Islamic extremists came to the fore. Of this latest phase I can cite no literary reflection: most likely it stems from deeper layers of Islamic societies, which do not show much interest in modern literary production, dressed in garbs of Western genres. Here is an indication of the limited appeal of modern Arabic literature: had it been able to create for itself a readership from among the various strata of Arab society, we would not have been at a loss to find one literary work which might be considered as a clear reflection of attitudes so disturbingly expressed in the political sphere.

Ceza Draz: When you wrote an introduction to your *Experiments in Literature and Criticism,* you declared criticism to be your hobby, while teaching was your profession. Since you teach your hobby, how do you figure each activity is projected on the other?

Shukry Ayyad: I don't remember clearly what I wrote in that introduction, but what I meant was probably that I am not a professional writer. For I have often insisted on this point: that I cannot consider writing as a profession. To me it is essentially a free activity, which means also that I cherish it more than teaching. The reason is clear: being obliged to take up a profession, I took up teaching. And it is enough that you are obliged to do something to feel rather reluctant to do it. It will become bearable only when you can sneak out of it to go on your own escapade. And I should be grateful to my literary escapades because they did not make teaching just bearable, but even enjoyable. In my class I am in direct contact with other minds, and we start together a kind of play. The lesson begins to take shape of its own free will, as it were. I think that my teaching has also influenced my writing. I could never present myself to my readers as a mere entertainer.

Ferial Ghazoul: Non-Arab readers do not find a book which introduces them to the peculiar charm of Arabic literature. I know that you are actually writing an English book on this subject. Will you give us some information about your work? What guidelines did you follow in writing it? To what kind of audience is it addressed? Did you think of the general reader or the one specializing in Arabic culture?

Shukry Ayyad: There is a course at the American University in Cairo called "Modern Arabic Literature in English Translation." I taught this course in the second semester of 1981–82. I noticed that the students—most of whom were non-Arabs—responded easily to my efforts to arouse their interest in this, to them, alien subject. Of course, living in Egypt, with various everyday contacts with the Egyptian people, they must be expected to show some interest. But I felt that the steadily growing importance, politically and economically, of the

Arab world will, perhaps, impel all enlightened readers in different parts of the world to look for a book both informal and informative enough to give them a more or less intimate knowledge of Arabs as human beings.

I embarked on the subject with the kind assistance of Nancy Witherspoon, who is an assiduous reader of English and other European translations of, and studies on, modern Arabic literature. The book developed into a rather stout volume, covering all literary genres and trying to refer their development not only to Western influences but also to the cultural tradition and the social environment. As I said it is not just information; it tries to put the reader in direct contact with Arab life, as expressed in the medium of literature. This means that it is not 'public' criticism either, if by this we understand a technical study of literary form; the changing and variegated forms of modern Arabic literature are explained in terms of cultural development. The whole thing is, of course, a venture. Only time will show how authentic or how valid or how useful it might be. All I can say is that it attempts to strike a balance between sympathy and objectivity, novel ideas and necessary information, and, of course, the eternal poles of enlightenment and entertainment.

Jabra Ibrahim Jabra

❖

On Interpoetics

Najman Yasin: You once said that the short story is an easy art. And yet you yourself have written a collection of short stories: *'Araq wa qisas ukhra* (Sweat and other stories). Do you think it was your earlier contentment with the easiness of the short story that led you to make this statement and finally to stop writing short stories?

Jabra Jabra: What I said is that the short story is an easy art in relation to the greater task of the novel. The story, that is, is an easy art if a writer imagines that the events and characters central to the story can be expressed in a limited number of pages—which is, of course, a wrong assumption. The easiness here lies in the attitude of the writer towards an extremely complex artistic issue. If every Arabic short story writer handled the short story as did Maupassant, Chekhov, or Hemingway, for example, then we might have said that the short story writer had met a difficult task with a suitably incisive weapon. But what has actually happened during the long development of the Arabic short story is that the task has come to be taken for an easy one. The Arabic writer came to dread facing the larger endeavor, namely the novel, because he realized that the novel could not be written as a short story is written, because the novel is not to be undertaken except over a long period of time in the writer's own life and through actual anxiety and suffering. To the Arabic writer the short story was a transition from the poem *(qasida)* which is characterized by an outpouring of emotion—or, more specifically, a single private outpouring, which neither goes far into nor penetrates the labyrinths of the human soul. The Arabic writer, in his 'poetic' attitude to the short story, treats it as an easy art. Such an attitude makes him, in the end, unable to encompass the vast visionary experience which is part of Arab life today. Thus I ask that Arab writers attempt the more difficult art, that they not finish writing something in a few hours, or a few days, and imagine that they have accomplished a miracle of art. I want Arab writers to live with their characters, to struggle with them and argue with them, and through this to participate in depicting at least a part of that overwhelming process: the transformation of our society. Furthermore, they should portray the constant intellectual interaction between writer and society. The novels of Balzac and Dostoevsky not only reflect their times, but express as well the influence of those times on the minds of two geniuses busy taking and giving with their age. For over ten years, yes, I myself wrote short stories. And although at eighteen I had written some short stories, I came to neglect them and returned to the form again in 1946, when the first story in my collection *'Araq* (1956) was written. At the same time I wrote two short novels in English: the first entitled *Echo and the Pool,* and the second, *Passage in the Silent Night,* which I later translated into Arabic with the title *Surakh fi laylin tawil* (Cry in a long night). And yet even while I continued writing short stories, such as the ones included in *'Araq,* I came back to the novel in 1953, and began *Hunters in a Narrow Street,* in English, while at Harvard. I worked on it for three years, writing at the same time short stories in Arabic. However, when I finished the novel I felt I should either write novels or move to other literary arts, such as poetry or literary criticism. If I haven't written a short story since, it is because I feel that it no longer meets my needs. I must confess though that I have not written many novels either—with only five novels to my credit, one of them still in typescript.

Najman Yasin: Poet, critic, painter, translator, short story writer, and novelist—do these diverse interests of yours cause you to branch out in different directions, or do they converge finally in unified creative vision?

Jabra Jabra: Had I not been all of these at once, I would probably have been none of them. The man, or thinker, or creator, in me is integrated through being all of these together. Nor have I ever felt that I was divided among them. Rather, each one of them was a help in supporting the other person in me. What I couldn't say as painter I said as poet, and what I couldn't say as poet I said as novelist. It was necessary for me to express diverse aspects of myself through diverse means. These means complement each other. Even the translations I have done have been an extension of my literary interests. And because I breathe through translation just as I breathe through my short stories and novels, the books which I have translated are closely connected within my own intellectual disposition. In the one activity I find help and support for interpreting the other. My lust for creation is characterized by a greed which, though rightful, almost tortures me. And yet it is through this lust alone that my life realizes its meaning.

Najman Yasin: It has been said that your novel *al-Safina (The Ship)* adopted some of the techniques and stylistic traits of Faulkner.

Jabra Jabra: Those who claim that I have borrowed Faulkner's stylistic devices should name some of them. Perhaps I was the first writer to introduce Faulkner to the Arab world. My first article on *The Sound and the Fury* appeared in *al-Adab* in 1954 and was followed by my translation of the novel.

I realized then that Faulkner had so broadened the potential of narrative structure that it was no longer possible to write a novel without considering his achievements. Faulkner, however, when he wrote his novel, was himself accused of imitating the styles of James Joyce and Virginia Woolf. And so *al-Safina* is criticized for being an imitation of Faulkner. Faulkner, too, realized that Joyce's accomplishments in narrative technique could not be ignored if he was to write a novel that went beyond *Ulysses*. When the early Renaissance discovered perspective in painting no painter could neglect this breakthrough, and perspective became part of the work of every artist. This never meant, however, that one artist was copying another. Narrative technique, if somehow expanded, becomes the property of every writer. What is important is what each writer accomplishes through technique and whether he himself contributes to its potential, to its possibilities. Thus I still believe that *al-Safina*, in assimilating earlier narrative techniques, actually went beyond them. It achieved a style I want to realize specifically in the Arabic novel, which is still traditional and unaware of the techniques of architectural structure—at least in most of the novels I come across and in most of the writers whose works I read.... Perhaps the reader will perceive the continuous interaction between technique and language in *al-Safina*. Language here is part of the energy I explode into different forms. The character, furthermore, is determined by his or her language as much as by the event in that character's life. The embodiment of cultural values, an embodiment to which the writer aspires, can be accomplished only through language. Language to the Arab is food and drink. It is the means of giving substance to his dreams and defining those inner ways which lead to the cultural identity he seeks for himself. It is to precisely this end that I use language in *al-Safina*. And I hope to have done so in my next novel as well. Is this taken from Faulkner or Joyce, al-Jahiz or al-Mutanabbi or al-Ma'arri? Man's imagination is the complex result of a complex understanding of a culture deeply rooted in history and in the national unconscious. It is this national unconscious which must ultimately have the final say.

Najman Yasin: That your novels have benefited from the other creative arts is clear, and it seems appropriate to ask you about the relationship you see between the novel and these other arts.

Jabra Jabra: The novel is one of the latest of man's art forms. It crystallized in the form we now know only in the last two centuries and was preceded by the epic *(malhama)*, the poetic story *(qissa shi'riya)*, the fable *(hikaya)* told by the animals, and the *maqama* or séance. The tales of the *Arabian Nights* followed, and were an addition to those folkloric narratives which make use of the story in depicting man's conflict with nature or in portraying the wisdom (or proverbs, *hikam)* man derives from his accumulated experience. The novel that we know today benefits from all of this and adds much that was unknown to earlier cultures. The contemporary novel may derive more than one of its powers from the epic, the play, the dialogue, and the fable, but it has become (adding as it does the analysis of the human character, of the event, connecting these two analyses, and carrying them to their explosion point in the human imagination) a vision that its earliest practitioners could not have foreseen. This addition, using the various means of diction and narration, developed over two centuries into what we today call the technique of the novel. . . . The novel benefited from painting, music, acting, and from poetry as verbal energy and suggestion. It became the meeting point of the creative arts known to man since earliest times. Unaware of this, the novelist cannot write a good novel. In other words, the novelist should know how to use techniques belonging originally to musical composition, such as rhythm, harmony, and crescendo, for example. If he doesn't know to use chiaroscuro (the combination of light and shadow in a certain way which seems to give concrete shape to an image), then he will be will be unable to master his art. But the novel benefits as well from the newer arts. It has profited a great deal from the cinema and its use of montage. Though the film relied at first on the novel, it created a special technique of its own that the novel then used to its own end. As you see, the arts are interconnected, and the novel attempts to combine them all in order to realize the purpose of the novelist. Having mentioned all of that, however, we have yet to talk about analytical psychology, about anthropology, about historic events or periods—and the combination of all these put to technical or stylistic use by the novelist. The novelist, having combined the sense of the psychoanalyst, the social scientist, the historian, the philosopher, and the artist, might well claim with D. H. Lawrence that "his book is the golden book of life" upon which he prides himself.

Najman Yasin: Apropos *al-Bahth 'an Walid Mas'ud* (In Search of Walid Mas'ud), your forthcoming novel of which two chapters have already appeared in *al-Adab* and *Afaq 'arabiya,* could you tell us something of the experience of childhood and the pathway leading to its world, a world whose rules and imagining lie beyond the norms and traditions of the outside world?

Jabra Jabra: You must have noticed my interest in childhood in all of my writings. Childhood is, for me, an eternal spring of creativity, as it is for every man. In Wordsworth's words, "the child is father of the man." In the child lie those beginnings that determine the future's identity and direction. However, going back to childhood in one's writings is not always as easy as you might think. The childhood must be both active and alive in the writer's mind: in my case, the world of childhood takes me back to my homeland, back to the absolute innocence known in the soil on which I was raised. It has always symbolized for me the world of purity, representing the purity of my country. It continually affirms and reaffirms the necessity of going back through the wounds of experience, through exile and homelessness, back to the primordial innocence which is a hidden spring in the life of the nation. One cannot speak of an absolute childhood, only of one's own. The clever or lucky man is the man who can make of his childhood a mirror of the reader's childhood and of the childhoods of all men. In my last novel, *al-Bahth 'an Walid Mas'ud*, I made the child the counterpart of the active, mature man. What I intended to do was to create an alternation in narration between the events of the hero in childhood and youth on the one hand, and the events he goes through later in his life, on the other. It remains, however, for the reader to see if there is such a connection between these two poles which are far apart in time and place and which continuously interlock as a determining factor in the hero's course of thought and action.

This is, of course, only one partial aspect of childhood in my novel. I do not deny that, in choosing my method in this novel, I took, as it were, a leap in the dark. As you may have noticed, I usually construct a kind of timeframe for the single work of art. This depends on a specific and intended unity from which I then derive some of the symbols of that work. The timespan in *Surakh fi laylin tawil*, for example, is one night. In *Hunters in a Narrow Street*, it is one full year which begins in autumn and ends with the last days of summer: there is a kind of shift in the climate of the novel, whose symbols are in turn connected with the seasons' changing. In *al-Safina*, on the other hand, the timespan comprises just one week. The attempt here to define a span of time for the novel corresponds to the attempt to describe a man's life during one week, whose hours in fact enclose a whole age lived by each character in the novel.

In *al-Bahth 'an Walid Mas'ud* the timespan is half a century. This, obviously, is a very risky thing in a work of art. I took great pains, however, to make these fifty years converge with each other in an artistic unity, a unity which is intended to express, at least in part, the novel's meaning. The importance of childhood in this novel is therefore greater than in my other novels, which is not, however, to diminish its role in them at all. The issue is, on the one hand, psychological and personal, and on the other, technical and artistic. What is most important to me is to combine these two aspects.... Have I succeeded? I just don't know ....

Najman Yasin: Abdelrahman Munif has said in an interview that *al-Bahth 'an Walid Mas'ud* is a pivotal novel for two reasons. The first is its technique and originality, which represent a great breakthrough for the contemporary Arabic novel. The second reason is that you, Jabra, have at last thrust your hand into the fire of revolution. Tell us about this novel of yours. Do you consider it a turning point in your thought and style?

Jabra Jabra: Abdelrahman Munif's approbation gives me confidence in this novel. As for the novel's being a great innovation in contemporary Arabic novel-writing, this is something I aspired to even in writing its first lines. And as for my having thrust my hand decisively into the fire of revolution, this may be due to our having become, one and all, a part of this fire, a fire which we want to continue burning in the Arab mind. It must burn in Arab achievements of the present as well as in those which are to come. If in the work of art there is no fire into which the artist can thrust his hand, he will never be able to strike such a fire in his reader's soul. And perhaps the highest aim to which a novelist can aspire is to ignite this flame—this revolutionary fire which becomes a kind of immanence in man's life.... I do not think that this novel is a turning point in my thought and style in any decisive sense. It is a logical extension of my first attempt at novel-writing. It seems to me at times that the creator discovers he has something to say early in his life. He says it, if only in part, repeats it, and adds later to it. Each attempt then to repeat it seeks to say that which had been left unsaid in its earlier iterations. We do not repeat ourselves in each of our works, but rather add, polish, and modify in order to complete the great work already begun. It is strange that in every attempt of this kind the previous attempts are not cancelled out, but their value is instead reconfirmed... am I contradicting myself? Even if a given work of art seems a turning point in the thought and style of its author, it is in fact (once its implications and recesses are probed) part of an ascending line which can be traced back to his starting point.

Hassan Fathy

❖

On the Poetics of Space

Introduction

But if we 'listen' to the design of things, we encounter an angle, a trap detains the dreamer . . .
—*Gaston Bachelard*[1]

Mushtaq: I shan't forget what I have experienced in this *mashrabiya*. Its decoration is like a melody struck on strings of a lute.
Nadim: Listen, is not what you hear music?
Mushtaq: Strange, I used to think that this house, which seemed dominated by silence, was uninhabited. It's as if I were sensing music, not *mashrabiya;* or *mashrabiya* and not music.
—*Hassan Fathy*[2]

To my mind, architecture is like the shell of a snail, the soft part secreting calcium carbonates, and by natural forces making the form by movement and surface tension.
—*Hassan Fathy*[3]

Everything that has form has a shell ontogenesis, and life's principal effort is to make shells. . . . The function constructs its form from old models, and life, although only partial, constructs its abode the way the shell-fish constructs its shell.
—*Gaston Bachelard*[4]

Hassan Fathy has not read Gaston Bachelard's *Poetics of Space*. But whoever knows Hassan Fathy—the artist who sculpts harmonious spaces out of walls, vaulted roofs, and domes, who creates a triumphant interplay of the intimate and enclosed with the overt and exposed of interior with exterior, or of the vast and lit with the narrow and dark; the architect who domesticates space in *iwans*,[5] alcoves, steps, and levels, or variegates it in patios and courts, where *mashrabiya* lattice-works screen out the sun and fountains bring in water; the man who repeats the phrase from St. Exupery's *Citadelle:* "the house of my father, where each step has a meaning," as a definition of what architectural design is expected to realize out of space—whoever knows Hassan Fathy and his work knows that he has not only anticipated much of Bachelard's definition of the poetics of space in his beliefs, but has embodied the poetics of space in architecture.

It is therefore by no coincidence that in an article on Bachelard's writings in a Lebanese weekly *(Beirut al-masa')*, published in 1982, a photo of one of Fathy's houses was used as the only illustration to the text, without any identifying caption, as if that architecture naturally illustrated Bachelard's theory and analysis of space: its poetics, expression, and reflections.

When I suggested to Hassan Fathy that I interview him on his interpretation of the poetics of space, I indicated my own interest in drawing parallels between his works and Bachelard's analysis. "The poetics of space" I said. "How can we discuss the subject?"

"The musicality of space," he replied at once. "It is a very important subject. When I think of the poetics of space, I see Venice, Fez, or Isfahan."

In the following dialogue, held in the fall of 1984, Hassan Fathy describes the meaning of space, felt space and built space, as implied in architecture, which he defines as "the space between the walls, and not the walls." But perhaps he is simply elaborating on the Goethean description of architecture as "frozen music."[6] For he believes in architecture as space, so woven and composed that one can listen and hear melody, and in town-planning as the creation of a sonata.

—*S. Samar Damluji*

❖ ❖ ❖

S. Samar Damluji: Hassan Bey, can we discuss 'the poetics of space' in architecture?

Hassan Fathy: In discussing the musicality of space there are three factors to be considered: melody, harmony, and counterpoint. The ensemble of notes simultaneously gives harmony and if both are played comprehensively they can give us a sonata. The expectations and surprises we experience in moving from one melody of a sonata to another are also experienced when we move from one building to another in a town: each building is a melody. Surprise contrasts with expectation. There is teasing: the composer gives you something different from what you expected there should be, which may sound dissonant at first, but which he ultimately resolves, until it becomes pleasing.

In discussing *space* we must differentiate between interstellar and enclosed space. Exterior or interstellar space cannot be felt, because it expands to infinity. To be felt, it has to be cut out and enclosed within walls. If this enclosed space is spherical there is not much for me to feel; it does not give me much to judge, since in a spherical shell my eyes go round and round without my knowing where I started and ended my looking within a circle. But if space is cubical, with plane surfaces like the walls, roof, and floor of a room, the eye will go to and fro, up and down, focusing along the lines of intersection of the planes that enclose the space, and the character of the space will be defined. Physiologically the eye doesn't perceive a line instantaneously but point by point, sending the experience to the brain where the line is conceived as in music; when you have a melody you hear it note by note and you send the experience to the brain through the ear, where we conceive the melody.

If the lines of the intersection of the walls that enclose the space are harmonious, then the space is pleasing, as in the Arab *qaʻa*,[7] where we have the dimensions (length, width, and height) ruled by phi (Φ), the Golden Section, and pi (π). In contrast, if the dimensions are hectic then the felt space is disagreeable and disturbing, like the lobbies of modern hotels, which are very large, long and have very low ceilings. The space is not harmonious and you feel that you want to push the ceiling upwards, but that it keeps coming down. You feel like Sisyphus endlessly carrying the stone to the top of the mountain.

S. Samar Damluji: You always define architecture as "the space within the walls and not the walls." Doesn't this definition mean that when designing or planning you are primarily concerned with the quality of space and composition? In essence, aren't you concerned with the poetics of space?

Hassan Fathy: Yes. Suppose you take a simple example, a theater. You have the porch outside, which is only an arcade. You leave your car and enter the vestibule, where you have a cloak-room and where you don't stay long. But then you enter the lobby. And in the lobby, because one arrives before the action starts, you see friends and talk to one another and it must therefore be larger in space, and of a certain form. You have thus proceeded from the porch, to the vestibule, to the lobby. Then you go to the hall itself, where everybody is seated. In each of these successive spaces you have had expectations as to what the size will be. The main hall takes in everybody, seated, not standing or walking, and you thus have particular expectations here, expectations not only as to the size and the height, but also as to the decoration. In the lobby again at the *entr'acte,* two-thirds of the audience have left their seats in the hall and reappeared, you see friends again and talk to them because the *entr'acte* takes ten minutes.

Such are the expectations we have in a theater, the feelings by which we can judge a theater. And what that means is that as you design a theater, you are aware of these expectations.

The ceilings of a modern theater get higher and higher as you go in. The ceiling of the porch is low, the vestibule's is a little higher, the lobby's is even higher, and the main hall's is the highest. But when you enter an ancient Egyptian temple you go from high to low. The ceiling gets lower as you proceed while the rooms get smaller, until you come at last to the sanctuary, which is the smallest space and where you have the statue of the Deity. So in such a building you have concentration, you are concentrating.

These are the kinds of feelings you must have when you are designing, expectations that you feel but you do not necessarily think about as if they were something visible. They are in the back of the mind, I mean to say.

Another point, of course, is the absolute and the relative. If you have both a small theater and a large theater in the same building, for example, they demand different spaces in the kind of succession I just described.

Intimacy needs small spaces, like in a bedroom, while in the living room you have a larger space, because you meet people there, different people, and the intimacy is reduced. And when you go outside, you lose intimacy altogether. So that a space itself can either evoke intimacy or, at the opposite extreme, a loss of intimacy amounting to anonymity.

S. Samar Damluji: I have noticed a feature in the design of all the bedrooms in your plans: the bedroom space is large, but you create corners of intimacy with the *iwans*. The feeling is not of a large dispersed space but of a space that has simply been composed of smaller, separate, more intimate spaces brought together to form a single larger unit.

Hassan Fathy: Yes. You have the beds in those small *iwans*. Naturally, when a bedroom is an alcove, small and completely closed in, it becomes dull and you feel imprisoned within. But if you use a *durqa'a*[8] or the principle of the *durqa'a*—a large space with the *iwans* off it, where you can sit and look onto the larger space—you have intimacy and at the same time the feeling of space, which is pleasant. It is a question of domesticating space, in this instance a large space.

S. Samar Damluji: Doesn't the concept of intimacy apply not only to interior architectural space, but to town-planning as well?

Hassan Fathy: Of course. When you walk in a *hara*[9] it is intimate. Children play and people meet, and the relationship between them is different from when you have a large street—what you call a boulevard—where you have cars and where people don't meet.

S. Samar Damluji: Hassan Bey, can we say that traditional Arab architecture is an architecture that expresses the poetics of space, providing a feeling of domesticated space, as you put it, in both architecture and townplanning, which is actually lacking or absent in contemporary architecture?

Hassan Fathy: This is what I was trying to say in my paper "Cairo of the Future."[10] We have to return this feeling of belonging to the space that surrounds us.

S. Samar Damluji: Do you mean the intimate space that results from the planning or interplay of exteriority and interiority?

Hassan Fathy: You have certain spaces which are both large and intimate. If you are at a football field, for example, you have an amphitheater and all the people are concentrating on the sport, that is to say, they are together, they belong together, and the result is amusing, like harmony, a kind of music. The space is large and is not in itself intimate, but there is intimacy here because all the people are sharing the same feeling, even if their allegiances are opposed, some for one team and some for the other. At least you have everyone's attention drawn to the football players and the match. So you see, in these different kinds of spaces, whether the bedroom, living room, or a football field, you have different feelings, but in each case it is a question of combining intimacy with space without losing the sense of belonging to the space you are in.

S. Samar Damluji: Bachelard wrote: "Often it is from the very fact of concentration in the most restricted intimate space that the dialectics of inside and outside draws its strength."[11] How is intimacy affected by the interplay of the outside and inside, by the combination, for example, of exterior space with interior space, as in the Arab house with a courtyard?

Hassan Fathy: The outside differs from the inside, whether the outside is the sky above, or, at ground level, the desert or a street or a square, the feeling in each is different. In the Arab house you have the courtyard, which is a little piece of the infinite space, the sky, which man has cut out to his own proportion, in harmony with his size and to satisfy his feeling of privacy, his wish for intimacy. And whether it's a large house or a small house, the courtyard provides the private piece of sky which belongs to man who lives there.

S. Samar Damluji: It represents a private piece of sky, a private portion of water in its fountain, and of earth in its trees or plants. Isn't the courtyard the private piece of the 'outside', i.e., the exterior, made intimate and domesticated?

Hassan Fathy: When we are 'outside', we are lost in interstellar space, but when you have a floor and four walls and a ceiling they enclose a private space. When the desert dweller became sedentary, he preserved his contact with the sky through the design concept of the courtyard house, as can be seen in the houses of Fustat, Iraq, and North Africa. And later on, with the development of urbanization, he transposed the concept of the courtyard and the *iwan* into the *qa'a* with the *durqa'a* and *iwans* off it. He made the *durqa'a* higher and with a roof, symbolizing the sky, i.e., its dome, as if it were a covered courtyard. These are musical compositions available to you when you want to play with the feelings—different feelings so not just to have intimacy alone and *finito*. You have to have intimacy but without either limiting or losing the feeling of space and without creating the feeling of being imprisoned.

S. Samar Damluji: There is also the concept of 'transition', from the exterior to the interior. Isn't that also an important factor in design?

Hassan Fathy: Of course. The transition from one space to the other is very important, because of our expectations.

S. Samar Damluji: This reminds me of when you used to discuss the plan of the Sultan Hassan mosque. You would point out the entrance, which leads from the street to the vestibule and then into the *majaz,* the long, narrow, dark corridor which opens onto the vast courtyard of the mosque. So that, in effect, the contrast between darkness and light and the transition from the public street outside to the private interior of the mosque is realized by the *majaz,* which creates this interlude in space. Although the private interior in this case is a large court, it is extremely secluded within the mosque's private space.

Hassan Fathy: The feeling of separation between the profane space of the street and the sacred part of the mosque's interior is effected by this meandering corridor, which joins the vestibule with the courtyard. It creates the succession.

S. Samar Damluji: So that architecture becomes the interplay and articulation of spaces and is equally evident both in the design of individual housing or buildings and in traditional Arab town-planning?

Hassan Fathy: Absolutely. In architecture we deal with the rooms as units in a system, which is the building. At the same time we deal with the buildings themselves as units in a system, which is the city. If you have to put together a group of houses in the street, there is an infinitude of possibilities for arranging these houses, for composing the space of the street.

When you have on one side of the street the harmonious play of silhouettes, forms, and textures as each building is looked at in succession, if it is aesthetically harmonious, then it is like a melody. And when you have another melody opposite in the facing row of houses, our alternative response to the one and the other is like counterpoint.

Or we could say that our vision is like a billiard ball, caroming from one side to the other and ending up in the pocket. Then you are excited.

S. Samar Damluji: This interplay of spaces, musicality, succession, and transition weaves a specific cultural identity, which is reflected in the buildings. How is it realized?

Hassan Fathy: The eye goes from one node to the other, from one side to the other. If you enter an old street like Sharia Saliba, which goes between Ibn Tulun and Sultan Hassan, you have closed vistas with successive nodal points—a minaret here, a house there, another building here, or another minaret there—the occurrence of which comes harmoniously. The eye moves from right to left as we walk along, we have counterpoint, and you say, "Ah, voilà!" You feel that it is intentional, that it is not haphazard, that it has been deliberately created.

S. Samar Damluji: The experience of walking down those streets trains the eye to be expectant. When the eye moves slowly, as one walks from one corner to another, it is waiting with expectation, surprised by each interruption and variation.

Hassan Fathy: From one nodal point to the next: it is like a movement in a sonata, and you have the succession of the musical movements in the street as you walk.

To understand the value of this experience only imagine that the same street offered the same houses repeated in a straight line, what expectation would you have? You would have nothing.

Notes

1 Gaston Bachelard, *Poetics of Space,* trans. by Maria Jolas (New York: Orion Press, 1964), p. 144.
2 This epigraph is drawn from Hassan Fathy's play *al-Mashrabiya,* an unpublished manuscript written in 1942. Mashrabiya, sometimes rendered in English as 'moucharaby', refers to a projecting oriel window with lattice work enclosure, typical of Arab houses.
3 "Hassan Fathy Speaks" in Renata Holod, ed. *Architecture and Community Building in the Islamic World Today* (Published for the Aga Khan Award for Architecture by Aperture, a division of Silver Mountain Foundation, Inc.: Middleton, N.Y., 1983), pp. 241–45.
4 Bachelard, *Poetics of Space,* pp. 112–13.
5 An *iwan* is a hall or a niche (generally vaulted), walled on three sides and opening directly to a larger unit (such as a courtyard or a room).
6 "Ich habe unter meinen Papieren ein Blatt gefunden... wo ich die Baukunst eine erstarrte Musik nenne." Goethe, *Gesprache mit Eckermann,* 23 March 1829.
7 A *qa'a* is a large reception hall formed by a central unit *(durqa'a)* with a high ceiling (sometimes covered by a dome) flanked by two *iwans* which are slightly raised and covered by a flat ceiling.
8 A *durqa'a* is the central unit of a *qa'a* (reception hall) usually with a recessed floor, a high ceiling, and a fountain in the middle.
9 A *hara* is a street (usually a dead end) in a popular neighborhood.
10 "Cairo of the Future," a paper presented to the Agha Khan Architectural Award Seminar devoted to "The Expanding Metropolis: Coping with the Urban Growth of Cairo," (Cairo, November 1984).
11 Bachelard, *Poetics of Space,* p. 229.

Mohamed Choukri

❖

Being and Place

Edwar al-Kharrat: You have mentioned that you consider *al-Khubz al-hafi (For Bread Alone),* an autobiographical novel, more of a social document than art. My question is: Do you honestly believe that you have not produced a work of art by writing *For Bread Alone?* Is it quite impossible for a social document to be literary, or rather, that a literary work can never be a social document precisely because it is artistic?

Mohamed Choukri: When I said that my autobiographical *al-Khubz al-hafi* is more of a social document than a work of art I meant that I had actually attempted a semi-documentary endeavor about an oppressed social group that included myself and my family. A work of art, be it a novel, a short story, a play, or a poem is more condensed, symbolic, and inspirational. In other words, it requires the writer to be more detached from the events he is depicting. This does not mean that an autobiography can never aspire to the realm of genuine art. It would have been so had I written it with an intellectual orientation where the philosophical and psychological levels are fused together in a similar way to Jean-Paul Sartre's *Les Mots,* James Joyce's (to some extent) *A Portrait of the Artist as a Young Man,* Colin Wilson's *Journey Towards a Beginning.* There are many others who did the same in ancient and modern times: Cicero, Saint Augustine, Jean-Jacques Rousseau, Goethe, Somerset Maugham, Jean Genet in his *Journal du voleur,* Pablo Neruda in *Residence on Earth.* Those and others wrote autobiographies laden with the cultural heritage they had nurtured since their childhood within their social and parental environment. In my autobiography, however, I did not overload my characters (including myself) with cultural dimensions except as befits their simple social status.

Most literary works stem from a combination of social and political experiences that are often closer to a documentary such as Dostoevsky's *The House of the Dead,* André Gide's *Voyage au Congo,* André Malraux's *L'Espoir* and *La Condition humaine,* Hemingway's *For Whom the Bell Tolls,*

John Steinbeck's *The Moon is Down.* Arab writers, on the other hand, are still struggling to get rid of the three swords dangling over their heads: politics, religion, and morality. In this way, had Tawfiq al-Hakim been a Frenchman— as Ihsan 'Abd al-Quddus said in his book *'Aqli wa qalbi* (My mind and my heart)—he would have been another Jean-Paul Sartre. And had Einstein been an Arab, he would have ended up like Hafez Ibrahim or Ahmad Shawqi, at the most. This is because we are still afraid of everything democratic and scientific.

I would like to recount a tale from the days of King Hassan I. The king sent Moroccan students on missions to Europe in the same year that Japan sent students too. When the Japanese mission members returned to Japan, they were welcomed and honored and awarded jobs that suited their qualifications. As for our mission, their members were either persecuted, assassinated, or driven away by bigoted officials. Those who managed to escape had to live under disguise and work as shoemakers or vegetable vendors.

Edwar al-Kharrat: In your opinion, what is the relationship between *al-Khubz al-hafi* and the stories of *al-shuttar* (the picaros) in folk literature such as *The Thousand and One Nights*, and the tales of 'Ali al-Zaybaq and the like. Is there a relationship? To what extent has historical time influenced the development of the picaresque model, that is, if this model already existed in your consciousness?

Mohamed Choukri: I confess that I have not yet read the stories of picaros in Arabic literature. Neither have I read *The Thousand and One Nights* or any other book related to picaresque literature in the East or the West.

I have recently acquired a copy of *Lazarillo de Tormes* written by an anonymous writer, as was *La Celestina*. These two works preceded *Don Quixote de la Mancha.* You will be surprised to know that I have not yet read Taha Hussein's *al-Ayyam* (Days) (which I only bought recently), the autobiography of Ahmad Amin (I read a few pages of it in 1958 because I had borrowed it and had to return it before I finished reading it). As for *Fi-l-tufula* (In childhood) by the Moroccan writer Abdel Mejid Ben Jelloun, I could not carry on beyond the first few pages because it was boring and verbose. To tell you the truth, I am not a good reader of Arabic literature because with the exception of a few old texts, I do not find it liberating.

Edwar al-Kharrat: Are there any differences between the Arabic text of *al-Khubz al-hafi* and the English version *For Bread Alone*, which Paul Bowles said was a direct translation of colloquial Moroccan, spoken orally? In other words, did you translate your spoken language into classical Arabic in the process of writing *al-Khubz al-hafi?* Or did you write it in classical Arabic to begin with? Which came first? The English or the Arabic text?

Mohamed Choukri: In 1972, the English publisher Peter Owen visited Tangier. According to his own statements to the press, he is dishonest in his treatment of writers. He knew Paul Bowles. He had already published the autobiography of a Moroccan young man who used a pseudonym, Idris al-

Sharadli, actually called al-'Arabi al-'Ayashi. It was called *Hayat mali'a bi-l-thuqub* (A life full of holes) and its original title in colloquial Moroccan was *al-'Aysha al-mathlula* (Servile life). Then, he published a story by another young man, Mohamed al-Murabit, called *Hubb bi-bid' shu'ayrat* (Love with a few hairs). Both men did not write but recorded their tales on tape, which were then translated into English by Paul Bowles with the help of the narrators. The first young man has emigrated to the United States, and has obtained a degree and hopes to get a teaching position in an American university. The second one still goes fishing, breeds birds, and frequents popular cafés where he listens to the folktales told by old men.

Paul Bowles had already translated many of my short stories: two appeared in the American magazines *Harper's* and *Anteus*, others came out in the English *Trans Atlantic*.

Peter Owen had heard from Paul Bowles snatches of my vagabond life and suggested to him that he ask me to write an autobiography. Until then, I had only published stories and articles in the Lebanese magazine *al-Adab* and in the cultural supplement of the newspaper *al-'Ilm*. To tell you the truth, I wanted to publish my first book at any price to prove to myself that I was a writer. When Paul Bowles asked me to write my autobiography, I immediately replied, "But it is already written. I have had it at home for some time." Needless to say, I had not put down a word on paper, but it was all there in my mind. I was planning on writing it after I had gained some literary glory. And, since all my life has been a response to one challenge after the other, I went to Bowles on the following evening with my first chapter written in classical Arabic. This (and the chapters that followed) were identical with what appeared in the Arabic edition, apart from a few changes that I made when Tahar Ben Jelloun asked for the manuscript in 1980 to translate it into French.

It took us, Paul Bowles and I, two or more days to translate one chapter into English. Meanwhile, I would finish the following chapter. I used to dictate to him in Spanish (which he spoke well) and sometimes, a French sentence would save the day. As for the claim made by Paul Bowles that he translated directly from colloquial Moroccan, it is an outright lie. I recall using a few colloquial words, and I do not mean to sound condescending about the colloquial language that Paul Bowles was only slightly familiar with. As for myself, I am incapable of writing in colloquial Arabic as I am ignorant of its aesthetic qualities. At the end of the sixties, I had tried to rewrite my play *al-Zilzal* (The earthquake) in colloquial Arabic to be performed on stage in Tangier and I failed. This is my story with Paul Bowles and *al-Khubz al-hafi* in English.

Edwar al-Kharrat: Do you consider *al-Khubz al-hafi* an indictment (as you have said), or rather, a confession, a disclosure? Can it be both? How? Which dimension is more important, do you think?

Mohamed Choukri: In my autobiography, I merged the indictment and the confession, as you say. But, I think that the social dimension predominates and it is less aesthetic and artistic than the confessional. Indictments spoil the aesthetic qualities in literature as they strive to provide logical explanations for everything, whereas the confessional dimension touches the heart and softens the sharp edge in human life.

Edwar al-Kharrat: Would you say that *al-Khubz al-Hafi* is a non-ethical work in the philosophical sense and not in the practical sense of the term? Or, does it stem from a deep ethical sense, that it even calls for a deeper kind of ethical awareness?

Mohamed Choukri: In *al-Khubz al-hafi*, I depict immoral scenes to search for morality and ideals. My characters are not content with their immorality: they do not rejoice in their corruption as they are compelled to act corruptly under the strain of disgraceful social oppression. Their life is commodified and they consequently lose their humane values. My life among them is emblematic: I got an education then made education my profession. I used my writing to protest against oppressive exploitation. It is an attempt to set things right, regardless of whether I win or lose.

Cherifa Gharari: Can you make a comparison between Kateb Yacine and Tahar Ben Jelloun?

Mohamed Choukri: No. I cannot compare these two writers as I am not well read in the works of Kateb Yacine. I have only read his novel *Nedjma* which is the most important Arabic novel in the Maghreb that draws upon Arabic tradition.

Cherifa Gharari: From your point of view, what is Maghrebi culture?

Mohamed Choukri: This is a very general question. It needs a long interdisciplinary study. My friend Mohamed Barrada is more qualified to answer this question as it lies within his field of specialization.

Cherifa Gharari: How do you view Maghrebi critics who have emigrated, or who are in exile? Does their writing deal with the real problems in their homeland?

Mohamed Choukri: I am only familiar with the work of Idris Chraïbi, Mohamed Khair Eddine, Tahar Ben Jelloun, and Edmond Amran El-Maleh, and in my view, they are not critics. Idris Chraïbi and Edmond Amran are novelists while Mohamed Khair Eddine and Tahar Ben Jelloun write novels and poems, even though Tahar Ben Jelloun is a specialist on the various problems of immigrants and has written many books on the subject, such as *Qimat al-'uzla* (The epitome of isolation) and *Fi diyafa firinsiya* (French hospitality).

Those writers are not lost to us simply because they write in French, as some dogmatic critics maintain. In their writing, they try to reinstate the identity of their homeland within their own specific cultural context. Chraïbi is the least important writer.

Cherifa Gharari: Why did you write about Jean Genet and Tennessee Williams? What do they represent for you?

Mohamed Choukri: When I first met Jean Genet in Tangier in 1968, I had not finished reading any of his works except for a number of articles that were written about his work in Spanish and Arabic magazines (his work was banned in the Franco era). I introduced myself to him as a Moroccan writer even though I had only published two short stories in the Lebanese magazine *al-Adab*. We immediately became friends. During the few days he spent in Tangier in November, I recorded our daily conversations, after I returned home, about books, writing, and about various forms of Moroccan life that he started to be acquainted with. He knew very little about Arab thought. He had read Kateb Yacine because he was a friend of his, he said. His visits to Tangier recurred at long intervals. He would then look for me in the cafés and bars I usually frequented. In 1973, he suggested to Paul Bowles to translate my memoirs with him. I dictated them to him in Spanish and they appeared in a short book published by Ecco Press in both paperback and hardcover editions. It was simultaneously published in Canada by Macmillan. I still have the second part of my memoirs with him because, in the last few years, Genet came often to Morocco for personal reasons and because of the strong cultural contacts he had established with Moroccans like Mohamed Barrada and Laila Barrada.

Jean Genet and I share many things especially in the way we judge life. Both of us had led the life of a vagabond. There are differences, of course. For example, he began writing when he heard a fellow prisoner recite a poem. Genet challenged him and vowed that he could write a better poem and he did. Then he began writing his first novel to amuse himself. When he realized that writing was an important thing that could release him from prison, he continued writing until a group of French artists and intellectuals championed his cause and he was granted amnesty for his life sentence.

As for Tennessee Williams, I met him through Paul Bowles and was introduced as a friend of his. We never developed a close relationship like the one I had with Genet. Tennessee was very temperamental in his relationships, as I witnessed them here. As creative writers, however, I considered both of them to be really great artists. This is so in spite of the fact that they did not appreciate or recognize each other, especially Genet, who once said that what Tennessee Williams wrote did not matter to him in the least. He had already made a similar remark about Albert Camus whom he said wrote like a bull.

Cherifa Gharari: *Al-Khubz al-hafi* appeared a long time ago. Do you feel that you need to add to it or revise it?

Mohamed Choukri: I wrote it quickly, as I used to write every day, and Paul Bowles would translate at night. My aim was to publish my first book, in a Mau Mau dialect if necessary. I left out a great deal that I consider important to add now. Nevertheless, these lapses come in handy as topics for short stories. I am now writing the second volume of my autobiography, entitled *al-Shuttar* (The picaros). Whereas the first volume was finished in less than two months, I have only written sixty typed pages of the second volume as I write at long intervals. I believe that the fact that my Arabic books are banned makes me lazy. I need to be spurred on to do any work. In 1980, my friend Mohamed Barrada suggested that I begin writing this second volume, to be published in the Moroccan newspaper, *al-Muharrir*. I started writing and several chapters were published. But, I had a literary misunderstanding with the newspaper that made me stop writing and resume my life as a drunkard.

Cherifa Gharari: Is there a woman whom you think represents the feminist movement in Morocco?

Mohamed Choukri: It is Fatima Mernissi. She is courageous and expresses very progressive ideas about the Arab and Moroccan woman in her research papers, and particularly in two of her books: *Sexe, ideologie et Islam* and *Le Maroc raconté par ses femmes*.

Barbara Harlow: When you wrote *al-Khubz al-hafi*, which is an autobiographical work, were you influenced by Western literature or by the traditions of Arabic literature? And, is the term 'influence' relevant in this context?

Mohamed Choukri: It is well known that I received an education in Arabic at the age of twenty. Only four years and three months later, I became a teacher in elementary schools where I taught pupils between the ages of six and eight. Besides Arabic, I also studied some Spanish. From my reading of texts originally written in Arabic and others translated into Arabic, as well as texts originally written in Spanish and others translated into Spanish, I discovered that there is a vast difference between Arabic and Western literature. Western literature is more liberated than contemporary Arabic literature, which is still chained to the dark ages. Notwithstanding, classical Arabic literature is one of the most liberated literatures of the world in spite of the oppressive forces that worked against it at certain periods of time. Consequently, it has its martyrs: Tarafa Ibn al-'Abd, Imri' al-Qays, al-Hallaj, Abu Hayyan al-Tawhidi, Bashshar, Ibn al-Muqafa', Ibn al-Rumi, al-Mutanabbi; all of them were persecuted and murdered by tyrants and thieves. Due to my rebellious nature in the face of everything that is static, corrupt, or tamed, I found freedom of expression in the way Western literature treated problems of Being. I read many of the classics of world literature both modern and ancient. Actually, I have always admired the biographies of great men and women more than their creative writing. This is probably due to my adventurous nature.

If Rimbaud, for example, had not stopped writing to embark on his adventures, I would not have admired him. Again, Baudelaire, for all his calm, if he did not possess this raging rebellion against his mother's reproaches, I would not have liked him. (I dislike writers like T. S. Eliot and Borges.) There are many, of course, starting with Prometheus and going on to Cervantes, Byron, Kierkegaard, Kafka, Nietzsche, Dostoevsky, Jack London, Esenin, and Mayakovsky. My nihilistic nature is probably quite annoying, but this is the way I think.

As for influence, it does not apply to my particular case. I am not Julien Sorel in Stendhal's *Le Rouge et le noir*. I have assimilated many lives, styles, and techniques which make me what I am in my life and writing.

Barbara Harlow: Even though *al-Khubz al-hafi* was originally written in Arabic, it first appeared in the French translation by Tahar Ben Jelloun and in the English translation by Paul Bowles. The Arabic text was published years later. Why did this happen? Was it for literary reasons, or ideological ones? Was it related to the reading public or to problems of censorship and publication?

Mohamed Choukri: Your comprehensive question presupposes all the possible reasons. If I were to arrange these reasons in order of importance they would look like this: 1) ideological reasons; 2) moral and ethical reasons; 3) publishing (publishers are big cowards; they are also thieves who are only after guaranteed profit—all their claims about being progressive and about promoting literature are hypocritical postures); 4) censorship (it only satisfies those who approve it); 5) the public (the real public wants to know about what is and what can be).

Ferial Ghazoul: In his introduction to your collection of short stories *Majnun al-ward* (The rose madman), Mohamed Barrada maintains that you are drawing a "secret geography" for the city and its underground. Can we say that, in these short stories, you are trying to depict the features of Tangier by reversing the discourse of tourism that you have practiced, that is, by writing an anti-orientation discourse? If so, do you consider writing to be a refutation of what you have to do in everyday life? Or, is it an extension of, and a new variation on, the means of survival in a society of oppression and repression?

Mohamed Choukri: For me, writing is a struggle between reality and imagination. Through our life and our imagination, the visionary writing happens; objects and a world of beyond are created. Writing will always be lacking in its relation with the world of events. I cannot live an experience, conceptualize it and enact it at the same time of its occurrence. In other words, identification is not inevitable. Everything is controlled by paradox. In my writings about Tangier, I object to everything that abuses its beautiful features, everything that violates her, invades her, and destroys her. Brian Gysin, a man who lived the best moments of his life in Tangier in the company of his friend William Burroughs says, "We belong to the place which we violate." This is the attitude of invaders. Reeling under the pressure of oppression and subjection, as you say, I am forced to dream of things that may never come true. I dream that Tangier becomes a new Arcadia, a land of peace and happiness.

Ferial Ghazoul: In spite of your bold style and your candid description of sexual details, your writing shows signs of childlike innocence, totally unaware of sin or evil. How did you manage to overcome a sense of guilt? Or was it never there in the first place?

Mohamed Choukri: A sense of guilt presupposes a deliberately criminal intention. If I have indulged myself in taboo pleasures, it was because my need for the gratification of my instincts was stronger than my moral consciousness. We only become aware of the pernicious consequences of our actions after it is too late. The harmful effects of sexual deviation (in its largest sense), for example, can only be theoretically realized after it has handicapped us for life. Our society, which does not provide us with a healthy sexual education, multiplies the possibilities of chronic deviations. I was lucky enough to grow up in the streets, away from parental authority. What gave one pleasure was permitted: this is the philosophy of the rootless *(les déracinés).*

Ferial Ghazoul: Two of the short stories in *Majnun al-ward* stand out as exceptional: "Children are Not Always Idiots" and "Vomit." The first contains the symbolism of an allegory and the second resonates with poetic rhythm and tempo. Do these two stories represent two marginal strands? Do their styles reveal the literary dimension that you deliberately curb? Do you write, as usual, in a non-poetic, non-symbolic style to assert your difference to the more dominant literary trends? In short, do you consciously strive to marginalize yourself in the world of literature?

Mohamed Choukri: Every story imposes its own style. "Vomit," "The Rose Madman," "The Tent" (published in Morocco), "The Little Paradise" (published in Morocco), "Bald Trees" and others were written specifically to be read in literary conferences or meetings. Oral presentations of stories require a certain amount of poetic vibration to elicit a response from the audience. In these stories, the analytic dimension is overshadowed by the smooth flow of ideas and metaphorical description. In one story, you can find a mixture of several literary trends: realism, symbolism, and expressionism, all at the same time. Literary genres will inevitably produce a stereotype of human beings and of time and place. The various disciplines of the humanities that were once part of the field of literature have gained a separatist independence which resulted in a reluctance on the part of writers to analyze social behavior.

Edwar al-Kharrat

❖

The Relative and the Absolute in Avant-Garde Narration

Sabry Hafez: Edwar al-Kharrat is one of the few authors whose writings have contributed to the shaping of a new artistic sensibility and in the foundation of a measure of creativity and literary experimentation, whose mere existence has led to a transformation of the dominant critical norms and postulates of the cultural movement. His writing has thrown a shadow of doubt on what were considered, for a long period of time, great literary accomplishments. That is because Edwar al-Kharrat, both in his creative works and his criticism, proposes a new conception of the process of literary writing, thus offering a new idea of art and the role of the writer.

This new conception, which confronts us from his very first collection of short stories, *Hitan 'aliya* (High walls) (1958), through his last collection of stories, *Ikhtinaqat al 'ishq wa-l-sabah* (Suffocations of passion and the morning) (1979), is not of a static nature but rather is a dynamic structure that contains some constant elements, of course, as well as other variable, evolving, and changing elements.

At the beginning of this interview, we will set the constant elements of this overall, distinctive, and original view of art and the artistic process, and its relationship to the role of art and society as a whole.

Edwar al-Kharrat: I will try to tackle your last point that deals with the constant and changeable elements.

I think that there are indeed constant elements that form—if I may use this expression—my concerns, which have never left me since I started writing, and have been my companions since the beginning of my 'consciousness' even though, naturally, they were in a primary and embryonic form. One of these concerns, that would instantly be apparent to any reader interested in investigating what I am trying to do, is the issue of man's loneliness or estrangement; whether it is his estrangement from himself, his estrangement and loneliness in society and in the company of others, among his companions, peers, and kin; his loneliness even in the most intimate relationships he creates, relationships that are the closest to himself, in which, supposedly, all walls of loneliness should collapse. Then there is man's loneliness in this universe, in a world that is made out of mute rocks, not carved out for him nor made to respond to his desires, urges, or passions. This estrangement, this loneliness, this isolation is what creates the fact that man is an island unto himself—this is a constant concern of mine. At the same time, you find an irresistible desire and a burning urge towards communication; towards breaking down these walls; towards communion—even more, infusion—with himself, between man and woman, between himself and his companions, comrades, and peers in society, and finally between man and the universe. I imagine that these two courses, or concerns, are part of the constant elements in my writings. There are also other constant themes that complement these two elements, which propose other issues I believe, such as the relationship between the temporal, transient, fleeting moment and the eternal, durable, and everlasting; or between what we can call the 'relative' and the 'absolute'; or in short, what has come to be known as the intimate, significant, burning relationship between the 'human' and what can be named as the 'divine'.

There are also the dreams of quest for freedom, justice, and truth.

These are the things that I think constitute my constant concerns.

But I do not know what you assume to be the differences between the constant and changeable elements. In your opinion, what are the dynamic or variable elements, or changes, that you find in a work that took about forty years, from the time I first wrote *Hitan 'aliya* till the last of my works, *Ikhtinaqat al 'ishq wa-l-sabah?*

Sabry Hafez: Before I move on to talk about evolving or changeable elements, I want to raise a question that was brought up by your answer dealing with the idea of the high walls of loneliness that man desires to bring down. Are these walls created by the self, seeking communication, or are they the making of the society that comes between man and fulfillment?

Edwar al-Kharrat: They are not created by the self, certainly, but rather are imposed upon it. From where are they imposed? And how are they imposed? I think that there are many levels in this sphere.

There is the imposition which stems out of what might be called the inevitability of the human condition, the inevitability of the unique being of man, the inevitability of consciousness, since the human being, ultimately, is consciousness: the inevitability of human consciousness, and the uniqueness and aloneness of this consciousness. Perhaps this aspect is one that is hard to investigate and discern, hard to attain or to delve in its various layers.

There are, of course, and in obvious and self-evident ways, the walls that are imposed by the social system. This is so evident that it hardly needs any demonstration. In the various forms of oppressive systems, in which man lives, there are these walls. And these walls are not imposed by absolute powers; they are self-imposed barriers and walls—given the self in a comprehensive sense. They are barriers imposed by the various interests and the various aspirations and greed on the economic, social, and political levels and others. These are truths—or facts if you like—that are impossible to doubt and whose importance it is impossible to overlook. Also it is impossible to underestimate the necessity and burning urgency of the endeavors to eradicate them.

But the issue goes far beyond this.

It goes beyond this, because the human condition that is ordained to be contingent between the moment of birth and the moment of extinction is a condition that, in itself and in the absolute, poses this value: the value of aloneness.

This condition, can never be solved except in the naivest of visions, such as those offered by 'science fiction', for example.

But within this transience, within this temporality, within this evanescent transition, there is something that cannot be grasped. There is something durable and ungraspable. Why is there this inclination towards durability? Why, in man, is there this urge towards what is called immortality? And it is an inclination that is preordained to be frustrated; this contradiction between the basic human transience and the no less basic human immortality is unsolvable.

This may be one of the most important elements in the essence of man's aloneness, and the walls within which the human being lives out his life.

Sabry Hafez: I suppose this last element brings us to what you called the variable elements, because this last element is more prominent and exists more tangibly in *Ikhtinaqat*, with its complexity and density.

Edwar al-Kharrat: Maybe it is more prominent and tangible in *Rama wa-l-tannin* (Rama and the dragon).

Sabry Hafez: Certainly. *Rama wa-l-tannin* will be discussed later, separately. The relationship between *Hitan 'aliya* and *Ikhtinaqat al-'ishq wa-l-sabah* (and of course, I hope that we could also talk about *Sa'at al-kibriya'* (Moments of pride) which is the collection published in 1972, between the two other collections) indicate a more tangible evolvement of an art form, upon which you embarked as a distinct adventure, since the forties. That is why the decisive period, between what was written in the mid-forties, approximately, and the last stories of *Ikhtinaqat* (1979), are the ones that can be used for critical purposes, to discover some of the variable elements that I would like us to talk about, on a more abstract level, and in a manner that would formulate some of the theoretical concepts regarding your particular understanding of art. The first collection, *Hitan 'aliya*, was published at a time when the prevalent concept of art—or even the general, prevalent concept among most artists—in different degrees, from the most mature of concepts available since the fifties to the most simplistic and naive ones—was, in my opinion, a single concept: that art is a mirror that reflects, either in a deep manner, or in a photographic manner, what seems to be reality, or what the writer sees as the real. In the endeavor of many of the writers to portray an image of the real, they sometimes trapped reality in the talons of their naive concepts of it. They thus made reality appear not only simple, but very simplistic, and to a great extent naive. Consequently this era produced, in my opinion, art that does not reach the desired levels of what we may call art.

During this period, *Hitan 'aliya* (1958) appeared, proposing a completely different concept of art. This concept was comprehensive, beginning with the relationship of art to reality, including all the elements that contribute to the shaping of the artistic experience. I mean that its conception of language, the artistic structure, and characterization were different. Nevertheless, within this conception there are constant elements, and I do not mean elements that are related to content, subject, or concerns which the collection attempts to propose, but I mean the specific concept that is related to the role of art. What is art during that period? Is it those prevalent writings, or is it something else that calls for adventure, search, and an attempt to reach something far more dense, deep, and complex than what was circulating during that period?

Hitan 'aliya, to my mind, has achieved or aspired to achieve this.

But when I consider the journey which begins with *Hitan 'aliya*, passing by *Sa'at al-kibriya'*, and reaching *Ikhtinaqat*, I find in this very conception, some variable elements. These variable elements appear when we examine some of the stories which employ an obvious degree of symbolism, realistic writing, and references which seem as if they are close to the concepts which were predominant during that period, although of course, they are different.

But the last collection poses an additional concept to all this. This is what I wanted to have clarified. Naturally, you will object; that it is criticism which is concerned with determining those distinctions. But I am trying here to find out what the writer was attempting to offer, or what the writer sees to be different in the experiment, and that is different in his conception of art.

Edwar al-Kharrat: Here you are dealing with an issue that has engaged writers, critics, philosophers, and those occupied with aesthetics, etc. It can be divided into two: the first is concerned with the role of the artist; the second with the question of the artistic treatment or the creative role of conveying or creating the experience.

As to the role of the artist, I will not address this here, except in a very simplistic manner. I do not think that the artist should be a publicist of anything; at least for me, I do not want to propagate, present, or even deal with a cause in this abstract, simplistic, or cerebral form.

To my mind, art has a comprehensive, epistemological value that partakes in the human experience in all its complexity. This is especially so in this era, an era of electronics and mechanics, programming and standardization. I believe that the artist's role approximates that of the old prophets of the past: a role that transcends the philosophical, social, and even the aesthetic techniques, almost reaching an ardent, intimate experience of communication, revelation, and creation that has the ecstasy of prophesy and also its illumination. It verges on knowledge that transcends—and incorporates also—intellectual cognition. Hence comes its particular aesthetics, with its renewable laws, each and every time (in spite of the obvious importance of intellectual cognition, in its own field, of course, and I would not attempt, in any way, to belittle that).

Maybe this concept has to do with what I attempted in *Hitan 'aliya* and other works, to find what I called the new sensibility. *Hitan 'aliya* was, of course, a leap in the dark. It was going against all the prevailing currents when it appeared.

And I will not hide this from you, if we move to the problematic of artistic treatment—provided we can use such a term—I would like to admit two things. The first is that I always felt a certain uneasiness as to the success of some of the stories in *Hitan 'aliya* in fulfilling what I aspired to: how to condense and distill this knowledge that I talked about within one comprehensive focus. (And please forgive me this tone of speaking that sounds a bit pedantic. I would have liked to deal with the idea I have in much simpler words than these, but I don't know how.)

I felt somehow that there are, at least in some of the stories, two different levels. There is a level that could be called the external reality—however it has been acquired, conceived, or recreated by an internal experience—and a second level, that is, the level of another world which we could call the purely internal world. There was a fissure or a separation in some cases between the two levels: the reality and the dream, the external and the internal.

I think that in *Ikhtinaqat*, I might have succeeded in attaining a kind of intimate fusion between elements that seem contradictory even though they are in essence one.

Sabry Hafez: I imagine that this approximates, to a great extent, the attempt to discover the variable elements between the two collections.

Edwar al-Kharrat: Maybe there is another factor also in what you called evolvement or change in *Hitan 'aliya*, and this is another point I must confess, as I have lately realized, where I might have been unfair to myself. Meaning that however hard I tried to make society and life between people an essential element in the stories of *Hitan 'aliya*, the main preoccupation, the main concern was directed towards dealing with the lonely, isolated human being, who is almost separated, though not actually, from his society. (And I hope that I have not, once again, been unfair to myself by making this confession, for social concerns are very obvious in *Hitan 'aliya*.)

In *Ikhtinaqat*, I realized that in this preoccupation, there is a great injustice done to myself and to what I am trying to do, in such a manner that I feel that it is impossible for the artistic treatment to attain what I want it to, unless the concerns of the individual man are integrated into the concerns of the community in which he lives as a fundamental, inseparable component. Even though this treatment is not conveyed in a direct manner, nor by confrontation, but rather through what I called the infusion of the conflicting or, at least, different elements of reality.

Though I give myself the excuse—if you will allow me—that *Hitan 'aliya* was written at a time when social concerns were predominant and occupied the foremost place in art, obliterating other broad human concerns in such a manner that it was necessary to say in an art form, no, this is not true, and it is possible to treat social concerns in a more truthful manner and to fulfill the exigencies of these very social problems by means of the specific artistic concept that I adopted.

This confrontation, or this necessity, that has been discarded lately, might have made me, in *Hitan 'aliya,* deviate a bit towards, or delve too deeply into the specific, intimate, and individual aspects. The ground is now more accommodating for a better kind of balanced equilibrium.

Sabry Hafez: It is so in the sense that there has been a continuous interaction between the creative process in its complexity and the predominant sensibility during the period in which you were writing.

If the relationship here is, as it were, a negative relationship—meaning, the element of internal reality, as you call it that seems completely neglected at a specific period of time is somewhat exaggerated to a certain extent—then the process started gradually as I see it. *Hitan 'aliya* projected the main protagonist, the man surrounded by these high walls (as the title of the collection suggests) who wishes for release and liberation. This, in turn, required focusing on nocturnal life, and on life's limitations and narrowness, expressed in detailed sensory symbols. Then this attitude (that looked as if it were a negation of the prevalent artistic sensibility) started slightly to change in *Sa'at al-kibriya'*, where the high walls turned into a concrete monster, running in the streets, devouring all the dreams and aspirations of the character, making the grip of oppression and death apparent. The protagonist of *Sa'at al-kibriya'*, despite his solidity, stoicism, and pride, seemed not to have fulfilled his dreams of demolishing high walls. He started fiercely struggling with death, and external reality began to materialize in a more sensory manner and with more presence.

In *Ikhtinaqat,* the process of an almost complete merging appears between the two levels, and also between the various levels of expression, between dream and reality, and between the sensory detail, the illusory detail, and, to a certain extent, the fantastic.

This began to be reflected in a very important issue, which I would like to take up in this discussion. It is the issue of language. Your language, distinct as it was from the start, began to move more towards poetry. It is true that we are now taking a big leap—since *Rama wa-l-tannin* preceded *Ikhtinaqat*—but in *Ikhtinaqat* the language appears artistic, purified, suggestive, and devoid of direct symbols, that is, of obvious allegorical symbols (which appeared, to a certain extent, in some of the stories of *Hitan 'aliya*). In *Sa'at al-kibriya'*, this language began to show changes in its artistic formulation, and this is particularly obvious in the important stories of this collection, such as the story "Open Wound," or "The Old Tower," or specifically the story "In the Streets." Here, all this begins another stage, a transitional stage, for it was not possible to write *Ikhtinaqat al-'ishq wa-l-sabah* before the transitional stage in *Sa'at al-kibriya'* was completed. Not because this is what actually happened, but because the language of narration needed this transition to reach the point it has. Probably, it also needed the experience of *Rama wa-l-tannin*, which I hope we will come back to discuss later. So what do you think of this?

Edwar al-Kharrat: This account, on the whole, I feel is correct. I would like to elaborate or expand on this idea regarding what is directly related to the style or the language of narration.

I admit here that *Sa'at al-kibriya'*, as you remarked, was published exactly as it was written, meaning that the draft of *Sa'at al-kibriya'* is identical to what you find published. I gave myself to the density, turmoil, and incandescence of the language. So the stories in this collection appear—if we may say this—dark and ardent at the same time.

I will not deal with *Hitan 'aliya* from the technical point of view because it is composed of two parts: a juvenile part, so to speak, and another part in which the venture resides—in the simultaneous delight and fear of discovery. I am talking now of the writer's feelings: finding fulfillment and being frightfully apprehensive of it.

In *Sa'at al-kibriya'*, I was able to give myself free rein, so as to blend the images, language, symbols, and words until they formed a thick paste of this darkly ardent writing.

And maybe it was not possible for *Ikhtinaqat* to be written except through the experience of *Rama wa-l-tannin*. There is in *Ikhtinaqat*—I hope—an amount of serenity, distillation, concentration, and cohesion that also does not renounce density, but it succeeded in extracting itself from the circle of this ardent mixture that might characterize *Sa'at al-kibriya'*.

I repeat, that if I had not passed through the experience of *Rama wa-l-tannin*, I would not have been able to reach that kind of experience in *Ikhtinaqat*.

Sabry Hafez: It seems that the time has come to talk about *Rama wa-l-tannin*, which has been characterized by a number of critics as an experiment that has no past tradition in the Arabic novel. An experiment that has no past tradition means, of course, a negation and a confirmation in both its positive and negative sense, with respect to the achievement of Arabic novels preceding it. It is an experiment that would have been impossible without the Arabic novel passing first through the long journey, from the beginning of Muhammad Hassenein Heikal, through Naguib Mahfouz, till the latest works of the most recent newcomers in the field of the Arabic novel, like Jabra Ibrahim Jabra, Abdelrahman Munif, or Tayeb Salih, etc.

Edwar al-Kharrat: Does this mean that it was a logical outcome of this itinerary?

Sabry Hafez: No ... no ... no .... I mean it was difficult for this novel to have been written before the Arabic novel established certain traditions and certain artistic conventions that enabled such negation. It would have been very difficult for the Arabic novel to start with *Rama wa-l-tannin*; but it was also difficult for *Rama wa-l-tannin* to appear before the Arabic novel passed through this long journey.

I agree with a number of critics who said that *Rama wa-l-tannin* has no tradition in the Arabic novel; nevertheless these rules and traditions had to be established before it appeared. It would have been different for such a novel to come about without them at all. It would have been very difficult for James Joyce to write his novel *Ulysses* before the Western novel had passed through its long journey. To my mind, *Rama wa-l-tannin*, begins by an attempt to negate the established traditions in the field of the Arabic novel.

Edwar al-Kharrat: And these traditions should have been established?

Sabry Hafez: They should have been established in order to be negated.

Edwar al-Kharrat: They should have been negated after being established!

Sabry Hafez: Of course, this is the other face of the same proposition. *Rama wa-l-tannin* is an experiment which I hope will be followed by other experiments and adventures that will enable the creative sensibility to assimilate what it attempted to propose.

Edwar al-Kharrat: And I hope that it will be given the evaluation and critical consideration that will allow this.

Sabry Hafez: Of course, this is the role of criticism, an important role which should be accomplished. Unfortunately, *Rama wa-l-tannin* appeared in a period of literary and critical stagnation and vacuity. Thus a great number of people who could have received sympathetically this experiment, and could have tried to mobilize a literary current around its visions and ideas, were unable to tackle it. It is unfortunate that some of them were even unaware of its existence, but this is another issue.

Let us go back to the question I tried to begin with, and which the title of the novel itself proposes: *Rama wa-l-tannin*. Rama, as any one who reads the novel knows, is the name of the main heroine but the dragon does not strike the reader except in the verses quoted from al-Hallaj, at the end of the book. The question proposed throughout the novel remains: What is the dragon? Is it meaninglessness? Is it the impossible? Is it the absurd? Is it the others? Who, or what, is the dragon in this novel? If it is possible to put this question to the writer ...

Edwar al-Kharrat: It is really very hard to abstract the dragon, to say what it is specifically. Probably the whole novel is an attempt to recognize the dragon, and not just even to gain cognition of it, but also to seek and do battle with it.

Let us start with discarding. I do not think that the dragon is the other. Hell, here, is not the other. At least this is not the basic aspect. Undoubtedly, this aspect is reflected in the novel; the other is implied in the dragon, if you like, but it is not its main aspect.

Many of those who read the novel and gave their opinions talked about the obvious meanings of the dragon: The dragon representing evil, as apparent in mythology, and as oppression. The dragon, in a certain sense, is taken as frustrated love, or the impossibility of love.

So may I venture to say that the dragon is the absolute, the divine, doing battle with the inclination towards the impossible within the heart of man? May I, once again, venture to say that this impossible, inasmuch as it is divine, is also satanic? Maybe this is the first time that I have admitted a kind of suspicion that has sometimes come to my mind, but had never been definitely formulated, that now, I see the dragon, in this manner, after I have finished with the novel and washed my hands of it.

Sabry Hafez: If the dragon here is the human, is it then the absurd? Is it meaninglessness? By this question, I intend to get closer to the human dimension, rather than the absolute.

Edwar al-Kharrat: At this point, may I here ask you a question that is basically philosophical and metaphysical? It might be one of my innermost concerns that the absolute, divine, and satanic are basically human; and that there is nothing other than the human being, so to speak, that is outside the human consciousness. And that the human being includes and encompasses, besides the relative, the absolute.

I have to return here to the fact that I am an Arab–Egyptian–Copt; in the following order: Coptic, Egyptian, and linguistically Arab. Arab culture has become one of the components of both my individual and collective life.

Being a Copt points to the issue, which is not only an intellectual one. The core of Egyptian orthodoxy is specifically the incarnation and the fusion of the absolute in man. The absolute is man, and man is the absolute without division: not even for one moment or a blink of the eye; it is the communion of the human and the divine. This is the issue, even more, the creed of Egyptian orthodoxy, and the essence of being a Copt. I claim that this also is basically the essence of being Egyptian. This differs from other Christian doctrines.

This concern is not new to me, but I have endured it as an idea and preoccupation since childhood. That is why I do not think it is a coincidence that this is my understanding of the interpretation of the dragon, regardless of the experience I embarked upon in the novel itself. This is what I am venturing into right now. The dragon is the absolute and he is this consummately sacred and satanic within man. In this sense evil is absolute, inasmuch as good is absolute, but they are both human, and relative, also contingent and eternal. There is no 'Manicheanism' here, and differing with some interpretations, there is no duality, or at least there is no complacency in, or consignment to, duality, but there is a perpetual yearning for oneness and 'Monophysitism'.

I do not know how much you will react to this interpretation, but it is possible—and even legitimate and necessary—to include the other interpretations that have been given to the dragon. I think that the novel—or more correctly the relationship between Rama and Mikhael, and their relationship with the world and society—allows for the other interpretations that some readers and specialists have been able to deduce.

This is a question on my part and not an answer.

Sabry Hafez: Of course, this answer opens for us perspectives and interpretations of various levels of meaning in the novel, which seems on one level as though it is a story of man's quest for communing with the other in order to know himself, not for the sake of knowing the other in itself.

Edwar al-Kharrat: I have a basic objection to this. I do not think that knowing the self—in this special meaning—is concordant with Socrates' well known dictum. "Know thyself" means "know the other."

Sabry Hafez: "And know the world." I have not yet expressed myself fully. I said that the endeavor of man to commune with the other is for the sake of self-knowledge, for the sake of getting to know the other, and in order to understand the world around him. This quest appears in *Rama wa-l-tannin*, as though it were itself the journey—where the histories, important events, wars, and the story of the society as a whole are transformed onto the canvas of a painting, into the material of the quest itself, the material through which man knows himself. In other words, the process of communing is itself also a process for self-knowledge, and not only the knowledge of the other; however, I do not negate either of them in favor of the other.

Edwar al-Kharrat: Shall I say that knowing the self is conditioned by the other?

Sabry Hafez: Of course. This is what the novel proposes at one level.

Edwar al-Kharrat: Let me present another question. Were not Mikhael's endeavors, concerns, and sufferings all an attempt to know Rama? I imagine my endeavor, at some level, is this aspiration that is also nearly impossible, and yet fulfilled in very short and very dazzling flashes: knowing the other or, to be more precise here, knowing Rama (because Rama is the other, and maybe she is the intimate side of the self at the same time). Knowing the other, knowing Rama, is the issue that primarily concerns Mikhael.

Sabry Hafez: It is the issue of the novel in another sense, because the knowledge of the other is Mikhael's attempt to defeat his loneliness, to conquer his estrangement, an attempt which began in the first collection, *Hitan 'aliya*.

Edwar al-Kharrat: It seems to me now, as I recollect the novel (and I had nearly forgotten it), that Mikhael was in no need of knowing himself, or was under this illusion. He thought that he knew himself very well. It was neither his problem nor concern to know himself. What really concerned him was the other's knowledge of himself, what the other conceived, that is, Rama's conception of him and not his own concept of himself.

Sabry Hafez: This leads us to the technique of the novel itself. Now I put forward a concept which I proposed before in my discussion of the novel, namely that the novel—to my mind—offers us this Osirian myth inverted, in which Osiris seeks Isis and not the opposite. Through his picking up of its parts, the image of Isis, that is, the image of Rama, takes shape and at the same time, with it, the image of Mikhael takes shape. Of course, Mikhael was not seeking his own self, but he was trying to defeat this loneliness and this estrangement and to realize this ardent desire to commune with the other. Through this search, which appears as though directed to the other and not directed to the self, we, ourselves, come to understand Mikhael and Mikhael gets to know his own self.

But the novel also poses the problem that love, as a means of salvation, is at the same time, impossible. Love, as knowledge of the self, of life, of the world is almost a hope for the absolute.

Edwar al-Kharrat: Exactly. It has to do with the problem of the relative and the absolute, the problem of contingence and eternity. I think the novel managed, in certain instances, to convey that time has vanished, contingency has vanished, that even the problematic of temporality and eternity ceases to be posed at all. Such opposition itself seems negated, and the experience transcending it towards another level, where neither the eternal and transient, nor the relative and absolute, nor the temporal and everlasting, are posed any longer. What exists is a level that verges on mysticism in transcending both contradictory sides. There exist, in the novel, these focal and central moments that formulate its core and nucleus, which are succeeded, incorporated, preceded, and always followed by a consciousness, painfully aware of the existence of the two contradictory poles. Here I am on the verge of correcting your statement about the impossibility of love. Possibility and impossibility, here, are like the two poles of the relationship. There is another level that I aspire towards, a level of incandescence that makes it almost impossible to communicate. Art here is gambling with what is nearly its negation by communicating an experience that is incommunicable, and by expressing something that is impossible to express. And yet it does. That is, it brings about and creates what nearly verges on being impossible to express and communicate.

Here both possibility and impossibility are negated and we reach a level where the two concepts are almost no longer posed. Love and knowledge exist on this quasi-mystical level.

Sabry Hafez: This is so, in the sense that the moment of attainment, the moment of incandescence, occasionally surpasses all our conceptions of possibility and impossibility.

Edwar al-Kharrat: And it transcends the level of expression as well; it transcends the possibility of expression itself. It knocks on, it penetrates, the gates of the impossible—the impossible in the real sense—given that it expresses what cannot be expressed making it exist. How does this happen? It is impossible . . . and it yet is . . .

Sabry Hafez: And yet it is possible as well.

Edwar al-Kharrat: It actually happens.

Sabry Hafez: Here we come back once more to the issue which we referred to before, namely the issue of language. The tense of the verb also disappears as a definite time, where the past, present, and future tenses merge into one single time.

Edwar al-Kharrat: Or into one 'timelessness'.

Sabry Hafez: Of course; and the various levels: the external level, the internal level, the illusory, the wished for, the desired, and the frustrated, are all set on one experiential level.

Edwar al-Kharrat: Or on another level that transcends them all.

Sabry Hafez: Is that what art is?

Edwar al-Kharrat: This is the artistic experience that the novel tries to explore: how can it be so.

Sabry Hafez: I would like to move from the question of how the apparently impossible can be somehow realized, to Edwar al-Kharrat the critic, who can explain to us, perhaps, the possibility of the impossible.

To my mind, Edwar al-Kharrat is basically a creative writer who is attempting to propose these new visions, some of whose traits we have been trying to discover, and we are still, up till now, attempting to understand from a distance.

Is Edwar al-Kharrat the critic separate, to a certain extent, from Edwar al-Kharrat the creative writer? Or is the critic here attempting, what could be called concentration, propagation, or raising interest in what seems to be close to his own creative venture?

Edwar al-Kharrat: From the outset, I do not tire of repeating that I do not consider myself a critic, at least not in the generally accepted and conventional sense. For me, criticism is also a kind of creative experience. I do not deny, nor do I try to deny, that the way I deal with literary works is quite close to the way I deal with life's experiences. In the same way as I deal with, for example, the stories "Open Wound" or "In the Streets," I deal with the works of Yahya Taher Abdullah or Ibrahim Aslan, as an *expérience vécue* that I reconceive through coexistence and through recreation. I am not bound, in this, to a specific methodology, at least one that is clear to my mind. The methodology might exist from within the treatment on a background level, so to speak. But in my case, I consider that critical writing hardly differs from narrative writing itself, except on a certain level or in a sort of quantitative form. So I try to present to the reader these literary works, which I relived through a perception that nearly recreates these works; hence, I can hardly deal with a piece of work unless I perceive or sense an echo or a correspondence with what concerns me as a fiction writer.

Sabry Hafez: Does that mean that you sense these echoes and correspondences only in the positive? Or also in the negative?

Edwar al-Kharrat: Both, and since I am confessing I imagine when I take a look at some of my few critical writings, that in dealing with a writer like Naguib Mahfouz or Ibrahim 'Abd al-Qadir al-Mazni I recognize in the writer the concerns that preoccupy me. That is why I write about him and bestow on his writings a certain conception that might be, to an extent, foreign to him.

Sabry Hafez: Is this a kind of shifting or transposition?

Edwar al-Kharrat: Exactly: transposition and interaction. But it is not, I hope, in any way, a kind of imposition. When I read what I wrote on Naguib Mahfouz in 1962, I see that I wrote about my own concerns and not about his concerns as a fiction writer, and I discovered in him what might have not been there, even though it is not entirely unrelated to what he wrote. There is a kind of relationship that I discover and sense and focus on, between what the novelist, or fiction writer, I am dealing with writes, and what I write or care to write about, as a novelist and a fiction writer; because of that, it might not be apparent to another critic, not only because it is not generated by that novelist, but because it is generated from the interaction between myself and him.

And this is my critical experience, which I do not think is entirely futile or useless. Through interaction, true and valid aspects of the writer whom I am critically analyzing are made clear, I should think; but they are not made clear except through their interaction with the concerns that preoccupy me as a fiction writer basically.

Sabry Hafez: In a sense, your critical writing should be viewed as a mirror that reflects some of the concerns which are assumed to be expressed and formulated in your own fiction.

Edwar al-Kharrat: Exactly. But it is not, I hope, unrelated. However, I think that it emerges from a very close relationship with the works of the writer I am critically dealing with, and not just an imposition from me on it, but rather my interaction with it, and transposition between me and it, so to speak.

Sabry Hafez: If we try to make Edwar al-Kharrat, the critic, look at the artistic issues which *Rama wa-l-tannin* raises, what would he say?

Let's begin with the problem of the artistic form. *Rama wa-l-tannin* starts with one chapter that tries, in some way, to present the whole novel. After that came the process of repeating the novel once more through the rest of the chapters of the work. These chapters diffuse and unfold the things which were said in the first chapter in a concise, allusive, poetic, mysterious, and integral

The Relative and the Absolute in Avant-Garde Narration 241

way. This technique, which appears in the formation of its independent circular chapters, caused the writer himself to publish some of them as if they were autonomous short stories. It is a technique that creates a large work and at the same time includes in it this episodic structure, that is, forming a totality out of autonomously constructed parts, though they are fused into the basic structure at the same time. Was there, in this structure, some connection to the degrees of the meaning in the work as a whole? Or was the vision condensed, then unfolded, consequently imposing this structure on the novel?

Edwar al-Kharrat: There are many aspects to this question, and I will start by asking a question myself. Is there any coincidence in art? The answer is yes, and the answer is also no; there is no coincidence in art.

I started *Rama wa-l-tannin* as a short story called "Mikhael and the Swan."

Sabry Hafez: It is the first chapter in the novel.

Edwar al-Kharrat: I was intending to consider it a short story, and intentionally the matter ends. This is a 'historical' fact, that is, it actually happened. But I will not keep it a secret; before this first story ended, before I finished the last word in the last sentence, it became apparent to me, inevitably, necessarily, and inescapably, that it was no longer a short story but the first chapter in a novel. And it was published as a short story at the same time that the whole novel started becoming apparent to me. When the rest of the chapters were published, at least as far as I am concerned, they were not published as short stories, but I pointed out when publishing some of them that they were chapters of a novel.

We are left with the issue of the episodic structure; it is not easy for me to define the basic structure of the novel. It is clear that there is an almost rigorous structure, when I look at it now, after I have been done with it for a time, but I cannot define it exactly, because it was not intended when I was writing the novel. Maybe this comes into the sphere of the secrets of the artistic process that are hidden from the artist himself, and possibly for the critic as well, unless he is patient with it.

If I go back in memory to the composition stage, I find that I had some conceptions. One of them has to do with the levels of meaning, as I said before, and their relationship to formulation. I mean the formulation that distinguishes the Arab culture (and even before that, the pharaonic culture), namely repetition that could be probably linked again to the relation between the relative and the absolute.

If we return to the miniatures, or ornamentations or arabesques, we find that the circular repetition is infinite by its very nature, where the elements that constitute it are limited, small, and even minute, so that it almost becomes partial by nature. This coupling of the partial, finite, and minute with their infinite repetition transcends itself into the absolute and comprehensive. This was at the back of my mind while I was writing. In a way, I wanted to bring together and incorporate the cumulative infinite layers within a boundless circle that does not have a beginning or end, where motifs—that is, what you call episodes—evolve from one motif to the second, to the third, and so on infinitely, in an accumulation that reminds us of hieroglyphics and the repetition one finds on the walls of tombs and old temples. It is like the closed cartouches and the abstract form that is repeated, reaching beyond the limits of the wall and fusing into another sky, that brings everything together in a comprehensive and rigorous unity. And this is what has been best fulfilled in Arabic formulations, on the walls of the mosques, as well as shrines, and in the miniatures, abstract ornaments, and arabesques.

This is also linked to the technique used in *The Thousand and One Nights,* in which the story evolves into another story, into another, and so on; then it finally comes back to the first story once again.

There is no conformity to this formal structure, but rather an inspiration and revival of this form that is embedded in our cultural heritage, and which I hope I have made contemporary and alive.

This, I suppose, is one of the aspects of the basic structure in the novel. I think that there are other specific aspects that some of the critics pointed out, and there are other aspects that I hope other critics will discover.

Sabry Hafez: Is it possible that we should regard the game of alliteration in the language, that is, the paragraphs that play on the letter *ha'* (h), or the letter *mym* (m), or the letter *syn* (s), as belonging to the tradition of the Arabic miniatures, or does it have its origins in a similar experiment in the Western tradition, like the experiment of James Joyce? If we try to identify the origins of the experiment, then what do we say? Play is no doubt one of the elements of art, and it seems that this is one of the favorite games which is part of the creative process itself. So to which of these two does this game belong, in your opinion?

I wish to make clear, at least to the reader, that I am referring to specific paragraphs in the novel of *Rama wa-l-tannin* in which every word appears to have the letter *ha'*, for example, and other paragraphs which seem to have in every word the letter *mym*, or the letter *syn.*

Edwar al-Kharrat: I think that it is found throughout the novel, and that it is a system and a temperament.

Sabry Hafez: Not with the same rigor and not with the same precision. There are paragraphs that have this rigor, and other paragraphs where a certain letter, or a certain sound, or silence predominates . . .

Edwar al-Kharrat: This is linked to several elements. I do not want to confine it to a single one. To my mind, there are several affiliations whether they are from the West, the Arab culture, or otherwise.

But I believe that the significant dimension originates from emotional and expressive necessity. The letter *ha'*, for example, comes in a moment of heat, incandescence, and ardency that was imposed by necessity itself. I imagine that it was a compulsion dictated by the emotional stance on the expressive form, to an extent that transforms us into the realms of incantation, amulets, and direct magical transformation of emotion through a certain vocal necessity. That is, it is not only mediated through expression—even though there is a clear rendition and a definite meaning—but also through the direct liaison with the initial sources of emotion: with sound, rather than the written letter, rather the letter as sound, or music, or as a refrain and echo of the turmoil of the internal movement. In other words, it is an attempt to create or bring into being. Here I am not exaggerating when I say that some paragraphs were inflamed by a spontaneous gush that, naturally, later on I polished and modified. But in the paragraphs that entirely include words that begin with the letter *ha'*, three quarters, or even more, were written just like that, in one go, without any premeditation, then were completed later. This happened in many of the paragraphs where I noticed, after writing them, that the letter *syn* was predominant, or the *qaf* (q), etc., without any intention of mine, but in a kind of direct liaison with the sources of inspiration or creation, between the available funds of language and the experience that the writing deals with.

Sabry Hafez: If we try to move on from this point to the question of the sources of creativity or creation, or rather the sources of inspiration or the creative experience, can we say that they come as vocal sources, or as sources formulated in the shape of an image, concept, abstraction, experience, or story? What are the sources which you feel are the sources of your creative experiment? To which of these kinds do you belong?

Edwar al-Kharrat: Really this is a hard question.

Sabry Hafez: Do you start from an image or a sound?

Edwar al-Kharrat: I guess it is an image. But it is also an image that is penetrated by sound, and that is ultimately connected immediately and directly with language. Even though it is a visual image and at the same time has resonance, the sound or resonance originates in language and not from abstract intonations. The image at once finds for itself the language and words without premeditation or intention. After all, it is not a silent film but a spoken film in the Arabic language: it is the precisely Egyptian Arabic that I write, which is connected simultaneously to sensory ideas and objects. That is, the images are not just shadows that follow each other, but visual and sensory pulses that have their own idiom and emotion. I do not start off with a plot or subject. This comes in the second stage; they both come in a later stage. As for cognition or abstraction, they directly coincide with this sensory concretized image that voices language in expressing itself.

I imagine that image, language, movement, and sensual passion bring with them an abstraction or cognition. They come, all at once, in first place. Then comes, in second place, the plot and its refinements, the embellishments of the narrative, and the adjusting of the narrative process and sequence, which are the object of artistic cunning, if you accept this expression. It is also the object of the conscious endeavor in establishing the complexity of refinement, succession, narration, and storytelling. It is an endeavor that comes after the first outburst of experience.

Sabry Hafez: Therefore, if we try to differentiate between description and narration in your work, it is the image which comes foremost.

Edwar al-Kharrat: Description—in its comprehensive sense and also as a certain kind of storytelling and narration—does have the foremost position. Yes. In fact, the narrative sequence and succession of events come in second place. Maybe this specific mechanism is why I am not a conventional novelist who starts with narration, storytelling, and chronological narrative succession. Maybe this is due to a certain psychological mechanism, or a mechanism in my own process of artistic creation where straight narration, a well-made plot, and a reasoned-out sequence, unlike the qualitative consequence, are foreign to me. As for the logic of qualitative consequence, that is, the qualitative associations, then it is primary and basic regardless of the conventional linear chronological order.

Sabry Hafez: And probably, in my opinion, this is the reason why the stories and novels of Edwar al-Kharrat propose another conception, a different conception of art.

Edwar al-Kharrat: Because the experience is just this; and it comes thus. So there is no need to impose generally accepted traditions and conventions artificially, especially when we find that the modern era's sensibility is in concordance with this.

Sabry Hafez: This is the reason why I am saying that there are other, new conventions—which are not new to literature in general—but are new, maybe, to Arabic literature. These conventions appear in the Western, modern novel, and you are one of the few writers who constantly keeps up with the modern novel, and there is an apparent correspondence with it in your work. So is it possible to say that besides the influences, the effort to return to ancient roots—the roots of ancient Egyptian art, Arabic miniatures, and ancient Arab art—there are also obvious Western influences? Can you mention to us some of the writers whom you feel have actually influenced you in your experiment, in some way?

Edwar al-Kharrat: This also is a hard question. A writer might feel that he is impressed or influenced by certain writers but his actual writings negate these feelings. For example, among the writers who very deeply influenced me—and I am not alone in this, but along with the whole of my generation—are the classic Russian writers especially Dostoevsky, and later on D. H. Lawrence, the English Romantic poets: Shelley, Keats, Byron, and so on. This influence was common to the whole generation, during the period when the Apollo school emerged; and at that time the poet Mounir Ramzy was with us. I even assiduously embarked upon a personal and private translation into Arabic of Shelley and Keats, followed by Baudelaire, during my early youth. I imagined at one time that I was greatly influenced by them, but does this show in my work?

Sabry Hafez: I imagine that there is a more obvious influence by James Joyce, for example, or Proust.

Edwar al-Kharrat: These I read at a relatively late stage, so that I did not feel the same tumultuous effect that Dostoevsky and Lawrence, and before them Shelley and Keats, exercised on me in my early youth. It is possible that the influence of Joyce and Proust—which I was exposed to immediately after this—was subtler and deeper. When I read *Ulysses*—which was an incredible thing at the time—I did not feel that tumultuous effect, but I was moved more by his collection, *Dubliners*, since I wrote short stories at the time. But I think that *Ulysses* had its deeper invisible, residual influence which may come back and resonate later. It is almost not consciously realized, sedimenting in some vicinity, a little beneath consciousness, and much deeper than it seems. But reading, influences, and the assimilation of artistic works are all part of life's work that, of course, never ceases.

Sabry Hafez: If we move from this interaction—I do not want to call it influence—but the interaction with the readings of Western works, which exists either in the area of the conscious or the vicinity beneath it; is there some kind of interaction with the Arabic readings?

Edwar al-Kharrat: Deep and basic. For me, the Arab heritage is something alive, potent, and very contemporary, both on the popular level, where I read and lived the tales of *The Thousand and One Nights* as a child, and which has almost not left me till now, and on the classical level from the *jahiliya* to al-Qadi al-Fadil and *Subh al-'asha* that I read in secondary school. And of course there is the Christian and Coptic literature whose effect is, up till now, deep-rooted and lacerating.

As for contemporary Arabic literature, with the exception of Gibran Khalil Gibran, Salama Mousa, and al-Mazni, and in spite of my readings—and I imagine, from the amounts I have read, that it includes everything—I think that my significant interaction with it is not much.

Latifa al-Zayyat

❖

On Political Commitment and Feminist Writing

Somaya Ramadan: In her essay "The Blank Page and the Issues of Female Creativity," Susan Gubar says, "For the artist, this sense that she is herself the text means that there is little distance between her life and her art. The attraction of women writers to personal forms of expression like letters, autobiographies, confessional poetry, diaries, and journals points up the effect of life experienced as an art or an art experienced as a kind of life, as does women's traditional interest in cosmetics, fashion and interior decorating" (in *The New Feminist Criticism*, edited by Elaine Showalter, New York: Pantheon, 1985. p. 299). How would you comment on that?

Latifa al-Zayyat: I have used part of my personal experiences in *al-Shaykhukha wa qisas ukhra* (Old age and other stories), in addition to personal forms like diaries and memoirs. This use does not necessarily denote a close distance between life and artistic creation, whether to me or in the text. It does not mean that I consider myself the text; moreover it does not denote a life experienced as art, or art experienced as a kind of life diminishing the boundary between life, on one hand, and artistic creation, on the other.

Because of my own self-image, the concept of creativity that I adopt, and my extreme attentiveness to artistic and technical requirements of writing, the line between the lived and the artistic, between life on one hand and art on the other, has constantly been distinct.

Susan Gubar, moreover, argues that women, due to upbringing and the dominant traditional male perspective, sometimes adopt an image of the self as the object and of the man as the creator of that object; the woman as an artifact and the man as artisan. Such a woman would consequently see herself as an artistic work or an *objet d'art*. This perspective leads to a confusion between life and art. She lives her life as if it were an artistic work. In writing she exhibits this artifact which is herself in a manner that is necessarily narcissistic and usually destructive. Susan Guber's conclusion is that the feminine self in this case becomes the text, she is the 'blank page' written by the male; she is the statue not the sculptor, and the portrait rather than the artist. In this context a woman ceases to be a creator of art and is rendered into a text herself. She reflects and exhibits herself from a male perspective, deceiving herself into thinking this to be art. Fortunately Susan Gubar does not generalize such a judgment on all writings by women; she argues that some women have gone beyond this perspective in their creative writings.

I don't think that this analysis presented by Susan Gubar applies to my self-image or to my creative writings. To refute such a position I need to speak of myself: my life and my writing.

I have been exposed in my life, like any other woman, to different kinds of moral subjugation. The most serious, I believe, is that exercised by women on themselves. It was, at times, so hard to set oneself free, as if trying to get a hair out of dough, yet I did manage to overcome subjugation time and again. In all cases, what came to my rescue was a view of the self, formulated in the beginning of my awareness and deepened in my undergraduate years between 1942 and 1946. This view of the self liberated me from the prisonhouse of the self, and it continues to do so. Each time I was rendered an active responsible human being, open to my country and my people, and preoccupied with their concerns. This view of the self as active and responsible formed the framework within which my life has been embodied, with its ups and downs. It has provided me with the criteria by which I have judged different periods of my life as positive or negative, as accepted or rejected. Therefore never at any time in my life, whether I regard the times positively or negatively, did I experience the luxury of feeling myself as if I were an artistic painting or an *objet d'art*. I have never sunk so low in life and experienced such a view of the self. Perhaps this is because I belong to a popular revolutionary movement, which cherishes the collective as opposed to the individualistic and subjective.

Since the onset of awareness, a persistent and demanding sense of responsibility was deeply rooted in me towards my country and towards others. I strongly felt the urge to be up to such a responsibility, and a responsible human being is necessarily a subject rather than an object. During my undergraduate years I went beyond the passive sense of responsibility to act accordingly in fulfillment of this responsibility. My political activity put me in a leading position in the National Committee for Students and Workers, which led the patriotic struggle of the Egyptian people in the late forties. In the view of others, men included of course, and in my own view, I was the maker and the mover of events, rather than a passive recipient floating along. During this period, and all through my life, my action acquired two simultaneous meanings: it was a collective action into which the self dissolved in the whole, yet which enriched the self by making it part of the whole. It was an anti-authoritarian action recharging one's intellectual and psychological abilities, while at the same time it was a continuous relation with others, and a strong longing for communication with others.

I am aware that in creative writing the unconscious lays bare what consciousness might conceal. I should, therefore, speak of *al-Shaykhukha* as a writer with a certain degree of critical awareness. I claim that in this collection I was the pen not the text, the sculptor rather than the statue, and the artist not the painting, thanks to my view of the self, which I have presented, and my concept of creativity which I sought.

It is true that a lot of women take the self as the theme of their creative work, and so do men. The important point marking the difference between creativity and non-creativity is how this self is used and to what end. Is the self an end in itself and in a process of exhibition, or is the use of the self functional, offering the reader an insight into life through aesthetic effect? What matters is whether the specific personal experience is confined to the level of the subjective and the particular, or transformed into the level of the general, impersonal, and aesthetic, offering the reader an insight into life. The important point is whether the personal experience is related as it is with all its lived details and chaos, or, alternately, a meaning in this experience is discovered through writing, and an order is imposed on it so that it falls into a pattern.

The difference between the two cases is, to me, the difference between art and non-art. Between art and non-art stands talent, the evaluation of which is left to the readers and critics. Between art and non-art stands also craftsmanship, which in my view is on the same level as talent. For the artist is primarily a craftsman. Perhaps craftsmanship is not apparent in *al-Shaykhukha* (and this in itself is craftsmanship), but the writing of *al-Shaykhukha* required an extensive technical knowledge and a relentless practice of craftsmanship.

It may or may not be that to some women writing is similar to interest in cosmetics, fashion, and interior decor, as Susan Gubar argues, but this is not necessarily true. For me artistic creation is first and foremost an emotional message which I try with all my artistic skill to relate to others. This message, rather than anything else, is my primary motive in creative writing.

I have used some of my personal experiences in stories of this collection. In all the cases where a personal experience has been used I have altered and modified to the extent that it bore hardly any relation to the real experience: I have stressed points and omitted others, and altered the actual chronological order. I aimed by all this to fit real life material into the framework of the theme in the story, thus moving from the particular to the general, from the personal to the typical. In all cases, I have been preoccupied with relating and communicating my vision to others. To achieve this I had to make use of many technical and rhetorical devices, in addition to an artistic and suggestive use of language implying the rise and fall of tension.

I believe that in *al-Shayhukha* I was successful in imposing the objective onto the subjective.

Somaya Ramadan: In *al-Shaykhukha* you write: "I have lost my self after [my husband] Ahmad's death. For nearly a year I never managed to finish a sentence I had started. I had to struggle to reconcile my 'subject' to my 'predicate'" (p. 46). What interests me in this sentence (which is typical of *al-Shaykhukha*) is the relation between the subject and the predicate regarding the gender of each. What is even more interesting, however, is the number of verbs concentrating on the idea of beginning and continuing, and the conflict between them. It is as if Isis is fighting distances recollecting the flesh of her husband. Could you comment on this, shedding light on the feminine artistic process in its dependence on the presence of the male as a main factor in women's creativity? How would you describe the role played by the male in the feminine creative process, which concentrates on the evaluation of the feminine self?

Latifa al-Zayyat: In the collection, I believe, the protagonist has, whether as a result of her emancipation or her age, developed beyond considering man as the central value in her life, although she was not free of a man-centered life at certain points in the past. Thus man is not the criterion of the self in *al-Shaykhukha*. Man, it is true, plays in it a prominent role, but not the central one. The protagonist writes, "I have lost myself after [my husband] Ahmad's death"; however, this feeling of loss is only a stage in a wider context whereby the protagonist is in fact recognizing her real self. In the collection as a whole, the protagonist develops beyond taking man as the criterion. Instead, she formulates her own specific moral values as the criteria of her action, opposing through them the dominant values in society adopted by both men and women.

The protagonist questions concepts of time, the absolute, human responsibility, and a number of other phenomena of the universe and society. She questions all these with her own specific values. I don't think that the issue of women's emancipation is a preoccupation of the writer in this collection; the central issue, rather, is that of human liberation regardless of gender.

Your question about the subject and the predicate, both of which are linguistically masculine by the way, did not stop me much. It was not a metaphorical use that I had made but a literal one, which is clarified by the preceding sentence: "I never managed to finish a sentence I had started." However, what attracted my attention was your perceptive critical comment on the "beginning" and "continuing," and the conflict between them, in *al-Shaykhukha*. For me, this process represents the law of life. I see life as a sequence of beginnings and responses to new beginnings punctuated by struggle. From this perspective, one has to be prepared and continuously vigilant—a continuity akin to that of breathing—for life presents us endlessly with challenges and tests at every single step. Life demands from us always and forever—through challenges and responses—new beginnings so as to survive. In fact I can put forward the theme of response and survival, and their variations, as the value permeating the whole collection; or as you have put it, the theme of beginning and continuity, and the conflict between them. I am pleased that the collection has suggested that pattern to you.

However, I must disagree with you in limiting the conflict between beginning and continuity to recovering the fragments of the husband, for the conflict in the collection, as I have already made clear, is much more comprehensive than recovering the fragments of a husband.

Somaya Ramadan: In the story "al-Shaykhukha" there is a sentence that says, "The experience of labor pains on paper after Ahmad's death was by no means easy." This is obviously a purely feminine expression, drawn from a biological experience exclusive to the female. Do you think that women's bodily qualities influence her choice of language, and to what extent does this happen in the process of writing?

Latifa al-Zayyat: This is a topic worth studying. I am not, however, qualified to give an answer. I can only draw attention to my use of another metaphor, besides that of "labor pains," based on bleeding, describing the protagonist's script as being so horrid that it bleeds and causes bleeding. I am not sure to what extent woman's physical nature interfered in the choice of such a metaphor. I wonder if such a use is restricted to women due to their biological qualities or if it includes a common storehouse for men as well.

Radwa Ashour: To what extent do your creative works *al-Bab al-maftuh* (The open door) and *al-Shaykhukha wa qisas ukhra* depend on autobiographical material?

Latifa al-Zayyat: I have answered the part of your question concerning *al-Shaykhukha* in the course of answering Somaya Ramadan. I have indicated the nature of my use of personal material in that work. What I have said of *al-Shaykhukha* applies also to *al-Bab al-maftuh*. Autobiographical material in this latter work, however, is much less than some critics believe.

When I started writing that novel, I entitled it *Arba' sanawat* (Four years). I intended then to write a novel on my undergraduate years, those years that set my life on a new course. During these years I became politically militant, adopted scientific socialism, and was overwhelmed by my desire for knowledge, which flowed like a torrent. It was during those years that the timid girl, who had carried her plump body as if it were a sin, developed into a group leader: daring, confronting, arguing, making rapid decisions, and thriving with pride in her abilities.

However, I was driven to relate that experience by the predominant passion of the woman who had once thrived on identifying herself with the masses, but was later frustrated in her isolation from these masses, although she retained her emotional identification with them. This predominant passion demanding expression crystallized during the 1956 aggression and its aftermath of confrontations, and around the enclosed self versus the open self (open to the homeland and the people) and around the fact that, paradoxically, one can only find one's self by initially losing it into a much wider issue than one's own subjectivity, into a reality bigger than one's own. The 'open door' was the opening up to the people and to the homeland, and thus the novel *al-Bab al-maftuh* came to be.

When we age, almost all our reservations concerning the self are dropped and we gain the courage to dissect the self in a painful and agonizing manner. This courage, however, could not be attained during such an old age unless one has reached a stage of maturity and a reconciliation with oneself, which enlist the history of the self into a coherent pattern and an intelligible and tolerable whole. No one can approach a vital subjective experience while agonizing—that is if he or she wants to treat it in an artistic objective way. No one can approach it in an attempt at an objective exploration except when the wound has healed, and when the emotional stress has been reduced and put behind one, rendering it an indivisible element in this acceptable and coherent pattern.

Al-Shaykhukha celebrated reaching such a stage of maturity and reconciliation with oneself. The tension in the collection, whether serving stylistic or descriptive functions, is a purely artistic, fabricated tension, by no means representing the state of reconciliation which the writer experienced at the time of creating it.

It would have been impossible for me to publish something like *al-Shaykhukha*, with its use of autobiographical material in 1960, the year of publishing *al-Bab al-maftuh*. For at that time I neither had the courage nor the reconciliation with the self. Yet the writing of *al-Bab al-Maftuh* as far as it presented openly my outlook on life, was a step on the long road which was finally enriched by courage and reconciliation.

Radwa Ashour: Was your use of the memoir form in the two stories "al-Bidayat" (Beginnings) and "al-Shaykhukha" (Old age) an intentional conscious use, or was it imposed by the fact that you incorporated your own memoirs into the stories? How far have you benefited from Doris Lessing's style in *The Golden Notebook*?

Latifa al-Zayyat: It was Lessing's *The Golden Notebook* that suggested to me the idea of the mixture of styles presented in *al-Shaykhukha*. However, I have used that style to achieve different ends from those of Lessing. In Lessing's book this mixture aims at foregrounding the partiality and fragmentary nature of any vision of reality—both the subjective and the objective. It thus serves one of her favorite themes, the theme of the fragmentation in the vision of reality. I used the same technique in order to create an impression of a relative completeness of that reality.

I have used the technique of mixing styles in two stories in the collection. In "al-Bidayat" (Beginnings) I used both diaries and narration; while in "al-Shaykhukha" I used both forms, diaries and memoirs. Both stories are structured around two points: first a moment of recognition that sheds light on the protagonist's whole life; and second, the gradual accumulation of the consciousness of the protagonist which leads to that moment of recognition. Where accumulation meets with discovery, the narrated experience becomes united and moves from the fragmentary to the whole. In both stories I used the diary form in recording the moment of recognition. I was attempting to create an artistic pattern equivalent to that which takes place in life. I wanted to capture the living moment of recognition in all its complexity and intensity. I wanted to mark all the stages leading to consciousness and understanding, starting from the state of unconsciousness and unawareness. One resists consciousness and understanding then stumbles in agony before finally reaching the stage of consciousness and understanding. In short, I wanted the moment of recognition to be present in the process of becoming from its onset to its completion, just as the lived moment of recognition is characterized by such a process of becoming. I believe that the form of diaries has helped me evoke artistically this state of becoming, for the action takes place under the reader's eyes as its parallel does in life.

In both stories the moment of recognition achieved by the protagonist is the cumulative outcome of a number of lived experiences which have already been analyzed and evaluated in the past; I had therefore, to look for another form in addition to diary form. Thus I chose to mix the diary form, on one hand, with story-within-a-story technique on the other, in "Beginnings"; while in "al-Shaykhukha" I used both the diary form and a special form of memoirs.

In both stories I made use of the same artistic device made possible by the nature of the memoirs used in *al-Shaykhukha*. These memoirs are like conventional short stories in that they analyze a past action seen from the perspective of its conclusion. In both cases I aimed by this mixture of styles to convey a wholeness to the experience by recording the moment of becoming while holding on to the roots of this becoming.

In the story of "al-Shaykhukha" I was led to the use of both memoirs and diaries for an additional reason, namely to write in the first person rather than the third person. To convey the intended emotional and intellectual message embodied in the story, it was necessary to make the reader face him or herself and to question many of the deeply rooted concepts of his or her own self. This is no easy task and the writer is required to help the reader attain this state. The use of the first person painfully engaged in dissecting the self should dismiss many of the reader's reservations and encourage a similar self confrontation. Thus the circle of reception could be completed, or so I hope.

Radwa Ashour: You have translated T. S. Eliot's critical essays into Arabic. Don't you see that as somewhat surprising, considering your social orientation, and his association with the extreme right?

Latifa al-Zayyat: I published a translation of some of Eliot's critical essays in the early sixties. I had been teaching those essays to the undergraduate students of English literature since the early fifties. In this context, I translated the essays for the benefit of my students. I undertook the task of translating those essays as an academic challenge, since I consider Eliot's critical essays extremely sophisticated and complex on all levels—from the construction of the sentence up to the overall meaning.

I realized later on the mistake I had made by publishing such a book without a theoretical introduction refuting Eliot's critical views on the nature of the literary text, its function, its dependence on the emotional rather than the intellectual, the negation of its cognitive nature, as well as the rest of his critical views which draw an arbitrary line between literature and life, and render literature as a means of reinforcing social reality rather than changing it. I believe that a critical and a careful reading of these essays is indispensable for a professional in literature or criticism. However, I failed to realize at that time that such a reading was one thing, while publishing the essays without a critique was quite another.

There is a great deal that we could learn from the extreme right, with which Eliot is associated, as long as we appropriate what we learn to our social orientation. Extreme right-wing critics may add nothing of theoretical importance concerning the nature of literature—its function, its genesis, its relation to its source in reality—or concerning the readers of this literature. However, some of them shed light on the literary text per se: its texture, structure, and its makeup that grants it relative autonomy. I have learned much from the critics of the American New Criticism school—who belong to the extreme right as well—concerning the formation of the literary text, and methods of analyzing and uncovering the relationship between its different parts. I have gone beyond what I have learned as a critic to reach the comprehensive meaning of an artistic work, and show its relationship to life in its totality. From Kenneth Burke, who is wrongly supposed to belong to this school, I have learned a great deal about the mechanisms of the literary text and its rhetorical devices that aim at producing artistic effects on the reader.

Radwa Ashour: Some claim that you are lazy and that but for this laziness you would have been able to produce much more work than you have done. What is your response to such an accusation?

Latifa al-Zayyat: I don't know whether to dismiss such an accusation in relation to creative writing or to accept it. Had I considered myself a creative writer by profession, rather than an amateur, I might have been able to subject emotions to craftsmanship, and would have produced a great deal. However, as far as I am concerned, and as far as my limited and modest works in this field are concerned, creative writing has been a communicative process relating me to the reader and shattering my isolation and what at the time I believed to be my uniqueness. Creative writing to me has always been a restless urge to share with others my vision of things discovered artistically. However, only when I formulate a crystallized vision at a moment of emotional and intellectual resolution of my on-going internal conflicts, do I feel this urge to write. Throughout a person's life, such moments of resolution are very rare.

What makes it even more difficult for me is the ever-developing critical faculty in me that often threatens the completion of the creative process, leading me to seek unattainable perfection. A critical faculty is essential in the creative process as long as it does not threaten the completion of that process and its realization. There is, moreover, this dreadful fear of the reception of my work or of descending from a certain level which I had formerly achieved. To send *al-Shaykhukha* to the publisher required on my part a conscious psychological effort, arguing with myself: let it be. Among my numerous unpublished papers there are many uncompleted works. Other completed works are still unpublished, however, on account of the developed critical faculty and that dreadful fear of not being able to live up to the standard I had formerly achieved. Among those completed but unpublished works there is a novel, a three-act play, a long story, and a number of short stories.

My psychological makeup, the nature of my creative writings, and both my finished and unfinished projects make it hard for me to accept the accusation of being lazy.

Farida Marei: In *al-Bab al-maftuh* the heroine's falling in love is concurrent with her political consciousness and her desire to take part in issues of national liberation, contrary to the protagonist in *al-Shaykhukha wa qisas ukhra*. Why is there this change (in *al-Shaykhukha*) when our struggles are as impelling and urgent as ever?

Latifa al-Zayyat: Literary works are primarily historical, products of their age, whose conditions determine the writer's vision; products of the people of that age, whose sensibility forms the circle of reception, while the values of those people constitute the common ground from which the writer begins the attempt to change these values. *Al-Bab al-maftuh* was written in a time of rising revolutionary tide—the years 1946 to 1956—which represented a crystallized and integrated chapter in Egyptian national history, leading towards more progress, or so we believed in those days when we saw our path opening up into an infinitely wide horizon. This openness allowed the ending of my novel to offer a new beginning for Egypt and for the characters. This novel was written in the presence of a large reading public possesing common sentiments, shared values, and a collective sense of belonging, and of whose nature the writer was fully aware beforehand.

A novel like *al-Bab al-maftuh*, considering all the economic, political, and social changes that have been taking place since 1967 to the present day, is now an impossibility: the outlook has become more complex; roads to salvation are blocked; the common ground of shared values seems to break down into multiple different sets of values according to the varied social strata; the common sensibility and its language is no more; people lacking national unity are divided and subdivided until each is turned into an insular island; all these changes resulted in marginalizing the sense of belonging and national struggle.

In the late fifties, while I was writing *al-Bab al-maftuh*, I was addressing a large reading public. I was aware beforehand of the values they accepted and those they rejected. I was also aware of the kind of rhythm that would produce an emotional response, and the correct note to play to get an effect. In the early eighties, when I was writing the collection of short stories, I was like a person jumping blindfolded into the sea. The circle I addressed was necessarily narrower due to the multiplicity of values and sensibilities. I had to play a tune, while ignorant of the note that readers might respond to. In such times *al-Bab al-maftuh* would be an impossibility. I, then, had to address the individual with his or her most intimate personal problems.

Yet, as in all works of art, there is an inherent political point of view in *al-Shaykhukha*. Political action in its highest form is transformed into the realm of sensibility, values, and behavior. It is in this realm that the collection works, sometimes running against the main current, attempting to change those dominant and deep-rooted values, and expressing disagreement with such values. In the collection, the concept of time, for example, especially as revealed in the first two stories, is a progressive concept contradicting and refuting the concept of time which is deeply rooted in the common consciousness. Time in these stories is an ally, rather than an enemy to (wo)man. It is not treacherous time bringing to crises helpless men and women, as it is usually believed to be. In these stories, time—in its totality if not in its constituent parts—is seen as a constructive element. It brings understanding to (wo)man of what was before unintelligible; it brings knowledge, and an ability to go beyond and move on. Time thus brings integrity rather than decline. One owns time insofar as one manages to control and direct the course of one's life.

Farida Marei: In your view, what is it that *al-Bab al-maftuh*, the novel, succeeded in conveying to the reader which the film (based on it) failed or neglected to express?

Latifa al-Zayyat: Things are relative. Considering the technical and financial limits of the Egyptian cinema in the sixties, *al-Bab al-maftuh*, directed by Henry Barakat, starring Faten Hamama and Mahmud Mursy, is a good film. It is a film reminiscent of a bygone period in Egypt's national struggle, and whenever it is shown on TV it arouses feelings of admiration and nostalgia. I have always felt grateful to Henry Barakat and Faten Hamama, who were both very enthusiastic to present this novel in the cinema. However, it is true that the cinematic view deviated from that of the novel.

The change which the novel's ending suffered in the film has impaired the novel's overall meaning. In the novel the protagonist's liberation is achieved by herself, and through her own action she develops herself, while the film presented her liberation as dependent, to some extent, on the male character, which is precisely what I tried to evade in the novel.

The paradox that came into my mind when I watched the film was that the novel presented a panorama of characters, events, demonstrations, and battles, all of which, surprisingly, the cinematic perspective narrowed—so unlike cinematic photography.

Moreover, other intended aims of the novel were unfulfilled in the film. However, due to the nature of film audiences, I wouldn't have expected those aims to be fulfilled.

I wanted the novel to be an innovation in narrative technique in Egypt. So, whereas description rather than dramatization was the dominant narrative technique until the sixties, in *al-Bab al-maftuh* dramatization dominated. The novel was built as a sequence of significant and intense dramatic moments, adopting a technique very similar to that of the impressionists. I imagined, then, the cinematic technique to be more adapted for expressing such an untraditional context, but I was disappointed.

In the novel, I aimed at crystallizing three levels of meaning, none of which, I believe, was present in the film. These levels were all interwoven into the structure and the texture of the novel forming a harmonious whole. The first level deals with the development of the female protagonist, and is related to the second, which deals with developments in Egypt at that period. As for the third level, it incorporates a commentary on the values of the middle class and its practices and how they prevent the class, and thus the country, from a takeoff.

Ibrahim al-Hariri: Through your activity in the project for change, have you experienced, as an intellectual, as a creative writer, a conflict between the political and the intellectual spheres? How? When? Where? How did you deal with it? Did you take the side of the intellectual or the political? Or did you make a sort of compromise?

Latifa al-Zayyat: I don't normally experience such a conflict. Usually, the emotional and the rational within me are incorporated into one whole, where the political seems like an extension of the intellectual, and vice versa, both interwoven into the framework of the project for change. It is during the critical times of national crises that things differ. I, then, react in an extremely emotional way, as though the national event were my own individual predicament, as painful as personal suffering. A reaction of this sort sets the political and the intellectual within me into conflict, and things lose their correct proportions. Usually, the political gains the upper hand during such times, but only temporarily; for once the excitement is over, I start to face things rationally.

After the 1967 defeat, I hated words and, consequently, literature. I confined my readings to history and economics, and I wrote that a single bullet against the enemy was more significant than all the words in the world. I also lost interest in a three-act play I wrote in 1966 on the theme of love versus possession. Beside the horror of the defeat, the play's subject seemed trivial. I don't see it that way anymore; and my not publishing it is due to its artistic shortcomings that require rewriting. In the field of creative writing I experienced this dilemma only once. Usually, however, the emotional and the rational within me are integrated, pointing a way out despite all hardships, and making sense in the face of unintelligibility. My only political commitment in the field of creative writing is my preference to keep quiet rather than to send the reader a message of despair.

In the period between 1961 and 1965, I wrote a novel in which I placed the protagonist in an extreme situation. Her journey was one of deprivation and loss of human support. The novel's vision seemed existential to me, and thus contrary to my social orientation. I left that novel behind, thinking that I had resolved the conflict in favor of the political. I realized later on that I was mistaken and that what made me reject this novel in the first place was its lack of artistic unity, for structure and texture were pulling it in two opposite directions.

Ibrahim al-Hariri: Everywhere and on all fronts things are shaking dramatically. Does this stirring raise questions in your mind? What are these questions? Of what nature? Have you managed to formulate primary answers?

Latifa al-Zayyat: I am faced by hundreds of questions, as an Egyptian Arab, as a Third World citizen, and as a woman to whom socialism has been and is still a life's dream. Those questions so overwhelm me that I stumble under their weight.

As an Egyptian Arab citizen I feel deeply the horrors of dependency. I resist, to the best of my ability, while the fronts for struggle are endlessly multiplying. I see people around me changed, transformed, and accepting what they wouldn't have accepted in the past, adapting themselves to changes in the Arab world, and in the whole world for that matter. I then wonder: Is it all beyond remedy? I am reminded persistently of the story of the man who was collecting signatures against nuclear war. Someone asked him: Do you believe in the effectiveness of such signatures? The man answered in the negative, adding: Show me another way that will justify my existence. I march with those who march. I have lived to see the world map redrawn twice: once in favor of socialism after World War II, and now a second time in favor of capitalism. I feel shaken, twice, first from the point of view of a socialist; and second, from the point of view of a Third World citizen whose dependency is reinforced by the new world changes, and whose issues of national liberation are now bracketed, blocking the way for the right of self-determination. Hundreds of questions follow while I cling to the dream of socialism even if no proper application of it has taken place on earth. I cherish the thought of the Palestinian Intifada, the Lebanese resistance to Israel, the liberation movements in South Africa and Latin America, which ignite free will in the face of the dominant current and in opposition to it. Then a better future for humanity reasserts itself, and I wonder when the winds of freedom would blow on us in the Arab world.

Ferial Ghazoul: The Marxist thinker Antonio Gramsci has distinguished between two means of repression of the masses. The first is the 'coercive', subsuming assassination, murder, imprisonment, house arrest, banishment, exile, etc. The second is the 'ideological', which propagates and builds up reactionary ideologies and false values, aborting every potential for revolution before crystallizing. And in his writings, Michel Foucault has investigated in a most careful and detailed manner the ideological apparatus. He has revealed the role of the network of official culture with its institutions in persuading, silencing, and repressing people, without resorting to explicitly coercive means. Edward Said has, moreover, revealed in his trilogy *Orientalism*, *Covering Islam*, and *The Question of Palestine* the role played by First World institutions, including universities, academic organizations, and the press, in obscuring, misrepresenting, and distorting the issues and characteristics of the Third World. A conscious citizen is thus incarcerated—even outside prison— within the walls of the dominant culture, controlled through ideological hegemony, as the Kurdish/Turkish film director Yilmaz Güney has revealed in his masterpiece "Yol" ("The Road").

In the light of your experience as a militant both outside and behind the walls of prison, and as a citizen who has suffered the authorities' coercion as well as ideological repression, do you find an essential difference between the two experiences, the two means of repression Gramsci identifies? And does the specificity of the prison experience qualify it for identifying a genre of literary writing? There is an increasing interest among critics in what is termed 'prison literature'. Do you see this interest as an openness to a specific literary experience which has not been dealt with before, or is this interest only an expression of the critics' attraction to prison as a vivid metaphor for the suffering of contemporary man?

Latifa al-Zayyat: The differentiation made by Gramsci between means of repression is not an essential one. Both forms of repression are directed at denying people's free will, denying the ability to think critically, whether regarding personal issues or social issues. It is also directed at rooting out the desire for change, and even the ability to bring about this change. However, both means may differ in appearance and in degree of seriousness. The practice of coercive repression is nowadays confined to culturally and technically underdeveloped countries.

The dominant social class in culturally and technically advanced countries manages to achieve cultural and ideological hegemony over society. It imposes a unified culture, the culture of the socially dominant class, on a society made up of varied class cultures. In such countries the state needs not practice coercive repression extensively, for the cultural and ideological hegemony it practices represses people and defeats the will for change. In the age of sophisticated means of communication, an advanced country like the United States is able to extend its cultural and ideological hegemony over other societies, uniting these societies in cultural dependency, which is what the United States is actually doing in Third World countries, and in the whole world for that matter.

In underdeveloped societies, however, it is beyond the means of the socially dominant class to impose its culture and thought on all other classes to create a unitary culture. This is because it is a class living on a shabby and dependent culture, unable to impose absolute hegemony on society. Such a class, therefore, has to combine ideological repression with coercive repression in order to confront the will for change and to root out the potential for this change. In this sense the difference between the two cases is a cultural difference between an advanced state capable of imposing hegemony ideologically, with no need to resort to coercion, and an underdeveloped state whose cultural means are inadequate in realizing absolute hegemony, and therefore combines both means of repression.

Ideological repression, it is true, aims at a wider range of people, while its results, in the long run, are much more serious. As the writings of Gramsci, Foucault, and Edward Said reveal, it is a kind of repression achieved on multiple fronts. It is an intangible repression that one cannot physically and consciously feel. Like poisonous gas, it infiltrates a person rooting out potentialities of change without the person knowing it. It is the sort of repression that lodges within a person inside the home. Nevertheless, it is the institutional repression, as Gramsci argues, which is possible to confront through institutional opposition. It is not an inescapable destiny, as it seems in the writings of Foucault. Coercive repression, on the other hand, is a physical and tangible repression. It is a form of repression that sharpens human abilities for defiance and endurance; it is also a form of repression whose echo is so widespread that it stirs up a broad spectrum of people to stand against it in defiance. Only the leading few are affected by this form of repression, while ideological repression is practiced against the great majority of people.

Incarceration is usually an extension of the kind of repression practiced against a person prior to the experience of prison, whether or not one was aware at the time of such repression. I believe that repression is much more serious and hard to endure when it takes us unawares. When I was imprisoned in 1981 I learned that my home had been videotaped during the previous three years. For a time I felt as if I were addressing walls which were ordering my silence, not only to preserve myself but also to preserve others. I had to pass through an agonizing pain caused by this violation of my humanity and my privacy. I had to fight hard to retain a spontaneity of expression, and consequently the ability to think freely and independently. Morally, it was a life-or-death struggle realizing that my free thinking and free expression were at stake. This was my main struggle during imprisonment and for a period following it. The experience of prison, with all that goes with it—denial of freedom, degradation and humiliation, being cut off entirely from the outside world, prevented from reading, writing, or listening and watching any form of mass media—all of this constitutes an attempt to destroy the human will, and exterminate a person's free thought and expression.

The challenge that one is faced with while imprisoned—the attempt to destroy the will—could either strengthen a person or lead to moral death. To confront ugliness in prison requires that one drop all reservations, abandon elegance and delicacy, become tough and coarse, and be able to face the challenge with a counter challenge.

Prison is a rich experience, provided one manages to discover one's inherent human potential, and to hold to this with all the pride of a human being capable of adapting to all circumstances and also capable of surmounting all circumstances. If we were to describe the experience of prison metaphorically, it would be that this experience reveals the person's fundamental nature, either as clay (lacking in form and will), or alternately as ceramic revealing the human ability to shape the self and to create beauty.

However, I don't think that the experience of prison is such a specific experience that it could form an independent literary genre. It might be so only if we consider prison as an extreme situation which the character is put into, as in the existential novel; it is the kind of situation that could take place outside prison though in prison it is much more complicated, intensified, and extreme. In the memoirs that I wrote inside prison, in spite of the prohibition of writing, I found myself concerned with my internal world and with my reactions rather than with prison in its totality, as a kind of microcosm. After being set free I felt the need to discover how to use the material of these memoirs for literary narratives rather than publish it as it was.

In my view the critics' interest in prison literature expresses the extent of the critics' attraction to prison as a vivid metaphor of the suffering of contemporary man, as you say. Prison is a small and closed world that intensifies and exaggerates, like the lines of caricature, all the repression that could befall human beings—all the humiliation, degradation, starvation, and deprivation that takes place in the wider world.

Edward Said

❖

People's Rights and Literature

Jonathan Rée: You wrote somewhere that the Palestinian experience is so fragmented that classical concepts don't apply to it. What about the concept of 'rights'?

Edward Said: Well, we are in a unique position of being a people whose enemies say that we don't exist. So for us the concept of 'rights' means the right to exist as a people, as a collective whole body, rather than as a collection of refugees, stateless people, citizens of other countries. It has, in a certain sense, the most urgent meaning for us, since, from the beginning of our struggle against the Zionist movement, and later against Israel, our principal goal is to get to step one. We are still a long way from 'national rights'. In the current climate of peace talks, the so-called 'peace process' that the Americans speak about, there is no phrase signaled by the Americans or the Israelis that suggests that we have 'self-determination' or 'national rights'. We are very much at the starting point.

Jonathan Rée: You talk about 'national rights' and 'self-determination'. But is a nation really a 'self' that ought to have rights to determination?

Edward Said: It's a tricky question, but I think that in the case of the Palestinians, yes. We have a long history of inhabitants on the land of Palestine. We were a coherent society with a collective memory, a language—Arabic, of course, which is like the language of other Arab people in other Arab countries—even if ours is a distinctive brand of Arabic. We had sent members to represent us to the Ottoman parliament in the 1870s, and part of the battle, the intellectual and cultural battle, that we've had to fight since the beginning of the twentieth century, has been to show that we are a 'people'. And as a 'people', there are two things open to us: one is subservience and finally suppression and extinction; the other alternative is to exist in a national state with the rights that are now the rights allowed to most peoples in the world today. We have opted for the second.

Jonathan Rée: But isn't the very idea of a 'national state', or a 'state-nation', or a 'nation-state', one which contains all sorts of traps? I mean one view would say that the idea of a nation is a kind of con trick whereby the ruling elites of different jurisdictions make it sound as though any injury to the elite is actually an injury to every person who lives under their jurisdiction, and the idea of 'national identity' and the right to 'national identity' serves to make for that illusion, so that in international law you get the idea that invading a nation state is a matter of violating every individual within it. Isn't that an illusion? Or do you think that's too cynical a view? Or what is it?

Edward Said: It is partly cynical and partly incomplete. In our case, it has to be remembered that there are two levels to Palestinian nationalism. On the one hand, it is an urgent necessity for people, the large majority of whom today, I would say, enjoy no rights at all, precisely because of their national origins. For example, there are over 400,000 Palestinians in Lebanon, all of whom exist as stateless people, and who have pieces of paper saying, "You are stateless." So in a certain sense, this is invidious nationalism. On the other hand, that level can be addressed, as you said, by founding a national identity, having a state, all of the traditional, one might say conventional, attributes of nationalism about which one has mixed feelings because this can lead to all sorts of abuses. But the other level for the Palestinians, which is more important as far as I'm concerned, is that the Palestinian struggle in the Middle East, in the Arab world in particular and with regard to Israel, is a vanguard struggle in that it is a secular struggle in a part of the world where religious nationalism is very, very powerful. I mean the nationalism of Islam in places like Iran, Algeria now, Jordan—Jewish nationalism too as the right-wing organism which has dominated Israeli life for the last twenty years—are examples of that, as well as Christian fundamentalist nationalism in Lebanon. So we are different. We are not a religious movement. We are a nationalist movement for democratic rights. The second attribute is that the Palestinian struggle is a vanguard struggle because it is a struggle for democracy in a part of the world where there is no democracy. We make it very clear in our national declaration of independence in 1988 that we are a secular struggle with democratic rights for all people, men and women, religions, creeds, and sects. In that respect, we are much more than a small or petty nationalism; and in that respect, it is a brilliant and important struggle.

Jonathan Rée: Jews, of course, are likely to feel threatened by the sort of thing you are saying. You wrote somewhere that Zionism is a touchstone of political judgment in our time. Could you explain that?

Edward Said: Yes. Jews, insofar as they are Zionists, are people who believe in a return to Palestine, that is to say, the ancestral homeland of the Jewish people. They are people who believe that they are entitled for the most part to sole rights in Palestine. What that overlooks, of course, is that there was another people there, and there is another people there now, most of them under occupation in the West Bank and Gaza since 1967, and about 800,000 who are the remnant of the Palestinians who have been driven since 1948, as second- or third-class citizens in a state which is described as the state of the Jewish people, not to say of its citizens (a very important distinction). Now, Zionism achieved very important things from the standpoint of Jews. But from the standpoint of its victims—and Zionism has always had victims—it's a catastrophe that the state of Israel was constructed. It is a conflict, if you like, of tragedies. On the one hand, here were the remnants of the Jewish people, who were massacred in Europe by Western anti-Semites, coming to Palestine. They had come before World War II, but the status and the state of the survivors, and the construction of their state, were on the ruins of our society. This is not a metaphor, because I remember. I was a boy, and I grew up in Palestine. I remember what it was like to leave. One's whole family left. From that point of view, it is a conflict between a group of people who came as victims and who, in turn, produced other victims: us—we are the victims of the victims—and it is a most difficult choice, but, I think, a required choice on the basis of rights. You can't deal with the rights of one people at the expense of the rights of another.

Jonathan Rée: Your work as a critic links up in quite deep and subtle ways, I think, with your concerns as a spokesperson for the Palestinian cause. But I think in particular of the fact that a theme in a lot of your criticism is space and geography. One could say that for a lot of previous criticism the main theme had been time and history. You have changed that, or perhaps you and Raymond Williams would be mainly responsible for that.

Edward Said: Well, you know, that isn't to say that if you're interested in geography, space, territory, you aren't also interested in history. I am really interested in the interaction between the two. But I do, it's true, give primacy to geography because it seems to me that the history of the last three hundred years is, in fact, world history, and it is a globalized history. What makes it intelligible, or one of the main things that makes it intelligible, is the struggle over territory. By 1918, 85 percent of the world was under the domination of a handful of states in Europe and America. Since that time, one can understand the cultural and historical experience, say the period after World War II, as the struggle to get back territory that had been taken from people of color in the colonized world. So, that's why it's terribly important to me. I see my own history, and the history of my people, as a function of that struggle over territory; and it was always territory. The interesting thing is that it was never territory taken for the sake of territory. You didn't simply go there, and just say, "Well I like this; I'm going to take it."

I am interested in the antecedent justifications. Australia, for example, is perfect for England because it is far away. It is the antipodes; we could put all our unwanted populations, the felons, there. America is the promised land, so they go there and they colonize it because it is a new Eden. Palestine was the country of the reclaimed promised land for the Jews. But what always happened was a conflict of these justifications with, you might say, the bodies, the realities of the people there. Therefore, it is a struggle over geography, but also over justification and philosophy and epistemology, and whose land it is. Is it the right of the people who live there? In the case of Palestine, for example, one of the main arguments in early Zionist writing—and not only early Zionist writing, but early European writing about Palestine in the twentieth century— was that it was uninhabited, and if it was not uninhabited, it was a land full of neglect, which is a similar argument to that used by French settlers in North Africa when they took Algeria: it was simply an empty land. In other words, the right to use land, or the right to imagine the best use for the land, is a right given to the European, to the white man. That seems to me to be the foundation, not only of actual political struggle, but also of the construction of cultures. It is impossible to understand European culture without some sense, for example in England, of the role played by India or Australia or the Caribbean in English domestic life. All of that strikes me as a fantastically interesting field, and bears always the connection, the relationship, to Williams' *The Country and the City*, the overseas territories, and so on.

Jonathan Rée: You talked about epistemology, and certainly in your work on the geography of imperialism the leading theme, I think, is the idea that the East was constructed as a mystery which it took the West to know about. There is a curious way in which your work on that subject has been caught up in the logic which it, itself, designated—I mean that people have criticized you for writing so exclusively about the European view of the East, and for neglecting agents who actually were in the East. What do you think of the way that this has developed?

Edward Said: Well, I think that to a certain extent they are right. That is to say that when I was writing *Orientalism*, I was really talking about European conceptions of the Orient, which are in some instances so far beyond any local conception of what that geography might be, that they constructed a field and a subject all their own. Even now, retrospectively, it seems to me perfectly okay to talk about it, because it constituted itself as an object that had very little to do with what people there thought. What I have done since then, however, is to look at the struggle over competing conceptions of geography. In my latest book, *Culture and Imperialism*, which will appear in a few months, I really spend half the time looking at how nationalist struggles in Africa, in places like Ireland, in the Caribbean, in India, really had to begin, you might say, with the reconquest of that territory, to do it initially epistemologically. In other words, to reimagine it in the way, for instance, that Yeats reimagined the history of Ireland in terms of its fairies and heroes and great fighters, and so on and so forth. The fact produces—as somebody like Neruda does in Latin America—a new geography which is a reclamation of the land. You find really competing conceptions there. I think that I've been trying to do that, but what is very striking is the extent to which the prevailing conceptions in Europe, in the West, are very difficult to dislodge, because so much is invested in them. It is not just a matter of someone having an idea—but scientific institutions are built around these ideas, like the Royal Geographical Society in England. Rodney Murchison, for example, was a man who, as a geologist, as a geographer, as a surveyor, didn't only think that he was exploring Africa. He actually said it was like a military campaign, and what he was trying to discover about the geography and the geology of Africa was, in a certain sense, adding to the realm of England. Along with that went an enormous institution—the Royal Geographical Society. Those are the things that one has to take seriously and not say, well, you know, they are just Western fictions.

Jonathan Rée: What about that situation of people in the English language, but not in Britain or America? I'm thinking of people, say readers, in Africa reading Conrad, in the Caribbean reading *The Tempest*, in India reading Kipling and Forster. What's that experience of reading?

Edward Said: Well, it's a very different one. I mean, let's say that you wanted to read as a Caribbean native a novel by Jane Austen, who is, perhaps of all English novelists, the most tied to a particular locale which is very, very English and extremely insular in that respect. But if you read with the eye of a Caribbean, or the eye of an Indian, a novel like *Mansfield Park* or *Persuasion* or *Pride and Prejudice*, you'll find very careful notations there of overseas territories that are very much held. In *Mansfield Park*, for instance, the estate of Sir Thomas Bertram is held by Bertram in Antigua, and the importance of Antigua, therefore, to the economy of *Mansfield Park* is absolutely central. But at the same time you have a kind of illusion of it. It ceases to be important once it is mentioned that he had to go there and take care of it. And it was a slave sugar plantation. If you read with those eyes, you can, then, see that the history of the English novel, great form that it is, is constructed with precisely those territories held in the imagination as they are held in England. A totally different experience emerges from the reading of the novel *A Passage to India* for example. Even more so, Conrad's *Heart of Darkness* becomes not just the explorations of Marlow and Kurtz of that bit of Africa, but really becomes the symbol for Africa and the enslavement and partition and the scramble for Africa. That entails, of course, a much different reading than simply reading as you would for a test or for an English course. You read as Ngugi [wa Thiong'o] and people like Chinua Achebe have read it. You have to read it in a decolonizing way. You have to strip from it all the assumptions that are there; and very often you have people like Achebe and Ngugi reading it and in some cases rejecting it and rewriting its history in terms of their own apprehension of the river and the territory, and so on. In my opinion, it is a much more lively and invested process to read and interpret literature of that sort from the point of view of the colonies, and above all of the decolonizing colonies.

Jonathan Rée: You've mentioned Ngugi and Achebe, so that raises the question of being a writer of English outside Britain and America, the situation of Yeats or [Derek] Walcott. [Seamus] Heaney has a phrase somewhere about how those people are in a situation of being on a forked stick of their love of the English language.

Edward Said: It is not inherent to English by the way. It is the case of French writers too. There is a whole group of very interesting and important Algerian novelists, like Kateb Yacine who writes in French, but was very much a part of the Algerian resistance to French colonization, and of Moroccan writers, like Abdelkebir Khatibi who writes in French. I think it is a very interesting case which, in a certain sense, Ngugi has finessed by proceeding to write in the native language. He rejected English after having written several very distinguished novels, saying that he wanted to write in his native language. But the challenge is there. That is to say that the language is a field which one can work in, and it depends often on the premises. It is not the language itself which is infected. For example, Achebe says that Conrad shouldn't be read at all, that he is such a racist that *Heart of Darkness* is an unreadable text for Africans, and then he goes off and writes his own novel in English. But I think that the struggle within the language for values, for perceptions, for geographies exactly, is a continuing one, and in a certain sense has to be understood in domestic terms. It is not everybody in England who writes from neo-colonial or imperial premises using English. One can always find alternatives to it. I think that's the great task of criticism today—to read novels, not to reestablish the orthodoxies and the perceptions of the dogmas, etc. that anchor the work, but rather to read to understand these, to try also to understand them as dislodged to allow for other places. As Aimé Césaire says, "there is room for everyone at the rendezvous of victory." That was a great example for someone like C. L. R. James—that you could write the history of the French Revolution from the point of view of the great slave revolt in Haiti. That seems to me to be the interesting alternative, not what language would you write in.

Jonathan Rée: Yeats is a particularly interesting example here, I think, because a lot of people would be surprised to see him regarded as a poet of anti-imperialism rather than a poet of modernist internationalism.

Edward Said: Absolutely! I think Yeats is a particularly interesting case because he was very reactionary, at the same time somebody who believed in great houses, in eighteenth-century nobility, and he was Anglo-Irish. After all, he belonged to the Ascendancy. But in a certain sense, Yeats was a national poet, and he was one of the people who forwarded precisely this decolonizing imagination that gave rise to the Irish Renaissance, and continues today to do so. I think it is possible to see Yeats in two ways: on the one hand as a man who slid off at the end of his life into a kind of terribly reactionary, even fascist, politics, but whose poetry, particularly up to the "Tower," and even after it, in the twenties, was really the nationalistic poetry that, I think, can be seen . . . I mean, in the Irish context, he became a reactionary. But if you compare him with nationalist poets of his time, or like Aimé Césaire later, or Neruda, or

Tagore in India, you could see him as belonging to the decolonizing culture, which was an international culture. They knew about each other, and worked from similar premises in local situations that differed widely. To see Yeats as simply a modernist internationalist, as he has been taken, is to miss, I would say, a good part of the vigor and arrogance of his verse. For an Irish person to speak the way he did, to talk about Irish history in the way he did, is an act of *lèse-majesté* whose force is undeniable.

Jonathan Rée: Your first book, *Joseph Conrad and the Fiction of Autobiography,* was described by you as an attempt at a phenomenological kind of criticism, and you talked of Sartre and Merleau-Ponty as the inspiration of the book. Is that still the inspiration of your work, or has its direction changed?

Edward Said: I would say probably yes, but I wouldn't, perhaps, use the word phenomenology. What interested me about those people, Sartre and Merleau-Ponty and Husserl, at the time was that they seemed to situate the study of forms, or it was possible through them to understand the study of forms, as taking place in a context, in a whole environment. And when I grew up as a student, and as a graduate, I was living in an era of high formalism where the work itself—the Cleanth Brookses, the New Criticism—was really the dominant thing. I found that in somebody like Conrad—who at the time was scarcely known (this is in the late fifties and early sixties) except as a writer of highly polished formalist kinds of things—something was missing. And what was missing was what I answered to in his work, the tremendous dimension of exile and dislocation and so on. There was a vocabulary at hand in the works of the phenomenologists and the existentialists that I made use of shamelessly, exploited, to be able to look at Conrad in that way. It was a study of Conrad's life in his work—not as anecdotal events, that he had been to Africa, or that he had been to Borneo, and put that in a story, and so on—but rather that he was always trying to reconstruct his experience in a whole way, in the forms that would yield to insight and investigative analyses, usually unsuccessfully (I mean Conrad's own unsuccessful attempts to get to the bottom). I found that stimulating, and in a sense, since I have gone on to try to do that, seeing works in a "situation," as Sartre says, in a context, remains very important to me. But all the heavy jargonistic and metaphysical language that goes along with it is now for me irrelevant in a way.

Jonathan Rée: One of the themes in the Conrad book is Conrad's total expatriation, his separation, the way that he tried to relate himself only very artificially to the tradition of novel-writing in English, because he was a well-traveled Pole and all that. It seems to me that this theme was taken up in your works of the seventies on 'beginnings' which, if I understand it correctly, was a sort of definition of what modernism means, defined in terms of having beginnings rather than origins, of situating yourself in relation to tradition by adjacency rather than by continuity. Do you still think that this idea of a break with tradition is adequate as a characterization of modernism?

Edward Said: It is a break with tradition up to a point, and I think that is an accurate definition of it, in that something cataclysmic happened. In the case of modernism, it was probably World War I, changes in the economic and political topography of Europe, and a number of other things. Later on, in my current work, I have a new theory of modernism that accomodates itself to precisely this, that one of the things that is directly involved in the creation of what we call European modernism (that would include people like Joyce, Eliot, Thomas Mann, Proust, and all the rest of it) is, in fact, the crisis in the imperial world. One has a sense that in the horizon of their works there is some disturbance at the peripheries which is having an effect, like the plague in *Death in Venice* which comes from the East, and becomes a metaphor for the change in Europe such that it can no longer exist on its own. Therefore, what the writer does is to reconstruct.

It is a break with tradition, but an attempt, sometimes a desperate attempt, as in the case of Eliot, to rebuild, and that's why the great metaphorical figure, for me, was provided by Vico in *The New Science*, that book on beginnings, where Vico is the great theorist of self-invention. The figure he uses, you recall, is that there is a big flood, and after the flood men are left lying around the great giants. In order to live as human beings, they make the choice to construct societies. They have to construct marriage, religion, civil institutions; and that becomes the metaphor for the new world in *The New Science*. I saw that as inspiring the onset of European modernism. But underlying that for me, you see, was the 1967 war in the Middle East which was a great crisis in my own life. I had spent most of my time there. My family was in the Middle East. I had gone to America as a student by myself and I had, more or less, lived as much as possible a life as a student and later as a scholar in America without reference, really, professionally or even emotionally, to this world I'd left behind—and which was shattered in 1967. The rest of Palestine was destroyed, or taken over by the Israelis. The Arab world, as I had known it, grown up in it, had completely changed. This then was my autobiographical impetus, to rethink the whole question of what it means to start again, to begin. It involved acts of choice, acts of designation, rather than things coming from heaven. That is why the emphasis on the secular is so great, as far as I'm concerned. It is a congeries of things, a number of things, working at the same time.

Jonathan Rée: Your most recent book is about music and it's about the pleasure that you personally take in music. It is a curious combination in a way because it contains a lot of discussion of a kind that people would have expected in a book by Said. That is to say, it talks about the development of the institutions of Western classical music, the definition of Western classical music versus the East, and the rise of the cult of soloists and celebrities and solitary listening, and the influence of technologies of reproduction and all of that. But in the midst of that, there is an emphasis on pleasure at a time that people wouldn't quite have expected it. Is this a new development in your work?

Edward Said: I shouldn't like to think so. No. It has been there all along. I must confess to feeling at times rather beset by these contests that I find myself in because I am a Palestinian or because I belong to one or another school of literary or philosophical or political criticism. And it seemed to me that what had been happening, at least in the United States, was that one becomes almost entirely a creature of those things which are completely professional—or professionalized, which is worse. You lose any contact with whatever it is that you're doing. It becomes just a matter of earning your honorarium or, more, your salary. I like to think of myself in many ways, that I'm moved by what I like, what I want to do, rather than what I don't like or what I am forced to do. So it seemed to me that one thing to do would be to write about music, and to focus on those aspects of music that are completely intimate, and provide a very sustaining kind of pleasure, which has been there all through my life, from my earliest consciousness.

Jonathan Rée: Given that you were born in Jerusalem, how did you become inducted into European literature?

Edward Said: I grew up really biculturally. I always went to English schools. Both Palestine and Egypt, where my family subsequently lived, were British colonies. I guess I belong to the elite of our country and we were sent to British schools. So I grew up studying English in school and speaking Arabic at home and with my friends. So I have no memory of not looking at European books. It has really been a very serious study all my life. But I always felt I wasn't European at the same time. Perhaps it was the schools I went to that made me feel that, because there were always English teachers and mostly Arab boys (I went to boys' schools). One felt sort of excluded, and that being educated in the language and the literature was a process of trying, unsuccessfully, to acculturate to it. One was always found wanting.

Jonathan Rée: Would it be facile to say that it was an easy assimilation to make because so much modern, modernist, European literature is about exile and displacement, and that you were exiled and displaced, so it was your literature?

Edward Said: I wasn't always exiled and displaced. I always felt slightly divided, because I come from a Christian minority, and within that minority in Palestine—about 10 percent of the Arab population of Palestine which is mostly Muslim—we were a Protestant minority, even smaller, so there was always a sense of being slightly askew, off from the center. The fact that I went to these schools and became good at speaking English and French was added to the peculiarity of the whole thing. So, in a certain sense, I felt peculiar, and this literature seemed to resonate with what I felt. Not all of it seems that way, but certainly modern literature does, yes, and that's what I am interested in. I never really felt completely at home in earlier periods of literature when I was getting my professional degrees as a scholar of literature. I loved the eighteenth century, but it seemed like almost studying a foreign culture, whereas the twentieth century, particularly with its expatriate figures, its wanderers—like Joyce and so on—was much closer to me.

Jonathan Rée: People with a taste for periodization or even a mania for periodization, tell us that modernism is over, and we are now in the epoch of postmodernism. What do you think of that?

Edward Said: I suppose it's true to people who think exclusively in terms of America and advertising culture and the media, pastiche, and that sort of thing. But if you are aware of other worlds than, say, Madison Avenue and high-tech architecture, you will realize that the battle for the modern, and therefore modern as in 'modernity', is, for example, in parts of the world that I am familiar and affiliated with, like the Middle East, a very important one. It is, indeed, *the* battle. Don't forget, we live in an age where the whole question of what the tradition is, and what the Prophet said, and the Holy Book said, and what God said, and what Jesus said, etc., are issues that people go to war over, as in the case of Salman Rushdie, who was condemned to death for what he wrote. That is for us the battle—the battle over what the modern is, and what the interpretation of the past is. It is very important in the Arab and Islamic worlds. There is a school of writers, poets, essayists, and intellectuals, who are fighting a battle for the right to *be* modern, because our history is governed by *turath*, or heritage. But the question is, who designates what the heritage is. That is the problem. For us, the crisis of 'modernism' and 'modernity' is a crisis over authority, and the right of the individual, and the writer, the thinker, to express himself, or herself, for it is also the battle over women's rights. So the whole question of postmodernism to us is an interesting sort of Candidean question in the West. But for us, modernism, as in modernity, is the issue of the moment.

Jonathan Rée: I've noticed that in several contexts recently you described yourself as being on the conservative side in certain debates. And, I think, you were talking in particular about cultural debates in the United States about the authority of the canon. One of the ways in which this has been formulated is in terms of the idea of political correctness, 'PC', very much an American tele-phenomenon. Is the question about PC, from your point of view, just another 'red scare', the idea that there are people on the campuses who are trying to gag anybody whose views they don't agree with?

Edward Said: Yes and no. The idea that there is a small left cabal in the American universities who are running things and are declaring what can and can't be read, that's total tommy-rot, total bullshit. But on the other hand, there is an important and interesting debate, and that is, what do we people, let's say, the subalterns, or the oppressed, or the formerly suppressed, or whatever designation, people of color, what do we do as we confront the canon? The alternatives are generally formulated, in my opinion, in rather impoverishing ways. One way to say it is, if we are people of color we are not going to read anything by whites; if we are women, we are not going to read anything by men;

if we are gays, we are not going to read anything by straights; and so on. That is to replace one canon with another. I have no sympathy for that, because it simply condemns us, you, to a new marginality. There is nothing easier for political-correctness bashers—who have turned themselves into an industry in America today—the people who write books like *The Tenured Radicals* or Dinesh D'Souza's book on "illiberal education." It's all tommy-rot . . . let's see what these people want; let's give them departments of African-American studies; let's give them gay studies; let's give them all that; but let's get on with it.

The other alternative is not to substitute one canon for another, not to become Afrocentric where you were first Eurocentric, gynocentric where you were first phallocentric, but rather to say, let us try and understand the construction of the canon and what these objects serve. That's number one. And number two, most important from my point of view, is how are they related to each other. In other words, it seems to me that the history of imperialism and the history of colonization, the history of oppression as experienced by blacks, by Palestinians, by gays, by women, all that is built upon segregation, on separation. The worst thing ethically and politically is to let separatism simply go on, without understanding the opposite of separatism, which is connectedness. In that respect, I am very conservative. I want to see how everything works. I am not just interested in Palestinian themes in American literature, or Palestinian themes in French literature. What I am interested in is how all these things work together. That seems to me to be the great task—to connect them all together—to understand wholes rather than bits of wholes.

Denys Johnson-Davies

❖

On Translating Arabic Literature

Ferial Ghazoul: How did you come to be a translator of Arabic literary texts?

Denys Johnson-Davies: Having made a somewhat arbitrary decision to study Oriental languages at university, I soon discovered that I was not temperamentally suited to an academic career—though I did spend some enjoyable years teaching at Cairo University after World War II. After university I spent five years in the Arabic section of the BBC and it was these years, and the help my Arab colleagues gave me, that convinced me to specialize in modern Arabic and its literature. My general interests were in literature and I discovered that the modern Arabic literary movement was almost neglected by Arabists. It seemed that a useful task for me to perform would be to make known to the West, through translation, some of the products of the literary movement. On coming to Cairo in 1945, I got to know most of the literary figures of the time: Taha Hussein, Mahmoud Teymour, Tawfiq al-Hakim, Bishr Faris, Yahya Haqqi; the critic Louis Awad I already knew from Cambridge. The first book I translated and published—in Cairo—was a short selection of the stories of Mahmoud Teymour. Though he is among the easiest of writers to translate—and his importance today is mainly a historical one—I was made to realize what a difficult task it is to translate convincingly. I well remember the time and effort I expended in reading through all his collections in order to make my selection, then in translating the stories and checking and rechecking my translation by referring to Egyptian friends and to Mahmoud Teymour himself to make quite sure I had understood the exact meaning of every word. At long last the book was ready for the printers, when I decided as a last check to ask an English friend with no knowledge of Arabic to read it through. As one does on such occasions, I gave him the book that I might be reassured with comforting words; all I wanted from him was to hear "They read excellently." To my horror he informed me—and no amount of tact on his part could lighten the blow—that whereas he didn't doubt the accuracy of my translations, the stories simply did not read as English. I asked for examples and he was only too easily able to point them out to me. So, once again, I laboriously went through the stories, this time in an attempt to create a translation rather than merely to assure myself (and hypothetical readers) that I had understood the Arabic text. The fact is that during one's studies no attempt is ever made to teach translation as such; translation, at school and university, remains one of the methods by which a foreign language is taught. When translating for examination purposes one should always be careful of being literal in case the examiner has doubts about one's understanding of the original text. As far as I know, marks are not awarded for elegance in translation.

With this, my first book, I discovered that a knowledge of my native language and of Arabic did not of themselves make me a translator.

While I myself have taught translation at various times I don't think I ever made an attempt at teaching the art of translation: I taught it—as I was required to teach it—as an adjunct to the learning of either English or Arabic. Possibly the only worthwhile practical advice I ever gave my students was: "Cut it up into small pieces."

Certainly I never consciously set out to be a translator. I do, though, remember reading very early on a book entitled *Intertraffic* by, I believe, a writer named Bates and being impressed by it. Also from an early age I read widely in various foreign literatures and was aware that this was made possible for me by the efforts of individuals other than the original writers. I have always regarded this intertraffic as of the utmost cultural importance.

I now recollect—something I had long forgotten—that one of the first pieces of writing I produced was an article on "Translation and Translators" in which I pointed out that creative writers of the caliber of Baudelaire, Proust and Lawrence, Dryden and Pope, and dozens of others, did not find translation too unworthy an undertaking.

The collection of short stories by Mahmoud Teymour was published in Cairo in 1946 or 1947 (the book bears no date) and it was not till twenty years later that my next book of translations, a volume of short stories covering writers from most of the Arab world, was published by Oxford University Press in 1967.

Ferial Ghazoul: You have translated *hadith,* poetry, short stories, novels, and drama. Presently, you are translating children's stories from Arabic. What motivates your choice of texts and genres?

Denys Johnson-Davies: Though I did for a time in London run an office specializing in all forms of Arabic translation—business and legal documents in the main—I do not find translation per se a particularly enjoyable occupation, or indeed a mainly rewarding one. Knowing from experience that translation is mainly a matter of hard slog, I suppose I choose works that are likely to demand the greatest amount of creativity. Though the element of choosing works which I believe should be made available to non-Arab readers plays a part, I am largely motivated by my own personal likes. Having translated many millions of words in order to make a living, I now indulge myself by translating only those things with which I feel in sympathy. One gives a lot of oneself when translating—not only time—and I am deeply unwilling to do this in respect of a writer with whose work I cannot communicate emotionally.

Translation, too, is a form of challenge and so, I suppose, I like to try my hand at as many genres as possible. My main literary interest is fiction, so most of my translations have been volumes of short stories or novels. I find translating dialogue, particularly dialogue written in the colloquial language, an enjoyable challenge and thus I recently decided to produce a volume of Egyptian one-act plays, all of which had been written in the colloquial language. In general, I have not been particularly interested in poetry, though for many years I have been a friend of Yusuf al-Khal, founder of *Shi'r* magazine, the magazine which radically changed the course of modern Arabic poetry. I was also a close friend of the late Tawfiq Sayigh, also of Jabra Ibrahim Jabra and other leading non-Egyptian poets. Never having thought of myself as a potential translator of poetry, it was really only at the suggestion of the late Ghassan Kanafani that I did a volume of selections from the poems of the Palestinian Mahmoud Darwish. I have since thought of doing a similar volume on Badr Shakir al-Sayyab, whom I knew just before the last unhappy days of his life, but haven't felt sufficient urgency to do more than a few as yet unpublished translations of some of the later poems.

Another sort of challenge is provided by *hadith*. This activity—which is a continuing one—was suggested to me by my cotranslator in this field, Dr. Ezzedin Ibrahim. The challenge here lies in the constraints imposed upon one when faced by a religious text. Here accuracy must have ascendancy over every other consideration.

The discipline is nonetheless enjoyable, and the experience of working with someone else—something of which I had not thought myself capable—is an added challenge.

Where the children's books were concerned, I happened to know the pubishers of a series where the quality of the writing and the illustrations impressed me. Here again it was a new departure for me and I greatly enjoyed the experience.

I should also add in this connection that my choice is motivated as well by the practical consideration of publication. Whereas original writing has an element of self-indulgence in it, the translating of someone else's work is only worthwhile if one is assured of publication. I cannot imagine a translator deriving any satisfaction from putting the efforts of his labor into a drawer of his desk. The fact that twenty years separated the publication of my first translated work and that of my second illustrates the difficulty of finding a publisher for anything out of the ordinary.

Ferial Ghazoul: What are the mechanics, techniques, and procedures of literary translation (including the problematics of idiomatic expression, connotation, and local references)? How do you compare the difficulties of translating Arabic into English with translating Romance languages into English?

Denys Johnson-Davies: By trying to treat literary translation creatively I endeavor to come to each piece of work in a fresh frame of mind. One of the difficulties is to be creative within the strict confines of the text in front of you; one must be self-effacing but at the same time there is no ignoring the fact that if you are any sort of a translator you are not mechanical and that your own style and personality will, to an extent, intrude. Where a novel is concerned one often quite quickly—if one is in sympathy with the writer—develops a style that approximates to the original—as far as any style in English can approximate to one in Arabic. One of the difficulties in, say, a volume of short stories written by various writers from different parts of the Arab world, is to try to accomplish in English not simply stories rendered into a readable and acceptable style but stories in a variety of styles which will give some idea of the varied flavors of the originals; the reader should, as far as possible, be made to feel that he is reading stories by different writers.

I am something of a purist in the matter of translation and believe that the first priority should be accuracy. If a story, for instance, cannot survive in translation unless changes or deletions are made, then it is best left untranslated. A translator must be bound by what he is translating—unless he wishes to become something else, an adapter for instance. Of course, if one is a creative person, one is at times tempted to 'go one better' than the writer, but the temptation should be resisted.

As has often been said, every attempt at translation is inevitably doomed to failure. It is merely a question of degree of failure. The problematics of idiomatic expression are, of course, immense when translating from and into two languages whose cultural backgrounds, ways of thought, etc., have so little in common. One must also continually bear in mind the knowledge, or rather ignorance, of one's potential reader. I remember once traveling in a Pakistan Airlines plane when the passengers were informed by the captain that we would be landing at our destination at such-and-such a time, "if God wills." The announcement was greeted by the passengers with laughter, some derisory, some a trifle uneasy. The captain, who no doubt experienced the self-same reaction each time he made his announcement in this manner, had to choose whether or not to comply with the Qur'an's injunction not to mention some happening in the future without adding the words "if God wills" despite his passengers' ignorance of the Qur'an. The translator from

Arabic continually faces similar problems. For instance, in colloquial Egyptian one man can call another, whom he perhaps does not know at all, any of the following: 'my son', 'my brother', 'my uncle', 'boy', 'man', 'my dear', 'my beloved', etc., all of which have quite different connotations according to the circumstances in which they are used. How is the translator to deal with them? Does he simply iron them out as best he can, generally by leaving them out altogether? The alternative is to translate them literally and bespatter one's translation with notes explaining their significance; this method though, carried to its logical conclusion, will leave one with a treatise on 'the manners and customs of the modern Egyptians' rather than a piece of fiction, which demands readability and continuity. On the other hand, to try to match Egyptian colloquialisms with near equivalents in English or American dialects is to run the risk of producing something incongruous and unreal.

These sorts of difficulties exist particularly where the languages concerned relate to such totally different social and cultural backgrounds, i.e., are more prevalent in translating from Arabic into English than say from French into English. This has been well summed up by Edward Sapir when he says, "The worlds in which different societies live are distinct worlds, not merely the same world with different labels attached." There is of course the additional purely linguistic difficulty, which is that Arabic grammar and syntax differ widely from that of English. Though I translate straight onto the typewriter, then correct extensively in pen, then retype again, and again make changes, I think that the thought processes I have trained myself to make are more complicated than those demanded of someone translating from a Romance language. In the Romance language the structure of the sentence is perhaps already determined for the translator, also the punctuation. In Arabic this is much less so.

Ferial Ghazoul: You have often discovered talents and introduced them to the world through your translations, even before their work has been published or widely circulated. How do you find manuscripts and single out stories often appearing in obscure or inaccessible periodicals?

Denys Johnson-Davies: I have read widely in modern Arabic fiction—and indeed in fiction generally. I also for a time edited an Arabic literary magazine. I therefore believe (who doesn't?) that I have an eye for talent. Having too a foot in both camps, in the literary worlds of the East and the West—in the same way that you have, and being, like you, highly suspicious of the establishment in its evaluation of writers, I come to modern Arabic writing with an open mind. I have, too, no political axes to grind, though one is forced to the conclusion that most talent lies to the left of center.

My friends in Egypt are almost exclusively creative writers and I also carry on a correspondence with other writers in the Arab world. There are, therefore, a number of people whose literary judgment I respect and who are kind enough to put me on to the track of possible new talent. The system of publishing in the Arab world, which is so different from that in the West, and the comparative lack of serious criticism, means that one must make one's efforts in sifting the wheat from the chaff. Sadly, too, criteria other than literary excellence often weigh with the establishment in selecting those writers it will publish and promote. It is this pioneering role in uncovering and furthering writing one believes is intrinsically valuable that gives to the work of the translator from a language such as Arabic an added dimension. The fact that I am one of a very small group of people interested in translating modern Arabic literature and that it is I who choose what I shall translate and am not commissioned by a publisher to translate a particular work, gives me perhaps an excessive, and certainly unsought, power. It may well be that the seventeen writers represented in my volume *Modern Egyptian Short Stories* are not necessarily the 'best' writers of short stories in Egypt; certainly many of them are not among the most well-known. The selection is, naturally, a subjective one. Perhaps, too, undue importance has been given by Arab writers to their writings being published in translation; many of them regard being translated into a foreign language as a stamp of excellence. In looking around for material for translation one is conscious of the fact that the English or other foreign publisher—like the eventual foreign reader—is ignorant of the Arabic literary scene: for them fame in the Arab world is irrelevant. A lot of translations have in fact been made of so-called established Arab writers and many have failed to find publishers in the West. The practical criterion of publishability is basic to one's choice of material, and in making one's choice it should be borne in mind that no one in the West is interested in modern Arabic literature per se but only in writing of genuine talent.

Ferial Ghazoul: It has been observed that erotic themes dominate modern Arabic narratives which you have translated. Is this an accurate statement? If so, is eroticism an essential feature of modern Arabic writing or is it privileged by you for its universality (as the philosopher Bataille once remarked: "Eroticism is a universal problem in a way that no other problem is.")?

Denys Johnson-Davies: I was not aware that anyone had made this observation. In any event, it's most likely an accurate statement. I suppose you are thinking primarily of *The Smell of it* by Sonallah Ibrahim and *Season of Migration to the North* by Tayeb Salih. In fact, though, I was interested in Tayeb Salih's writing before he wrote *Season*, as I had already translated several short stories by him, also the novella *The Wedding of Zein*. Yes, the erotic has always interested me—years ago the late Tawfiq Sayigh and I had plans to do a book together on 'the erotic in Arabic literature', i.e., in classical Arabic literature. While the humorous, the dramatic, the tragic only too often fail when transported across linguistic frontiers, the erotic remains effectively erotic. I wonder, though, on reflection, whether that is quite true. I suppose, however, that any writer worth his salt in the Arab world today is perforce a rebel, and one of the more interesting ways of rebelling is—as a writer—to rebel against the puritanism that has ruled the Arabic literary renaissance. The Arab world was shocked—and many Arab readers still are—by the sexual frankness of passages in *Season of Migration to the North.* In fact the novel, which was translated from manuscript, contained several other sexually explicit passages, which Tayeb Salih decided against including in the original but which he suggested be retained in the English translation. I objected that if anyone were to compare the original with the translation, he would come to the inescapable conclusion that the additional passages were of my own composition. Reluctantly, therefore, we decided to exclude them both from the original and from the translation. Whatever one's views about *Season of Migration to the North*—and it does not, in my opinion, rank among his best writing—the scene of some of the old people of the village sitting around and chatting idly about sex is one of the most delightful in modern Arabic literature. After novels like *Portnoy's Complaint* eroticism in Western literature has about run its course. In Arabic it still has a lot of mileage.

Ferial Ghazoul: As a translator do you feel bound by any theoretical position? Would you endorse—as Walter Benjamin did—the startling statement of Rudolf Pannwitz: "Our translations, even the best ones, proceed from a wrong premise. They want to turn Hindi, Greek, English into German, instead of turning German into Hindi, Greek, English. Our translators have a far greater reverence for the usage of their own language than for the spirit of the foreign works . . . The basic error of the translator is that he preserves the state in which his own language happens to be instead of allowing his language to be powerfully affected by the foreign tongue."

Denys Johnson-Davies: I didn't know of Pannwitz's proposition, but I find it thought-provoking. It posits, of course, the fundamental question: What's the purpose of translation? What, one asks, is the point of having one's language 'powerfully affected' by a foreign language? By the act of translating is one, primarily, making known ideas, moods, new ways of thought, opening doors on creative talents, or seeking in some way, through language, to change the processes of thinking in one's own language? The attitude expressed by Pannwitz questions the very process of translation. Should it even be attempted? It brings to mind Robert Frost's cynical and defeatist dictum that "poetry is what gets lost in translation." Of course no one would deny that something gets lost in all translation. In the last resort, as George Steiner pointed out in his introduction to *The Penguin Book of Modern Verse Translation,* "Arguments against verse translation are arguments against all translation." It may well be that a piece of literature is, in the process of translation, denuded of its 'soul'; it may nevertheless, in the hands of a sympathetic translator, be endowed with a new, a similar though slightly different, soul. Scholars have tirelessly pointed out that Fitzgerald's renderings of 'Umar Khayyam are not exact. And how true to the original are Ezra Pound's translations of Chinese poetry? True or not, English poetry would be the poorer without them.

Ferial Ghazoul: If you were to make up a program for future translation, what would you include in it?

Denys Johnson-Davies: The last ten years or so haven't achieved the promise shown in the fifties and sixties. The political instablity and rapid social changes of the area are not, I think, conducive to producing great writing. I would be very surprised if there was an Arabic Proust or James Joyce lurking in the wings. The sort of talent combined with integrity that Yahya Taher Abdullah possessed is rare indeed—and he himself was hindered by the material and other circumstances in which he lived; his was essentially a spontaneous talent. Perhaps his short novel should be made available in translation, though it is a flawed work. I hear that attempts are being made to translate Edwar al-Kharrat's very difficult novel *Rama wa-l-tannin* (Rama and the dragon); it is certainly impressive in Arabic—a new departure, in the same way as his stories in *Hitan 'aliya* (High walls) represent in Arabic what *Dubliners* did for the short story in English. I wonder whether *Rama wa-l-tannin* isn't one of those works that almost defy translation. The Iraqi short story writer Mohammed Khudayyir deserves to be more widely known, both in the Arab world and outside.

On the whole I find modern Arabic literature today more remarkable for its quantity than its quality; the Arabs' newly found prosperity has made possible the publication of numerous magazines devoted to publishing mediocrity so that a quite prodigious number of short stories by writers without talent appear every week. The system, too, whereby writers pay for the publication of their own books, means that the market is flooded by small volumes of nondescript short stories and poetry, while writers of caliber are not assured publication.

Barbara Harlow: The "Arab Authors" series has now published nearly twenty volumes of translated Arabic literary texts. Among these are a number of short story collections. Is this because of greater availability of short stories in Arabic, or is it due instead to practicalities of translation? Could it just as well be attributed to the demand on the part of a Western readership? Do you see a significant role for the short story, as opposed to the novel or poetry, in modern literature?

Denys Johnson-Davies: Yes, I think the reason for the large number of volumes of short stories is, as you suggest, the availability of this genre of writing. Certainly the short story has been the most popular form of fictional writing in the Arab world, and it has—in people like Yusuf Idris—produced writers of genuine talent. I would say—talking at least of England—that publishers are not on the whole keen on volumes of short stories and prefer novels. I myself have always found the short story an interesting genre and felt sorry for its comparative decline in popularity in the West. Yes, I do find a significant role for the short story. Some of the world's greatest fiction has come out of the short story. Economically it has perhaps relied in the past on serious literary magazines, which—at least in England—scarcely exist today. I see no reason, though, why short stories shouldn't exist in their own right, independent of magazines, and be published directly in book form. One has only to see the outstanding reputation made by, for instance, Borges solely through the medium of the short story to be convinced that it still has a role and a readership.

Barbara Harlow: Many of the volumes in the "Arab Authors" series have been written by Egyptian writers. Is it that Arabic literary activity has been more highly concentrated and developed in Egypt? What role do you see the writer as having in the Arab world today? Does this role and function differ from country to country?

Denys Johnson-Davies: I think there is no doubt that there is more literary talent in Egypt than elsewhere in the Arab world. It is only in poetry, where the modern movement was centered on Beirut and mainly featured poets from Iraq, Palestine, and Syria that Egypt did not lead. Whereas what you say is, I think, true, I feel that modern Arabic literature, like classical Arabic literature, is the product of a single culture and language and that the actual nationality of a particular writer is largely irrelevant. It is, for instance, of no more than incidental interest that Conrad was a Pole. You are, though, right that there is a predominance of Egyptian writers represented in the "Arab Authors" series and this may be due to the fact that Arabists have for the most part interested themselves in Egypt to the exclusion of other Arab countries. Certainly in the series I would greatly welcome examples from, say, Iraq, Syria, and North Africa.

V. S. Pritchett, the short story writer and critic, made the observation the other day that serious writing had become 'a cottage industry'. One cannot but feel that this is particularly true of the Arab world where serious attempts at the short story and the novel are scarcely read outside a small coterie of literati. Fiction has still to gain respectability. Also, journalism and creative writing are not regarded by the majority as two quite separate activities; we thus find a novelist or short story writer turning a dishonest penny by giving his views in a newspaper on how the traffic problems of Cairo can be solved. Owing to the political setup in most of the Arab world today the writer's role is perforce restricted. Many of the 'emerging' countries want writers in the same way as they want football players; they merely want the prestige of being thought 'cultured' and they, of course, readily find suitably mediocre candidates.

Nels Johnson: Although it is obvious that a text is a culture (and vice versa) there obviously comes a point when a translator must emphasize one aspect of this unity over another. How do you deal with this dilemma? That is, how does one decide between conveying the sense of the text and making it comprehensible to the audience?

Denys Johnson-Davies: This is a dilemma that is at the very root of the art of translation. A reader who does not know Arabic cannot read a short story written in Arabic and must rely on my knowledge of Arabic (and of English) to convey it to him. The problem remains that the reader is not a passive recipient of the new short story I have concocted for him in English in place of the Arabic one. I cannot spoonfeed it to him; he has, as a reader, an active role to play and, depending on his degree of understanding and sensitivity, will 'experience' the story or not. Whereas though, by translating the story into English for him I have made up for his lack of Arabic, I cannot share with him the background knowledge I have acquired alongside my study of Arabic and my having lived in the Arab world. If the hero of the story makes his ablutions and performs the sunset prayer, I know how ablutions are made and I also know that for the sunset prayer he will perform three *rak'a* (and I also happen to know what a *rak'a* is), the first two aloud and the last under his breath. To the average English reader the word 'ablution' has a somewhat jocular connotation, while 'performing ablution' in Islam is a procedure the proper understanding of which requires a considerable amount of background knowledge. How important is this to the general understanding of the story?

The translator should not, I believe, have any hard and fast rules; he is the practitioner of an art and not a science and he must simply take a view as he comes to each dilemma. Ferial Ghazoul asked me whether I felt bound by any theoretical position, and I don't think I specifically answered her question, which is again raised to my mind by yours. While my first loyalty is obviously to the writer in conveying as well as I can what he has written, my second loyalty—and no less an important one—is to my reader who does not possess a knowledge of Arabic. My freedom from any theoretical position is thus the exact opposite of the scholastic approach, but then the scholar is writing for fellow scholars whereas I am translating for the man in the street. What, therefore, have I achieved if I make a perfect translation which is only comprehensible to a fellow Arabist?

One's criteria differ both in relation to the type of material one is translating and with the audience one has in mind. In translating a religious text, as for instance *hadith,* or the Sayings of the Prophet, one is continually conscious of the necessity of being accurate above every other consideration. My cotranslator and I also bear in mind that such translations are made, in the first place, for Muslims who do not possess Arabic as their mother tongue, and that they will be read in a devotional frame of mind. No efforts must, therefore, be spared to efface oneself wholly and to provide as exact a reproduction of the meaning of the original as possible, even if it means adding copious footnotes. Where translation of a literary work is concerned, one is to an extent forced to compromise between doing justice to the writer and presenting the reader with a piece of writing that is comprehensible and enjoyable. I myself enjoy reading modern Japanese fiction, but knowing no word of Japanese, never having visited the country, and possessing no backround knowledge, I recognize that my understanding, intellectual and emotional, of the translation of a Japanese novel is inevitably of a different order from that of a Japanese reader or of the Englishman or American who translated it. The latter may have captured in his own mind 'the mind's speech' of the writer, but is the English language adequate for reproducing it? And am I the reader sufficiently well-equipped to savour it? The presence of the translator merely aggravates the difficulties that already exist in the writer–reader relationship.

Nels Johnson: How does a translator deal with such questions from an author as "That's not what I meant"? Does there come a point, in other words, where the enterprise of translation takes on a creative momentum of its own such that it overtakes even the protestations of the author?

Denys Johnson-Davies: I am extremely careful with my translations and if I have the least doubt about something I ask the author, either in person or by letter. The fact of the matter is that the one person who really has to understand a text is the translator: the writer can shrug off any query by saying that it's not up to him to explain his writings, while the reader simply passes on to the next sentence; only the translator, if he's doing his job properly, must wholly get under the skin of every single word. Of course, there are times—I remember such a time when I was doing the volume of stories by Yahya Taher Abdullah—when the writer does insist that whereas something he has written does not appear to make sense, that is how he wants it, how he means it to be. The attentive reader can find such an example in Yahya Taher Abdullah's story "A Tale Told by a Dog," where I have knowingly retained in my translation something that is palpably illogical. If, however, what he writes is unacceptable in translation I would perhaps suggest to him that it be left out of the translation or I would decide against translating the whole work. Translation certainly does take on a creative momentum, and very often one is capable of translating at great speed, but this momentum relates directly to the text and is lost once one's own momentum comes up against something that is out of tune with it. As I've indicated, the obstacle is sometimes so great that one abandons the whole project.

I believe a translation is usually only successful when the original text generates a creative momentum in the translator. With some writers a particular translator finds himself capable of producing little more than a 'crib' to the text, with others the translation takes wings.

The importance of literary translation is acknowledged with delicate perception in Octavio Paz's words: "Every text is unique and, at the same time, it is the translation of another text. No text is entirely original because language itself, in its essence, is already a translation: firstly, of the non-verbal world and secondly, since every sign and every phrase is the translation of another sign and another phrase. . . . Every translation, up to a certain point, is an invention and as such it constitutes a unique text."

Sources

"My Experience With Writing" by Radwa Ashour appeared in *Alif* 13 (1993). This testimony was presented at a conference at Cairo University and was published in *Actes du colloque international de narratologie et rhétorique dans les littératures française et arabe* (4–6 April 1988). Translated by Rebecca Porteous.

"On Reading the Earth" by Saadi Youssef appeared in *Alif* 13 (1993). Translated by Ferial J. Ghazoul.

"Intertextual Dialectics" by Gamal al-Ghitany appeared in *Alif* 4 (1984). Translated by Samia Mehrez.

"Language, Culture, and Reality" by Adonis appeared in *Alif* 7 (1987). It was written in 1970 and published as a chapter within a section entitled "Concerning Poetry and Revolution" in Adonis's well known and manifesto-like book *Zaman al-shi'r* (The age of poetry), which was first published in Beirut by Dar al-'Awda in 1972 and then reissued by the same press in 1978. The book includes articles and studies written by Adonis in the sixties and seventies.

"Thoughts on Change and the 'Blind Language'" by Ghassan Kanafani appeared in *Alif* 10 (1990). It is based on a lecture Kanafani gave on March 11, 1968, reprinted in two parts in *al-Hadaf*, no. 919 (July 17, 1988), pp. 46–49, and no. 920 (July 24, 1988), pp. 43–45.The lecture was later published in the journal *Muhadarat al-nadwa* (June 1968). Introduction by Barbara Harlow. Translated by Barbara Harlow and Nejd Yaziji.

"The Image of the City: Wounded Beirut" by Mona Takieddine Amyuni appeared in *Alif* 7 (1987). Written in Beirut in the summer of 1986, this article developed out of a public lecture given a few months earlier at the Department of English and Comparative Literature at the American University in Cairo.

"Brecht and the Egyptian Political Theater" by Mahmoud El Lozy appeared in *Alif* 10 (1990).

"Naguib Mahfouz and the Sufi Way" by Hamdi Sakkut appeared in *Alif* 5 (1985). Translated by Noha Radwan.

"The Mythmaker: Tayeb Salih" by Ahmad Shams al-Din al-Haggagi appeared in *Alif* 3 (1983). This article is dedicated to Sheikh Muhammad 'Abd al-'Aziz al-Uqsuri. Translated by Omaima Abou-Bakr.

"Opaque and Transparent Discourse in Sonallah Ibrahim's Works" by Ceza Kassem Draz appeared in *Alif* 2 (1982).

"Force and Transitivity: Bayram al-Tunisi and a Poetics of Anticolonialism" by Marilyn Booth appeared in *Alif* 7 (1987).

"Poetic Experimentation and the Institution: The Case of *Ida'a 77* and *Aswat*" by Samia Mehrez appeared in *Alif* 11 (1991).

"On Criticism and Creativity," an interview with Shukry Ayyad, appeared in *Alif* 4 (1984).

"On Interpoetics," an interview with Jabra Ibrahim Jabra, appeared in *Alif* 1 (1981). This is a selection from a larger interview that appeared in Arabic in a journal published by the University of Mosul, Iraq (*al-Jami'a* VIII: 4, December 1978, pp. 46–53). Translated by Alaa El Gibali and Barbara Harlow.

"On the Poetics of Space," an interview with Hassan Fathy by S. Samar Damluji, appeared in *Alif* 6 (1986). Introduction by S. Samar Damluji.

"Being and Place," an interview with Mohamed Choukri, appeared in *Alif* 6 (1986). Translated by Hoda El Sadda.

"The Relative and the Absolute in Avant-Garde Narration," an interview with Edwar al-Kharrat, appeared in *Alif* 2 (1982). Translated by Maggie Awadalla.

"On Political Commitment and Feminist Writing," an interview with Latifa al-Zayyat, appeared in *Alif* 10 (1990). Translated by Lamis al-Nakkash.

"Peoples' Rights and Literature," an interview with Edward Said by Jonathan Rée, appeared in *Alif* 13 (1993). The interview took place originally as part of a program entitled "Talking Liberties," broadcast in June 1992 by British television's Channel Four.

"On Translating Arabic Literature," an interview with Denys Johnson-Davies, appeared in *Alif* 3 (1983).

Notes on Contributors

Omaima Abou-Bakr (Egypt) studied in Egypt and the United States, where she specialized in Comparative Literature and the Middle Ages. She has taught Comparative Literature and Arabic language in the United States, and currently teaches in the English Department at Cairo University. She is the author of several articles on Sufism and medieval mysticism, including studies of Shushtari, St. John of the Cross, and Rumi.

Adonis (Syria) is the pen name of 'Ali Ahmad Sa'id. He was educated in Damascus and Beirut and has served as the representative of the Arab League at UNESCO in Paris. He is one of the most influential poets in the Arab world. He has been the editor of *Mawaqif*, a cultural and literary journal, and was co-editor of *Shi'r*, an avant-garde quarterly. He has written several poetic collections, a critical trilogy, and numerous books on poetic theory, including *An Introduction to Arab Poetics*.

Mona Takieddine Amyuni (Lebanon) was educated in Beirut and Paris. She now teaches at the American University of Beirut. She is the author of a number of articles on Naguib Mahfouz, Adonis, Georges Schéhadé, and Tayeb Salih, and the editor of *Tayeb Salih's Season of Migration to the North: A Casebook*.

Radwa Ashour (Egypt) was educated in Egypt and the United States, where she specialized in African-American Literature at the University of Massachusetts. She is currently Professor of English Literature and chair of the English Department at Ain Shams University in Cairo. Among her published works are *al-Tariq ila-l-khayma al-'ukhra: dirasa fi a'mal Ghassan Kanafani* (The path to the other tent: a study in the works of Ghassan Kanafani) and *al-Riwaya fi gharb Ifriqya* (The novel in west Africa). She has also written several creative works: *al-Rihla: ayyam taliba misriya fi Amrika* (The journey: an Egyptian student's days in America), *Hajar dafi'* (Warm stone), and *Ra'aytu al-nakhl* (I saw the palm trees).

Maggie Awadalla (Egypt) was educated in England and Egypt, specializing in comparative literature at the American University in Cairo, and wrote a thesis on Virginia Woolf and Edwar al-Kharrat. She has published in Arabic and English on Bedouin women, postmodernism, the literary depiction of Alexandria, and on painting and poetry, and has translated modern Egyptian poetry into English. She is the editorial manager of *Alif*.

Shukry Ayyad (Egypt) has taught literature and literary criticism in Cairo, Algiers, and Riyadh. He has written short stories, poetry, and plays, as well as criticism. His influential works in criticism include *The Hero in Literature and Myth* and *The Music of Poetry*, and he has also translated Aristotle's *Poetics* into Arabic.

Nancy Berg (United States) was educated in the United States and Egypt. She is a scholar in comparative Middle Eastern literatures, and teaches presently in the Department of Asian and Near Eastern Languages at Washington University in St. Louis.

Marilyn Booth (United States) studied in the United States, Britain, and Egypt. She is the author of *Narrative and the Egyptian Context of Mahmud Bayram al-Tunisi, 1919–1938*, and several articles on colloquial Arabic poetry. She is the translator of a collection of short stories by Egyptian women writers, entitled *My Grandmother's Cactus*.

Mohamed Choukri (Morocco) is a writer who became internationally known after the publication of his autobiography *For Bread Alone (al-Khubz al-hafi)*. He is also the author of collections of short stories and novels, including *Majnun al-ward* (The rose madman) and *al-Suq al-dakhili* (The inner market).

S. Samar Damluji (Iraq) is an architect who was educated in Iraq and England. She has taught at universities in Beirut and currently teaches Islamic architecture at the Royal College of Art and is Senior Tutor at the Architectural Association School of Architecture, London. She is general editor of *Islamic Art and Architecture: The System of Geometric Design*, and is also the author of *A Yemen Reality* and *The Valley of Mud-Brick Architecture*, and editor of *Zillij: The Art of Moroccan Ceramics*.

Ceza Kassem Draz (Egypt) has taught literature at the American University in Cairo and Cairo University. She has published several articles and books on Arabic and comparative literature, and has co-edited *Flights of Fantasy*, a collection of modern Arabic short stories translated into English.

Hassan Fathy (Egypt) was an internationally known Egyptian architect and the author of influential works on architecture, including *Architecture for the Poor* and *The Arab House in the Urban Setting*. He received the Aga Khan award in 1980 and the Union of International Architects Gold Medal in 1984. He died in 1989.

Ferial J. Ghazoul (Iraq) was educated in Iraq, Lebanon, Europe, and the United States. She is presently Professor of English and Comparative Literature at the American University in Cairo. She is the author of a number of studies on comparative, medieval, and modern literature, including *The Arabian Nights: A Structural Analysis* and *Saadi Yusuf.* She has translated creative and critical texts from Arabic, English, and French. She is the editor of *Alif.*

Alaa El Gibali (Egypt) was educated in Egypt and the United States. He is presently an associate professor in the Arabic Language Institute at the American University in Cairo. He is the author of several studies on bilingualism and on Arabic linguistics and stylistics, including *Beginning Colloquial of Cairo*, *Advanced Colloquial of Cairo*, and *Around the World: An Intermediate Arabic Broadcast Media Course.*

Gamal al-Ghitany (Egypt) is a prominent writer and literary journalist, and is presently the editor of *Akhbar al-adab*. He has studied and taught carpet design. He has written a number of influential novels including *al-Zayni Barakat, Khitat al-Ghitani,* and *Kitab al-tajliyat.*

Cherifa Gharari (Algeria) was educated in Algeria and has lived in Cairo, where she taught French at Cairo American College. She writes short stories in French, and teaches French and North African culture at the Foreign Service Institute of the US Department of State.

Sabry Hafez (Egypt) was educated in Cairo and London. He has taught in Sweden and the United States and is presently a professor of Arabic Literature at London University (SOAS). He is the author of several books and articles on modern Arabic literature and critical theory, and numerous studies on the Arabic short story and the sociology of narrative, including *The Genesis of Arabic Narrative Discourse.* He is an editorial advisor to *Alif.*

Ahmad Shams al-Din al-Haggagi (Egypt) is a professor of Arabic literature at Cairo University. He has written on the origins of classical Arabic drama and on the mythic dimension in the modern Arabic novel, and has published a study on myth in contemporary Arabic drama.

Ibrahim al-Hariri (Iraq) is a creative writer and journalist. He is the author of novellas, short stories including *al-Inqilab* (The coup d'état), and dramatic works. He has also translated American short stories into Arabic.

Barbara Harlow (United States) was educated in the United States and Europe. She teaches English and comparative literature at the University of Texas, Austin. She has translated Jacques Derrida and narrative works of Ghassan Kanafani into English. She is the author of *Resistance Literature* and *Barred: Women, Writing, and Political Detention*, and is an editorial advisor to *Alif*.

Jabra Ibrahim Jabra (Palestine) was educated in Palestine and England. He is a novelist, short-story writer, poet, critic, translator, and painter. Among his novels are *Hunters in a Narrow Street, al-Safina (The Ship)*, and *al-Bahth an Walid Mas'ud (The Search for Waleed Mas'ud)*. He has translated Frazer, Faulkner, and Shakespeare into Arabic.

Nels Johnson (United States) was educated at the University of Illinois and McGill University. He has conducted anthropological field research with the Kwakiutl Indians in western Canada and with Palestinian refugees. He has taught anthropology at the American University in Cairo and now teaches at Richmond College in England, and is the author of *Islam and the Politics of Meaning in Palestinian Nationalism*.

Denys Johnson-Davies (United Kingdom) is the leading translator of Arabic literature into English. He has published many volumes in English of the works of Arab writers, including Tayeb Salih, Mahmoud Darwish, Naguib Mahfouz, Salwa Bakr, Nabil Naoum Gorgy, and Tawfiq al-Hakim. He served as editor of Heinemann's "Arab Authors" series, and has recently translated *The Journey of Ibn Fattouma* and *Arabian Nights and Days* (forthcoming) by Naguib Mahfouz and a collection of short stories by Mohamed El-Bisatie.

Ghassan Kanafani (Palestine) was a novelist, critic, short-story writer, and a prominent leader in the Popular Front for the Liberation of Palestine. Kanafani's literary writings in English translation include *Men in the Sun and other Palestinian Stories, Palestine's Children,* and *All That's Left to You*. He died in 1972.

Edwar al-Kharrat (Egypt) is a leading novelist, critic, and translator. He has translated Tolstoy, Marcuse, and Anouilh, among others, into Arabic, and among his works translated into English are *City of Saffron* and *Girls of Alexandria* (forthcoming). He is the author of *Hitan 'aliya* (High walls), *Sa'at al-kibriya'* (Hours of pride), *Rama wa-l-tinnin* (Rama and the dragon), *Ikhtinaqat al-'ishq wa-l-sabah* (Suffocations of love and mornings), *Mahattat al-sikka al-hadid* (The railway station) *al-Zaman al-akhar* (The other time) and *Makhluqat al-ashwaq al-ta'ira* (Creations of flying passions).

Notes on Contributors

Mahmoud El Lozy (Egypt) was educated in Egypt and the United States. He is an actor and director, and is assistant professor of drama at the American University in Cairo. He has written on the theater of Chekhov and contemporary Egyptian playwrights, published a translation of Tawfiq al-Hakim's *The People of the Cave,* and written articles in English on the politics of satire.

Farida Marei (Egypt) was educated in Egypt and the United States. She is a short-story writer and film critic, and is a senior librarian at the American University in Cairo. She has published several articles and essays on Egyptian and Japanese cinema.

Samia Mehrez (Egypt) was educated in Egypt and the United States. She teaches Arabic literature at the American University in Cairo. She has published several studies on contemporary Arabic and Francophone North African literatures, and on translation, most recently *Egyptian Writers Between History and Fiction.* She is an assistant editor of *Alif.*

Nur Elmessiri (Egypt) was educated in the United States, Egypt, and England. She teaches at the American University in Cairo and works as consultant to the English-language Cairo newspaper *al-Ahram Weekly.* She has translated modern Arabic poetry and co-translated short stories into English, including Muhammad al-Makhzingi's *In the Cold Night* and *Anthology of Palestinian Short Stories* (forthcoming).

Lamis al-Nakkash (Egypt) was educated in Egypt and England. She is a translator and an English Language Instructor at Cairo University. She is writing a comparative thesis on Herman Melville and Sonallah Ibrahim.

Rebecca Porteous (United Kingdom) graduated from Cambridge University in Arabic and Middle Eastern Studies, presenting a final dissertation entitled *The Debate About Music in Egypt, 1932–1992.* She has lived intermittently in Cairo over the last five years and now works for *al-Ahram Weekly* and as a freelance translator.

Noha Radwan (Egypt) received her M.A. from the Department of Arabic Studies at the American University in Cairo. She has worked as a freelance journalist and translator, and has published a collection of her short stories, *Ahla min al-safar* (Better than traveling). One of her stories was translated for *Opening the Gates,* an anthology of Arab women writers.

Somaya Ramadan (Egypt) was educated in Egypt and Ireland and has taught at the American University in Cairo. She is a creative writer and has published on feminist and literary issues. She now teaches at the Academy of Fine Arts in Cairo.

Jonathan Rée (United Kingdom) teaches philosophy at Middlesex University in England. He is the author of *Philosophical Tales* and the general editor of the series "Ideas," published by Methuen.

Hoda El Sadda (Egypt) studied in Egypt and England and teaches English literature at Cairo University. She has translated two collections of Arabic short stories into English: *Evening Lake* by Ibrahim Aslan and *Such a Beautiful Voice* by Salwa Bakr. She is the author of several articles on English, Egyptian, and Caribbean literatures, and is the co-editor of *Hagar*, an Egyptian journal on women's issues.

Edward W. Said (Palestine/United States) was educated in Palestine, Egypt, and the United States. He holds the position of University Professor and teaches in the Department of English and Comparative Literature at Columbia University. He has written extensively on literary and cultural theory. His many works include *Joseph Conrad and the Fiction of Autobiography*; *Orientalism*; *The Question of Palestine*; *Covering Islam*; *The World, the Text, and the Critic*; and most recently *Culture and Imperialism*.

Hamdi Sakkut (Egypt) was educated in Egypt and England. He is a professor of Arabic literature and chair of the Department of Arabic Studies at the American University in Cairo. He is the author of a study on the Egyptian novel and a number of articles in Arab and Western journals. He is the editor of a bio-bibliographical source-book series on modern Egyptian writers.

Abdel Moniem Tallyma (Egypt) is a professor of Arabic literature and has taught for many years in Japan. He is the author and editor of a number of books on literary theory and aesthetics, including *Muqaddima fi nazariyat al-adab* (An introduction to literary theory) and *al-Adab al-'arabi* (Arabic literature).

Nancy Witherspoon (United States) has taught English composition at the American University in Cairo and now teaches English to non-native speakers at the City University of New York. She has published articles on travelers to Egypt and interviews with Egyptian playwrights, and she is the co-author (with Shukry Ayyad) of *Reflections and Deflections: A Study of the Contemporary Arab Mind Through its Literary Creations*.

Najman Yasin (Iraq) is a creative writer and a critic. He teaches history at the University of Mosul, Iraq, and is the author of several collections of short stories, including *Dhalika-l-nahr al-gharib* (That strange river) and *Murad Daghestani*.

Nejd Yaziji (Syria) studied literature at Damascus University and is completing a dissertation at the University of Texas at Austin entitled *Narrative Refigurations of a Post-colonial Conflict: The Question of Palestine*.

Saadi Youssef (Iraq) is a distinguished poet and activist. He was educated in Iraq, where he studied Arabic literature, and has lived in several Arab and European capitals. He has published many collections of poetry, including *Ba'idan 'an al-sama' al-'ula* (Away from the first sky), *al-Akhdar Ibn Yusuf wa mashaghilih* (al-Akhdar Ibn Yusuf and his concerns), *Qasa'id Bayrut 1982* (Beirut Poems 1982), and *Qasa'id Baris: shajar Ithaka* (Paris poems: the trees of Ithaca). He has translated into Arabic the works of Whitman, Cavafy, Ungaretti, Ritsos, and Soyinka, among others. He is currently editor of *al-Mada*, a literary quarterly.

Latifa al-Zayyat (Egypt) is a prominent novelist and critic. She teaches English Literature at Ain Shams University in Cairo. She has published a number of studies in Arabic and English on modern literature and critical theory, and is the author of *al-Bab al-maftuh* (The open door) and *al-Shaykhukha wa qisas ukhra* (Old age and other stories). She has also written on the image of women in literature and on Naguib Mahfouz. She chairs the Egyptian Committee for the Defense of National Culture.

Index

'Abd al-Quddus, Ihsan 221
'Abd al-Nasser, Gamal 137
'Abdallah, Muhammad 'Abd al-Halim 19
Abdel Karim, Abdel Maqsud 183, 187
Abdul Saboor, Salah 181, 182, 184
Abdullah, Yahya Taher 239, 279, 282
al-Abnudi, 'Abd al-Rahman 138
Abu 'Ali al-Qali 18
Abu Nuwwas 185
Abu Tammam 29, 185
Achebe, Chinua 265, 266
al-Adab 222, 224
al-Adib 18
'Adli Pasha Yakan 173n23
Adonis 54, 68–71, 183
al-Ahram 94
al-'Alim, Mahmud Amin 184
Amin, Ahmad 221
Apollinaire, Guillaume 69
Arabian Nights (The Thousand and One Nights) 209, 221, 242, 245
Aristotle 3
al-'Ashry, Galal 189
al-'Askari 199
Aslan, Ibrahim 239
Aswat (journal) 179
Auerbach, Erich 74n4, 199
Austen, Jane 265
Avicenna 3
Awad, Louis 187, 272
Awwad, Tawfik Youssef 54, 56, 57, 65
Ayyad, Shukry 2

Bachelard, Gaston 213
Badawi, Muhammad 183
Bally, Charles 199
Balzac, Honoré de 208

Barakat, Henry 255
Barakat, Salim 191
Barrada, Laila 224
Barrada, Mohamed 223, 224, 225, 226
Barthes, Roland 143
al-Barudi 201
Bashshar 225
Bataille, Georges 277
Baudelaire, Charles 69, 225, 244, 273
Beckett, Samuel 66
Beguin, Albert 75n16
Beirut al-masa' 214
Ben Gurion 44, 46
Ben Jelloun, Abdel Mejid 221
Ben Jelloun, Tahar 222, 223, 226
Benjamin, Walter 278
Blake, William 76
Borges, Jorge Luis 225, 280
Bowles, Paul 221–22, 224, 226
Buddha 100
Burke, Kenneth 253
Burroughs, William 226
Byron, Lord George 225, 244

Cabral, Amilcar 36
Camus, Albert 224
Cervantes, Miguel de 225
Césaire, Aimé 266
Chekhov, Anton 18, 207
Chraïbi, Idris 223
Cicero 220
Conrad, Joseph 265, 266, 267, 280
Curzon, Lord 174

D'Souza, Dinesh 271
Dalton, Roque 183
Dar al-Kutub 18
Darraj, Faysal 34, 36

Index

Darwish, Mahmoud 73n3 274
Dostoevsky, Feodor 17, 208, 220, 225, 244
Dryden, John 273
du Gard, Martin 18
Dunqul, Amal 22

Edel, Leon 18, 20
Ehrenburg, Ilya 18
Einstein, Albert 221
Eliot, T. S. 69, 225, 252, 268
Eshkol, Levi 46
Esenin, Sergei Aleksandrovich 225

Fanon, Frantz 36
Faraj, Alfred 77, 82–87
Faris, Bishr 272
Faulkner, William 208
al-Firdawsi 20
Fitzgerald, Edward 278
Forster, E. M. 265
Foucault, Michel 258, 259
Freud, Sigmund 19
Frost, Robert 278
al-Funun 149

Gallery 68 179
Gandhi, Mahatma 150
Gebeyli, Claire 54, 60–65, 66, 68, 71
General Egyptian Book Organization 181
Genet, Jean 220, 223–24
Gibran, Gibran Khalil 245
Gide, André 220
Goethe, Johann Wolfgang von 220
Gordeyev, Foma 18
Gorky, Maxim 18
Gramsci, Antonio 36, 257, 259
Gubar, Susan 246–47
Guiraud, Pierre 141
Güney, Yilmaz 258
Gysin, Brian 226

Habiby, Emile 21
Hafez, Sabry 177
al-Hakim, Tawfiq 19, 204, 221, 272
al-Hallaj 24, 26, 76, 185, 225
Hamama, Faten 255
Hamroush, Ahmed 94
Haqqi, Yahya 19, 204, 272
Hasan, Salim 19
Hassan I, king of Morocco 221
Hawi, Khalil 73n3

Heaney, Seamus 267
Heikal, Muhammad Hassenein 235
Hemingway, Ernest 207, 220
Henein, Georges 183
Higab, Sayyid 181
Higazi, Ahmad Abdel Mu'ti 186
al-Hilli, Ahmad Kamil 149
Hochhuth, Rolf 83
Hugo, Victor 17
al-Huseyni, Hoda 76n19
Hussein, Taha 15, 183, 221, 272
Husserl, Edmund 267

Ibda' 190, 191, 193
Ibn Abi Rabi', 'Umar 185
Ibn al-'Abd, Tarafa 225
Ibn 'Arabi, Muhi al-Din 23, 24, 26
Ibn al-Hakam 19
Ibn Hayyan, Jabir 32
Ibn Iyas 19, 21, 24, 26
Ibn al-Muqafa' 225
Ibn Qutayba 18
Ibn al-Rumi 225
Ibn Sab'iyn 24
Ibrahim, Ezzedin 274
Ibrahim, Hafez 221
Ibrahim, Muhammad 'Id 183, 187, 191, 195n26
Ibrahim, Sonallah 277
Ida'a 77 (journal) 179
Idris, Yusuf 19, 97, 134, 279
al-'Ilm 222
Imam al-Sha'rani 24

al-Jabarti, 'Abd al-Rahman 19
Jabir ibn Hayyan 32
Jabra, Jabra Ibrahim 235, 274
al-Jahiz 199, 209
James, C. L. R. 266
James, Henry 18
Jesus 100, 118–19
al-Jili, Sheikh 'Abd al-Karim 21, 23, 24, 26
John the Baptist 118–19
Johnson, Samuel 17
Jonson, Ben 17
Joyce, James 18, 209, 220, 235, 245, 268, 279
al-Junayd 24

Kaf nun 179
Kafka, Franz 66, 225
Kanafani, Ghassan 3, 274
al-Karmal 191
al-Katib 181
Keats, John 244
Khair Eddine, Mohamed 223
al-Khal, Yusuf 274
Khalaf, Samir 53
Khallaf, Muhammad 183
al-Kharrat, Edwar 179, 188–89, 191, 279
Khatibi, Abdelkebir 266
Khatwa 179
Khoury, Elias 54, 65, 69, 71
Khoury, Nadia 68
Khudayyir, Mohammed 279
al-Khuly, Amin 18
Kierkegaard, Søren 225
Kipling, Rudyard 265
Kipphardt, Heinar 83
al-Kitaba al-sawda' 183, 184, 193
Kitabat 179
Kongstad, Per 53
Kuprin, Alexander 18
al-Kurrasa al-thaqafiya 179

Labib, 'Abbas Ahmad 171
Lawrence, D. H. 244, 273
Le Guern, Michel 140
Lebanon 50–51
Lessing, Doris 251
London, Jack 225

al-Ma'arri 200, 209
Mahfouz, Naguib 19, 21, 55, 135, 205, 235, 240
Majallat shi'r 179
El-Maleh, Edmond Amran 223
Mallarmé, Stéphane 31
Malraux, André 220
Mann, Thomas 268
Mansur, Ibrahim 179
Mao Zedong 36
al-Maqqari 18
al-Maqrizi 19
Marj Dabiq, battle of 20, 24
Matar, Muhammad 'Afifi 181, 186
Maugham, Somerset 220
Maupassant, Guy de 207
Mayakovsky, Vladimir 225

al-Mazni, Ibrahim 'Abd al-Qadir 203, 240, 245
Merleau-Ponty, Maurice 267
Mernissi, Fatima 225
Michaux, 76
Milner, Lord 156, 170
Mis'id, Rauf 136
Misriya 179
Moses 118
Mousa, Salama 245
al-Mubarrad 18
al-Muharrir (Lebanon) 20
al-Muharrir (Morocco) 225
Mumford, Lewis 72
Munif, Abdelrahman 211, 235
Munir, Walid 181, 183, 193
al-Murabit, Mohamed 222
al-Muraqqish the Younger 13
Murchison, Rodney 265
Mursi, Ahmad 179
Mursy, Mahmud 255
al-Mutanabbi 200, 209, 225

al-Nadim, 'Abdallah 149, 179
al-Naqqash, Raga' 185, 190
Neruda, Pablo 220, 264, 266
Ngugi wa Thiong'o 265, 266
Nietzsche, Friedrich 76, 225
al-Niffari 26, 185

Omar al-Khayyam 14
Orwell, George 18
Owen, Peter 221–22

Palácios, Asín 200
Pannwitz, Rudolf 278
Paz, Octavio 282
Perse, Saint-John 13
Piscator, Erwin 83, 84, 85
Plato 32
Pope, Alexander 273
Poulitzer, Georges 19
Pound, Ezra 75n15, 278
Pritchett, V. S. 280
Prometheus 225
Prophet Muhammad 119
Proust, Marcel 245, 268, 273, 279

Qabbani, Nizar 74n3
al-Qadi al-Fadil 245
al-Qassas, Gamal 182, 193

Index

al-Qassas, Muhammad 18
al-Qays 225
al-Qilish, Kamal 136
al-Qushayri 24

al-Ra'i, 'Ali 77
Rabin, Yitzhak 46
Rachide, Amina 200
Ramadan, 'Abd al-Mun'im 182, 183, 186, 191, 193
Ramzy, Mounir 244
Rayyan, Amgad 183, 190
Rilke, Rainer Maria 13
Rimbaud, Arthur 69, 76
Rousseau, Jean-Jacques 220
Rushdie, Salman 270
Ryan, Marie-Laure 135

Sabatini, Raphael 17
al-Sabbak, Abu Bakr 102
Sadat, Anwar 25, 194
al-Sadr, 'Abd al-'Aziz 149
Said, Edward 36, 258, 259
Said, Khalida 76n24
Saint Augustine 220
Salih, Tayeb 76n19, 205, 235, 277
Salim, 'Ali 77, 78–82, 88
Salim, Hilmy 182, 184, 187, 192
Sallam, Rif'at 180, 182, 187
Saltykov-Shchedrin, Mikhail Evgrafovich 18
Sanabil 181
Sartre, Jean-Paul 31, 220, 221, 267
Sayigh, Tawfiq 274, 277
al-Sayyab, Badr Shakir 274
al-Sayyid al-Badawi 100
al-Shabab 149, 151, 153, 164, 167, 181
al-Sharadli, Idris 221
Shawqi, Ahmad 201, 221
al-Shaykh, Hanan 74n3
Shelley, Percy Bysshe 244
Shi'r 203, 274
Shu'ayb 118, 119
al-Siba'i, Yusuf 19
Socrates 14
Sophocles 99
Spence, Lewis 99
Spitzer, Leo 199
Stack, Sir Lee 164

Steinbeck, John 221
Steiner, George 278
Sue, Eugène 17
al-Suhrawardi 24
Sulayman, Muhammad 181, 182, 183, 191
Sulayman, Sidqi 140

Tagore, Sir Rabindranath 267
Taha, Ahmad 183
al-Tawhidi, Abu Hayyan 23, 26, 225
Teymour, Mahmoud 272, 273
Tibi, Lina 195n26
Tilib, Hasan 182, 187
Todorov, Tzvetan 140
Tolstoy, Leo 18
Tuéni, Nadia 54, 56–60, 63, 65, 68, 70, 72
Turgenev, Ivan 18

al-'Ujayli, Abd al-Salam 204
Umm Kulthum 14

Vadeyev, Alexander 18
Walcott, Derek 266
Waltari, Mika 17
Waraqa ibn Nawfal 119
Weiss, Peter 83
Williams, Raymond 263
Williams, Tennessee 223, 224
Wilson, Colin 90, 220
Witherspoon, Nancy 206
Woolf, Virginia 209

Yacine, Kateb 223, 224, 266
Yared, Nazik 74n3
Yeats, William Butler 266, 267
Youssef, Saadi 2
Yunan, Ramsis 183
Yusuf, Magid 183

Zaghlul, Sa'd 157, 158, 161, 167, 173n23
al-Zahawi 201
al-Zaybaq, 'Ali 221
Zaydan, Jurji 17
Zola, Emile 17
Zoroaster 100